Understanding
RAINER WERNER FASSBINDER

UNDERSTANDING MODERN EUROPEAN AND LATIN AMERICAN LITERATURE

JAMES HARDIN, *Series Editor*

volumes on

Ingeborg Bachmann
Samuel Beckett
Thomas Bernhard
Johannes Bobrowski
Heinrich Böll
Italo Calvino
Albert Camus
Elias Canetti
Céline
José Donoso
Rainer Werner Fassbinder
Max Frisch
Federico García Lorca
Gabriel García Márquez

Juan Goytisolo
Günter Grass
Gerhart Hauptmann
Christoph Hein
Eugène Ionesco
Milan Kundera
Primo Levi
Graciliano Ramos
Erich Maria Remarque
Jean-Paul Sartre
Claude Simon
Mario Vargas Llosa
Franz Werfel
Peter Weiss

UNDERSTANDING

RAINER WERNER
FASSBINDER

Film as Private and Public Art

WALLACE STEADMAN WATSON

UNIVERSITY OF SOUTH CAROLINA PRESS

Published in Columbia, South Carolina, by the
University of South Carolina Press

Manufactured in the United States of America

00 99 98 97 96   5 4 3 2 1

Library of Congress Cataloging-in-Publication Data

Watson, Wallace Steadman, 1936–
    Understanding Rainer Warner Fassbinder : film as private
and public art / Wallace Steadman Watson
        p.   cm.
    Includes bibliographical references and index.
    ISBN 1–57003–079–0 (cloth)
    1. Fassbinder, Rainer Werner, 1946– —Criticism and
interpretation. I. Title.
PN1998 . 3 .F37W38 1996
791.43'0233'092—dc20   95–41780

In memory of my parents,

Myra Steadman and Thomas Coburn Watson

CONTENTS

ILLUSTRATIONS

EDITOR'S PREFACE

Understanding Modern European and Latin American Literature has been planned as a series of guides for undergraduate and graduate students and non-academic readers. Like its companion series, *Understanding Contemporary American Literature* and *Understanding Contemporary British Literature,* the aim of the books is to provide an introduction to the life and writings of prominent modern authors and to explicate their most important works. We have chosen to include the film director R. W. Fassbinder in this series because of the extraordinary link between film and literature in his work. In this connection one thinks especially of his magnum opus *Berlin Alexanderplatz,* based on the well-known novel (*Berlin Alexanderplatz,* 1929) by Alfred Döblin. In adapting works of literature, such as the Döblin work and Nabokov's *Despair,* Fassbinder obviously does not slavishly adhere to the text before him; rather, he makes his own creative statements, coming to terms with not only literary but also with cinematic traditions such as the French New Wave, film noir, and Hollywood melodrama.

Modern literature makes special demands, and this is particularly true of foreign literature and cinema, in which the reader must contend not only with unfamiliar, often arcane artistic conventions and philosophical concepts, but also with the handicap of reading the literature in translation, or, in the case of the film, hearing the work in a foreign language while aided by subtitles. It is a truism that the nuances of one language can be rendered in another only imperfectly (and this problem is especially difficult in fiction), but the fact that the works of European and Latin American writers are situated in a historical and cultural setting quite different from our own can be as great a hinderance to the understanding of these works as the linguistic barrier. For this reason the UMELL series will emphasize the sociological and historical background of the writers treated. The peculiar philosophical and cultural traditions of a given culture may be particularly important for an understanding of certain authors, and these will be taken up in the introductory chapter and also in the discussion of those works to which this information is relevant. Beyond this the books will treat the specifically literary aspects of the author under discussion and attempt to explain the complexities of contemporary literature lucidly. The books are conceived as introductions to the authors covered, not as comprehensive analyses. They do not provide detailed summaries of plot as they are meant to be used in conjunction with the works they treat, not as a substitute for the study of the original works. It is our hope that the UMELL series will help to increase our knowledge and understanding of the European and Latin American cultures and will serve to make the literature of those cultures more accessible.

J. H.

PREFACE

Rainer Werner Fassbinder was by far the most prolific and, in the minds of many, the most talented filmmaker in an impressive "New German Cinema" which emerged on the international film scene in the 1970s. When he died at age thirty-seven in 1982, he had compiled a remarkable artistic record, completing in a professional career of a little over fifteen years more than forty feature-length or longer films, in addition to substantial work in the theater. All of these films are intellectually, emotionally, and aesthetically challenging, and at least a dozen of them have been generally ranked among the most significant products of the postwar international cinema. Fassbinder's films explore both intimate psychological relationships (often referring directly or indirectly to his private life) and the complex political, social, and cultural aspects of his world, the Federal Republic of Germany. This book describes and interprets his work within those private and public contexts.

As my textual and bibliographical notes make clear, there is need for a comprehensive, accurate, and well documented critical biography of Fassbinder. This book is not intended to meet that need. Chapter one does, however, consider in some detail the director's unusual childhood and adolescence, correcting the published record at a number of points. For readers not specifically familiar with postwar Germany, that chapter and chapter seven also summarize those aspects of political and cultural life in the Federal Republic which most directly impacted Fassbinder's creative life and output—including the postwar reestablishment of literary and theatrical activity in West Germany, the development of the so-called Young and New German Cinema, the political and cultural rebellion of "the Generation of '68," and the left-wing terrorism of the 1970s and the reactions it produced in West German society. Chapter two traces in some detail the beginnings of Fassbinder's artistic career through late 1969 (his twenty-fourth year), which took place primarily in the theater, considering that early theater work particularly in the context of the late Sixties' rebellion.

The remainder of the book concentrates on the films, grouped thematically within the three major periods of Fassbinder's career as a feature filmmaker: a frenetic apprenticeship of twenty months in 1969 and 1970, which produced eleven movies on a variety of themes and in widely differing styles; a middle phase (1971–75) characterized by relatively straightforward, accessible critical melodramas; and a more complex final phase (1975–82) in which both private and public themes are blended into unusually dense cinematic texts. Obviously, such a scheme must not be applied mechanistically. Many of Fassbinder's films do not fit neatly into any single phase or category. But as he himself once observed, he was inclined to work on related projects at the same time.[1] In any case, an understanding of these major periods and groupings is useful in approaching the almost overwhelming quantity and variety of Fassbinder's cinematic production. Furthermore, given the self-referentiality of much of his work, it is helpful to have the total corpus in mind in considering any single part of it. Thus I comment at least briefly upon all of Fassbinder's plays and films, providing information also on costs and other material conditions of this production. I analyze in considerable detail fifteen of the films that seem to me most significant, and which illustrate all phases of the director's career and his major themes and styles. They include two adaptations of novels whose transformation into particularly personal films are examined in separate chapters. Along with these analyses, I engage some of the theoretical discussion which Fassbinder's films have recently generated among critics and scholars of the cinema, the theater, and popular culture—representing historical-materialist, feminist, psychoanalytic, and gay and lesbian perspectives, among others.

Throughout the book I draw often upon Fassbinder's own writing and interviews, the latter of which constitute the richest source of his ideas about his life and work. Most of what he had to say in this format seems to me both perceptive and candid, though I have tried not to privilege unduly his opinions and stated intentions. Moreover, Fassbinder sometimes changed his mind on specific points, and he was not above putting his interviewers on, or playing different roles for different audiences.

I have seen all of the extant Fassbinder films and video productions with the exception of the television version of *Bolwieser*. For the opportunity to view this material, I am especially grateful to Enno Patalas and his staff at the Munich Filmmuseum, and I appreciate also the cooperation of the following institutions: The Rainer Werner Fassbinder Foundation (Berlin); the Video Department of Ludwig-Maximilians-Universität (Munich), the Munich Stadtbücherei, the Goethe Institut Berlin, and Westdeutscher Rundfunk. Helpful information and materials were made available by Oskar Törne of the Stiftung Deutsche Kinemathek (Berlin), Ingrid Scheib-Rothbart of the Goethe House New York, the Deutsches Institut für Filmkunde (Frankfurt am Main), the Bayerishe Staatsbibliothek (Munich), the British Film Institute (London), the Department of English and Norlin Library of the University of Colorado—Boulder, the New York Public Library, the Mugar Memorial Library of Boston University, and New Yorker Films.[2] I am grateful to Duquesne University for granting me a leave for research on this book and, for additional support, to my department chairperson, J. J. Keenan, and the deans of Duquesne University's

College and Graduate School of Liberal Arts, John J. McDonald and Constance Ramirez.

I have received particularly helpful materials and information from the previous and current directors of the Rainer Werner Fassbinder Foundation. They are Fassbinder's mother, the late Liselotte Eder, who acted in twenty-five of her son's film and assisted him in other ways, establishing the foundation in 1986 to protect his legacy; and Juliane Lorenz, Fassbinder's film editor for the last six years of his life and his intimate companion for the last four, who took over direction of the Foundation in 1992.[3] My interviews with both of them and my extensive correspondence with Ms. Lorenz, cited frequently in the text and notes, have provided significant new information (including the first published excerpts from Fassbinder's much-discussed farewell letter to his lover Armin Meier), and close views of a director whose personal life was inextricably bound up in his films. Moreover, Ms. Lorenz generously pointed out factual errors in a typescript of this book and shared with me unpublished materials, including prepublication copies of several of her interviews with Fassbinder's coworkers.[4]

I am especially grateful to Donna L. Hoffmeister, who encouraged me to undertake this project, who has been my most consistent supporter and most helpful critic, and who has time and again given me the benefit of her expertise in German language and culture. I thank also my patient and perceptive series editor, James Hardin, and production editor, Bill Adams, as well as the many other individuals who have given me significant advice and help—including Harry Baer, Sir Dirk Bogarde, Gerd Gemünden, Kent Casper, Rosemarie and the late Rainer Jahnke, Bruce Kawin, Richard Korb, Al LaValley, Leo Lensing, Susan Linville, Ron Miriani, Cornelius Murphy, James Palmer, Brent Peterson, Jonna Potuwa, Carmen Stonge, Michael Töteberg, and Krishna Winston, among others. I am of course responsible for whatever errors or misjudgments appear in the book. Finally, I am grateful to my three children—Stead, Amy, and Joanna—who have encouraged me throughout my work on this project, patiently accepting a fascinating interloper's demands upon their father's attention.

Material in the introduction and in chapters 7 and 10 that first appeared in different form in *Sight and Sound* and *The Literature/Film Quarterly* is published here by permission of the editors, Philip Dodd and James M. Welsh, respectively. Quotations from Fassbinder, *The Anarchy of the Imagination,* are used by permission of The Johns Hopkins University Press, Baltimore, and those from *Fassbinder* (edited by Tony Rayns), courtesy of the British Film

Institute. Unpublished letters from Tom Stoppard to Dirk Bogarde are quoted by permission of the Mugar Memorial Library, Boston University, Mr. Bogarde, and Mr. Stoppard. Correspondence between Dirk Bogarde and Fassbinder is quoted by permission of the Mugar Memorial Library, Mr. Bogarde, and the Rainer Werner Fassbinder Foundation.

Production information for the plays and films is based primarily on Hans Helmut Prinzler's data section in the latest edition of the Jansen and Schütte Fassbinder handbook; information in the catalogue of the 1992 Fassbinder exhibition in Berlin (RWFF Cat. 258–64); and letters from Juliane Lorenz. Film production years given in parentheses indicate the years in which they were shot. English translations of German and other non-English titles of books and films are given in parentheses or brackets, using italics to indicate titles which have appeared in English-language versions, and roman type to translate titles apparently not released in English. Abbreviations for interviews with Fassbinder and for several frequently cited sources are indicated in my bibliography. Throughout, translations from German and French are my own unless otherwise indicated.

Notes

1. *Anarchy* 156.

2. Fassbinder materials previously held in the Lorenz collection at the Stiftung Deutsche Kinemathek are now in the archives of the Fassbinder Foundation.

3. Liselotte Eder said in 1990 that she hoped the foundation would be able to provide assistance to young filmmakers "after everything is straightened out" (interview with author, 21 and 24 September). Juliane Lorenz noted that, in addition to its support of the 1992 Fassbinder retrospective and exhibition in Berlin and subsequent programs in many countries, the Foundation is engaged in such activities as protecting original negatives of Fassbinder films, arranging for theatrical release of his television films, and cataloguing archival materials (interview with author). The foundation's address is Kurfürstenstrasse 17, D-10785, Berlin.

4. Those interviews, as well as my own with Juliane Lorenz and Liselotte Eder, translated into German, are included in Lorenz, ed., *Das ganz normale Chaos*.

CHRONOLOGY

Note: Unless otherwise indicated, italicized titles indicate films, which are listed in the years in which shooting was completed. Films were both scripted and directed by Fassbinder, except as indicated in parentheses (cs = coauthor of script; ns = not credited for script; cd = codirected). RWF is credited with editing or coediting seven of his films during 1969–70 and seven during 1976–82. English titles are given for films released in English-language versions or with English subtitles; otherwise, the German titles are translated in parentheses. German titles of all the films are given in both the text and the filmography.

1945–46	Born 31 May 1945 in Bavarian spa city, Bad Wörishofen. As infant, moves with parents (Dr. Helmut and Liselotte Pempeit Fassbinder) to Munich, where father sets up medical practice. Spends six months of first year with paternal uncle and aunt in a village in the Black Forest. Returns to parents in spring 1946; apartment now shared by relatives of mother.
1950	Mother hospitalized for several months with tuberculosis.
1951	Parents divorce. Father moves to Cologne; mother begins work as translator.
1951–55	Attends public school for one year, and private Rudolf Steiner School, Munich, for three years. Writes stories and poems, makes audio tapes of plays performed by friends, begins seeing movies regularly. Mother hospitalized again. RWF variously cared for by family friends and neighbors, mostly in Munich.
1955–61	Attends four *Gymnasien* (high schools), including two boarding schools in Augsburg (1956–9) and two in Munich. Mother hospitalized for two years; undergoes surgical removal of portion of lung; marries free-lance journalist Wolff Eder (1959).
1961–63	Lives approximately two years in Cologne; helps father in his real estate business; completes high school certificate through night classes. Writes plays, poems, short stories, film scripts.
1963–	Returns to Munich, where he will live until his death, in various group arrangements, and with several individuals, with occasional interruptions (including vacation trips to southern Europe, North Africa, and the United States; visits to his apartment in Paris; and stays in Cologne, Berlin, and other West German cities during filming projects).
1963–66	Works part-time in archives of Munich newspaper, *Süddeutsche Zeitung;* assists and acts in several documentary and training films;

makes 8 mm films. Takes private acting lessons (September 1963–February 1964), then a two-year evening course at Fridl-Leonhard Actors School, Munich (1 March 1964–31 May 1966), where he meets future star of his films, Hanna Schygulla.

1966 Shares third prize in dramatic competition for a four-act play, *Nur eine Scheibe Brot: Dialog über einen Auschwitzfilm* (Just a Slice of Bread: Dialogue about an Auschwitz Film, unproduced during his lifetime). Makes 8 mm films (lost), including *This Night*. Unsuccessfully applies for admission to new German Film and Television Academy, Berlin. Makes 16 mm film, *Der Stadtstreicher* (The City Tramp, 10 min.).

1967 Makes 35 mm film, *Das kleine Chaos* (The Little Chaos, 9 min.). Performs several theater and film acting roles. Fails in second application to German Film and Television Academy. Becomes creative leader of the Action-Theater, Munich, directing one and codirecting another production.

1968 Writes and codirects play, *Katzelmacher,* for Action-Theater. With nine others previously associated with Action-Theater, organizes the "antitheater," which stages performances in several Munich locations. Writes or cowrites four free adaptations of others' plays for the antitheater; directs or codirects five performances; writes and codirects his original play, *The American Soldier.* West German student protest movement climaxes in April "Easter disturbances."

1969 Writes two original plays, coauthors another, and writes two dramatic adaptations; directs two and codirects two antitheater productions. Four feature-length films, produced by antitheater-X-Film: *Love Is Colder Than Death, Katzelmacher, Gods of the Plague, Why Does Herr R. Run Amok?* (cs). Performs roles in seven films (three of his own). RWF "Showdown" in Bremen features two Fassbinder films and two of his plays. Begins one-year liaison with Günther Kaufmann.

1970 *Whity, Die Niklashauser Fart* (Journey to Nicklashausen) (cs), *The American Soldier, Beware of a Holy Whore, Pioniere in Ingolstadt* (Army Engineers in Ingolstadt), all produced by antitheater-X-Film. Performs roles in eight films (own and others'). Writes and directs two radio plays. Marries Ingrid Caven (August). Begins eight-month pause in filmmaking.

1971 Sees films of German-American director Douglas Sirk and visits him in Switzerland; determines to make films appealing to wider audiences. Dissolves antitheater. Forms production company, Tango-Film Rainer Werner Fassbinder (producer or coproducer of many later RWF films). Begins liaison with El Hedi ben Salem. *The Merchant of Four Seasons*. Stepfather Wolff Eder dies; mother Liselotte begins to assist in financial record-keeping for Tango Films. Four Fassbinder theatrical productions (written and/or directed by him) staged in Bremen, Nuremberg, and Frankfurt; writes and directs a radio play.

1972 *The Bitter Tears of Petra von Kant, Wildwechsel* (Wild Game Crossing), *Acht Stunden sind kein Tag* (Eight Hours Don't Make a Day), *Bremer Freiheit* (Bremen Freedom). Directs a play in Bochum, under three-year contract with city theater. Writes and directs a radio play. Divorce from Ingrid Caven (27 September).

1973 *Welt am Draht* (World on the Wire) (cs), *Nora Helmer* (ns), *Martha, Ali: Fear Eats the Soul, Effi Briest* (begun 1972). Ends liaison with El Hedi ben Salem. Directs two plays, in Bochum and Berlin. Ends commitment to Bochum theater. Performs in three films.

1974 *Fox and His Friends* (cs), *Wie ein Vogel auf dem Draht* (Like a Bird on the Wire) (cs). Directs three plays in Frankfurt, two at the Theater am Turm (TAT), where he takes position of managing director. Performs roles in two films. Begins liaison with Armin Meier. First Fassbinder retrospective at Paris Cinématheque.

1975 Leaves TAT during controversy over his unproduced play, *Garbage, the City, and Death*. Begins to talk of leaving West Germany. *Mother Küsters Goes to Heaven, Fear of Fear*. Cowrites and performs a major role in *Shadows of Angels* (directed by Daniel Schmid), film version of RWF play *Garbage, the City, and Death*. Fassbinder retrospective at New York Film Festival.

1976 *I Only Want You to Love Me, Satan's Brew* (both begun in 1975); *Chinese Roulette*. Performs role in one film, directs a play in Hamburg.

1977 *The Stationmaster's Wife* (begun 1976); *Frauen in New York* (Women in New York), *Despair* (ns). Climax of the West German terrorist crisis. *Germany in Autumn*. Performs roles in two films.

1978 *The Marriage of Maria Braun* (cs). Letter of farewell to Armin Meier (2 May) and Meier's death several weeks thereafter of drug overdose. *In a Year of 13 Moons*. Performs one film role. Begins living with film editor Juliane Lorenz.

1979 *The Third Generation* (begun 1978).
1980 *Berlin Alexanderplatz* (begun 1979); *Lili Marleen* (cs). Dictates screenplay for *Hurra, wir leben noch* (Hurrah, We're Still Alive—unproduced).
1981 Writes screenplay for *Kokain* (unproduced); *Lola* (cs); *Theater in Trance; Veronika Voss* (cs), which wins Golden Bear at 1982 Berlin Film Festival. Three roles in others' films.
1982 *Querelle*. Two roles in others' films. Dies early morning, 10 June.

Sources: Fassbinder's "Lebenslauf" and "Gesamtwerk in chronologischer Reihenfolge," in Rainer Werner Fassbinder Foundation, *Rainer Werner Fassbinder* (RWFF Cat. 258–64; production data by Hans Helmut Prinzler in Peter W. Jansen and Wolfram Schütte, eds., *Rainer Werner Fassbinder,* 1992, 271–300; author's interviews with Liselotte Eder; letters from Juliane Lorenz.

Understanding
RAINER WERNER FASSBINDER

Introduction

Death at an Early Age

Early in the evening of 9 June 1982, nine days after his thirty-seventh birthday, the West German filmmaker Rainer Werner Fassbinder retired to the bedroom of his Munich apartment—but not to sleep. As always, he had work to do. This night he was making notes for what would have been his forty-fifth film in fifteen years, *Rosa L.,* based on the life of Rosa Luxemburg, a martyr of the German Communists who had been murdered in 1918 while held prisoner by the government. Shortly after one o'clock in the morning Fassbinder talked on the phone with his longtime friend and coworker Harry Baer, who reported that he had just found an ideal shooting location in a nearby discotheque for their next planned movie. Tentatively titled *Ich bin das Glück dieser Erde* (I Am the Happiness of This World—after a song by the German rock singer Joachim Witt), it would tell the story of three failed detectives who make good in the German New Wave rock music scene. "Great," said Rainer, and he told Harry to close the deal. "Are you okay?" asked Harry. Like many other Fassbinder associates, he was concerned about the effects of the director's extraordinary pace of work and reckless lifestyle on his health. The reply was reassuring: "I'm watching television, video, and reading in between. I have some more things to do."[1] That was apparently Fassbinder's last conversation, and it was altogether characteristic of the filmmaker who had never been satisfied to do one thing at a time or to relax between projects. At 4:30 A.M., his film editor and companion Juliane Lorenz found Fassbinder dead in his bed, lying on top of his notes for *Rosa L.*

The cause of his death was a presumably accidental overdose of sleeping pills and cocaine. Initially, many speculated that Fassbinder had intentionally killed himself, since he had several times recently talked of that possibility with interviewers. Others have said that his frenetic style of living and working was in fact suicidal. In his mid-twenties, the director had told his mother that she would outlive him, and many of his friends and associates recalled his frequent talk of dying young. On the other hand, some who were closest to him have insisted that, for all the distress in his private life and his unhappiness with conditions in his world, Fassbinder was by no means ready to opt out of life at age thirty-seven. Harry Baer said that he showed a new lust for living during his last two years, with plans for at least fifty films, and he wrote movingly of the pleasure Fassbinder shared with his coworkers while they were making what turned out to be his final film, *Querelle*.[2] Juliane Lorenz, who lived with Fassbinder for his last four years, has emphasized that, contrary to the morbid speculation about his state of mind during his last years, she witnessed no letup in his pleasure in making films and his "big, big capacity for love."[3] Asked a few months before his death if his extraordinary pace of making films ever tired him, Fassbinder responded with an enthusiasm that seems to have been characteristic of his lifelong approach his art: "Oh, no. Because each one is new, fresh, an exploration for me and the others."[4]

Fassbinder's Career: An Overview

Fassbinder's artistic productivity, in a professional career that lasted just over fifteen years, is astonishing. He directed (mostly from scripts he authored) thirty-six feature-length films, two filmed television series (of five and fourteen parts, respectively), four other short narrative films, two documentaries for television, twenty-four stage plays, and four radio plays. Moreover, he performed roles in six theatrical productions and in thirty-six of his own and others' films.

In their variety, Fassbinder's films constitute a virtual catalogue of cinematic styles, self-consciously and often ironically reflecting film traditions as different as the chiaroscuro lighting and pessimism of film noir, the slick surfaces and emotionalism of Hollywood melodrama, the gritty naturalism of Italian Neorealism, and the startling incongruities of the French New Wave. The result is a body of films extraordinarily rich in cinematic texture and thematic interest.

Most of Fassbinder's films combine both public and personal themes. On the one hand, his work constitutes a substantial critique of modern German society, culture, politics, and economic arrangements. The films often suggest that the horrors of the Third Reich were not a historical aberration but rather expressions of xenophobic and authoritarian strands in the German character which could also be seen in the materialism, intolerance, and reactionary tendencies of postwar West Germany. They also look intently at individual lives, dramatizing in many different circumstances what Fassbinder identified as his central theme, "the exploitation of feelings"[5] and the deep-seated anxieties that accompany this exploitation. But even his bleakest films contain moments of comic irony (often ignored in the predominantly somber commentary on his work). And most of them are infused with yearning for satisfactory personal relationships, as well as for a utopian society in which "each person can be an artist," as the director once put it.[6]

Fassbinder's artistic life developed in several fairly distinct phases. After making several short films in 1966 and 1967, he spent two years (starting in the fall of 1967) as a potent force in Munich's underground theater. He quickly became the dominant member of an acting troupe calling itself first the "Action-Theater" and then the "antitheater."[7] Their aggressively left-wing and stylistically unconventional theatrical work is fascinating in its own right, and it was crucial to the formation of Fassbinder's consciousness of himself as an artist and to the development of his cinematic directorial style. After the antitheater group made its first film in April 1969, he devoted most of his energy to filmmaking, although he continued to work extensively in the theater for several years after that.

Under Fassbinder's increasingly strong direction, the antitheater produced over the next twenty months eleven feature-length films, of remarkable diversity. The first was *Liebe ist kälter als der Tod,* 1969 (*Love Is Colder Than Death*), a bleak story of powerlessness and emotional manipulation among alienated Bavarian youth, articulated in the language of American gangster films noir of the 1930s and 1940s. Two variations on this theme followed in the next sixteen months. Another 1969 film, *Katzelmacher,* portrays the inarticulate despair of a group of young suburban Bavarians who take out their frustrations in mistreatment of a foreign worker. Other films of this apprentice period include a sardonic cinema verité-style study of the banality of contemporary lower-middle-class family life; a comedy about escaping contemporary West Germany to search for lost treasure in Peru; film versions of two antitheater stage productions (from eighteenth-century Italy and early twentieth-century Germany, respectively); a technically impressive if dramatically improbable domestic tragedy set in the nineteenth-century American West; and the story of a fifteenth-century revolutionary preacher set in contemporary West Germany.

The next-to-last film of this early period, *Warnung vor einer heilige Nutte,* 1970 (*Beware of a Holy Whore*), marks a major transition in Fassbinder's artistic development. It is a stylish study, both amusing and disturbing, of a tyrannical film director who feels himself the victim of his dependent cast and crew, with obvious autobiographical references. It is also a formal farewell to the antitheater's ideal of an artistic collective. That cinematically reflexive film was followed by an eight-month pause in making movies, during which Fassbinder discovered the films of the German-American director Douglas Sirk. The model of Sirk's highly crafted but critical melodramas of American life in the 1950s inspired and helped Fassbinder as he sought now to move beyond what he already considered the self-indulgent films of his apprentice period to make (as he put it) "German Hollywood-films," critical melodramas with broad audience appeal.

Fassbinder lived up to his intentions in the five-year period that followed (1971–75), producing nine relatively straightforward stories of individuals trapped within systems whose oppressive mechanisms they internalize. In contrast to the often convoluted plots and erratic cinematic styles of his earlier work, these films largely follow the conventions of the classical-realist Hollywood "well-made film." At the same time, they insistently work against the grain of that dominant cinema through such alienating devices as obtrusively stylized framing, parodic use of music, and unconventional angles, lighting, and editing. They probe the prevailing ideologies of postwar West Germany with the cinematic polish of Sirkean melodrama, but also with more critical bite than Sirk's films, which Fassbinder found intelligent and sympathetic but only mildly subversive.

These films of the early 1970s also mostly avoid the self-conscious personal references of the apprentice work in their exploration of sociological themes and conflicts—mostly within middle-or lower-middle-class families. *Händler der vier Jahreszeiten,* 1971 (*The Merchant of Four Seasons*), for example, tells the story of a fruit and vegetable seller rejected by his bourgeois family. Similar class prejudice is dramatized, in a gay context, in *Faustrecht der Freiheit,* 1974 (*Fox and His Friends*). Other films of this period portray generational conflict, prejudice against foreign workers, and the problems of working-class people both at their jobs and in their domestic lives. A number of them focus on the personal problems of female protagonists, recalling the Hollywood "women's pictures" of the 1940s and 1950s made by Sirk and others. The first of these, *Die bitteren Tränen der Petra von Kant,* 1972 (*The Bitter Tears of Petra von Kant*), is a stylized but moving dramatization of a frustrated lesbian love affair. *Fontane Effi Briest,* 1972–73 (*Effi Briest*), one of the more successful Fassbinder films of this period, adapts a well-known novel about a young woman's oppression in nineteenth-century North German society.

The final and most complex phase of Fassbinder's brief artistic career be-

4

gan early in 1975, during a period of crisis in both his private and his professional lives. Most of the films of this period exhibit considerably increased stylistic and thematic complexity. The psychological oppression of children is explored with new intensity in *Chinesisches Roulette,* 1976 (*Chinese Roulette*), a mannered drama of tense emotional game-playing, and *Ich will doch nur, dass Ihr mich liebt,* 1976 (*I Only Want You to Love Me*), a largely naturalistic account of an abused son taking indirect revenge against his oppressive father. Problematic aspects of bisexuality and homosexuality are dramatized in complex ways in *In einem Jahr mit 13 Monden,* 1978 (*In a Year of 13 Moons*), a study of the last hours in the life of an abused transsexual, and in *Querelle,* 1982, a ritualistic reenactment of Jean Genet's 1953 novel of male sexuality, murder, and betrayal.

More public themes are explored simultaneously with personal melodrama in a new group of Fassbinder "women's pictures," which constitute a sort of cultural and political history of modern Germany. *Bolwieser,* 1976–77 (*The Station-master's Wife*) reveals provincial narrow-mindedness and authoritarianism during the late Weimar era. *Lili Marleen,* 1980, blends a story of private love and betrayal with an examination of the Nazis' use of spectacle as a means of manipulating mass psychology. Three of these late women's films portray personal and official corruption during the celebrated postwar West German economic recovery: the cold-hearted pursuit of financial success in *Die Ehe der Maria Braun,* 1978 (*The Marriage of Maria Braun*); criminal collusion between public officials and real-estate developers in *Lola,* 1981; and a conspiratorial abuse of official power in *Die Sehnsucht der Veronika Voss,* 1981 ([The Longing of] *Veronika Voss*). Sardonic criticism of postwar politics of the left is offered in two other films of this period: *Mutter Küsters Fahrt zum Himmel,* 1975 (*Mother Küsters Goes to Heaven*) and *Die dritte Generation,* 1978–79 (*The Third Generation*). Fassbinder's most direct revelation of his intensely subjective engagement with public controversies of his day came in his contribution to *Deutschland im Herbst,* 1977 (*Germany in August*), a collaborative film in which several West German writers and filmmakers reacted to their government's heavy-handed response to escalating political terrorism in the Federal Republic.

Two other major projects during these last years are highly personal adaptations of novels set in the later years of the Weimar Republic: *Despair—Eine Reise ins Licht,* 1977 (*Despair* [A Journey into the Light]), based on a novel by Vladimir Nabokov, and Fassbinder's magnum opus, a fourteen-part film made for television, *Berlin Alexanderplatz,* 1979–80, based on a 1929 novel by Alfred Döblin.

Resources and Reputation

Fassbinder's first films were made on shoestring budgets with largely inexperienced and underpaid casts and crews. Beginning in 1969 with *Katzelmacher,* which won almost one million marks in prizes and state subsidies, he was increasingly able to attract government financing for all but the most personal and eccentric of his creative projects, from a variety of subsidy and award programs that the Federal Republic and the West German states had established to encourage younger filmmakers. Later, he arranged ever more ample funding through coproduction arrangements with West German television networks and from private financiers and producers. More than half of these later films were international coproductions, and their casts and production staffs consisted increasingly of well-known professionals (some with world reputations) gradually replacing many of the original team. For all of his unconventional and controversial personal lifestyle, Fassbinder established a reputation as a highly disciplined director who could usually be counted on to get a project completed on time and below budget.

During his lifetime Fassbinder's work was generally received more enthusiastically abroad than at home. As early as 1972, the National Film Theater in London staged a Fassbinder retrospective; the Paris Cinématheque did so in 1974—the same year he was given an award by the International Catholic Film Office (OCIC) at Cannes. Fassbinder's films were regularly featured at the New York Film Festival, starting with *The Merchant of Four Seasons* in 1972. He was the first of his West German contemporaries to enter the arena of international coproduction, with *Chinese Roulette* in 1976 and *Despair* in 1977. In 1978 *The Marriage of Maria Braun* projected its director into the international film spotlight as the dynamo of what critics were now calling a "New German Cinema." The following year, the Italian film industry awarded him its Luchino Visconti Prize for the complete body of his work and gave a special actress award to Hanna Schygulla for *Maria Braun.* In West Germany, Fassbinder was well known as the most productive director of the New German Cinema, and a number of his films and his coworkers on them received German Film Prizes (similar to the American Oscars). In the country's most prestigious film competition, the International Film Festival at Berlin, he won the second-place Silver Bear for *Maria Braun* in 1979 and the first-place Golden Bear for *Veronika Voss* in 1982. Nevertheless, Fassbinder's reputation in his homeland was entangled almost continually in controversy. As Juliane Lorenz has noted, he was for many years known to ordinary West Germans more as an enfant terrible than as a cineaste.[8] The boulevard press hawked sensationalistic stories about his gay lifestyle and his supposedly tyrannical directorial manner (although this latter charge was challenged by some critics who actually saw him at work). There were attacks from a variety of groups that his films offended. Pressures from both labor and industrial leaders prevented him from shooting episodes six through eight of his working-class television series *Acht Stunden sind kein Tag,* 1972 (Eight Hours Don't Make a Day). The Bavarian playwright Franz Xaver Kroetz sued Fassbinder over alleged obscenity in *Wildwechsel,* 1972 (Wild Game Crossing), based on a Kroetz play. Lesbian and feminist groups accused him of misogyny, in presenting women as complicit in their own oppression in his "women's pictures." Gays complained of betrayal by one of their own in *Fox and His Friends.* Rightists attacked him for his associations with the radical left. Leftists said he had sold out his political principles in his sardonic portrayal of manipulative communists and anarchists in *Mother Küsters Goes to Heaven* and of manipulated terrorists in *The Third Generation,* as well as in his collaboration with a right-wing producer in *Lili Marleen. Berlin Alexanderplatz* was moved to a late night television slot amid complaints that it was unsuitable for family viewing. The most vociferous West German criticism of Fassbinder came in response to his play *Der Müll, die Stadt und der Tod (Garbage, the City, and Death).* Its scheduled performance at the prestigious avant-garde Theater am Turm (TAT) in Frankfurt was canceled early in 1975 amid charges of anti-Semitism. In the turmoil, Fassbinder and his company were dismissed from the TAT, and the director complained bitterly about what he considered willful misrepresentation of his intentions. The publication of that play, and the release of a film adaptation of it (*Schatten der Engel* [*Shadows of Angels*], directed by Daniel Schmid and starring Fassbinder in a lead role), revived the furor. This controversy damaged Fassbinder's reputation with much of the German public and some of the critical press for the rest of his life. As late as 1985, disagreements over a production of *Garbage, the City, and Death* were causing diplomatic reverberations between Bonn and Tel Aviv.[9]

The enthusiastic responses to several Fassbinder programs in Germany in observance of the tenth anniversary of his death in 1992 (including the interest shown by former East Germans to whom Fassbinder's work was virtually unknown before German unification in November 1989) suggest that those old antagonisms on the part of Fassbinder's fellow Germans have largely dissipated. The most ambitious of those 1992 programs was a seven-week exhibition of Fassbinder materials at the Alexanderplatz in Berlin and screenings of virtually all his films and fifty of his favorite movies by other directors. It was well attended and widely covered in the German press. The Goethe Institute and the Fassbinder Foundation have arranged for versions of this exhibition to be carried to Paris, Moscow, Athens, Jerusalem, Buenos Aires, Mexico City, and other cities, in most instances with retrospective film screenings; it will be shown in at least eight United States and Canadian cities starting in the fall of 1996. In the United States, the Bravo cable television network programmed seven Fassbinder films in 1992, and five Fassbinder films previously unseen here were released in 1993. These exhibitions and screenings, along with increasingly sophisticated critical commentary on the director's films in professional and academic journals in many countries, indicate that Fassbinder is finding a permanent place of honor among the major artists of the postwar international cinema, both at home and abroad.[10]

After Fassbinder's death in 1982, many of the people who had come to depend on him emotionally and professionally were in despair over what they would do with their lives.[11] One of Fassbinder's most attentive critics concluded that with his death "the heart, the beating, vibrating center" of the New German Cinema had departed.[12] Many asked, "Is there a New German Cinema after Fassbinder?" The international reputation of West German filmmaking certainly did decline rapidly in the 1980s. Whether or not that can be attributed substantially to the loss of Fassbinder, as some have suggested, it is clear that his death at age thirty-seven cut short an extraordinarily accomplished and promising career. Had he lived longer, the creative energy and the capacity for self-examination and artistic growth which he demonstrated during his brief life would have insured his remaining a vital, if unpredictable, force in both German and international cinema.

Film as Autobiography: A Caveat

Few cinema artists have so openly bared their souls through their work as Fassbinder did. More than perhaps any other filmmaker (Ingmar Bergman, Federico Fellini, and Woody Allen being perhaps the most comparable, for all the differences among them), Fassbinder made use of his films to explore his private experiences and fantasies.[13] Time and again in his work one encounters characters and situations that seem to reflect or comment on his problematic childhood, his often troubled intimate adult relationships, or his public identities as disillusioned radical and compulsively driven artist. He regularly put his friends, coworkers, lovers and ex-lovers, and even his mother into roles which seem to dramatize aspects or possibilities of their real-life relationships with the director. There is considerable truth in the remark of one of his most frequent interviewers: "For Fassbinder there was no boundary between work and free time, between working colleagues and private friends, between art and life."[14]

Fassbinder did not discourage the tendency of critics to look to his personal life for keys to interpretation of his films. For all his reputed shyness in one-on-one encounters with strangers, he seemed to thrive on his status as a controversial celebrity. He invited interest in himself as a legendary artist with his trademark black leather jacket, battered hat, dark glasses, and the provocatively paunchy midsection of his later years. In the many interviews he gave, he talked candidly about the reflection in many of his films of such matters as his "childhood that was no childhood at all," his aggressive tendencies, his frustrating experiences in intimate relationships with both sexes, and his frequent despair.

Fassbinder's many cameo roles in his films are often pointedly self-referential. In the major roles he gave himself in several early films, he often seems to be projecting and exploring aspects of his private self (real or imagined) even further. This is true of Franz, the alienated and depressed protagonist of *Love Is Colder Than Death;* of Jorgos, the social outcast in *Katzelmacher;* and of the exploited working-class gay in *Fox and His Friends.* There are also less obvious autobiographical references—for example, in *Petra von Kant,* which Fassbinder once said was derived from "a particular relationship of mine"; *I Only Want You to Love Me,* which seems to reflect his emotional isolation as a child; and particularly *In a Year of 13 Moons,* which makes substantial reference not only to his dead lover, Armin Meier, but also to Fassbinder's own life.

However, there are considerable dangers in approaching Fassbinder's films with his personal history in mind. Some commentators have been content simply to identify parallels, in reductive fashion, inspired perhaps by such statements by the director as, "I have to deal with everything that I experience in one way or another, in order to have the feeling that I've really experienced it."[15] Certainly, autobiographical approaches to works of the imagination fly in the face of much modern and contemporary critical practice. Anglo-American New Criticism of the 1940s and 1950s discouraged consideration of the author's life and personal views (along with historical and social contexts) in analysis of literature. And while postwar film theory was dominated for many years by the idea of the film director as auteur, with creative power over his or her film as complete as that of the poet or novelist, that approach did not usually result in autobiographical readings of films. More recent literary and cinematic theory has downplayed the significance of the auteur as an autonomous and conscious creator of aesthetic artifacts, and even as a locus of critical interest, among competing systems of ideological and rhetorical significance.[16] However, Fassbinder's forceful and continually self-examining personal character poses a serious challenge to sweeping proclamations about the death of the film auteur. The complex interplay among the director's private and public identities and the imaginative reflections of these in his films are important aspects of the films' meaning. As Jane Shattuc has pointed out, interpreting a Fassbinder film without knowledge of his biography produces "a naive reading."[17]

But one must be careful in interpreting the autobiographical references in Fassbinder's films. In the first place, like any other artist he no doubt drew upon his observations of others' lives as much as his own in finding raw material for his films. Moreover, such material was often substantially altered in its transformation to film. One should not assume without evidence otherwise that any particular event or situation in his films directly reflects the director's own experience or observations. Fassbinder himself has emphasized the shaping power of his artistic imagination: "In the films I certainly deal with my own person somewhat differently from what I do in life. . . . There things happen that I can't direct, or don't want to direct. In my films, on the other hand, my characters behave just as I want them to."[18]

An American Perspective

Fassbinder's films hold particular interest for viewers in the United States. Hollywood films were a major component of his self-education in the cinema, and they are frequently cited in his work—along with many other components of American popular culture. Fassbinder found both in the American gangster film and in American film melodrama, particularly "women's pictures," important models for his films. Furthermore, he saw in the American movie a model of technical proficiency and popular appeal he hoped to achieve in his own films, even though he objected to the emotional and critical shallowness of the typical Hollywood movie.

Moreover, Fassbinder's films provide an incisive critique of postwar West Germany that has serious implications for American culture and American attitudes in the post-Cold War world. Many of these films offer direct or indirect critiques of West Germany's postwar "Economic Miracle," in which the country was transformed from a heap of rubble back into an industrial, technological, and economic dynamo. That miracle was financially launched by the United States, intent on creating in the Federal Republic a bastion against communism in Eastern Europe and the Soviet Union, in the form of a media-hyped, consumer-oriented, capitalistic culture based on the American model. Many in the United States assume that this is the unquestionably appropriate model not only for the supposedly backward former East Germans but also for the millions of other Eastern Europeans and former citizens of the Soviet Union experimenting with free-market capitalism after the fall of their communist regimes in 1989 and 1990. Fassbinder's films continue to pose provocative questions about the validity of the American model of social and economic organization in their depictions of cynical abuse of power, neglect of social responsibility, emotional exploitation, and personal ennui within a society motivated primarily by economic competition and consumerism.

Notes

1. Baer 202.
2. Baer 197–98.
3. Lorenz interview.
4. Haddad Garcia Int 51.
5. Fründt Int 179.
6. Fassbinder, *Anarchie* 179.
7. The latter title is spelled *antiteater* in German. The *h* is added in this book for the convenience of readers. See chapter 2, n. 66.
8. Lorenz, "Je ferai tous mes films avec toi" 67.
9. Lichtenstein 11.
10. In 1991 Hanna Schygulla, the most famous actress in the Fassbinder group, reported that when she appeared at a festival of German films in China she met students from film schools who were "studying [Fassbinder's] movies and writing about them in Chinese." Emerson 22.
11. E.g., Baer 202.
12. Schütte, "Sein Name" 63:
13. The comparison to Allen et al. is made by Limmer (11).
14. Thomsen, *Rainer Werner Fassbinder* 21.
15. Wiegand Int 68.
16. For discussion of recent theories of the film auteur and the "implied author" of a film, see Chatman, *Coming to Terms,* chapters 6, 8, and 9; of the "author" in the New German Cinema, Elsaesser, *New German Cinema,* ch. 3.
17. Shattuc, "R. W. Fassbinder as a Popular *Auteur*" 40.
18. Limmer, Int 68. Fassbinder said in another interview that he allowed his film characters "much more leeway than I give myself"—for instance, "to express their feelings directly"—and that this had helped him change himself (*Anarchy* 26). Critics must, of course, be cautious in dealing with such expressions of intentionality by any artist.

CHAPTER ONE

Fassbinder and His Germany

While Fassbinder's artistic work should not be interpreted reductively as simple dramatization of his personal history, his private life did provide important thematic material for many of his films. This chapter sketches in the most formative periods of his life—his childhood and adolescence—correcting at a number of points the accounts given in published biographies, and speculates on the implications of the director's complex relationships with his parents for his artistic work. It also summarizes political and cultural developments in Fassbinder's homeland, the Federal Republic of Germany (West Germany), whose development as a separate nation after World War II chronologically paralleled his life. Students of his films need to be aware of these developments, since much of the director's work is intensely engaged with public issues, and his artistic career was shaped by the particular conditions of West German literature, theater, and cinema.

Growing Up "Like a Little Flower"

Rainer Werner Fassbinder was born in Bad Wörishofen, a small health spa near Munich, the capital city of Bavaria, on 31 May 1945, just three weeks after the collapse of Adolf Hitler's Third Reich.[1] His father, Helmut, was a physician (with ambitions to be a poet) who had just been discharged from the German army. His mother, Liselotte, had studied German literature and history at the University of Munich but had not completed her degree because of the war and ill health.

Shortly after the birth of Rainer, his parents' only child, the family moved to Munich, where Helmut set up a medical practice with Liselotte's assistance. They rented two adjacent apartments, one for the medical practice and one for living quarters. Because of the poor condition of the building apartment, the infant was sent away from his parents in the fall, at Helmut's insistence, for six months or more. He stayed with his father's twin brother and sister-in-law (both of whom were physicians) in the village of Kippenheim bei Lahr, near Freiburg

in the Black Forest.[2] Liselotte recalled later: "For me, it was terrib
were extraordinary times."

When the child was returned to Munich in 1946, the family liv
were crowded with several lodgers, as well as Liselotte's parents, h
and her sister—who had fled the occupying Soviet army in the former
German (now Polish) city of Danzig (Gdansk). The grandmother, whom
called "a very domineering person," took care of the kitchen as we
baby. She became for Rainer "the person that I should have been
Liselotte—pointing out that, having herself been sent away from her p
home as a child to live with relatives, she was at the time enjoying being
again the child of her own mother: "I was a kind of older sister to Rainer.
boy's father paid him little attention: "He knew his father as little as he k
who I was among all those people." But he was "a lovely child, who was spo
by everybody," the mother recalled. Fassbinder would remember his childh
home as "semi-chaotic . . . a household that didn't conform to bourgeois norn
. . . I actually grew up almost without parents. . . . Nobody ever told me, 'This
how you do it' or 'You're not allowed to do that,' and so forth. I really grew u
like a little flower."[3]

The extended family in which Rainer spent his early years came apart in
1951, when he was six, an event his mother believed was traumatic for the
boy.[4] His parents divorced. Liselotte's relatives moved out of the apartment.
Helmut departed for Cologne, only occasionally visiting his son thereafter; when
he did, he would "read Faust with me on a tape or things like that," Fassbinder
later recalled.[5] Liselotte began to work as an English-German translator.[6] Her
ability to give her son personal attention was hindered by this work and—more
seriously—by recurrences of the tuberculosis that had plagued her for many
years and that now sent her to sanatoria, twice for several months each (in 1950
and 1953), and then for two years (1956–57), when part of a lung was removed.
During her earlier absences, Rainer was reportedly looked after by boarders
and friends[7]; his mother said he spent half a year with the mother of a friend of
hers in Ravensburg. During Liselotte's later hospitalization, he was sent to boarding schools (at his father's expense, according to Liselotte).

As a child, Fassbinder showed numerous indications of artistic creativity.
A friend of his mother who took him for walks starting about age three said he
had an insatiable appetite for stories.[8] He wrote many himself, often presenting
them as gifts to his mother. His childhood crayon drawings and paintings, many
of which his mother saved, make unusually imaginative use of color and form.
When he was about nine his mother gave him, at his request, an audiocassette

recorder, on which he recorded "radio plays" with neighborhood children. Fassbinder's imaginative life as a child was particularly fed and shaped by movies, especially American films of the 1930s and 1940s, which flooded German cinemas after the war. He recalled first seeing "covered wagon westerns," starting at age five. By the age of seven he had become a regular: "I actually went to the movies every day, and later, two or three times a day, if possible."[9] By age twelve, he later recalled, he had made up his mind to become a filmmaker: "For me there was no debate about the matter; it was only a question of time."[10]

Rainer's schooling was mostly an unhappy experience. His mother recalled that there were a hundred students in the public-school class in which he enrolled for the first grade. Once, she said, the teacher slapped him, provoking the boy to shout, "Help, police! You have no right to hit me!" For the second through fourth grades (1951–55) he was sent to the private, permissive Rudolf Steiner School in Munich, which was apparently congenial to his restless temperament.[11] But this was not true of his later schooling. From 1955 to 1961 he attended four different *Gymnasien* (German university preparatory high schools), starting with the Theresiengymnasium in Munich. For two years (1956–58), during his mother's long hospitalization and surgery, he was sent to Saint Anna's, a boarding school in Augsburg, thirty-five miles from Munich. This is presumably the school his mother said she selected for its humanistic orientation, hoping she could have the chance of studying Greek along with her son. But this kind of school "was not to Rainer's taste," so he was moved to the Augsburg Realgymnasium (a less classically oriented high school) for the 1958–59 term. He transferred to the Munich Realgymnasium for the two years 1959 to 1961 (living in a student rooming house, according to his mother).[12]

Fassbinder's performance in this schooling was uneven. He was not willing to study subjects that did not interest him and had to repeat several classes, according to his mother. His grades in mathematics fluctuated so wildly that his teacher once exclaimed to Liselotte, "I don't know what the matter is with that child. It's possible that he is a genius, or that he is crazy." His report card from Saint Anna's for the school year 1957–58 (the year he turned thirteen) shows mediocre-to-low grades in all subjects, with a warning from the director that he was in serious danger of not moving up to a higher level.[13] In 1961, at age sixteen, he dropped out of high school without having received the *Abitur* (German university-preparation degree).

While in his mother's home, Rainer experienced difficult relationships with two quite different kinds of father figures. The first was Liselotte's younger lover, who lived with them when her son was eight or nine years old. Rainer remembered him as being only seventeen years old at the time (his mother said he was twenty), and claimed that he "tried to behave like a father to me. All I

could do was laugh."[14] The second man was more significant in Rainer's life. He was Liselotte's second husband, Wolff Eder, a freelance journalist seventeen years older than she, whom she married in 1959. Fassbinder later spoke of his "touchy relationship" with Wolff Eder. His biographers have often cited this comment, but they have largely ignored his admitted indebtedness to the older man for his view that the Nazi regime was a natural outgrowth of German history and culture, not an aberration, a theme that is fundamental to several of Fassbinder's films.[15] The mother believed that Eder was "a very important authority figure" for her son, and that the example of his liberal-left criticism of the conservative West German government in the 1960s was an important factor in Rainer's refusal to follow the more radical forms of political protest that many of his friends pursued.[16]

According to his mother, it was following an argument with his stepfather that Fassbinder went to Cologne in 1961, at age sixteen, to live with his father, whom he had seen only occasionally since the breakup of the family ten years previously.[17] He had purchased some older buildings in Cologne, which he had subdivided into apartments for immigrant workers. During the two years he lived with him, Rainer helped his father set up a real-estate office and expand his rental business.[18] He also worked for a decorator in the evenings, painting and papering walls.[19] While in Cologne, he completed a high school certificate (but not the Abitur) through night classes, according to his mother.

Early in his adolescence, Fassbinder had identified himself as homosexual. His mother recalled that when he told her this, when he was about fourteen, she was perplexed: "I thought it was a sickness, and I said we should send him to a psychologist, to be cured."[20] When he talked about this matter to interviewers, he insisted that his homosexual preference had never seemed a problem to him, except insofar as others such as his mother found it so.[21] "Sexually speaking, I have no problems at all," he said on another occasion. "That is a point on which I have really no complexes and no inhibitions."[22] Fassbinder did have sexual liaisons with several women as well as with men. As will be seen, it may be more accurate to speak of his sexual orientation as bisexual rather than strictly homosexual.

Ties That Bind: Rainer and His Parents

The problems between parents and children frequently seen in Fassbinder's films have given rise to much speculation about the nature of the director's relationships with his parents. It seems likely that his childhood was emotionally damaging—considering his lengthy separation from his parents as an infant, his lack of parental attachment as a small child, and the breakup of the family in his sixth year. Many writers have concluded that his "childhood that was no childhood at all" almost entirely explains the recurrent theme of emotional exploitation and oppression in Fassbinder's films, as well as the difficulties he experienced in many of his own intimate relationships as an adult. Ronald Hayman, for example, asserts that Fassbinder spent "much of his adult life struggling against the memories of childhood,"[23] and he interprets many of the films accordingly. However, Fassbinder often insisted that, although his childhood situation was unusual, it was not damaging. "It was probably not a childhood like Truffaut experienced . . . not one that was all messed up; rather it just wasn't one. . . . I'm glad I had this remarkable kind of non-existent parental home."[24] Even in pointing out that his parents neglected him, Fassbinder acknowledged their reasons: "My mother was sick and my father had his own life." And he characterized the times that he did get their attention as "euphoric" episodes that seem to anticipate the "utopian" moments that occur in many of his films: "I saw very little of my parents as a young child, but when I did it was really great. There was always something happening. Before they had me, they had really incredible ideas about the kind of wonderful parents they would be, that they would really help their child come to terms with life. They aren't stupid people, but really sharp, and in the little time we were together they tried to give a lot of themselves to make up for lost time."[25]

There are few directly oppressive fathers in Fassbinder's films. Where fathers do appear, they are often well intentioned but ineffectual. But mostly they are absent. If Fassbinder's comments about Helmut are taken at face value, it appears that he was not particularly troubled by his virtual lack of a real father. He once noted matter-of-factly that, after having lived with him for two years in Cologne, he had no further contact with Helmut. Asked if his father was proud of his accomplishments, he said, "I can imagine rather that it is painful and frightening for him when people say, 'Are you the father of this Fassbinder?'"[26] As an adult he seems to have shared his mother's view that his father was "a broken personality," as well as her scorn for his literary pretensions.[27] "My father is a comical person. He is really a great artist, a great poet, who has only one handicap: he can get to work as an artist only when he is financially secure, and naturally that never happens. . . . I think he is completely crazy."[28]

But such offhanded comments may disguise serious disappointments and anxieties. One wonders, for example, how much the child Rainer believed the idealized version of Helmut that his mother says she gave him, and to what extent he was disillusioned by the contrasting reality he later experienced.[29]

Fassbinder's acknowledgment that there were substantial autobiographical grounds for the "fatherless heroes" of many of his films suggests a sense of emotional deprivation because of his absent father.[30] He may have been seeking to compensate for this lack later in his life both in playing (with such mixed emotions) the role of patriarch within his professional entourage, or again in the several close but presumably nonsexual relationships he had with older men, such as the film director Douglas Sirk, the writer and actor Gerhard Zwerenz, the actor Dirk Bogarde, and the wealthy film producer Horst Wendlandt.[31]

Fassbinder's relationship with his mother also seems to have been considerably more complex than he was often willing to admit. But it does not seem to have been nearly as obsessive as has often been reported, frequently by writers who have taken an unaccountably hostile attitude toward Mrs. Eder.

It was only after his parents had divorced, and Rainer and his mother were by themselves for the first time (when he was six), that the boy began to see her in her special role as his mother.[32] After the death of her second husband in 1971, Liselotte substantially assisted her son in his professional work, although she was otherwise employed full-time (at a research center in Munich, first as a programmer and later as editor of a periodical, *Statistical Software Newsletter*). She took responsibility for straightening out major problems with government tax authorities relative to the antitheater films (as discussed in chapter three), prepared financial reports for funding agencies, and typed some film scripts— in addition to taking roles in twenty-five of his films. For a decade after Fassbinder's death, she worked strenuously to protect his estate from the claims of some former associates and his father.[33]

Many of the books about Fassbinder that appeared within a few years after his death represent Liselotte as an aloof, self-centered woman who alternately neglected and oppressed her son during his childhood and adolescence. In casting her in many demeaning roles and in creating so many oppressive mother figures in his films, so this story goes, the director was simply punishing her for what she had done to him earlier. For example, Kurt Raab identifies the mother of the protagonist of *The Bitter Tears of Petra von Kant* simply as Liselotte, "cold, emotionless, interested only in her own well-being."[34] Robert Katz misleadingly sums up Liselotte's roles in the films (most of which are distinctly minor) as "a cold, hovering presence," and he describes her name as it usually appears in the credits, "Lilo Pempeit," as a "new name" her son imposed upon her as an instrument of his "endless revenge"[35]—when in fact it is nothing more than an informal version of her maiden name.[36]

Such speculation is not without its grounds in the films, of course. As will be seen, there are plenty of oppressive mothers there. And the three most significant roles that Liselotte Eder took in her son's films are problematic mother figures: the deceptively sweet mother in *Effi Briest,* the kindly but disapproving Mother Superior in *In a Year of 13 Moons,* and Liselotte Eder playing herself voicing reactionary sentiments, in the at least partly staged confrontation with her son in *Germany in Autumn.*[37]

Fassbinder often spoke as if the relationship he had with his mother after the breakup of the extended family in his sixth year was an uncomplicated friendship, but one with definite limits. "We had a wonderful relationship as pals, a friendly relationship to each other. When she then suddenly tried to make a son out of me, I put up a strong fight."[38] "Since we work, we get along. Work is the pacifier. But our relationship is not typical—of anyone. We are friends, but we give each other tremendous freedom. She is not Rainer's mother. She is herself."[39] But sometimes such comments take on a defensive tone that seems to be holding strong emotions in check: "My mother and I are buddies. I resist anything more than that. I don't need any mother-son contacts."[40]

Fassbinder's observations about Liselotte's recurring bouts with tuberculosis suggest another important factor in their "very complicated relationship," suggesting how closely such emotions as sympathy, guilt, and anger can be linked in intimate situations, as so often happens in his films: "I finally came to understand her as my mother at a time when she was very ill. On the one hand, that brought out pity in me, on the other hand, guilt, because in my egocentrism—as a child . . . I didn't have any authority figure who could have put me in my place—I saw her illness as my fault, which then brought out hostility in me."[41]

Some of Fassbinder's most intense feelings about his mother seem to be indicated in his discussion of a dream she once had that they were going to be married. His account implies that this happened many times in his childhood (but his mother said that it occurred only once, when he was about thirty years old).[42] "That always upset me," he said. "It scared me when I suddenly realized that I was so important for her, as an individual figure, as a human being." Did he respond with Oedipal feelings? "No. On the contrary, I treated my mother the way in Freud boys treat their fathers. They always kill the father; they have to kill him. Every time my mother got too close to me with those dreams of hers, I dealt with her in a way that certainly had something to do with murder. . . . I really tried to reduce her to total silence."[43]

With their emotional intensity and archetypal overtones, those remarks suggest clearly how Fassbinder's ambiguous feelings about his mother could have fed his artistic imagination. He may have imputed to the relationship between child and mother (that "primordial subject of the first demand," as the psychoanalytic theorist Jacques Lacan has put it) an undue proportion of his many other relational difficulties.[44] Once he admitted that he sometimes confused his recollection of the facts of his childhood with the examples of emotional "paralysis" within families which he had created in his imagination.[45] Another statement puts Fassbinder's ties to his mother into the same category with all the other personal relationships he so imaginatively projects into his films: "We had a lot to come to terms with. On the other hand, we tried to establish a normal kind of friendship. Perhaps that's the reason she is in my films. I always have my friends perform in the films, because that makes it possible for me to have a special kind of contact with people."[46]

Harry Baer takes a helpfully skeptical approach to the portrayals of the mother figure in Fassbinder's films, reminding one how much difference there may be between the actual components of an artist's personal history and their representation in works of the imagination. Baer observed that Liselotte seemed to follow humbly her son's directions in her roles both as actress and as mother. He wondered, therefore, about the unpleasant mother figures in the early films, and he was particularly puzzled by the discrepancy between the coldhearted mother Lilo Pempeit plays in *Gods of the Plague* and what he had observed of her personally. "We all thought: What is Rainer getting back at her for? Actually, she is a really nice woman, a little distant."[47] Baer ironically dismisses a frequently cited episode in which Rainer supposedly shouted at his mother during a shooting session: "You tried to poison me with green apples when I was a baby!" He implies that the episode was either a joke or (as Mrs. Eder has explained) highly exaggerated.[48] A homosexual himself, Baer comments: "Rainer and the apple. Perhaps he is guilty about his homosexuality, since, as we all know, Eve gave Adam the apple and, as is well known, all our unhappiness began with that." Baer concludes with a perceptive observation that should be taken as a warning to all critics and biographers inclined to take too literally the supposed autobiographical references in Fassbinder's films: "All these things are set pieces, which are randomly moved around in the great production that is named Rainer Werner Fassbinder."[49]

Postwar Germany: Zero Hour, Cold War, Economic Miracle

Like virtually every other large city in Germany, Munich was devastated when Helmut and Liselotte Fassbinder and their infant son moved there in the early summer of 1945. One fourth of all housing units in the country had been destroyed or made unusable in the Allied bombing raids. Food was in short supply, and transportation was paralyzed. Beyond the intended victims of the Nazi regime, millions of Germans had died or been severely wounded during the war that had been launched by Adolf Hitler six years earlier to establish the National Socialist "thousand-year empire."

The German people were not only in a state of extreme physical duress in the early postwar months. As a nation, they were "morally . . . bankrupt."[50] The Nazi regime had led the country—with its rich heritage of literature, music, art, philosophy, science, and theology, and its traditional ideals of piety and home—into an era of utter barbarism. Its most grisly achievement had been the systematic murder of six million Jews from Germany and elsewhere in Europe, along with additional millions of Gypsies, Slavs, homosexuals, political resisters, and other supposed undesirables. Thus, both physically and morally, it was for the Germans, as many then said, "Zero Hour."

The victors launched a program of "de-Nazification" in Germany after the war. In 1945 and 1946 an international military court at Nuremburg found nineteen major Nazi leaders guilty of war crimes and crimes against humanity and sentenced them to death or long prison terms. Later trials sent other Nazi criminals to prison, and the occupying military forces set about to exclude all former Nazis from positions of responsibility. But by no means all individuals tarnished by Nazism were thus disqualified and penalized, since many records had been destroyed as the war came to an end, and many former Nazis who were judged to have played only "nominal" roles in the party were allowed to take high-level positions in the effort to get the country running again.

Fassbinder lived in the Federal Republic of Germany, which officially came into being in May 1949 (when he was four years old), after the unlikely wartime coalition which had defeated Hitler had deteriorated into an ideological Cold War. The territory of pre-Nazi Germany—except for portions ceded to Poland and the Soviet Union—was divided into the Federal Republic of Germany (FRG) and the German Democratic Republic (GDR). The FRG (West Germany) was Western-oriented, democratic, and capitalist. It was initially divided into zones assigned to the three leading Western powers among the victorious allies—the British, the French, and the Americans—and the small city of Bonn was designated as its capital. A Soviet-dominated, communist government was in control of the GDR (East Germany). Its capital was the eastern sector of Berlin (the capital city of Germany before the postwar division of the country and after its reunification in 1990); the western sector of the city (controlled by the Western allies) was completely surrounded by GDR territory. The border between East and West Germany soon became the most sensitive dividing line between the two postwar superpowers, the United States and the

Soviet Union. It took literally concrete form in the Berlin Wall, erected in August 1961, which symbolized the virtual cessation of economic, political, and social commerce between the two Germanies until the late 1970s.

The Wall had been erected by the authorities of the German Democratic Republic to stop the flight of thousands of its best-trained workers to the Federal Republic, which was enjoying a remarkable postwar economic recovery. That "Economic Miracle" had been set in motion by U.S. Marshall Plan dollars and was built upon a combination of American-style free-market economics and a continuation of Germany's historic commitment to social welfare (so-called welfare-state capitalism). The demand for labor to support the Economic Miracle led to a large influx of foreign *Gastarbeiter* ("guest workers," as they were euphemistically called) into the Federal Republic from southern Europe during the 1950s and early 1960s. By 1975 they and their families constituted a resident foreign population in the Federal Republic of over four million. The social conflicts arising from this influx of foreigners into the relatively homogeneous "Fatherland" would be a central theme of two Fassbinder films, *Katzelmacher* and *Angst essen Seele auf* (*Ali: Fear Eats the Soul*).

Presiding over the Economic Miracle until Fassbinder's eighteenth year was the Federal Republic's first chancellor, Konrad Adenauer. *Der Alte* (The Old Man) was seventy-three years old when elected in 1949, and his shrewd, authoritarian style of leadership kept him in power for fourteen years. Strongly committed to free-enterprise capitalism, Adenauer built on Western fears of communistic Eastern Europe and the Soviet Union to gain for the Federal Republic full membership in the defensive North Atlantic Treaty Organization (NATO) and to build up West German armed forces, operating under NATO command.

Adenauer resigned in 1963 under growing pressure from the political left and an increasingly antagonistic younger generation. The young rebels objected to what they saw as a self-satisfied, conservative government in Bonn that had no interest in reforming social and political institutions "whose structures had originated in Germany's authoritarian past."[51] Adenauer was succeeded as chancellor from 1963 to 1966 by Ludwig Erhard (former economics minister and architect of the Economic Miracle). Then followed a three-year "Grand Coalition" of the three major political parties, headed by Chancellor Kurt Georg Kiesinger, a former Nazi who had "repented" and become a staunch defender of democracy in West Germany.[52] In 1969 a new coalition of the large, left-moderate Social Democratic Party and the small Free Democratic Party (Liberals) launched the so-called Social-Liberal Era, which corresponded almost exactly with the thirteen years of Fassbinder's career as a feature filmmaker,

21

from 1969 until 1982. The Social-Liberal coalition was first led by Chancellor Willy Brandt, the popular ex-mayor of Berlin. But Brandt was forced to resign in 1974, when one of his closest aides was discovered to be an East German spy; he was succeeded by Helmut Schmidt. The Brandt-Schmidt government turned significantly away from the conservative policies that had characterized the Adenauer era. It liberalized domestic policies on such matters as abortion, divorce, and pornography, and in its "Ostpolitik" (Eastern Policy) it took major steps to normalize relations with the Soviet Union, the German Democratic Republic, and other communist regimes in Eastern Europe. But it did not go nearly far enough to satisfy the younger generation and the more extreme political left.[53]

The Generation of '68: Revolution, Disillusionment, Terrorism

Like most other Western democracies, the Federal Republic in the late 1960s experienced dramatic political upheavals led by a radicalized younger generation. Throughout Europe and the United States thousands of demonstrators took to the streets to protest the "military-industrial complex," the Cold War, the nuclear arms race, the American war in Vietnam, racial prejudice and oppression from South Africa to the southern United States, environmental pollution, and educational systems that seemed to perpetuate and rationalize the power of privileged classes.

The most tumultuous year was 1968. Rebellious university students and workers virtually paralyzed France for a few weeks in May. (Fassbinder was arrested in Paris at the time—whether as a participant or an observer is not clear.)[54] In the United States there were widespread campus uprisings and violent confrontations between police and demonstrators at the Democratic convention in Chicago, and two major political figures, the presidential candidate Robert Kennedy and the civil-rights leader Dr. Martin Luther King, Jr., were assassinated. In the Federal Republic, some older leftists and many in the postwar generation had become increasingly disillusioned with the governing Grand Coalition. They concluded that the Social Democratic Party, which had been founded as a Marxist-socialist party in the nineteenth century, had sold its birthright in return for a bigger role in the administration of the Economic Miracle. Leftist students broke off from the Social Democratic Party in 1959 to form the German Students for a Democratic Society, which became increasingly active in opposing the coalition government in the 1960s. Claiming that opportunities for effective political opposition had been effectively shut down, an informal

22

Marxist-anarchist "Extraparliamentary Opposition" arose in the late 1960s, and it soon became a major force behind large demonstrations against the government in many West German cities. University students, who had begun protesting initially against West Germany's outmoded and hierarchical educational systems, became increasingly radicalized over political issues.

The scene was especially tense in the isolated western sector of Berlin. In the spring of 1967 in Berlin (where Fassbinder was unsuccessfully seeking admission, for a second time, to a newly established film academy), university students and police confronted each other in "increasingly brutal tests of strength."[55] By the next year, students all over West Germany were demonstrating in huge numbers, occupying university buildings, and (in Freiburg) storming a prison to release jailed colleagues. An International Vietnam Congress in February mobilized 12,000 demonstrators in West Berlin, demanding the dissolution of NATO. In April, "Red" Rudi Dutschke, the most brilliant theoretician of the student protest movement, was permanently disabled by a gunshot to the head, fired by a man who many believed was put up to the deed by the city government and the reactionary Springer press, publisher of the popular *Bild* tabloid newspapers. The same month, two Frankfurt department stores were torched by firebombs. Some of the bombs had reportedly been manufactured in the apartment of a man in whose theater in Munich Fassbinder and his colleagues were rehearsing and performing provocative antiestablishment plays.[56]

Like most of his friends, Fassbinder, who turned twenty-three at the end of May 1968, numbered himself among the radical Generation of '68. But he was not an active participant in the confrontations with the police. His artistic work apparently seemed to him an appropriate substitute for such activity. Besides, he was more interested in fomenting "private revolution" than direct political action, he said in 1969.[57] A decade later he would remark, "I don't throw bombs, I make films."[58] But occasionally in interviews throughout his adult life, Fassbinder wondered aloud whether or not he should be more directly involved in political protest and resistance.

The passionate hopes of the worldwide youth rebellion of the late 1960s, which many participants seemed to think would be able to overturn well-entrenched political and economic systems virtually overnight, were quickly dashed. The end came abruptly in West Germany. In May 1968 the Social Democratic Party and the trade unions separated themselves from the student movement by agreeing to a set of Emergency Decrees limiting constitutionally protected civil liberties, which the Kiesinger government had proposed as a means of protecting the country from subversives. For all their Marxist rhetoric, the students had never shown much interest in attracting German workers into their cause, and their tactics were quickly turning off the older generation of leftists. Germany's best-known postwar writer, Günter Grass (1927–), a close friend of Willy Brandt as well as an outspoken critic of the hard-nosed response of the Berlin police to student demonstrations, complained of "symptoms of fascism" in the student rebels and criticized the "middle-class élite and . . . scholastic theorists" who, he said, were manipulating them.[59] By the autumn of 1969, the major organization behind the young people's protests in the Federal Republic, the Socialist German Student Union (SDS), had split into factions and was giving way to other interest groups, including feminists. The revolutionary German students thus found themselves isolated, disorganized, and without clear goals.

The sudden disillusionment of the West German Generation of '68 is captured in the opening chapter of Harry Baer's 1982 book about his association with Fassbinder. They first met in 1969, Baer writes, after the revolutionary air had cleared. But 1967 and 1968—"those were the years":

> Back then I had gotten up and gone to bed with the battle-cry: "The Yanks are behaving like pigs in Vietnam, and if that doesn't inspire cold rage in you, then you're either ignorant or a pig yourself!" . . . Then came April 68. The revolt was at hand. Our total insurrection, our revolution! Easter in Munich. Stones flew, cars were destroyed, window panes, Springer's yellow journalism offices stormed, people died. In May, Paris on the barricades. "Our revolution has gone worldwide, you can see it!" . . . We are not alone. A single huge orgasm of solidarity. . . .
>
> And then came the laws [Emergency Decrees]. Everybody out! There is more bombing in Vietnam, and if we don't watch out our security guards will be allowed to start shooting too. Where is the exit?
>
> Mine led . . . into the theater. Into the antitheater.[60]

Some of the brightest and most radically committed members of this generation were not satisfied to channel their revolutionary fervor into offbeat plays and films such as Fassbinder and his companions in the antitheater were making. Nor were they interested in gradually bringing about their utopian ideals in a "long march through the institutions" (the universities, the press, and the government), as many of their disappointed fellows talked of doing. In their increasing desperation and despair over what they perceived to be a reactionary turn in West German politics, they set out on a course of terroristic actions that they hoped would inspire fascistic reactions from those in power. This strategy would, they thought, at least convince the world of the correctness of their political analysis of the nature of the Federal Republic, if not lead to the popular revolution some among them expected.

The actions of these terrorists, along with the government's extreme reactions, came close to paralyzing West German political society and almost undermined the still-new democratic tradition of the Federal Republic during the 1970s. Many on the left (including Fassbinder) were convinced that the official response was more dangerous than the terrorist threat; they concluded that the political instincts of the supposedly progressive Social-Liberal regime were close to fascistic. Fassbinder was acquainted with two of the early terrorists, and he sympathized with their ideological position even though he had serious doubts about their tactics. As will be seen in chapter seven, his ambivalent feelings about the terrorists and his abhorrence of the government's increasingly authoritarian crackdown on leftists during the 1970s were major ingredients in the crisis that marked the beginning of the final phase of his career.

Out of the Ashes: Postwar Literature and Theater

Fassbinder grew to maturity within a German cultural complex that had to rebuild itself substantially after the nightmare of the Third Reich.[61] Many artists and writers had fled Germany in the 1930s, since Hitler and his minions (particularly his minister of propaganda Joseph Goebbels) would tolerate artistic work only if it supported Nazi ideology. After the war, both federal and state governments in West Germany were anxious to convince the world that the Nazi era had been a tragic aberration and to restore respect for German culture through a quick revival of symphony orchestras and theater and opera companies, with the substantial governmental subsidies to which they had long been accustomed.

Literary publication began again in the Federal Republic during the first year after the war, mostly in the form of books from writers who had made the "inner emigration," that is, who had remained in Germany during the Nazi era but had held back manuscripts that they knew would not have passed Hitler's censors. This group was severely criticized by many of those who had really emigrated, most notably Thomas Mann (1875–1955), Germany's most prominent prewar writer, then living in the United States (and later in Switzerland). Many significant postwar West German writers were associated with "Group

47," an informal and changing group of authors who came together once a year from 1947 to 1967 to read and criticize each other's manuscripts. Group 47 nurtured such writers as the Nobel Prize winner Heinrich Böll (1917–1985); Günther Grass, whose 1959 novel *The Tin Drum* first brought international recognition to postwar West German literature; Martin Walser (1927–), another novelist noted for his ironical observations on contemporary German society; and the philosophical and socially committed Austrian-born poet and fiction-writer Ingeborg Bachmann (1926–1973).

By the 1960s most West German writers were explicitly or implicitly left-wing in political orientation. As one film scholar has pointed out, whereas in the 1950s most writers in the Federal Republic were nonconforming individualists, giving voice to "radical hermeticism and existentialism," by the end of the next decade they had begun to raise "a serious critical voice," influenced by the so-called Critical Theory propounded by the Frankfurt School of social inquiry.[62] The ideas of Herbert Marcuse and Theodor Adorno and other theorists of the Frankfurt School—which applied both Marxist and Freudian concepts in their analysis of the class bases of modern culture—also affected the work of many West German filmmakers, including Fassbinder.

Efforts to rebuild the theater in the Federal Republic after the war were inspired by the long tradition of German drama as a "moral institution," as the poet and dramatist Friedrich Schiller (1759–1805) had called it.[63] Within a few years most of the venerable and publicly subsidized West German theaters had been rebuilt and their repertory companies reestablished. Audiences were hungry for plays from the international repertory that had been denied to them during the Nazi regime, as well as new work, including plays from the "Theater of the Absurd" by such authors as the Irish-French Samuel Beckett (1906–89), the Italian Eugène Ionesco (1912–94), and the Swiss Friedrich Dürrenmatt (1962–90).

There was considerable interest in the plays of Bertolt Brecht (1898–1956), such as *Mutter Courage und ihre Kinder,* 1941 (*Mother Courage*) and *Der gute Mensch von Sezuan,* 1943 (*The Good Woman of Setzuan*). Brecht was the most important living German playwright, and his work had not been seen in Germany since the Nazi takeover in 1933, the year he began an emigration that took him as far as California. A committed Marxist, Brecht returned from the United States to live in East Berlin from 1949 until his death, managing his world-famous Berliner Ensemble theater. Brecht's most influential dramatic theory concerned the *Verfremdungseffekt* (alienation effect) that he sought to achieve in his plays. By breaking the illusion of realism, he intended to stimu-

late the spectator's critical thought about real-world injustices and inspire social action outside the theater. The influence of Brecht's leftist critique of bourgeois society, and of the alienation effects his plays so often employed, can be
felt in the work of many West German postwar playwrights and filmmakers,
including Fassbinder.[64] However, as Jane Shattuc has argued, Brecht's influence on Fassbinder should not be overemphasized. By the late 1960s Brecht's
theater had become an acceptable cultural institution in the Federal Republic.
To many in the West German counterculture, Brechtian theater represented
both the moderate and complacent "established left" of Willy Brandt and Helmut
Schmidt and the "more authoritarian left" of the German Communist Party—
neither of which had effectively challenged the American military-industrial
complex's war in Vietnam and its hegemony in West Germany.[65] Fassbinder
rarely spoke of Brecht, and he might well have been thinking of the work of
Brecht, among others, when he expressed in 1973 his disinterest in the kinds of
plays being presented at Munich's Residenz Theater and other mainline theaters in the city.[66]

Fassbinder's early work was much more clearly affected by two new phe-
nomena in the postwar West German theater scene—the revival of the Austrian
and south German *Volkstück* (folk play), and the "Living Theater" recently
imported from the United States. The folk plays were dialect dramas, with roots
in the popular theater of eighteenth-century Vienna, focusing on the everyday
lives of peasants and the lower bourgeoisie. In the 1920s they evolved into a
serious form of social and political analysis through the Bavarian "critical folk
plays" of Marieluise Fleisser (1901–74) and Ödön von Horváth (1901–38). Re-
vivals of Fleisser's plays in the postwar West German theater, along with new
works in the folk play tradition by Fassbinder, Martin Speer (1944–), and Franz
Xaver Kroetz (1946–), were important vehicles for a heightened political aware-
ness in the late 1960s and 1970s.[67]

The American Living Theater was even more politically engaged. This
communal acting company, founded in New York in 1951 by Julian Beck and
Judith Malina, toured Europe from 1964 to 1968 with psychologically and politically provocative plays which engaged in extreme forms of interaction with
their audiences, inspired by the "theater of cruelty" performed and theorized by
the French playwright Antonin Artaud (1896–1948). During 1968, the troupe
had sided passionately with the rebellious students in France, and it had aroused
great enthusiasm when it toured Germany.[68] It was through a German offshoot
of this tradition, which called itself the "Action Theater," that Fassbinder in
1967 began to find his métier as an artist.

Young and New German Cinema

During the first decade of the Weimar Republic, which in 1919 replaced the government of Kaiser Wilhelm II after its defeat in World War I, German cinema had experienced a golden age. With substantial government support, and working mostly in the tightly controlled environment of the large Universum Film A.G. (UFA) studio at Neubabelsberg, near Berlin, German directors set new international standards both for psychological realism and for artistic visual effects (many of their films contributing significantly to "German Expressionism"—one of the earliest nonnaturalistic modern European art movements). Among the most influential films produced during this period were the fantasy of madness and tyranny *Das Kabinett des Dr. Caligari,* 1919 (*The Cabinet of Dr. Caligari*), written by Hans Janowitz and Carl Meyer and directed by Robert Wiene; F. W. Murnau's much-imitated first Dracula film, *Nosferatu,* 1922, and his moving portrait of a hotel doorman, *Der letzte Man,* 1924 (*The Last Laugh*); G. W. Pabst's love story set within the political tumult following the Russian revolution, *Die Liebe der Jeanne Ney,* 1927 (*The Love of Jeanne Ney*); Joseph von Sternberg's account of a pedantic teacher ensnared in love for a showgirl, *Der blaue Engel,* 1930 (*The Blue Angel*); and Fritz Lang's *M* (1931), a complex exploration of the psyche of a child-murderer.[69]

By the time Hitler became chancellor in 1933, many of the directors and cinematographers, and some actors, of this golden-age cinema had fled Germany—most of them to Hollywood, where they significantly enriched American film for decades. Many who stayed in Germany contributed to the Nazi wartime film industry, which became, under the special attention of Hitler and Goebbels, an instrument of powerful propaganda, both directly and indirectly. The ideological messages were straightforward in the newsreels and documentaries that claimed both invincible power and idealistic motives for the Nazis. They were less direct in many UFA entertainment films of this era—such as historical dramas celebrating the military achievements of the eighteenth-century Prussian Emperor Frederick the Great and *Heimat* (homeland) films idealizing the lives of rural Nordic-looking Germans utterly devoted to the Fatherland.[70]

The initial revival of the West German film industry in the years following World War II was shaped in large part by the policies of the occupying Allied military powers. Their first priority was not the reconstruction of a German film production capability but the rebuilding of movie theaters and restoration of a German film distribution system, mostly under American control; by 1950 most of the eighty-five German film distributors had U.S. ties.[71] Conveniently,

Hollywood had on hand a great many films made in the later 1930s and early 1940s which the Germans had not had the opportunity to see. Since most of them had already recouped their costs, these films could be dumped on the German market at low cost, for easy profits. Hollywood producers successfully urged this policy on the U.S. government, arguing that these films would substantially assist in the Allies' denazification campaign and support "the worldwide ideological struggle for the minds of men."[72] West Germans streamed into the theaters by the millions to absorb the images, gestures, and idioms of the lonesome cowboys, the tough but vulnerable mobsters and gun molls, the valiant soldiers, and the upstanding citizens who had peopled the cinematic imaginations of Americans during the previous decades.[73] (Among those viewers was a lonely kid in Munich, whose mother would have preferred that her son play soccer instead of stopping by the movie theater on his way home from school every day. But he was headstrong, and she had to keep up her work as a translator.)

German film production began again in the Federal Republic almost immediately after the war, and it achieved considerable success with home audiences until the mid-1950s, when television began to draw viewers away from the theaters. Movie audiences had also begun to tire of the formulaic genres to which their directors repeatedly turned: "rubble films"; war adventure dramas; improbable romances set in exotic places; Heimat films; and, increasingly, soft pornography passing as educational sex films.[74] The absence of originality and creativity in West German cinema in the early 1960s prompted a leading international film magazine, *Sight and Sound,* to characterize West Germany as a "cinematic wasteland."[75]

The enervated state of the film industry in West Germany at this juncture contrasted sharply with exciting developments in cinema elsewhere in the world. Italian directors Luchino Visconti, Roberto Rossellini, and Vittorio De Sica had developed in the later 1940s the stark, moving style of Neorealism, and by the early 1960s their successors (Federico Fellini, Michelangelo Antonioni, Pier Paolo Pasolini, Bernardo Bertolucci *et al.*) had produced significant work in a second Italian film renaissance. Some of the most impressive achievements of the French nouvelle vague (New Wave) had already been completed in the early 1960s by Claude Chabrol, François Truffaut, Alain Resnais, Jean-Luc Godard, Agnès Varda, and Louis Malle—stimulated by the heady discussion of American film auteurs and cinematic theory in the influential journal *Cahiers du cinéma.* In many other countries, postwar filmmakers were establishing international reputations with their fresh and distinctive approaches to the cinema: Ingmar Bergman in Sweden, Tony Richardson in England, Roman Polanski and Andrzej Wajda in Poland, and Akira Kurosawa and Yasujiro Ozu in Japan, to name only a few of the major directors.

In February 1962 twenty-six young German filmmakers attending an annual festival of short films in the northwestern German city of Oberhausen issued a manifesto against what they called "Papa's cinema." They announced "the collapse of the conventional German film," whose "attitude and practice we reject." The successes which many of them had had in international short film competitions showed "that the future of the German film lies in the hands of those who have proven that they speak a new film language." They declared their intention "to create the new German feature film."[76] This Oberhausen Manifesto was the symbolic beginning of what would, within a decade, be recognized as one of the most vital and significant national cinemas in the world. Ironically, not many of the signers of the manifesto would occupy highly visible places in what was first known as Young German Film and then, starting in the early 1970s, as the New German Cinema—after a new generation of German filmmakers (including Fassbinder) had become prominent. It is also ironic that the New German Cinema was heralded more enthusiastically abroad than at home. Most of these films were received coolly by West German theater audiences and much of the critical establishment. But in New York, Paris, and London, the films of the Young and New German Cinema were showcased and its star directors celebrated.[77]

The complex history of the New German Cinema through the remainder of Fassbinder's life, including the system of state subsidies developed to encourage it, can be only summarized here.[78] It was always more an idea than a concerted program or organization. It developed in a series of small steps forward in the spirit of Oberhausen, with some major detours and regressions. At both federal and state levels, governmental authorities in West Germany were committed to a revival of a respected German film industry, presumably both for its potential as an economic export and as a means of building a positive image of the new Germany in the postwar world. They were willing to invest considerable money to encourage this revival—though not nearly as much as they spent on symphony orchestras, theaters, operas, and ballet companies, as the film community often pointed out.[79]

In 1962 the Institute for Film Design was founded in Ulm by several signers of the Oberhausen Manifesto, including attorney, fiction-writer, theorist, and filmmaker Alexander Kluge (1932–), "the most articulate spokesperson for the Young German Film since its inception."[80] Kluge and his colleagues were committed to the critical theory of the Frankfurt School and were more interested in effects created by camera perspectives and editing than in narrative.[81] The call of the Oberhausen Manifesto for the establishment of film schools was answered with the establishment of the German Film and Television Academy in Berlin in the fall of 1966 (Fassbinder was one of the unsuccessful applicants that year and the next) and a School for Film and Television in Munich in 1967.

One of the most important steps in the realization of the Oberhausen program was the establishment in 1964 of the Young German Film Board (Kuratorium) by the Federal Ministry of the Interior. Its purpose was to support the first and second films of new West German filmmakers. During its first three years the Kuratorium awarded five million marks to support twenty feature films by new directors.[82] These included the first films of Alexander Kluge (*Abschied von Gestern*, 1955–56 [*Yesterday Girl*]) and of Werner Herzog, who within a few years would achieve international recognition for such dark, romantic journeys into the depths of the human soul (and often into exotic geography) as *Aguirre, der Zorn Gottes* (*Aguirre, Wrath of God*, 1972) and his tribute to Murnau, *Nosferatu* (1978). The Kuratorium also supported the first feature film of Volker Schlöndorff (1939–), *Der junge Törless*, 1966 (*Young Torless*). Schlöndorff had been living in Paris, where he had assisted such well-known directors as Jean-Pierre Melville, Alain Resnais, and Louis Malle. He returned to Germany in 1961, the year before Oberhausen, "in order to make films, because they have none there."[83] He soon became one of the most widely recognized directors of the New German Cinema. In 1975 Schlöndorff collaborated with his wife, Margarethe von Trotta (who had acted in several early Fassbinder films), in making a popular and politically engaged film, *Der verlorene Ehre der Katharina Blum* (*The Lost Honor of Katharina Blum*), based on a novel by Heinrich Böll. In 1979 Schlöndorff completed his adaptation of the celebrated novel by Günther Grass, *The Tin Drum*. That film became one of the most successful products of the New German Cinema, winning a Hollywood Oscar as Best Foreign Film. The only graduate of a German film school in this era to achieve an international reputation was Wim Wenders (1945–), who attended the Munich film academy; many of his films display an ambiguous fascination with American popular culture as it impinged on West Germans, as in *Der amerikanischer Freund*, 1977 (*The American Friend*). Schlöndorff's former wife and collaborator, Margarethe von Trotta, later became one of West Germany's best-known directors in her own right. Her highly praised film *Die bleierne Zeit*, 1981 ([The Leaden Time] *The German Sisters*) is a moving story based on the life and death of terrorist leader Ulrike Meinhof, revealing the roots of 1970s terrorism in such elements of the German past as Lutheranism, male authoritarianism, and Hitler fascism. Another successful female New German Film artist of Fassbinder's era is Helma Sanders-Brahms (1940–), director of an important film set in World War II: *Deutschland, bleiche Mutter,* 1980 *(Germany, Pale Mother).*[84] In addition to these feature-film makers, a number of postwar German cinema artists—including Alexander Kluge, Edgar Reitz, Werner Schroeter, Ulrike Ottinger, Rosa von Praunheim, Hellmuth Costard, and Jean-Marie Straub and his wife and collaborator Danièle Huillet were making interesting, often politically provocative, avant-garde films, usually brief and nonnarrative in style.

Like their counterparts in many other European countries (but not the United States) postwar West German filmmakers drew substantially upon public monies for financing their projects. Kuratorium funding for new films was considerably reduced in 1968 in a complicated process by which the younger filmmakers were "outmaneuvered by the old guard."[85] But regulations were revised several times in subsequent years, each time opening up possibilities for new talent, particularly for those whose films were able to achieve ratings of "valuable" or "extremely valuable" in artistic quality by the Film Subsidy Board.[86] In addition, the Federal Ministry of the Interior gave annual German Film Prizes, as well as production grants. Moreover, the state-subsidized television networks began entering into production and distribution arrangements with West German theatrical filmmakers. By 1978 more than 34 million marks had been invested in such coproductions, which typically would be exhibited in theaters for two years before the networks showed them on television.[87] A final important source of support for the creators of the New German Cinema was the establishment in 1971 of the Filmverlag der Autoren, a filmmakers' cooperative organized as a production company and then expanded to distribute its members' films (Fassbinder was a founding member, and remained in the Filmverlag until 1977).[88] As Thomas Elsaesser has summarized the situation, the young filmmakers of postwar West Germany had to "nourish their creative habit by learning to combine their own limited resources with cash awards, subsidy grants and loans, co-production money from television, funds donated by private companies in order to gain a tax advantage, and the more traditional funding arrangements of the established commercial cinema."[89]

None among these young West German filmmakers was more skillful than Rainer Werner Fassbinder in making use of this complex system to pull together the financial resources he needed to transform his most personal fantasies and his most provocative observations on life in his homeland into memorable cinematic images. Within a few years after his return at age eighteen from Cologne to his home city, Munich—intent upon making a career in film but uncertain how to get started—he would become the best-known and most-productive filmmaker in the Federal Republic. As Sheila Johnston has written, Fassbinder's "colorful personality, the extreme visibility of the authorial inscription in his films, his inexhaustible and much-admired capacity for hard work and his entrepreneurial willingness to take financial risks all combine[d] to make him . . . *exceptionally* compatible with the requirements of the system within which he . . . worked."[90]

Notes

1. Until his death, Fassbinder's birthdate was usually reported as 31 May 1946. Katz interprets this as a deliberate deception practiced by Fassbinder and his mother to give him "an extra year of being a boy wonder" (Katz 13; see also Hayman 1). Fassbinder once told his mother that, while he never lied about his age, he enjoyed being thought of as a year younger than he was, after one of his first newspaper interviewers incorrectly calculated his birth year as 1946. "What should I have done about it?" his mother asked. "Write a letter to the editor? Why should Rainer and I have an argument over that?" This and all other references to statements made by Fassbinder's mother are based on the author's interview with her unless otherwise attributed.

2. The location is identified by Juliane Lorenz in a letter to the author, 29 July 1994. Liselotte said that the infant Rainer was well cared for by his aunt and uncle, who had two young children of their own, and nurses. The author understood from her that the absence was about six months; Lorenz received the same information from her (Let 7 April 1994). In an interview with André Müller, however, Liselotte is quoted as saying that the child stayed away from her for a year. "Der Tote Sohn" 17.

3. Wiegand Int 57. In another interview, Fassbinder spoke of the "remarkable" strangers in his parents' apartments, who thought it was "wonderful" to take care of a child. "But for me this constant changing, from one mother to another, was odd" (Müller Int 188). Liselotte recalled that her son "got a lot of love and care as a child from the family and from all the other people who were there. . . . He was a lovely child, who was spoiled by everybody."

4. Liselotte said that on their first Christmas by themselves, Rainer asked, "What? Only the two of us?" "It was like being stabbed in the stomach," she recalled.

5. Wiegand Int 57.

6. Liselotte Eder said that she translated the contemporary American writer Truman Capote's short-story collection *A Tree of Night;* two volumes written in English by Lin Yü-t'ang (1895–1976), a Chinese professor of English, editor, and writer: *The Importance of Understanding* and *The Chinese Theory of Art;* and "a lot of children's books."

7. Hayman 4.

8. Hayman 4.

9. Wiegand Int 62.

10. Brocher Int I.

11. Fassbinder's mother said that she selected the Steiner school primarily for its smaller classes, not because of its child-centered educational philosophy.

12. Names of schools and dates are taken from a brief curriculum vitae that Fassbinder submitted with his 1967 application to the Berlin Film Academy (reproduced in RWFF Catalogue 13 and in Spaich 20).

13. Spaich 21.

14. Limmer Int 47–48. Hayman identifies the young man as "Siggi" (1). Liselotte Eder said that this was not his name, but that her son often joked about Sigmund Freud as "Siggi." Perhaps he applied this tag to his mother's boyfriend.

15. "From my mother's second husband, with whom I always had a very touchy relationship, I learned incredibly much about the German past. It became clear to me then, that the Third Reich was not some kind of an accident on the assembly line of history, but that it came about through a rather logical development" (Limmer Int 89).

16. Liselotte Eder said that Fassbinder "acquired a certain equilibrium" through Wolff Eder, whom she described as "a dedicated Social Democrat." She said that when she started living with Eder in 1958, after her two-year hospitalization, Rainer continued living in boarding schools and visited her and Eder on weekends. She recalled his being present frequently at breakfast when Eder would read the newspaper and "sputter and fume" over policies of the Adenauer regime. She said her second husband arranged through friends of his in the education ministry for her son to remain in school after twice being held back; that he arranged a job for Rainer in the archives of the *Süddeutsche Zeitung* in 1963 through connections at that newspaper; and that he loaned Fassbinder his old Leica camera ("which was like a sacred object to him") for his entrance examination for the Berlin Film School in 1966. She interpreted the personal problems her son and second husband did have as the result of Eder's having taken away "the last person with whom Rainer had a primary relationship. Children are always jealous when their parents remarry."

17. Liselotte Eder recalled that when she and her second husband questioned Rainer about his future plans after he dropped out of school the boy repeatedly answered, "I couldn't care less." His stepfather, recognizing Rainer's talent for drawing and painting, recommended that he go to an art or graphics school, get a job as a theater set designer, or even apprentice himself to a housepainter. All these elicited the same response. Once when the boy was rude to his mother, Eder told him, "You don't talk to my wife that way!" It was then that Rainer said he wanted to live with his father in Cologne, and Eder told Liselotte, "Then he has to go. You must let him go." That was the only "serious incident" between Fassbinder and his stepfather, Liselotte said.

18. Fründt Int 175–6. Hayman writes that Dr. Fassbinder had by then been forced to give up his medical practice because of drunkenness or illegal abortions, and he was living off the rent from his apartments (13). Liselotte Eder disputed the drunkenness charge, pointing out that her former husband did not even smoke.

19. Wiegand Int 60.

20. Liselotte Eder said that she was particularly worried over the fact that in those days homosexuality was against the law. Her husband, Wolff Eder, did not share her

view that the boy's homosexuality was an "illness," but rather "a phase of his development," she said. Contrary to reports by Raab (48) and Hayman (15), the mother said that she and Eder frequently entertained her son "with his homosexual friends" in their home.

21. Limmer Int 75–76.

22. Müller Int 183–84.

23. Hayman 4.

24. Jansen Int 95–97.

25. Müller Int 188.

26. Fründt Int 175–76.

27. Liselotte Eder described Helmut Fassbinder as "brilliant in some ways . . . but disturbed and difficult to live with." She said he thought of his medical practice as a way of financing his desire to be a writer. She said that "the entire Fassbinder family" wrote dilettantish poems imitative of the early-twentieth-century German poet Rainer Maria Rilke, and that she did what she could to dissuade her son from such tendencies—by giving him building blocks and soccer shoes, for example. "If you were sure that your child would become a great poet, you would support that. But there are so many bankrupt poets and artists. A parent wants her child to learn to do something sensible."

28. Limmer Int 49. Katz reports, without documentation, that Fassbinder refused to return his father's telephone calls, in which he usually requested money (19, xxi, 1).

29. Not knowing whether or not her ex-husband would have to take charge of the boy because of her illness, Liselotte had characterized Helmut as "really a wonderful man. . . . He knows all about Einstein, space travel, poetry, literature." Fassbinder once recalled that his father could explain practically everything: "space travel, Dürer, politics" (Limmer Int 49).

30. Jansen Int 58.

31. The first three relationships are discussed in chapters 4, 7, and 8, respectively. Wendlandt, the producer of *Lola*, was also involved in *Lili Marleen* and *Veronika Voss*. Fassbinder and Juliane Lorenz lived in his penthouse apartment on Clemenstrasse, in the Schwabing district of Munich, for the last two years of the director's life; they did not live there free, as Katz implies (162), but paid 2,500 DM a month rent (Lorenz Let 23 June 1993). Lorenz writes that Wendlandt "really liked Rainer and understood his temper! And . . . he was intelligent enough not to force Rainer in any direction" (Let 3 June 1994).

32. Jansen Int 96.

33. Hans Helmut Prinzler's filmography in Jansen and Schütte lists Liselotte Eder in the casts of twenty-three Fassbinder films, usually under her maiden name Lilo Pempeit; she told the author, however, that she was certain that she had appeared in twenty-five. She characterized reports in Katz and elsewhere that Fassbinder had given away rights to some of his films to former associates as "nonsense," noting that there were no written records of such transactions. The father's claims, she said, were based on a proviso in West German law that both parents share the estate of an unmarried person dying without a will. Dr. Fassbinder thought that his share "would be millions" and would allow him at

last "to pursue his writing," she said. She was also concerned that the father's "enormous tax debts" might lead to a court seizure of the son's estate. After six years of negotiation, her ex-husband settled his claims by getting half the appraised value of the estate, which consisted primarily of rights to his films and writing. Liselotte said that she donated her share of the inheritance to establish in 1986 the nonprofit Rainer Werner Fassbinder Foundation as a means of protecting her son's legacy. With reference to her efforts on behalf of Fassbinder's estate, Liselotte told the author in 1990, "I will soon be 68 years old. I need now to withdraw from all this commotion. It's been really hard work." She transferred the management of the foundation to Juliane Lorenz at the beginning of 1992 and died in May 1993.

Juliane Lorenz said that on the few occasions when Fassbinder mentioned his father to her, he "spoke well" of him. But he told her that Liselotte was "the person who was important to him." She said that Liselotte never interfered in her life with Fassbinder, though mother and son met often on the set or arranged dinners together. She added that "all the things people accuse her of have nothing to do with the woman I knew," who became "very important" for her after Fassbinder's death (Int 10 June 1992).

34. Raab 162. Berling repeats this charge against the mother, without attribution (172). Raab's hostility toward Mrs. Eder is epitomized in the remark he made to a friend after Fassbinder's death: "I believe his mother can be quite happy over what she has inherited" (Raab 124). He characteristically pictures Liselotte melodramatically lamenting beside the bloodied wreck of a car Rainer had been driving in Turkey, "My Rainer, my son is dead!" (268), even though, by Katz's account (102), Raab was not on hand to see this scene but was at a nearby hospital with the other occupants of the car. One wonders how much of this is Raab's projection onto Rainer and his mother of his own extremely unhappy relationship with his mother, which he describes at length in his book. Ronald Hayman's 1984 biography uncritically recycles many of Raab's stories, including the charge that Liselotte frequently (and, by implication, irresponsibly) sent him out to the cinema or gave him money to buy a sausage from the street-corner stand, so that she could pursue her work as a translator (4). (She said that Rainer frequently volunteered to do this, seeing how busy she was.) Hayman repeats Raab's story that Rainer saw Irm Hermann, a frequent actress in Fassbinder films, simply as "a more pliable version" of his mother, "totally at his disposal," whom he sadistically punished "for the shortcomings of his mother" (21). Fassbinder once said to Wolfgang Limmer that this supposed similarity was an invention of Hermann and Hanna Schygulla (Limmer Int 85), but he also told Limmer earlier in their interview that perhaps both Irm Hermann and Hanna Schygulla "together corresponded to my mother" (63).

35. Katz 17.

36. On the basis of a two-day interview and subsequent correspondence and brief visits with Liselotte Eder, the author is unable to account for the hostility toward her expressed by many of Fassbinder's associates and by other writers. She appeared to be a competent, reasonable person who had seriously examined her sense of herself as a woman and her role as the mother of a controversial film director, who talked frankly about her insecurities and limitations (e.g., as an actress and an authority on film), while

remaining committed to the strenuous task of responsibly managing her son's artistic legacy. Liselotte said that her son once told her, "When I see what kind of mothers the others have, then I think I have been lucky having you."

37. In the other twenty films in which Liselotte Eder or Lilo Pempeit is credited in Jansen and Schütte, she appears in a variety of roles, by no means all of them unsympathetic: as a middle-class housewife or neighbor in seven, a mother in four, a nursemaid in one, an office worker or clerk in three, the wife of a major male character in two, and unnamed in three.

38. Limmer Int 64.

39. Haddad-Garcia Int 54.

40. Fründt Int 176.

41. *Anarchy* 20–21. In the "Childhood" section of the 1992 Fassbinder exhibition in Berlin was displayed a Christmas wish list "to the Christ child," which began with Rainer's hope that his mother would get well soon.

42. On the first page of his book Hayman, who interviewed Liselotte Eder, suggests that she frequently talked to her son about such dreams. Her account of this matter to the author of the present book is as follows: "I dreamed that Rainer came to me and said, tersely, 'We are going to get married.' In my dream, I thought: that isn't allowed, but if Rainer wants it, then he will certainly push it through. Then we went to some kind of bazaar, where there were many bolts of precious, expensive fabric. Many people from Rainer's circle were there, looking for material to buy for clothes for our wedding, at his expense. I was also supposed to look for some fabric for myself, but I was wearing a very simple office dress, which I had in reality bought the day before. I told Rainer that that was good enough—I didn't need a new dress. Then I woke up. I thought about it a lot, and I wanted to tell Rainer about it the next time I saw him. But I didn't go any further than 'I dreamed we were going to get married.' Rainer left the room with peals of laughter." She concluded that her discussion of this dream came "at an unfavorable time, when he was trying to cut the umbilical cord to the family—that is, from me personally, since there was no one else left." For her the dream signified that she had delegated her "creativity and power" to her son, as she previously had to his father and to Wolff Eder; she said it helped her begin a "process of . . . personal emancipation."

43. Limmer Int 52–54. There are interesting psychological implications in a comment Fassbinder once made to the effect that all his protagonists relate to their mothers as James Cagney relates to his mother in Raoul Walsh's *White Heat* (Wiegand Int 62). In that 1949 archetypal film noir, Cagney plays a short, tough gangster named Cody, whose only real emotional attachment is to his mother. She does her best to protect Cody and pushes him to live up to her high expectations—which, the film suggests, may be the cause of Cody's extreme headaches while she is alive, and his increasing megalomania after she is killed by Cody's sexy blonde wife (Virginia Mayo).

44. Cited in Kaplan, *Psychoanalysis and Cinema* 14.

45. Müller Int 188.

46. Jansen Int 96.

47. Baer 32.

48. The green-apple anecdote was still alive in 1992, when an interviewer asked Liselotte Eder about it. She replied that Rainer had gotten the story from his father, who once shouted to her, as she was trying to feed her three-month-old son a piece of green apple she had found (fruit rarely being for sale in those days): "For God's sake, you are killing the child." "Naturally, I didn't want to kill him," she said ("Der tote Sohn" 55).

49. Baer 33.

50. Turner 7. Unless otherwise indicated, this is the source for specific information given in this section.

51. Turner 83.

52. Turner 92.

53. Peter Demetz attributes the souring in the early 1970s of the "sweet hopes and almost unlimited expectations" of the Social-Liberal coalition government to various factors: economic problems (especially the oil crisis), which led to reductions in support of social programs; Brandt's resignation in 1974; and the disaffection of many intellectuals "untrained in the fair exchange of arguments and unschooled in the art of political compromise." *After the Fires* 81.

54. A 21 May 1968 *Süddeutsche Zeitung* theater review reported that production of Fassbinder's play *Katzelmacher* had been "postponed indefinitely" because of the arrest in Paris of the author and leading actor. Karsunke 5.

55. Demetz, *After the Fires* 62. Unless otherwise indicated, this volume (59–66) is the source for historical events cited in this and the next four paragraphs.

56. Katz 34; Lorenz Let 24 May 1994.

57. Färber Int 475.

58. This remark, which may have been made during the filming of *Die Dritte Generation* (*The Third Generation*) in 1978–79, was used by the Filmverlag der Autoren for promotion of that film (Lorenz Let 7 April 1994). In 1973 Fassbinder explained that his interest in collective theater during his early years did not mean that he desired to produce "political theater"; rather, he was primarily interested in staging "artistically demanding" works (Brocher Int I).

59. Demetz, *After the Fires* 374.

60. Baer 13–15.

61. This section is particularly indebted to Demetz, *Postwar German Literature* and to information provided by Donna L. Hoffmeister. As Demetz makes clear, there was considerably more carryover of German literary tradition into the immediate postwar era than has often been implied in the legend of "zero hour." See also Rentschler, *West German Film* 32ff.

62. Rentschler 32–33.

63. Demetz, *Postwar German Literature* 233. This book is the source of the specific details in this paragraph.

64. See H.-B. Moeller, "Fassbinder's Use of Brechtian Aesthetics," *Jump Cut* 35 (April 1990): 102–107.

65. Shattuc, "*Contra* Brecht" 37–38. See also Gemünden.

66. Brocher Int II. In 1971 Fassbinder said that it would be more accurate to compare

the films of his contemporary filmmaker Alexander Kluge with Brecht's theater: "Kluge's alienation is intellectual like Brecht's, while mine is stylistic" (*Anarchie* 41). He suggested that his work would better be compared with the theater of Ödön von Horváth (discussed in the paragraph following).

67. Hoffmeister, *Theater* 6. See also Rentschler, *West German Film* 110, which portrays these folk plays as critiques of the sentimental, politically retrogressive German tradition of rural *Heimat* (homeland) fantasies.

68. Hayman 30.

69. Two particularly influential studies of Weimar era film are Kracauer and Eisner.

70. For a discussion of Nazi-era film emphasizing ideology and financing arrangements, see Petley.

71. Phillips xi. Phillip's introductory essay is a major source for this section.

72. Elsaesser *New German Cinema* 9.

73. Eric Rentschler summarizes this cultural interchange as "a postwar Germany ready to accept the U.S. colonization of its fantasies as a way to escape its own haunting images from a troubled past" (*West German Film* 88).

74. Franklin 29.

75. Franklin 54.

76. Rentschler, *West German Filmmakers* 2.

77. For discussion of what was lost in the transition of the New German Cinema abroad—particularly its German political implications—see Rentschler, *West German Film* 51, 64–65, 90–92; on West German resistance to these new films, see 68–69, 136.

78. Two useful introductions to the New German Cinema for American readers are Pflaum, *Germany on Film* and Rentschler's more detailed *West German Film.* Earlier volumes by Franklin, Phillips, and John Sandford are also valuable, but somewhat dated. Timothy Corrigan, *New German Film* and Elsaesser, *New German Cinema* are important, more theoretical, studies.

79. Franklin 32.

80. Rentschler, *West German Film* 8.

81. Phillips 251.

82. Franklin 31.

83. Phillips 270.

84. For discussion of eight female directors of the New German Cinema, see Fischetti. Films by Sanders-Brahms and Helke Sander are discussed in Richard McCormick.

85. Rentschler, *West German Film* 44.

86. Franklin 32.

87. Phillips xix. According to Thomas Elsaesser, television coproduction arrangements served for the second wave of New German filmmakers as the Kuratorium had for the first ("Postwar German Cinema" 14.

88. Filmverlag der Autoren means, literally, "authors' film publishing house."

89. Elsaesser, "Postwar German Cinema" 15.

90. Johnston, "A Star Is Born" 71.

CHAPTER TWO

Starting Out . . . Mostly in the Theater

Although Fassbinder grew up on films as a child and adolescent and had made several short films by the age of twenty-two, it was in the theater that he first became a professional artist—as actor, writer, and director. Starting in the fall of 1967, the Munich theater troupe known first as the "Action-Theater" and then as the "antitheater" quickly gained, under his leadership, a reputation as one of the most exciting counterculture artistic collectives in West Germany. In less than two years Fassbinder and his entourage premiered thirteen new theatrical productions in several low-rent venues in Munich. But he was intent on making films, and in April 1969 he directed his first feature-length movie, *Love Is Colder Than Death;* he completed twenty-one more feature films by the end of 1974. Nevertheless, during this period Fassbinder was largely responsible for twelve additional theatrical productions. As his reputation rapidly grew, most of these plays were premiered in relatively well-established, if often experimental, theaters outside Munich. But by 1975 Fassbinder's work in the theater was virtually finished. He seems to have found the relatively free, if risky, entrepreneurial environment of film production much more congenial to his temperament than the security and the bureaucratic strictures of established theaters.

Although Fassbinder's films constitute by far the most important part of his artistic achievement, his plays are significant as cultural documents of their time, and most are interesting in their own right. He adapted six of them as feature-length films, three of which are among his most important movies. Moreover, Fassbinder's first two years in the theater, which this chapter chronicles in some detail, were crucial to his development as a professional artist. During this time he gained self-confidence as a writer and director, experimented with a wide variety of acting and production styles, and explored many of the themes central to the films he would later make.

Early Film Work, Writing, Acting School

When Fassbinder returned to Munich in 1963 at age eighteen, after spending two years with his father in Cologne, he was intent on making films but had little idea how to begin. "I wrote down a lot of stuff, began things, stopped them, began again, stopped again; I just didn't know what I should do."[1] To supplement the 200 marks a month his father was sending him he took on a part-time job in the archives of Munich's leading daily newspaper, the *Süddeutsche Zeitung,* where, as he said, he "read a lot of newspapers."[2] Doubtless he found there much discussion of the emerging Young German Film. In any case, he shared in the widespread euphoria about the future of filmmaking in West Germany.[3]

During this period Fassbinder had first-hand experience on a number of film and video projects.[4] He assisted the director of a documentary about handicapped children participating in sports, helped with the sound on a television film about unwed mothers in Italy, and acted in a training film for army auto mechanics.[5] Perhaps his most important study of the cinema was in going to the movies, which he said he was doing at the rate of three or four a day.[6] In much of that moviegoing he was joined by an older friend who had studied German and French literature and was also taking first steps toward a career in filmmaking, Michael Fengler; the two of them experimented with an editing machine and analyzed Federico Fellini's celebrated 1963 film-about-filmmaking, *8 ½.*[7]

Fassbinder's mother said that during this time her son discussed with her the possibility of completing the Abitur degree, which would prepare him for entering a university program in theater, as a basis for a career as a film director. She discouraged this, knowing his impatience with theoretical matters and his history of failure in school with subjects that didn't interest him. She suggested instead that he study acting—which would be much more likely to lead to practical work—and she arranged private acting lessons for him.[8] After about six months of these lessons, on 1 March 1964, Fassbinder enrolled on his own in one of Munich's specialized high schools for training actors, the Fridl-Leonhard Actors School. He later recalled that he did so because he had no better alternative in mind and anticipated that it would help him get into the new film school scheduled to open in Berlin in two years.[9]

Fassbinder studied at the acting school in the evenings for over two years, through May 1966.[10] One of his friends there was Hanna Schygulla, who was enrolled in a university teacher-training program and secretly (against her parents' wishes) attending acting school in the evenings. They were the only two, Fassbinder said, who maintained their integrity within an educational institution that seemed to him to exist only to exploit young people who had a "basically pathological yearning for the stage." One evening as he was sitting with her after class in a bar, it suddenly became "crystal clear" to him that she would "one day be the star of my films," though he did not tell her so at the time.[11]

Two Fassbinder plays from these years, neither performed in his lifetime, have survived. The first, which was apparently written in 1966 but not published and performed until 1994, was a ten-scene piece titled *Nur eine Scheibe Brot: Dialog über einen Auschwitzfilm* (Just a Slice of Bread: Dialogue about an Auschwitz Film), for which Fassbinder won third prize (shared with another writer) in a Munich dramatic competition. This first Fassbinder play shows him already wrestling with a number of ethical issues that would come up in his later plays and films, particularly the failure of West German filmmakers to deal concretely with the Nazi past. The protagonist is a young filmmaker, Hans Fricke, who is shooting a film about the Auschwitz death camp in Poland. In a series of conversations, Hans discusses the ethics of making money on such a subject as the death camps, the relationship between art and "reality," and neo-anti-Semitism. He bitterly accuses his father and an uncle of complicity with the Nazi regime and argues for the inclusion of documentary newsreels and interviews in the film. But his producer envisages the project only as "a fiction film about [past] events," and Hans is finally persuaded to omit these real-life elements. In the final scene the producer addresses the theater audience directly, informing them that the film was completed in time to be released just before Christmas and was launched as "a shocking, merciless portrayal of destiny in the spell of dark powers." He assures the audience that although they will be "gripped and thrilled" by the film, which has been officially evaluated as "especially worthy" and has won three state film prizes, they will be able to watch it "quite calmly."[12]

Late in November 1966 Fassbinder joined two other winners in this dramatic competition for readings in a gallery called Tangente near the University of Munich. Selections from his play were read by his live-in friend of that period, an unemployed actor named Christoph Roser. The playwright watched from a table where he sat with his mother. Another person in the audience, a young secretary named Irm Hermann, was immediately taken with the shy author.[13] She would soon become one of Fassbinder's most devoted and long-suffering supporters and an actress in many of his plays and films.

While the first surviving play of this early period anticipated public issues related to filmmaking that would be raised in much later work by Fassbinder, in the second, which was not produced until 1985, he focused on what would become the central private theme of his films: emotional exploitation within intimate relationships. This is a four-act piece, "a comedy with a pseudo-tragic ending" according to its title page, titled *Tropfen auf heisse Steine* (Drops on Hot Stones) . Written in a traditionally realistic dramatic form, with conventional dialogue, it is a literarily self-conscious play about a homosexual love affair between an older man (Leopold Bluhm) and a twenty-year-old (Franz

Meister), which disintegrates into everyday pettiness and emotional manipulations.[14]

As he neared the end of his acting course in the spring of 1966 Fassbinder set his sights on being admitted into the first class of the new German Film and Television Academy, scheduled to open in Berlin in the fall of that year. He reworked *Nur eine Scheibe Brot* into a film script and submitted it with his application, along with a short 8 mm film titled *This Night,* one of several he made that fall (none have survived).[15] These materials were impressive enough to earn him the right to take an entrance examination in Berlin. His stepfather, Wolff Eder, lent him his personal camera to use in the exam, and his mother wrote him a warm letter advising him how he might compensate for his lack of technical knowledge.[16] But all to no avail: he was turned down for admission along with two others who would later become recognized directors of the New German Cinema, Werner Schroeter and Rosa von Praunheim.[17] This failure was a substantial, but not decisive, setback to Fassbinder's career plans: "I didn't know then what I should do," he recalled. "I could have sat around, but that never interested me very much."[18]

What did interest him, obviously, was making films. Setting out to challenge the judgment of those responsible for his "sad and shameful defeat" at the Berlin film school,[19] Fassbinder proceeded, with more than a little help from his friends, to make two short films (ten and nine minutes in length, respectively), which have survived: *Der Stadtstreicher* (The City Tramp), shot in November 1966 in 16 mm format; and *Das kleine Chaos* (The Little Chaos), shot on 35 mm stock the following January. Both were made with money advanced by Christoph Roser, the friend who had given the reading from *Nur eine Scheibe Brot.*[20] Fassbinder assigned acting and production duties to Michael Fengler, Irm Hermann, and a few other people he knew; in the second film he took a substantial role himself, and he included his mother in a scene in her apartment—which was shot before she realized what has happening, she recalled.

Both of these short films demonstrate that the largely self-taught director had gained considerable mastery of cinematic techniques by the beginning of his twenty-second year. And both anticipate stylistic features and themes important in his later work. *Der Stadtstreicher* was inspired by Fassbinder's favorite film at the time, the French director Eric Rohmer's *Le Signe du Lion,* 1959 (*The Sign of the Lion*), which features a Paris bohemian born under the sign of the lion who loses everything and aimlessly wanders the empty streets of the city in the summer. Fassbinder's film is a sequence of sorts. His tramp

(Roser) walks around Munich in a bleak late-autumn day trying to get rid of a pistol he has found. He is threatened by sinister strangers who eventually take the gun from him and leave him lying on the ground in Munich's English Garden, pretending to shoot at them with his finger (in a gesture that would recur in several of the director's early films). This earliest surviving Fassbinder film demonstrates considerable sophistication in shot composition and editing. It also indicates the director's interest in pure visual form (in an abstract composition of rocks in a dry streambed) and in visual humor—the tramp raises his hands comically when a waitress returns the gun he had discarded by poking him with it in the back. (Fassbinder's second surviving short film, *Das Kleine Chaos,* which anticipated his use of the gangster movie genre in three of his early feature-length films, will be discussed with those films in chapter three.)

In managing to finance and produce these two films while undertaking other serious writing, as well as working evenings at the *Süddeutsche Zeitung,* Fassbinder was already demonstrating the persuasive skills, the energy, and the ability to make the most of his opportunities that would soon make him the most productive member of the postwar generation of West German filmmakers. But the road to his remarkable career in the cinema was soon to take a major detour by way of the theater. A film evaluation board in Wiesbaden denied to the first of his short films, *Der Stadtstreicher,* a special quality rating that would have reduced taxes on the film, claiming, absurdly, that the film was a "glorification of suicide." After that rebuff Fassbinder decided not to submit his second short film to the board.[21] Instead, he sent both to the Oberhausen Short Film Festival, West Germany's most important showcase for new film talent. But they were rejected. And although he took both films to Oberhausen with the intention of showing them privately, he "lost his courage" and did not do so.[22] He also included them both with a second application he made to the Berlin Film Academy in June 1967, but this time he was turned down without even being invited to Berlin for another examination.[23]

In spite of these setbacks, the aspiring filmmaker had clear ideas about what he needed to learn and the kind of environment in which he wanted to work. In a remarkably prescient memo to himself written in 1966 or 1967 (headed "How do I imagine my future professional work?"), he anticipated working within a "well organized group" in which he would be able to make in quick succession a series of inexpensive films "in order to realize fully the possibilities of my ideas." He wanted to gain "a comprehensive understanding of the technical problems of film," which he considered absolutely necessary for a director. He also indicated an interest in learning about the possibilities of making television films, as distinguished from theatrical ones.[24]

Action-Theater

Fassbinder had managed to find a few minor acting jobs, including one as a monk in a production of George Bernard Shaw's *St. Joan,* at the Munich Kammerspiel.[25] He also got the part of a soldier on trial in a 1967 television film, *Tonys Freunde* (Tony's Friends), directed by Paul Vasil, and he played roles in five additional films by other directors over the next two years.[26] Nevertheless, a half year after finishing his second short film he had little reason to be encouraged about his professional future in the cinema. "At that point," he later recalled, "everyone was starting to make films, but I didn't see any opportunity to do it myself."[27] He said that he was becoming pessimistic about the hoped-for future of Young German Cinema—and especially, one can suppose, his role in it—when, one evening in August 1967 ("when I didn't know what to do with myself"), he accepted the invitation of one of his friends from acting school, Marite Greiselis, to attend the opening night of a play she was in. She was one of four actresses sharing the lead role in an unconventional production of the classical Greek tragedy, Sophocles' *Antigone,* at Munich's Action-Theater.[28]

The performance took place in an old movie theater, which a married couple, Ursula Strätz and her husband Horst Söhnlein, had recently taken over—first to show foreign movies and films of the younger German directors, and then, after remodeling the auditorium, for theatrical performances. Fifty-nine chairs were grouped around saloon tables in what one critic called a "gloomy dive."[29] With a group of friends from acting school, the couple had begun producing plays in the provocative style of the American Living Theater, which had been performing in Germany and several other European countries its "Artaud-inspired happenings," including *Antigone.*[30] The Action-Theater's production was an aggressively political adaptation of Sophocles' tragedy, which dramatizes the revolt of a young woman against civil and military authority as embodied in her royal uncle. One unsympathetic critic compared this version of the play to a central African tribal celebration. It featured statistics on war dead from many eras chalked onto the black back wall, and a brutal battle scene (played into the audience), which the program notes claimed was derived from the West German army's rules for hand-to-hand combat. The dialogue had been developed spontaneously by the actors during rehearsals from several versions of the play, including Brecht's legendary *Antigonemodell* (1948).[31]

Fassbinder was fascinated. This play did not resemble any theatrical performance he had ever seen. It was, he said, "intensive theater" in which he felt a "concrete" force that took his breath away. He sensed between the actors and the audience "something like a trance, like a collective longing for a revolutionary Utopia." He made up his mind on the spot "to work with this group, here in this theater," without the slightest fear that he would not be accepted. He hung around the theater after that performance and came back every night afterward. When one of the actors broke a finger, Fassbinder offered to take over the role on one day's notice. And though he nervously muffed his first night's performance—forgetting all but the first and last lines of many of his speeches—he said that he handled his role with enough aplomb that Ursula Strätz found it exciting, like everything else Fassbinder did.[32]

Fassbinder quickly established his role as a leader within the group. After Marite Greiselis was crippled in a knife attack by one of the actors, he brought in his other friend from acting school, Hanna Schygulla, who won critical acclaim during the long run of *Antigone* as one of the four versions of the title character. As Fassbinder later recalled, some members of the group were resentful of the attention Schygulla was getting, and of her refusal to subject herself to "the fundamental group ethos, according to which each member owed complete allegiance to the demands of the collective effort and was expected to come forward automatically to help out with any aspect of production." Fassbinder said that only he and Peer Raben—who had directed *Antigone* and with whom he shared many conversations about producing theater different from that on subsidized stages—understood that a healthy group "in which all were equals" could accommodate such individual views.[33]

When *Antigone* closed, the collective had little idea where to go. Ursula Strätz and Peer Raben allowed Fassbinder to assume artistic leadership of the group, recognizing that his "compulsion to create something was irrepressible."[34] In addition, it was becoming increasingly clear to Fassbinder that, despite all their talk about it, the spirit of collectivity within the Action-Theater ensemble "had sunk into a kind of blissful Boy Scout camaraderie." Members of the group sat around singing to guitar accompaniment, or hung around the theater just to enjoy the free lodging, food, and beer, without recognizing the costs involved or the fact that "no theater has even a halfway chance of making it unless some serious acting is going on."

In October 1967 the Action-Theater opened its production of the popular satirical comedy *Leonce und Lena* (*Leonce and Lena,* 1835) by Georg Büchner (1813–37), which Ursula Strätz had long dreamed of producing.[35] The play features a prince and a princess who run away from a marriage their parents are forcing on them but then fall in love as supposed strangers, marry, and set up a free-spirited kingdom to replace the authoritarian rule of their elders. Like *Antigone,* this play was performed before a black backdrop, with virtually no scenes or props, and with heavy use of Beatles music.[36] In the spirit of collectivity, four directors were designated for the production—including Fassbinder, who also was given the small role of Valerio, a court fool. Although he muffed many of his lines on his second opening night, many in the audience were favorably impressed by the aggressive manner in which he responded to what he perceived as their hostility, and the play was generally well reviewed.

Meanwhile, relations between Fassbinder and Ursula Strätz's husband Horst Söhnlein were degenerating as a result of Söhnlein's insistence that the Action-Theater produce only politically relevant plays and his jealousy of Fassbinder's growing power within the group and supposed sexual liaison with Ursula Strätz (which Fassbinder claimed never really existed).[37] Late in 1967, apparently, Söhnlein wrecked the auditorium of the Action-Theater, which he had himself remodeled not long before. Fassbinder and Raben moved out of the Strätz-Söhnlein apartment near the theater, in which they had been living, into Irm Hermann's apartment (where they were later joined by Strätz). The housemates managed to scrape together barely enough to live on—supplemented by frequent visits of Fassbinder to his mother and Raben to his parents.[38]

The Action-Theater was repaired in time for a production in December 1967 of *Die Verbrecher (The Criminals,* 1928) by Ferdinand Bruchner (1891–1958). *The Criminals* is a technically complex play dealing with the incompatibility between justice and law. Fassbinder partially rewrote the text, and this time he assumed sole responsibility for directing. He later said he "learned how to be a director" with this play, which he rehearsed long and intensively. In contrast to the more spontaneous *Leonce and Lena,* he exercised in this production a great deal of control over the actors' performances, seeking to produce an extremely concentrated effect.[39]

During rehearsals for the play Fassbinder took the troupe to Paris for guest performances of *Antigone* and *Leonce and Lena,* with the support of a 4,000 DM state subsidy that Strätz had obtained. But the French sponsors had not prepared for their visit, and after single performances of each play "before three people" the group gave up the project amid accusations from some members that Raben was mishandling the subsidy funds. "It was a colossal financial debacle," for which he, not Raben, was largely blamed, Fassbinder recalled.[40]

It was becoming clear to both Fassbinder and Raben that it was necessary, even while working as a collective, to produce theater that was not as "chaotic" as their previous work had been; they decided that they should draw more substantially from "the things we had learned in acting school" and from "what we knew from good theatrical performances."[41] Perhaps Fassbinder had these goals in mind in his next effort, which was the first of his several ventures into the tradition of the German critical folk play. In February 1968 the group staged in Munich's Büchner-Theater a piece they called *Zum Beispiel Ingolstadt* (For Example Ingolstadt), Fassbinder's free adaptation of *Pioniere in Ingolstadt* (Military Engineers in Ingolstadt),[42] a 1928 play by the Bavarian playwright Marieluise Fleisser (1901–74). In the playbill Fassbinder described his adaptation, which he codirected with Peer Raben, as a "freely mounted dramatic reflection upon the psychological world of the middle class as experienced by Marieluise Fleisser."[43] Fleisser was upset because the group had announced the production without obtaining the rights to her play. When Fassbinder sent Raben to ask her for permission two weeks before the opening, she refused. But Fassbinder went ahead with his plans for the production on the grounds that his play was only inspired by Fleisser's work. Some members of the troupe then went to Fleisser in Ingolstadt and convinced her, through their "charm," to attend the dress rehearsal; after she saw how dirty the Büchner Theater was and how talented the young people involved were—and realizing the difficulty she would have in stopping the performance in any case—Fleisser gave the group permission to stage the play.[44] It ran for five nights, closing down after Ursula Strätz was injured in an automobile accident.[45]

Fleisser's play dramatizes the impact of an army bridge-building unit on a small Bavarian community, particularly its women. Alma, a prostitute, takes advantage of the situation to expand her trade, but her friend Berta, a naive servant girl, falls in love with and loses her virginity to one of the soldiers, who drops her without regret when the unit moves on. The play also shows the commanding sergeant's bullying of his troops and the shady dealings between the soldiers and the town folk. Much of the effect of the play depends on Fleisser's subtle dialogue, which transforms "the phraseology, cadences, and expressions of lower Bavaria" into a not-quite-realistic kind of speech that "calls forth . . . a critical, alienated view of precisely this spoken speech."[46]

After Strätz's accident her husband, Horst Söhnlein, took control of the Action-Theater and arranged for a well-known avant-garde film director, Jean-Marie Straub, to put on a play there. Straub, born in France in 1933, was making intellectually demanding films in Germany in collaboration with his wife, Danièle Huillet. For his Action-Theater production he worked a radical artistic experiment on another play by Ferdinand Bruchner, *Krankheit der Jugend,* 1928 (*Sickness of Youth*), compressing the original text to ten minutes' playing time. Over Sohnlein's objections Straub insisted on hiring Fassbinder, Schygulla, and Raben as members of the cast.[47]

Fassbinder was impressed by the seriousness of Straub's approach to theatrical direction and by his ability to engender a kind of detached self-awareness among the actors. Straub became "an important figure" for the younger man as he rehearsed the piece (in which Fassbinder played the role of a pimp) over a period of months. Fassbinder said that he was "really fascinated" by the "air of comic solemnity" with which Straub patiently lead him and the other actors to develop "the technique of looking at ourselves" and thereby creating a distance between themselves and their roles "instead of total identity."[48] Straub also encouraged Fassbinder's till-then largely frustrated interest in making films. Fassbinder showed him the two short films he had recently made, and Straub told him that he did not know anyone "with this much violence in his films."[49] In addition, Straub and Huillet made a film of this compressed version of the Bruchner play, which they titled *Der Bräutigan, die Komödiantin und der Zuhälter* (The Bridegroom, the Comedienne, and the Pimp). Fassbinder said that this project reactivated his own interest in filmmaking, and that in the process he absorbed from Straub a good bit of cinematic theory, learning "how to develop a film stylistically."[50]

To make a complete evening in the theater the group needed another play to offer along with Straub's ten-minute version of Bruchner. Söhnlein failed to book a production by the well-known director Vlada Kristl and was obliged to accept instead a forty-minute play that Fassbinder had written for the occasion: *Katzelmacher*.[51] This piece, which Fassbinder codirected with Raben, is a series of vignettes dramatizing the disruptive effects of a Greek "guest worker" of reputedly extraordinary sexual powers on a self-satisfied but unstable group of working-class young people living in a Bavarian village.[52] The minimalist dialogue and action of the play seem to have been inspired in part by the example of Straub.[53] The play is also clearly indebted to Marieluise Fleisser, to whom it was dedicated. Her influence can be seen in both the play's dramatic structure and its dialogue style: snippets of everyday life depicting passive people striking out against the limitations of their consciousness in an artificial, cliché-ridden speech heavily flavored with Bavarian dialect. It also follows Fleisser's play in depicting the disruptive effects of an outside presence on a closed community.

The Straub-Fassbinder double bill opened at the Action-Theater in April 1968. The critic Alf Brustellin expressed amazement at how effectively this leftist-oriented theatrical commune with virtually no money was thumbing its nose at the cultural establishment and challenging the liberal-bourgeois attitudes of its audiences. He praised *Katzelmacher* as "an often fascinating encounter-game" with constantly changing centers and arrangements, "a kaleidoscope of attitudes, prejudices, passions, dreams, and everyday cruelty."[54]

Later that spring Fassbinder's troupe produced at the Action-Theater two politically charged plays—*Axel Cäsar Haarmann* and *Chung*—in the midst of the so-called Easter disturbances against the proposed Emergency Powers Acts.[55] Fassbinder characterized *Axel,* which opened in April, as the theater group's own spontaneous reaction to the current political turbulence in the Federal Republic, with each actor privately developing his or her part, so that the play came together only during the performance: "no rehearsals, no safeguards, like jumping into cold water."[56] The program announced: "This has to do with Springer. . . ! (and the rotten democracy which allows him to have power)."[57] The play consisted largely of quotations from such diverse sources as the right-wing *Bild* newspaper, owned by Axel Caesar Springer; the West German constitution; the proposed emergency laws; court judgments; and demonstrators' slogans. The playbill announced that proceeds would be used to help pay medical costs for the wounded radical student leader Rudi Dutschke and to support the Socialist German Student Union legal rights fund.[58] At the end of the performance Fassbinder stood on stage with a water hose, recalling police handling of street demonstrators. A voice claiming to be that of the theater management announced over the loudspeaker that the production had been shut down and the audience must clear out; those who did not do so actually got doused, "which washed the happy smiles off the faces of the 'aesthetic left' quite totally."[59] *Chung,* which opened in late May or June, was even more direct, consisting of a series of leftist "agit-prop" scenes.[60] Some of the performances were conducted in the streets, among the thousands of people demonstrating against the emergency laws.[61]

Some time in April, Horst Söhnlein had left Munich for Frankfurt am Main with Andreas Baader and other leftist radicals (who had often shouted during Action-Theater performances that it was time to stop doing theater and get on with the action), carrying bombs Söhnlein had been secretly making.[62] The bombs were set off in Schneider's Department Store in Frankfurt, an act of violence that was a major escalation of the protest movement.

The quick clearing of the theater at the end of *Axel* was prophetic, for on 6 June the Action-Theater was permanently shut down by the Munich authorities. The ostensible reason was inadequate electrical conduits. When the objection was made that these problems had already been corrected, the city alleged that the theater would have been closed in any case, since it was operating more as a "political cabaret" than as a theater making "predominantly artistic statements."[63] The same day, Söhnlein was arrested in connection with the Frankfurt bombing.[64]

antitheater

Ursula Strätz refused to let Fassbinder's group reorganize itself as "Action-Theater II" to escape previous debts,[65] so in June 1968 they invented a new name for themselves, "antitheater," and began to look for a new home.[66] Fassbinder was depressed but not completely discouraged,[67] and the next month he produced at the Academy of Arts in Munich the antitheater's first play, one of the lighter works of the politically engaged German-Swedish writer, Peter Weiss (1916–1982), *Wie dem Herrn Mockingpott das Leiden ausgetrieben wird, 1963–68 (How Mr. Mockingpott Was Cured of His Suffering)*. Characterized as "a big flop" by the influential *Süddeutsche Zeitung* and other papers, the play attracted very small audiences and ran for only a few performances.[68]

In August the antitheater performed at the Büchner Theater an unusually free-spirited piece called *Orgie Ubuh*. The production was planned by the group, and the dialogue developed freely during rehearsals, in what Fassbinder, who directed it, said was "a great collective adventure—a really nice experience.[69] The play was based loosely on *Ubu-roi*, 1896 *(King Ubu)*, an anarchic attack by Alfred Jarry (1873–1907) on late-nineteenth-century French society and the conventions of naturalistic theater that has been a perennial favorite of counterculture theaters. According to one report, Fassbinder's production was a wild mixture of "Beat," popular television, marital in-fighting, group sex, West German chancellor Kurt Georg Kiesinger, transvestite striptease, soccer, Kafka, and boozing. The theater manager found the performance "too political and too obscene" and shut it down by turning off the electricity after fifty minutes on opening night. The press condemned the piece as "dilettante-theater," but everybody in Munich was talking about Fassbinder and the antitheater.[70] "I wouldn't say it was filthy," Fassbinder recalled five years later. "It was a little disgusting . . . but also very funny."[71]

The abrupt closing of *Orgie Ubuh* was a serious blow for the group, Fassbinder said, but it also motivated them to look for their own permanent theater.[72] Within a week they had found a location, the back room of a bar called the Witwe (Widow) Bolte in Schwabing, the Munich cultural and entertainment district. They were able to have it for their own use in the evenings— except for Thursdays, when "some sort of literary event" was scheduled—for as long as the management was satisfied with the amount of beer and food sold during the performances.[73] Following the well-publicized closing of *Orgie Ubuh* at the Büchner Theater, Fassbinder and his group packed the Witwe Bolte for ten or more performances of that play, until several members of the cast had to depart for other commitments.[74]

In October, Fassbinder directed at the Witwe Bolte his adaptation of *Iphigenia auf Tauris* (*Iphigenia at Tauris*), a heroic verse drama by the most celebrated of all German writers, Johann Wolfgang von Goethe (1749–1832). Undaunted by the classical aura of the play (itself inspired by the ancient Greek tragedy of the same name by Euripides and Jean Racine's French neoclassical *Iphigenia* [1764]), Fassbinder drastically altered Goethe's text, turning the play into a topical political satire, "an elaborately splintered wreck" of Goethe's play.[75] The production included quotations from political trial proceedings, Chinese Communist Party Chairman Mao Zedong's "Red Book," pop songs, and film music. It put the heroine in a "Hollywood-style swinging cage made of tubing and wire netting"[76] and presented her long-lost brother Orestes and his companion Pylades as defiant homosexuals. At one point Pylades sums up the meaning of life and highlights the tendency of Fassbinder and his contemporaries to mix American pop culture, European film culture, and serious political critique: "Musik, Autos, Tanzen [dancing], Rolling Stones, Jean-Marie Straub, Coca Cola, Karl Marx, Jean-Luc Godard. . . ."[77]

In December 1968 Fassbinder directed what he called "an archaic operetta from Sophocles" based on the classical Greek tragedy *Ajax,* a play about honor and jealousy among war heroes, adding a motto about creating "discomfort for the institutions of the bourgeoisie." In contrast to his treatment of *Iphigenia,* this production made only minor changes in the traditional text of the play, but it transferred the scene from antiquity to a West German army officers' quarters. This and other contemporary references were so heavy-handed, and the style of acting so slapstick, that the potential of the play for critical comment on contemporary events was lost, as Fassbinder himself later admitted.[78]

Wolfgang Limmer has summed up Fassbinder's substantial impact on Munich's cultural scene a year and a half after he happened upon the opening night of *Antigone* at the Action-Theater: "It was quickly spread about that here was a provincial Marlon Brando, bursting with pent-up energy, who was making exciting theater in a cozy student bar . . . a leather-jacket phoenix arising from the ashes of bourgeois culture . . . . While the conservative critics conscientiously did their duty and portrayed him as a bogeyman and a fright, the progressives more and more celebrated him as a hero of the new culture, who transformed such exciting and nostalgic notions as communes and collectives into artistically productive action."[79]

Fassbinder and the antitheater completed the eventful year 1968 with the staging in December of a tight little gangster play, *Der amerikanische Soldat*

(The American Soldier), with Fassbinder playing one of the three roles and codirecting with Peer Raben. The play concerns a hired killer who is unnerved when he learns that one of his intended victims is a woman. Its action is derived from a 1958 American film directed by Irving Lerner, *Murder by Contract.*[80] Fassbinder's 1970 film of the same name would evoke the American gangster-film milieu, but it would tell a substantially different story. Still, his evocation of American gangster movies in the 1968 play is a reminder that he had by no means forgotten his primary interest in cinema even while he was still heavily involved in theatrical production.

In fact, Fassbinder had for some time been pursuing the possibility of producing a feature-length screenplay he had written, *Love Is Colder Than Death,* which explicitly recalls the gangster-film genre.[81] When his efforts to raise money for the film failed, Peer Raben suggested that the antitheater group produce it, and he helped Fassbinder persuade the troupe to agree to withhold some of their salaries to support the project.[82] Raben also helped Fassbinder trade on his growing theatrical reputation in Munich to raise the rest of the money by accompanying him on a visit to an heiress of the Bosche automotive fortune, who agreed to put up 15,000 DM toward the project.[83]

Presumably early in 1969 the antitheater performed *Hilferuf,* 1967 (Calling for Help), a ten-minute *Sprechstücke* ("language play") by the Austrian writer Peter Handke (1942–). Fassbinder said that the production was motivated primarily by the group's desire to exploit Handke's current popularity in West Germany: "Everybody was talking about Handke—and in Munich nobody was doing Handke; let's do it." The production was "really insipid," he said; "we just didn't enjoy it at all."[84]

The antitheater's next production, which opened in February 1969, was much more to their liking. It was *Die Bettleroper,* Fassbinder's free adaption of the satiric operatic burlesque *The Beggar's Opera,* by the English writer John Gay (1685–1732).[85] Fassbinder called this play the antitheater's best production, "a hundred percent right for us."[86] He took the part of the cynical Mecki (Mack the Knife), and the play included many allusions to his personal experience of Munich's subculture, including pinball, one of his favorite pastimes in those days. Peer Raben (as Peach) raised extra money by begging from the audience during the (often repeatedly extended) overture.[87]

March 1969 saw the opening of *Preparadise sorry now,* a morbid play written by Fassbinder and directed by Raben. The play expresses the disillusionment and bitterness that was typical of many in Fassbinder's generation as they realized that their revolution of 1968 had failed—a mood that foreshadowed the somberness of most of his film work. The title refers ironically to

Paradise Now (1968), a Living Theater play that had "glibly suggested that the world could be redeemed by the endemic power of love."[88] Fassbinder's piece deals primarily with the so-called Moors murderers in England, Ian Brady and Myra Hindley. It summarizes and dramatizes Brady's delinquent childhood and youth in the slums of Scotland and Manchester; his fascination with Hitler and the Nazis, pornography, and murder mysteries; his gradual domination of Myra (whom he here calls "Hessie," after Hitler's deputy Rudolf Hess); and their murderous career in the name of racial superiority. Interwoven with their story are a number of "neo-realist vignettes demonstrating 'the fascistoid underpin-nings of everyday life'" in the oppressive behavior of pimps, landlords, teach-ers, and parents and "a series of Christian liturgical passages which reveal their basis in cannibalism."[89] The play's style has often been described as "kaleido-scopic" since, according to Fassbinder's instructions in the text, all parts of it may be moved around at the will of the director except for the Brady-Hindley narrative. Nevertheless, the play as performed by the antitheater seemed "very rigorous and symmetrically conceived," according to one critic.[90]

After spending most of April making their first film, *Love Is Colder Than Death,* the antitheater group was back on stage in June 1969 at Munich's Fo-rum-Theater with a cabaret-style political satire titled *Anarchie in Bayern* (An-archy in Bavaria), written by Fassbinder and directed by Raben. Identified in the program as "a naive science fiction," the play dramatizes with heavy irony the effects of an imagined socialist revolution in Bavaria, West Germany's most conservative state, on a family named Normalzeit (normal time). The motley cast of stereotypical characters includes "Marriage/Car," "Child-Murderer," "Old Romantic Love—Masculine," "New Romantic Love—Feminine," and "The Mother of all Whores," in addition to gangsters, soldiers, and bureaucrats. Dur-ing the short-lived era of anarchy that the revolution brings about in the play, the voice of the "German Chancellor" (apparently meant to represent the con-servative Bavarian political leader Franz Josef Strauss) is heard from Bonn, urging his "beloved brothers and sisters in the Bavarian homeland" to bear up patiently.[91] In the end, United States Army troops move in to restore the old order. A cautionary note in the playbill shows how it applies to the disappointed hopes of the previous year: it calls for revolution in the form of a "long march" that will change the consciousness of revolutionaries as well as the bourgeoisie, noting that "external changes will not suffice to bring about a basic change in the western consciousness, fixed as it is on repression and authority," a state-ment that articulates Fassbinder's "postrevolutionary" approach to public is-sues in most of his films.

Anarchie in Bayern was performed in Munich only three or four times. In July 1969 the antitheater ensemble staged at the Munich Academy of Arts a ten-minute pantomime show, with music from Mozart and Elvis Presley, about a woman from East Germany who falls victim to consumerism in West Germany. They called it *Gewidmet Rosa von Praunheim* (Dedicated to Rosa von Praunheim), after a West German filmmaker who had recently made a film on the same theme.[92] Then the group turned its attention to their second film, an expanded version of their play *Katzelmacher,* which was shot in August 1969.

Showdown in Bremen

A major step in Fassbinder's public recognition came in November 1969, when he was invited to present his work in Bremen at a theater whose manager had been impressed with the antitheater production of *The Beggar's Opera* in Munich. In what one local newspaper called a "showdown," Fassbinder screened his two feature-length films, *Love Is Colder Than Death* and *Katzelmacher,* and staged two plays, *Anarchy in Bavaria* and *Das Kaffeehaus* (*The Coffeehouse*), using actors from the Bremen theater along with some from the antitheater group. The latter play was an adaptation of *La bottega del caffè* (1750) by the Italian playwright Carlo Goldoni (1709–93); it had opened in Munich in September, directed by Fassbinder and Raben. In the words of its subtitle, the new play consisted mostly of "games from other games." According to the critic Peter Iden, it converted Goldoni's protagonist Don Marzio from "an irksome, parasitical chatterbox and gossip" into a melancholy figure characteristic of the Viennese playwright Arthur Schnitzler (1862–1931); and the styles of eighteenth-century Venice and the American West were blended in the staging of barefoot actors in period costumes with Colt revolvers on their hips.[93] This production would be the basis of Fassbinder's sixth full-length film, *The Coffeehouse,* shot on videotape in a Cologne television studio in February 1970.[94]

The "Fassbinder showdown" in Bremen marked the beginning of the end of the myth of his artistic "collective." Fassbinder was impressed by the working conditions in this state-supported theater, as well as by the professional skills of the Bremen actors.[95] And his name alone appeared on the banner over the Bremen Theater announcing the performances. The mass media all over West Germany began to celebrate the young director's artistic personality. "Fassbinder's talents became forcefully apparent that day; seldom had so much promising material by one artist been seen all at once," Peter Iden reported of the event in Bremen. "Everything was anarchic, from the staccato tempo and accentuated artifice of the Goldoni piece to Fassbinder himself, who was almost stupidly inarticulate in a discussion afterwards. . . . Still, it was clear that here was a talent to be reckoned with."[96]

Summing Up: Fassbinder in the Theater

In a little more than two years Fassbinder had emerged from obscurity, with no clear notion about how he might set out on the artistic career he hoped for, to become one of the most talked-about rising stars on the West German cultural scene. His success generated hostility on the part of many, from his theatrical associates who accused him of deliberately exploiting them to advance his career as a filmmaker to the Munich newspaper columnist who wrote that "the only thing he has to express are the blackheads on his face."[97] "The provincial critics reacted, if at all, sourly," wrote Yaak Karsunke, who found Fassbinder's work a model of genuinely subversive alternative theater—in contrast to the tame, if offbeat, performances in the basement workshops of the large subsidized theaters and the independent mini-theaters, who limited themselves to "regressions into theater history, particularly into Expressionism, with a few standardized Artaud imitations, and production after production of Jarry's sacred *Ubu.*"[98]

Fassbinder's later theater work, from late 1969 through September 1976, when he directed his last play, is summarized in an appendix. During these seven years he wrote the scripts for two more adaptations from other playwrights (Lope de Vega and Marieluise Fleisser), coauthored a play with Harry Baer, and wrote three original plays, two of which he later turned into films; he directed or codirected all but one of these productions. In addition, he directed seven plays by well-known authors from the standard dramatic repertory (Ferenc Molnár, Heinrich Mann, Henrik Ibsen, Peter Handke, Émile Zola, Anton Chekhov, and Clare Boothe Luce), two of which he filmed. For a few days in September 1978 he rehearsed the part of the villain Iago in Shakespeare's *Othello* in a production of the well-known director Peter Palitzsch.[99] By far the most important of Fassbinder's later theater work was his play *Der Müll, die Stadt, und der Tod* (*Garbage, the City, and Death*), which he tried unsuccessfully to produce at the Theater am Turm in Frankfurt early in 1975. That work, and the intense controversy surrounding Fassbinder's efforts to produce it on the stage

56

and adapt it to film, are discussed in chapter seven, where its artistic, political, and ethical implications can be more appropriately considered.

What is the significance of Fassbinder's work in the theater? Surely it does not deserve the dismissal a prominent American Germanist, Reinhold Grimm, has given it in a sweeping denunciation that seems to be inspired largely by *Garbage, the City, and Death*.[100] Grimm isolates specific portions of Fassbinder's theatrical texts that he finds offensive, taking little account of the serious themes in much of this work or of the light these plays shed on the political and cultural contexts in which they were originally performed. The brief survey given above suggests that, on the whole, Fassbinder's theater work from 1967 through 1969 constitutes an energetic and imaginative attempt to use the stage as a place of provocative discourse on contemporary cultural and political issues, played off against a variety of venerable texts. Much of this work seems to have been inspired by the idea of a "theater of cruelty" formulated by the French poet, playwright, and drama theorist Antonin Artaud. Artaud's influential book, *Le Théâtre et son Double,* 1938 (*The Theater and Its Double*) is a passionate manifesto for a radically antiliterary and interactive theater, one that makes "a believable reality which gives the heart and the senses that kind of concrete bite which all true sensation requires," a theater which allows its audience "to liberate within itself the magical liberties of dreams which it can only recognize when they are imprinted with terror and cruelty." Fassbinder would cite this book in two of his films, and he seems to be echoing such passages as this in many of his later comments about his hopes for liberating the imaginations of his film audiences.[101] If nothing else, Fassbinder's early work in the theater constitutes a fascinating record of the "Generation of '68" at a particularly critical moment in its history, as it moved from a free-spirited thumbing of its nose at the older generation and the bourgeois establishment (as in *Leonce and Lena*) to the much more ominous disillusionment embodied in *Preparadise sorry now*.

But one can make only limited claims for the importance of Fassbinder's work in the theater, which apparently did not fire his imagination nearly to the degree that the cinema did. Peter Iden wrote in 1974 that he could find no unity or coherence in this work. Fassbinder's plays seemed to Iden a series of disparate statements, often thrown together in a hurry under pressure, and neglected by the director after opening as he moved on to something else. His premieres "were eagerly awaited events, but the tense expectation was often followed by disappointment and complaints." It was fortunate for Fassbinder, Iden concludes, that so few playwrights in West Germany were writing about contemporary issues at the time he began his work in the theater.[102] This remark echoes an earlier judgment by another critic of the Munich theater scene, who in 1973 characterized Fassbinder's theater work as "an exotic, occasionally admired plant" in Munich's "mostly tired theater-life."[103] Still, there has been enough international interest in Fassbinder's theatrical writing to justify publication of translations in at least ten countries outside Germany.[104]

In any case, Fassbinder's work in the theater during these early years contributed significantly to his development as a film director. This is true in both the personal and the artistic spheres. The Action-Theater and the antitheater offered the young director a relatively supportive environment in which he could begin his artistic life. After a lonely childhood and adolescence marked by severe problems in school and frustrated efforts to begin formal training for a career in the cinema, he suddenly found himself at the age of twenty-two in the center of a group of young artistic coworkers, many just out of acting school, with whom he was able to test out his capacities for friendship, intimacy, and aggressiveness and with whom he could explore a wide variety of themes and theatrical styles. There was apparently a considerable enmity within the antitheater, and many in the group resented their extraordinarily driven leader. But most of them recognized their dependence on his creativity and energy and stuck with him for years (many with considerable affection), even though the communal ideal quickly ceased to exist as a practical model for their work together.

The general conditions in which Fassbinder undertook his early theater work provided a relatively safe context for artistic experimentation by the fledgling artist. The antitheater scripts and performances were flexible, changing from night to night, and the audiences in the Witwe Bolte were about half university students.[105] One assumes that most of the older patrons who found their way to these performances came expecting to be shocked, titillated, and at least verbally assaulted—if not hosed down! As Michael Töteberg points out, the dilettantish quality of the performance added something to its attractiveness.[106] It was for Fassbinder a time for exploring a wide range of authors, from Sophocles to Handke, even if their texts were more often merely occasions for creative play or political provocation than for serious reinterpretation. And it was a time for initial gropings with virtually all the themes his films would explore later: the damaging effects of unhappy childhood; the exploitative potential of intimate relationships, including (in its most vivid metaphorical form) vampirism; the oppressiveness and duplicity of governmental power; the problems of foreign workers and other social outsiders; and both the appeal and the futility of anarchy and utopian revolution.

Fassbinder found his work as a theatrical director and as a filmmaker satisfying in quite different ways. He once said that the theater "offers the greater possibility for control over the productive means and their further development."[107] On another occasion, he pointed out that in the theater he had more time to develop through the group; "the result doesn't interest me so much as the process." Filmmaking, on the other hand, is "tiring and sometimes very unsatisfying. . . . But the result is very exciting."[108] He observed that his early work in the theater and in film was mutually supportive. "In the beginning, it was pretty extreme," he said. "In the theater I would stage things as though I was doing a film, and then I made a film as if it was on the stage."[109] As has been seen, Fassbinder's collaboration in 1968 with the director Jean-Marie Straub helped him develop a sure-handed if often indirectly expressed kind of directorial control that produced a self-conscious style of acting that was distinctly different from what was usually practiced in realist theater and film.

Shortly after he finished his first film in 1969, Fassbinder—perhaps defensively—misrepresented his motives for starting out in the theater: "We did theater because at a certain moment a ridiculously large number of people were making films and hardly anyone was doing theater. So we thought, we'll do theater. And then when all these films that had been made turned out, at least for the most part, not to measure up to what we thought was possible, we came up with the concrete idea of making films."[110] Two later comments are more consistent with the history of his early theater work traced in this chapter. In 1971 Fassbinder said that he had wanted to make films from the start but, being "a trained actor . . . it was much easier to begin in the theater; it has paid off: when I *did* start making films, my previous work in the theater made it much easier to get credit . . . with theater enjoying more respect than film in Germany."[111] In the year before his death, he summarized: "Film was always more interesting to me [than theater]. But the problem of money was so difficult. I got involved with the Action-Theater at first actually just to have something to do, and then I found that really exciting." But in retrospect, it was for him "just a transition to making films."[112]

Notes

1. Brocher Int II 15.
2. Brocher Int II 15; Eder Int (on the monthly allowance).
3. Schygulla/RWF 202.

4. Fassbinder said that he had had experience in all aspects of filmmaking except music before he began making his first feature film (Steinborn Int 14).

5. Unidentified interview cited in Töteberg, "Einführung" 10.

6. Schygulla/RWF 200.

7. Hayman 41.

8. The acting lessons were with a director named Kraus, whom Fassbinder mentions in the *Lebenslauf* (curriculum vitae) reproduced in RWFF Cat 13 and Spaich 20.

9. Fassbinder, "Hanna Schygulla" 200.

10. Kurt Raab wrote that Fassbinder was so impatient that he studied at the Fridl-Leonhard school for only a two months (Raab 21). But a certificate from the school, which Mrs. Eder showed the author, indicates that was there for the twenty-seven months indicated here. Katz claims, without citing a source, that Fassbinder "was thrown out of acting school for having no talent" (25).

11. Schygulla/RWF 200–201.

12. See Brocher Int II 15 and Töteberg, "Fassbinders Theaterarbeit" 152–53 (cited hereafter in this chapter as "Theaterarbeit").

13. Katz 23, citing Irm Hermann.

14. *Tropfen auf heisse Steine* is published in *Anarchie in Bayern & andere Stücke* 7–62. It was first performed in Munich in May 1985. The older man's name is presumably a version of Leopold Bloom, the protagonist of James Joyce's famous novel, *Ulysses* (1922), though the two characters have little in common. The masochistic younger man, Franz Meister, seems to be the first of the many reincarnations in Fassbinder's works of Franz Biberkopf, the protagonist of Alfred Döblin's *Berlin Alexanderplatz* (1929), whose significance for Fassbinder is reviewed in chapter 10; his last name also recalls Wilhelm Meister, the protagonist of several *Bildungsromane* by Goethe.

15. Fassbinder, "*Lebenslauf*," RWFF Cat 13; Spaich 20.

16. Eder Int. See also Brocher Int II 15 and Wiegand Int 61.

17. Fassbinder's application papers to the Berlin film school, his responses to questions on the entrance examination, and the examining committee's evaluation are reproduced in RWFF Cat 56–76.

18. Töteberg, "Theaterarbeit" 153–54.

19. Schygulla/RWF 202.

20. Roser was given major roles in both films, and the money was apparently paid back, contrary to the impression given by Hayman (28–29) and Katz (25). Fassbinder said the total amount he borrowed from Roser was 15–18,000 DM, and that when he and Roser broke off their relationship shortly after the films were made, he signed a promissory note to repay the money at the rate of 300 DM a month (Wiegand Int 61).

21. Brocher Int II 15; Eckhardt 66.

22. Brocher Int I.

23. RWFF Cat 76.

24. *Kopf* 123.

25. Töteberg, "Nachwort," *Antiteater* 231. At some time during this early period, Irm Hermann, who had become Fassbinder's talent agent, reportedly managed to find

him a promising role in a television series which he was not able to accept since he was cooling his heels in a Turkish jail with Roser after they had been caught delivering stolen cars (Katz 25–27, citing Hermann).

26. Brocher Int II 273.

27. Wiegand Int 61.

28. Schygulla/RWF 203. Unless otherwise indicated, this essay is the source of the following account of Fassbinder's work in the Action-Theater; quotations not otherwise identified are from pages 203–211 of this text. For further discussion by Fassbinder of this period, see Brocher Int I and Int II 15–26 and Limmer Int 61–63.

29. Töteberg, "Nachwort," *Antiteater* 231; Eckhardt 66–67; Pluta 11.

30. Shattuc, "*Contra* Brecht" 43. As Shattuc has elsewhere observed, the performance of *Antigone* that Fassbinder saw that evening exemplified the propensity of late-Sixties avant-garde theatrical groups in West Germany to freely adapt "traditionally sacrosanct works" to fit their leftist political agenda (Shattuc, "R. W. Fassbinder as Popular *Auteur*" 42).

31. Töteberg, "Nachwort," *Antiteater* 232; Karsunke 3.

32. Brocher Int 17; Limmer Int 12.

33. Schygulla/RWF 205–206 and Brocher Int I. Raben would later serve as music director for most for Fassbinder's films. For Schygulla's account of the loosely structured rehearsals for this play, see Emerson 74.

34. Brocher Int I. Juliane Lorenz reports that Ursula Strätz told her that she and Raab let Fassbinder assume direction of the Action-Theater because of his "great 'aura'" and because "his ideas were extraordinary and good" (Let 24 May 1994). Fassbinder said that Raben's directorial style led him into many "psychological detours," while his own was "concrete" (Brocher Int I).

35. Brocher Int I.

36. DIF 11; Limmer 12; Karsunke 2.

37. Brocher Int I; Schygulla/RWF 211.

38. Brocher Int I.

39. Brocher Int II 20–23.

40. Brocher Int I.

41. Brocher Int I.

42. The most frequently used English translations of the German word *Pioniere* in the title are "Pioneers" and "Recruits," but neither is very accurate; "sappers" would perhaps be the best choice, if the word were more commonly known. Fleisser wrote this play at the suggestion of Bertolt Brecht (following what she later indicated was his too-strong advice), who directed a controversial revised version of it in 1929; it was based on incidents the author observed in Ingolstadt, her hometown. (Hoffmeister, *Theater* 44.) Presumably, Fassbinder's version has not survived; it is not included in his *Sämtliche Stücke*. Fassbinder would later produce two more versions of Fleisser's play: his eleventh feature-length film, shot in November 1970 (discussed in chapter 3), and a theatrical version staged in Bremen the following January. For discussion of the reciprocal influences between the Fleisser revival and the work of Fassbinder and his contemporary

playwrights Franz Xaver Kroetz (1946–) and Martin Speer (1944–) in the critical folk play, see Töteberg, "Theaterarbeit" 157 and Hoffmeister, *Theater* 22.

43. Karsunke 3.

44. This account of the dispute over the staging of *Zum Beispiel Ingolstadt* is given in Fleisser, "All meiner Söhne" 509–11. Fleisser writes here that when Fassbinder dedicated his 1969 film *Katzelmacher* to her, she realized that she had "given something decisive to a talented young man," who was thanking her for that in the dedication (510–11). Fassbinder said that he understood that the group had originally obtained legal rights to produce his version of the play (Brocher Int I).

45. Brocher Int I.

46. Hoffmeister, *Theater* 23.

47. The Bruchner play dramatizes the promiscuous lives of a group of disillusioned medical students. It is not clear whether Straub's wife and regular collaborator in filmmaking, Danièle Huillet, was involved in this theatrical project in the Action-Theater. The major sources for this discussion of the production are Brocher Int I and Schygulla/RWF 212–13.

48. Wiegand Int 63–64.

49. *Anarchy* 8.

50. *Anarchy* 8.

51. Brocher Int I.

52. The title has been variously interpreted as Bavarian slang for tomcat and "cock-artist" (Hayman 44) and as traveling Italian grocer (Töteberg, "Einführung" 16), all suggestive of the foreigner's supposed virility.

53. Töteberg, "Einführung" 15–16.

54. Eckhardt 71.

55. Hans Helmut Prinzler dates the performance of *Axel* in April (Jansen and Schütte 275), and Jane Shattuc, in June ("*Contra* Brecht" 44).

56. Schygulla/RWF 213.

57. Karsunke 4.

58. Limmer 13, Karsunke 5.

59. Karsunke 5.

60. This dating of *Chung* derives from Fassbinder's comment that the 6 June closing-down of the Action-Theater (noted below) occurred during the play's run (Brocher Int I). This production is not listed in Jansen and Schütte.

61. Limmer 13.

62. Katz 33–34, citing Peer Raben.

63. Karsunke 6.

64. Brocher Int I, note.

65. Brocher Int I.

66. The official new name of the company was *antiteater,* to which an *h* is added for ease of reading in this English text (at the suggestion of Krishna Winston, translator of *Anarchy*). Fassbinder said that he was not very happy with the name, which was

selected by the group in one night, in order to be able to meet an advertising deadline for the group's next play, *Mockingpott*. He regretted that the name was often interpreted as indicating opposition to the theater, rather than "a critical attitude toward society" (Brocher Int I). On another occasion, he remarked that the name did not signify anything important: it was "just a name we gave it, in the same way that another stage might be called the 'Schiller Theater'" (Thomsen Int 82). Töteberg dates the official founding of the antitheater as 6 June 1968 ("Nachwort," *Antiteater* 234).

67. Brocher Int I.

68. Brocher Int I.

69. Brocher Int I.

70. Eckhardt 76.

71. Brocher Int II.

72. Brocher Int II.

73. Brocher Int I.

74. Brocher Int I.

75. Karsunke 8.

76. Karsunke 8.

77. Fassbinder, *Antiteater* 20–21. For an analysis of both the political and the nonpolitical implications of such use of American pop culture in Fassbinder's theatrical and film work, see Shattuc, "*Contra* Brecht."

78. Töteberg, "Nachwort," *Antiteater* 235; Karsunke 9.

79. Limmer 14–15.

80. Töteberg, "Theaterarbeit" 165; "Einführung" 11.

81. Fassbinder had originally titled the film "Kalter Stahl" (Cold Steel). He said he came to write the script after an encounter with Ulli Lommel, a film actor with whom he had worked in *Tonys Freunde* and who had recently played a lead role in a French movie inspired by American gangster films, Jean-Paul Melville's *Ice-Cold Angel*. After they had together seen an Italian western movie with a progressive political message—Damiano Damianis' *Quien sabe* (German: *Töte Amigo* [Dead Friends])—they decided, "We have to make a film like that." Fassbinder then wrote the script for his first feature film and sent it to Lommel, who returned it to him by way of a film director friend, Martin Müller, who added a note, "This film has got to be made." Lommel tried unsuccessfully to use his connections to interest a production company in the script (Töteberg, "Einführung" 12–13).

82. The members of the antitheater troupe agreed to donate half their earnings, according to Limmer (16); according to Töteberg, they refused this plan but agreed instead to a more complicated arrangement for later reimbursement ("Einführung" 13).

83. Töteberg, "Einführung" 13; Brocher Int II 26–27.

84. Fassbinder, Brocher Int I. This production is not listed in Jansen and Schütte.

85. Gay's play was the inspiration for *Die Dreigroschenoper* (*The Threepenny Opera*, 1928), the well-known musical satire by Bertolt Brecht and Kurt Weill.

86. Fassbinder, Brocher Int II 27.

87. Karsunke 9; Töteberg, "Theaterarbeit" 160. The production followed both "the Brecht/Weill tradition of satiric operetta" and that of the Living Theater, in its "quick succession of silly doggerel and prayerlike dialogue" and a closing in which the actors crawled about and barked (Shattuc, "*Contra* Brecht" 44).

88. Hayman 108.

89. Calandra 10.

90. Karsunke 9.

91. *Anarchie in Bayern* 109.

92. This production is not listed in Jansen and Schütte. Töteberg indicates the date of the premiere and reports that the text is lost ("Theaterarbeit" 160). Rosa von Praunheim's 1969 film is entitled *Rosa Arbeiter auf der goldener Strasse* (Rosa Worker on the Golden Street). If the play seemed to be an ironic put-down of Rosa von Praunheim's film, it may have been one of the first shots fired in a long-running public battle between Fassbinder and the gay filmmaker Praunheim. See *Anarchy* 68 and Praunheim, "From Beast to Beast," in Rentschler, ed. *West German Filmmakers on Film: Visions and Voices* (New York: Holmes and Meier, 1988) 201–204. Praunheim's hostility to Fassbinder continued as late as the summer of 1992, when during the Fassbinder memorial exhibition in Berlin he asserted in a newspaper essay, "I couldn't bear Fassbinder, because he loved slaves," among other charges ("Schwul").

93. Iden 17–18.

94. The German playwright Botho Strauss wrote that Fassbinder read through Goldoni's *The Coffeehouse* and then "wrote down what inspired him in the speeches in a newer form," thus replacing the witty wordplay of the original with a restrained and even "elegiac" verbal style. "It is not even a comedy anymore, but becomes a really very sad play." *Theater heute* (October 1969): 16 ff.; quoted in Roth/AF 213.

95. Brocher Int I. The Bremen actors included Margit Carstensen, who would later replace Hanna Schygulla as Fassbinder's leading female star for several years.

96. Iden 13.

97. Quoted in Baer 26.

98. Karsunke 2. Antonin Artaud is discussed later in this chapter.

99. Braun. Lorenz points out in this interview that Fassbinder gave up the role of Iago, for which he rehearsed for a few days at most, because he disagreed with Palitzsche's conception of Iago as a pensive, guilt-ridden "egg-head" (he wanted to play him as "an energetic intriguer") and because he was unimpressed by the actress cast as Desdemona.

100. Following his charges against *Garbage, the City, and Death* (which will be considered in chapter 7), Grimm accuses Fassbinder of plagiarism (in the ending of his production of *The Beggar's Opera*), racism (in *Petra von Kant*), physical and psychological "brutality," exploitation of the theme of Nazism, and "incomprehensible and inexcusable unscrupulousness"—concluding that the director's theatrical work is "a heap of inflated nothingness" (with the exception of *Katzelmacher* and possibly *Bremer Freiheit* and *Petra von Kant*). Grimm admits that he is not familiar with Fassbinder's films.

101. *The Theater and Its Double* 85–86. Artaud is quoted in *Satan's Brew* and *Theater in Trance*. Jane Shattuc helpfully distinguishes between Bertolt Brecht and the "anarchist and antirationalist" Artaud, who refused to participate in either bourgeois culture or leftist politics ("*Contra* Brecht" 45–6). See also Töteberg, "Das Theater der Grausamkeit," cited by Shattuc 53, n. 37.

102. Iden 15.

103. DIF 16.

104. A list dated 11 April 1991 provided to Liselotte Eder by the West German publisher of Fassbinder's plays, Verlag der Autoren, indicates translations of those plays in Brazil, Japan, and the United States, in addition to seven European countries.

105. Färber Int 474

106. "Nachwort," *Antiteater* 241.

107. Iden 14.

108. Scherer Int 98; see also Töteberg, "Theaterarbeit" 163. Shortly before his death, Fassbinder indicated the kind of personal satisfaction he found in theatrical work, when asked if he might return to work in the theater: "Oh, I'll do that for sure. It's really nice to work in the theater for six or eight weeks, when you're doing it with friends. . . . But I have no interest at all in doing theater with just anybody" (Steinborn Int 2).

109. *Anarchy* 14

110. Färber Int 472.

111. Thomsen Int 82.

112. Limmer Int 64.

CHAPTER THREE

Film Apprenticeship as Marathon Race

Once their commitment to make films was clear, Fassbinder and his antitheater group plunged into what one writer has called a "marathon"[1] and another "an explosive ecstasy of production."[2] In the nineteen months after the completion of *Love Is Colder Than Death* in April 1969 they made ten full-length feature films of widely varying styles and themes: seven based on original scripts by Fassbinder, three adaptations of plays they had previously produced (two written by Fassbinder), and one using an outline script. Other work went on as well. During this period, under the name of the antitheater, Fassbinder put on four more stage plays and two radio plays, produced one film for another director, wrote another screenplay, and played roles in seven films directed by others.

Fassbinder's energy, chutzpah, and charisma held the antitheater group together and kept them on a productive course under difficult circumstances. He sometimes claimed that his pace of work was not unusual, as in a 1970 remark comparing his work schedule with those of factory and office workers: "I don't know why at twenty-four I shouldn't work as hard. And when you work all year, you can accomplish a lot."[3] He made it clear that he was not one of those "3000 guys who loaf around Schwabing and complain, 'Yeah, if I just had a nice apartment, I'd write a terrific novel, and if I had a million, I'd make a great film.'"[4]

One of the main reasons Fassbinder kept so busy was his need to pay off the debts he was accumulating making films, he told André Müller in 1971.[5] Funding was always uncertain, even after he was awarded 950,000 DM in prizes and subsidies for *Katzelmacher*. This sum covered the costs of that 80,000-DM production many times over, but it was not enough to balance the books for his many other projects. Fassbinder seems to have disregarded the disadvantages of flooding the West German market with so many of his films in such a short time. It did not help matters that the group's production company, antitheater-X Films, was never officially registered as a corporation or that Peer Raben, the music director to whom Fassbinder delegated the responsibilities of financial officer, was so disorganized in this function that a federal tax assessment board ruled that the company owed 300,000 DM in unpaid income taxes when it was dissolved at the end of 1970 (the amount due was eventually reduced).[6]

During this period of frenetic production Fassbinder and his colleagues mostly taught themselves the craft of filmmaking. He had had only limited experience in film acting and in film production, and most of his colleagues had considerably less. The first cameraman he hired (for *Love Is Colder Than Death*) had bad eyesight, of all problems, which cost the group six shooting days. His replacement, Dietrich Lohmann, who was brought into the project on only one day's notice, had done some work with Schlöndorff and others, but only as an assistant cameraman.[7] Fassbinder, however, not only strongly believed in his own ability to make films, in defiance of those who had turned him down for film school, but he also had a remarkable ability to give others confidence in their ability to learn by doing.[8]

Looking for Love: Hollywood Gangster Style

The first antitheater film, *Love Is Colder Than Death,* filmed in April, 1969, was one of three early Fassbinder films, all made in black and white, which evoke the milieu, moods, gestures, and dialogue of the film noir-style American gangster films of the 1930s, 1940s, and 1950s—films that had themselves adopted the chiaroscuro lighting, tightly enclosed urban settings, and fatalism typical of many films made during the Weimar-era golden age of German cinema.[9]

Many of the situations and themes of Fassbinder's three feature-length gangster films were anticipated in his short film, *Das Kleine Chaos,* which he shot on 35 mm black-and-white film in February 1967. In that wry nine-minute piece three young people in Munich, frustrated in their attempts to sell magazine subscriptions, rob a middle-class woman in her apartment at gunpoint. Fassbinder plays a cocky, wise-guy hoodlum with a cigarette dangling from his lips. His name is Franz—the first of many references in Fassbinder's films to Franz Biberkopf, the protagonist of Alfred Döblin's famous 1929 novel *Berlin Alexanderplatz.* The well-dressed woman with her classical records and modern-art prints seems to represent the bourgeois establishment, and the Fassbinder character enacts a little ritual of defiance of middle-class conventionality in threatening her with sexual domination and setting fire with his cigarette lighter to a small print pinned on her wall (a Picasso-like nude). But none of this seems intended to be taken particluarly seriously. The film contains a number of stylistic tricks, such as a quick-cut montage of similar shots showing each of the three companions having a door slammed in his or her face by a potential magazine buyer (one of whom is Fassbinder's mother in the first of her roles in her son's films), and the sudden loud strains of classical symphonic music as Franz burns the print on the wall. Already in Fassbinder's second surviving short film there are inside references to his own work: a still from his first short film, *Der Stadtstreicher,* and a poster of Rohmer's *The Sign of the Lion,* which inspired it (along with posters from two Hollywood gangster films).[10] This cinematic reflexivity is comically underscored in the final shot of the film. As the three petty thieves divide up the money from the robbery, one of them asks what they will do it. Fassbinder's Franz responds with a knowing smile at the camera: "I'm going to the movies."

Like *Das Kleine Chaos,* Fassbinder's three feature-length gangster movies are all set in his home city, Munich. Their central characters are aimless young men who seem to be longing for companionship and love. But they can express their emotions only through the clichés and gestures of gangster movies, including bullying the women in their lives. Fassbinder said that he was not trying in these films to remake American gangster films, but rather to use their relatively "simple" structure to express "what was basic to me and to my interests."[11] What he did express in them can be interpreted on both public and private levels. On the one hand, the films dramatize the stultifying conditions of a postwar German bourgeois society trying to bury its consciousness of an unspeakable recent past in its pursuit of the Economic Miracle. In contrast to the "outsider" protagonists typical of American gangster films, Fassbinder's gangsters and small-time thieves are "actually integrated into society," he said. They are "victims of the bourgeoisie, not rebels," who do essentially just what the capitalists do, only outside the law.[12] Moreover, Fassbinder was drawn to these gangster stories as a means of commenting indirectly on what he saw as the increasingly police-state mentality developing in West Germany in response to the radical left-wing protests and terrorist acts; he said it was not possible at the time to make films directly on the latter subject.[13] At the private level, these films portray several painful aspects of intimate relationships, particularly as experienced or enacted by males: longing for dependable comradeship, fear of exploitation through love, and abuse of women as compensation for male impotence. In general, these three films show that, like a number of French postwar film directors, Fassbinder found in "the egocentricity of the outsider, the slightly self-pitying pessimism, and the latent misogyny" of the Hollywood film noir a point of departure for a "tortuous discourse about a world of false images and real emotions, of public failures and private fantasies," as Thomas Elsaesser has observed.[14]

Love Is Colder Than Death (1969)

Fassbinder's first full-length film was shot on 35 mm black-and-white film in April 1969. Produced by antitheater-X Films at a cost of approximately 95,000 DM, it premiered at the Berlin Film Festival two months later and opened in West German theaters the following January.

Fassbinder plays the lead role of Franz, a small-time pimp who refuses to cooperate with a crime syndicate. The organization assigns one of their own, a good-looking young man named Bruno (Ulli Lommel) to implicate Franz in a crime so that they can force him to work for them.[15] Franz is so taken with Bruno that he invites him to visit him in the apartment where he lives with Joanna (Hanna Schygulla), a prostitute, and even to share her sexual favors. Later the two men carry out a bank robbery in which Bruno is shot dead after Joanna tips off the police. Franz and Joanna escape with Bruno's body in the large black Cadillac they have brought to the robbery. They foil the pursuing police by tossing the corpse onto the highway, and as they drive away into a trashy-looking countryside Joanna tells Franz that it was she who had called the police, to which he responds simply, as the film ends with a fade to white: "Whore."

Love Is Colder Than Death evokes a hopeless world in which personal and intimate relationships are both uncertain and threatening. "Here are poor people," Fassbinder commented, "who can't get started, who have been put down, and for whom nothing is possible."[16] Although Franz tells Bruno that he loves Joanna, their passive gestures of affection and erotic interest suggest otherwise. Their alliance seems to be mutually exploitative: early in the film he pockets most of the money from her last prostitution client; and her chief interests are, she says, a house, a child, and some peace. The conclusion of the film certainly implies an unpromising future for Franz and Joanna. It has sometimes been suggested that Franz's attachment to Bruno, which is implicitly homoerotic, is portrayed in more idealistic terms than his relationship with Joanna. The attraction, however, comes primarily from Franz's side, anticipating the naive and misplaced trust in a male friend by many a later Fassbinder protagonist named Franz.

Love Is Colder Than Death well illustrates the director's frequent assertion that the gangster world is essentially bourgeois. He called the prostitute Joanna's longing for home and family the main point of the film; she is "totally bogged down in bourgeois values."[17] Although the film does not fully support that reading, it is presumably Joanna's bourgeois dreams that lead her (irrationally, if she wants to settle down with Franz) to tip off the police about the bank robbery. The furniture in Joanna's one-room apartment is a far cry from middle-class—consisting of a sleeping-couch, a plain table, a folding chair, a throw rug, a small stereo set atop a low table, and a toilet just off camera but not out of earshot. Still, in one scene late in the film, the three friends enact a quiet parody of bourgeois domesticity, Joanna sitting (topless) on the bed stitching a blouse while Franz and Bruno work quietly at an adjacent table, one on a crossword puzzle and the other on a machine gun. The middle-class tastes of the criminals are more directly indicated in the furnishings of the syndicate office: a classical bust on an antique chest, Danish-modern table and chairs, and a large cubist painting.

For the most part the visual effects of Fassbinder's first feature film are stark, consistent with the empty, constricted lives of its protagonists. The lighting of interior shots is often unusually bright, as in Joanna's bare-walled apartment and the glass-partitioned police station where Franz is questioned about the murders Bruno has committed. The outdoor shots depict mostly the dreary lower-middle-class Munich neighborhood where the protagonists live. By day it is depressingly gray; by night it is threateningly dark, in the tradition of film

Love Is Colder Than Death, 1969. Joanna (Hanna Schygulla) sews, while small-time mobsters Bruno (Ulli Lommel) and Franz (Fassbinder) complete the parody of domestic bliss in Fassbinder's first feature film, which evokes the film noir gangster genre. (By permission of the Rainer Werner Fassbinder Foundation, Berlin)

noir. This effect is particularly evident in a traveling shot, more than four min-utes long, indicating Bruno's entry into Franz's neighborhood, which Jean-Marie Straub gave Fassbinder to use in his film.[18]

Straub's influence on the visual style of Fassbinder's first feature film goes far beyond this one piece of footage, however. The director with whom Fassbinder had collaborated the previous year at the Action-Theater seems to have been a major inspiration for many aspects of the film's self-conscious stylization—for example, the formal framing, the long-running shots, and the static camera setups and acting (interrupted at times by heavily choreographed scenes).[19] At some points this nonnaturalistic style escalates into pure comedy, particularly in a scene in a department store in which Franz, Bruno, and Joanna steal three pairs of sunglasses while confusing the saleswoman (Irm Hermann), and a lyrical shoplifting romp through a supermarket, accompanied by a highly mobile camera and the strains of Richard Strauss's 1911 opera *Der Rosenkavalier.*

Gods of the Plague (1969)

Fassbinder made the second of his three gangster films, *Götter der Pest* (*Gods of the Plague*), in October and November 1969, largely on credit and faith in the future, according to Harry Baer.[20] Filmed on black-and-white 35 mm film at a cost of 180,000 DM, *Gods of the Plague* premiered at the Venice Film Festival in April 1970 and opened in West German theaters three months later.

Gods of the Plague is reminiscent of the earlier gangster film in several ways, but it is significantly different in style. In place of the high-contrast light-ing, static camera work, relatively simple plotting, and fast pace of *Love Is Colder Than Death,* this is a dark mood-poem, with much more mobile camera work, enigmatic dialogue and plotting, and unusually slow-paced action. As Töteberg notes, the film is a kind of elegy, with a mood of unrelenting weari-ness and sadness.[21] Fassbinder said in 1974 that this was his favorite film, if not his best, because of the way its "very strong atmosphere" evoked for him that time "after the revolution, when one just didn't any longer know where things were leading, whether one should take an interest in politics or not, and one was really fed up with all that."[22]

The casting of the film reinforces the interpretation of it as an unusually personal project as those remarks of the director suggest. The protagonist, Franz Walsch (Fassbinder's pseudonym as film editor), is played by Harry Baer, a new friend of Fassbinder's, whose emotional account of his generation's sudden political disillusionment in 1968 was discussed in chapter one. Franz's mother, who is utterly unable to break through the emotional wall her morose son has put up around his ego, is played by Fassbinder's mother. Franz's closest friend, who is also the killer of his brother, is played by Günther Kaufmann, a black Bavarian (the son of a German woman and an African-American soldier), with whom Fassbinder had recently begun the first of his three most significant gay love relationships.

Moreover, the career of this Franz, who at one point uses the last name Biberkopf as an alias, closely parallels that of Franz Biberkopf, the protagonist of Alfred Döblin's *Berlin Alexanderplatz,* a novel that had for many years fascinated the director and which he would in 1978 turn into his most ambitious film. As in Döblin's book, Franz's story in *Gods of the Plague* begins with his being released from prison. Professing a desire to go straight, he goes passively from woman to woman, then masochistically attaches himself to a male companion who destroys someone he loves and leads him back into a life of crime and eventually to his downfall. Like Fassbinder's first gangster film, *Gods of the Plague* dramatizes many of what would become recurrent themes in the Fassbinder film corpus: the fruitless search for friendship and love, intimacy as an instrument of manipulation and betrayal, and an oppressive society's entrapment of vulnerable individuals who are unreflectively dependent on predetermined codes of communication and behavior in a futile effort to express their own personalities.

Fassbinder's second gangster film carries over a number of characters and plot details from *Love Is Colder Than Death.* For example, early on Franz's brother mutters: "Bruno is dead," and Franz responds, "I know" (there is no further mention of Franz's late friend). Also continued from the earlier film is Joanna (again played by Hanna Schygulla), now a nightclub singer, who is Franz's girlfriend at the beginning of the story. As in the first film, Joanna betrays Franz to the police. But this time she does so only after he has deserted her and after she has become romantically entangled with a hardboiled police inspector. As a result of her betrayal, Franz is killed at the end of the movie when the inspector surprises him and his friend in a supermarket store holdup.

Consistent with the elegiac mood of *Gods of the Plague,* the enigmatic protagonist is extraordinarily passive. Franz of *Love Is Colder Than Death* is able to assert his will against the syndicate bosses who want to control him, and he survives the final shoot-out. In this film, however, Franz mostly broods in silence, responds hardly at all to the affections of women, and merely follows along with his friend's plan for the robbery that results in his death. Franz's despondency seems to be rooted in his family ties. His emotional distance from his mother is dramatized poignantly when Franz visits her bourgeois apartment. In an extremely slow-moving scene Franz sits slumped despondently in a chair as his mother attempts to cheer him up with a record she has recently bought (a ludicrously upbeat Italian workers' marching song, to which he listens without comment) and then offers him money. "I have enough," he mutters, without showing the slightest emotion. Franz does seem to be strongly drawn toward his brother, Marian (Marian Sydowski), early in the film. His only response to Joanna's plaintive assurance—"I love you so much"—as they sit in a restaurant shortly after his release from prison is to go to the telephone to call his brother. However, when Franz finds Marian dead in his apartment shortly thereafter, he merely looks at the corpse, strokes it passively, and leaves, taking care to wipe his fingerprints off the door handle.

Franz finds little comfort in his relationships with women. He simply walks out of Joanna's life, apparently for no other reason than that he is smothered by her affection and attention. He then gets involved with his brother's cast-off mistress, Magdalena (Ingrid Caven), who rescues him from a beating by immigrant workers after he has stolen one of their suitcases, and takes him into her apartment. Franz remains despondent and passive as Magdalena undresses him and speaks in a dull monologue of her sad life as a woman alone in a big city, abused as a child by her uncle and brother and now deserted by Marian. The scene ends with a shot of Franz lying in Magdalena's lap, like Christ in the lap of Mary in the *Pietà*.

Franz does make the effort to seek out in her workplace the third woman with whom he takes up, Margarethe (Margarethe von Trotta). Perhaps they have known each other before, since they have exchanged knowing glances in previous scenes in a bar and a restaurant. In any case, the two passionately embrace when they meet at this later point in the film, but Franz settles into his usual passivity once he moves into Margarethe's apartment. In one painfully slow-moving scene, he unenthusiastically suggests a walk, responds not at all to Margarethe's offer of ravioli, listlessly takes the glass of schnapps she offers, and then listens to her recording of "Der Maskenball der Tiere" ("The Animals' Masked Ball"), a nonsense song by Karl Valentin, a popular Bavarian dialect comedian of the prewar period, with no more emotion than he showed listening to the marching song in his mother's apartment.

The theme of homoerotic love in *Gods of the Plague* is suggested both in Franz's passive and despondent relationships with women and in the excitement and utopian promise of his relationship with his old friend Günther Schlöndorff.[23] Günther appears suddenly in the story, as Franz and Margarethe are walking along a business street. The men greet each other in a mixture of

73

feigned violence (a pretended fight) and unabashed enthusiasm. Franz mutters "Crazy!" as they alternately spar and embrace.[24] The two men admire Günther's sporty convertible and spontaneously decide to drive into the country for a visit with an older gangster, Joe (Micha Cochina), who lives on a farm. They bring Margarethe along almost as an afterthought. The imagery of the film suggests how liberated Franz feels by his encounter with his pal. The scene shifts from constricted, gloomy Munich to the open country as the car speeds along a mountain road. On the way Franz asks Günther if he knows anything about his brother, Marian, and if Günther had slept with Joanna while Franz was in prison. Günther replies "Yes" to both questions. Then he adds a laconic comment on Marian: "He sang. It was an order." To these revelations—that his friend had slept with his girlfriend while he was in prison and killed his brother for the mob—Franz mutters, "I love you." Like Döblin's Franz Biberkopf, this Franz seems masochistically drawn to the friend who has hurt him. Fassbinder matches Franz's declaration of love with a dramatic cut to a lyrical helicopter shot showing them speeding through the lovely Bavarian countryside.[25]

Later, in Margarethe's apartment, Franz, like his earlier embodiment in *Love Is Colder Than Death,* offers to share his lover with his friend. Günther takes him up on the offer, and Margarethe, unlike Joanna in the earlier film, goes along with the plan. Margarethe talks about practical possibilities for getting more money, but the men talk dreamily of going to an island somewhere to the south and living off fish, crabs, and hunting. "We don't need money," says Franz, and Günther completes the fantasy: "since we love each other." When the two men reveal that they are going to get money, in any case, by robbing a supermarket, Margarethe, like Joanna in *Love Is Colder Than Death,* tries to dissuade them, and she offers to supplement her salary by taking on work as a prostitute—"for you, Franz." For this loving interference in her man's affairs, Franz rewards her with a slap across the face.

Franz shows no apparent feelings as he goes with Günther into the supermarket and as he callously betrays another friend, Martin, the store manager. When Günther grabs Martin to begin executing the robbery, a police inspector who, tipped off by Joanna, has followed them into the store opens fire. He kills both Franz and Martin and mortally wounds Günther, who escapes and makes his way to the apartment of a female pornography-seller and police informer who he assumes has tipped off the police. Günther ties her to a chair and shoots her in cold blood just before he dies, muttering melodramatically in English, "Life is very precious, even right now."[26]

Ruth McCormick, among others, has pointed out the misogyny in this and Fassbinder's other two gangster films.[27] But the antagonism toward women is the attitude of the male characters in the film, not of the film as a whole. Among these three films, *Gods of the Plague* focuses the most sympathetically on the bleak lives of its long-suffering women, anticipating the director's many variations on the melodramatic Hollywood "women's picture" in his future work. Joanna's oppression and exploitation by the police inspector, following her desertion by her beloved Franz, are markedly drawn. In one poignant episode Magdalena and Joanna come together to comfort each other, even as each maintains that Franz belongs to her. A particularly downtrodden female victim in the film, and a key element in the dense plot, is the police informer and pornography-seller Carla Aulaulu (played by the actress of the same name), a figure presumably inspired by a character in an American gangster film Fassbinder particularly liked.[28] After Carla gives Günther's name and address to Franz, she pathetically asks if he would like to come home with her, and he turns down her offer. Just before she is gunned down by Günther in the penultimate scene of the film she plaintively sings the theme song from an American film melodrama, Robert Aldrich's *Hush . . . Hush, Sweet Charlotte,* 1965, as she makes up her face before a mirror. It is the women in the film who dominate the melancholy concluding shot as Franz is buried in a bleak Munich cemetery under a gray late-autumn sky. His mother, Margarethe, and Joanna look on as the priest intones the ritual words about the hope of purgation from guilt. Joanna walks weeping toward the camera, muttering, "I loved him so much."

In *Gods of the Plague,* the police have taken the place of the syndicate bosses of *Love Is Colder Than Death* as representatives of the powers who control the world that so oppresses the individuals portrayed in the film. The far-ranging power of the police is symbolized in a large Munich street map that dominates the commissioner's office. Their corruption is suggested in an early shot of an officer caught by his superior in the act of kissing a secretary. Their cynicism is dramatized in the commissioner's demand that the inspector get results in his fight against crime in the city, no matter what "tougher" methods are required, and in the inspector's responses to that charge: he seduces Joanna, cold-bloodedly kills her lover and his friend in the supermarket, and places the death weapon in the hand of the dead Franz.[29]

Fassbinder maintains in this film the balance between heavy-handed melodrama and ironic narrative modes that was characteristic of his first feature film and that would appear in most of his later work. This balance is achieved by various stylistic gestures that call attention to themselves, thereby reminding the viewer that this is not reality but a film, and an allusive and self-conscious one at that. These distancing effects are achieved here in various ways, beyond the many references to American gangster movies and other films. Fassbinder sometimes makes use here of the Straub-inspired stylistics seen in *Love Is Colder Than Death*: static setups and camera work and excruciatingly long-running shots. The highly contrastive black-and-white visual style of *Gods of the Plague* is pointedly reminiscent of American film noir and its forebears in the films of Weimar Germany. A notable example is an evocative scene in the Lola Montez nightclub, in which Joanna, in a glittering black dress and feather boa, sings (actually, mouths) Marlene Dietrich's "My Blonde Baby."[30] The film also includes a number of obviously symbolic visual and aural allusions and quotations—such as the large print of the legendary King Ludwig II of Bavaria that Margarethe buys for Franz and the Ray Charles song "Here We Go Again" to which Franz and Margarethe dance as the opening credits come up.

The song suggests what Thomas Elsaesser calls the Fassbinderian "cinema of vicious circles," which is strongly felt in this early film. Elsaesser writes of the "circularity" in which Fassbinder's protagonists find themselves, "an almost unbearably self-lacerating pessimism shot through with moments of ecstatic (and in the event gratuitous) optimism."[31] The occasional moments of escape from the nearly overwhelming gloom of this film do seem arbitrary, and their abrupt interruption of the realistic narrative work as alienation-effects in the film. So too do the occasional moments of pure comic relief: for example, Franz's successful efforts to sneak past the doorman at the Lola Montez, and an American tourist's frantic search for her money at the hotel desk while Franz makes his escape without paying.

There are occasional indications of amateurishness in *Gods of the Plague,* and the plot is sometimes too dense to follow. All in all, however, this was an ambitious and accomplished piece of cinema work for the inexperienced director and his still largely uninitiated filmmaking group, and a considerably more moving and more personal adaptation of the conventions of the gangster film to a distinctly postwar West German setting than their first effort had been.

The American Soldier (1970)

Fassbinder took his leave of the gangster movie with *Der amerikanische Soldat (The American Soldier)*, filmed in 35 mm at a cost of approximately 280,000 DM, during August 1970, almost a year after *Gods of the Plague*. The film, which was first shown at Mannheim Film Week in October 1970 and opened in theaters the following month, is in some respects similar to the play of the same name that the antitheater produced in 1968, particularly in having as protagonist a hired killer who receives his orders over the telephone. In keeping with the conventions of the gangster genre, Fassbinder returned in this film to black-and-white stock, after having made four color films. In spite of some serious production difficulties that resulted in last-minute recasting, rewriting, and hurried shooting and post-production work, this is an accomplished piece of filmmaking.[32]

The milieu and major characters of this story are reminiscent of the earlier gangster films: dark enclosed interiors, dingy Munich exterior scenes (with shiny film noir streets at night), corrupt police, and ruthless killers. But the overall effect is altogether different from the somber, elegiac *Gods of the Plague*. Fassbinder produced this time a cool parody of the Hollywood gangster film, and of his own earlier efforts in the genre. He said in 1974 that he considered this film "quite concrete and professionally made," much more polished than the two earlier, more personal, gangster films. It was, he said, a "more conventional fictional-narrative film" and its quotes from such Hollywood directors as Raoul Walsh and John Huston "were, in retrospect, more important than the political interpretation I gave it at the time."[33]

The plot of this film is relatively simple, unlike the action of *Gods of the Plague*. At its center is a German-born American veteran of the Vietnam War, Ricky von Rezzori (Karl Scheydt), who has been hired by some shady Munich

The American Soldier, 1970. Ricky's brother (Kurt Raab) in his mother's apartment. (By permission of New Yorker Films, courtesy of the Museum of Modern Art/Film Stills Archive, New York)

police officers to kill several underworld characters they cannot get rid of them-selves.[34] With his broad-shouldered suits, pistol strapped under his jacket, Fe-dora hat, and ice-cold emotions, Ricky evokes many a hero of Hollywood gangster films. Fassbinder cast himself as an old friend of Ricky's, Franz Walsch (that name again!), in a role altogether different from the brooding Franz of *Gods of the Plague*. Ricky follows his instructions from the police, murdering a gypsy and then a pornography-seller and police informer (and a man who hap-pens to be with her). He also cold-bloodedly kills Rosa, the mistress of one of the police officers who, sent to spy on him pretending to be a prostitute, falls in love with him. Preparing to leave Munich, he asks his friend Franz to meet him at the train station, in case there is trouble. But the double-crossing police, tipped off this time, apparently inadvertently, by Ricky's mother (Eva Ingeborg Scholz), are waiting to arrest Ricky. Franz arrives a few moments later and gets the drop on the police, until he and Ricky are distracted by the unexpected arrival of Ricky's mother and brother, Kurt (Kurt Raab), whom the police have called to the station, and both friends are shot and killed by the officers.

The film contains melodramatic themes that Fassbinder would play out to full effect in later films, though here they often come across primarily as parody. For instance, the potentially sad case of the chambermaid in Ricky's hotel (Margarethe von Trotta) is merely ludicrous: she goes into raptures over Ricky's attentions and then melodramatically commits suicide while talking to her boy-friend over the telephone, as Ricky and Rosa walk by, hardly noticing her. Her story about a tragic love affair between an older German woman and a young immigrant worker, however—which she tells to no one in particular as she watches Ricky and Rosa caress each other as they lie naked on a bed—is mov-ing, for all its incongruity. (Fassbinder would recycle the story in his 1973 film *Ali: Fear Eats the Soul*.) Similarly, the problematic relationships among Ricky; his cool, aloof mother; and his strangely withdrawn brother, Kurt, are the stuff of somber melodrama in many later Fassbinder films. But here these weighty possibilities are overshadowed by baroque stylistic effects, such as in a scene in the mother's *haute-bourgeois* apartment, dominated by an illuminated painting of the Virgin Mary, a poster of Clark Gable in *Gone with the Wind*, and a pin-ball machine.

"A Greek from Greece": *Katzelmacher* (1969)

By far the most successful of the seven additional films Fassbinder made during his apprentice period was an adaptation of his 1968 stage play,

Katzelmacher, dramatizing the effects of a Greek "guest worker" on a provincial Bavarian community. This was his second full-length film, shot on 35 mm black-and-white stock in nine days in August 1969 (four months after the filming of *Love Is Colder Than Death*) on a budget of approximately 80,000 DM. Like the play, the film was dedicated to Marieluise Fleisser, whose Bavarian folk plays of the 1920s had been an important influence on the stage version of *Katzelmacher,* as noted in chapter two.

Katzelmacher premiered in October 1969 during the Mannheim Film Week, where it was acclaimed as the highlight event even though it was not in the festival's official competition. In addition to the 950,000 DM the film earned from five federal government film prizes and a later subsidy to support future films, it won awards from a major film magazine, a Protestant church film board, and the German Academy of Performing Arts as well as receiveing an "excellent" mark from the official film rating office in Wiesbaden, which had refused such a designation to Fassbinder's first short film. *Katzelmacher* constituted Fassbinder's breakthrough as a film artist onto the German cultural scene.[35]

The eighty-eight-minute film was substantially expanded from Fassbinder's play, which had run for forty minutes on stage. The forty-seven brief stage scenes were increased to ninety film scenes, each consisting of a single shot, in most cases running no more than a minute or two. The location was shifted from a country village to a suburban apartment complex near Munich. Several characters and relationships were changed, and the dramatic rhythm and mood of the story were significantly modified. The most important change was to delay the entrance of the "outsider," the Greek worker Jorgos (played by Fassbinder, as in the stage production), from the first scene of the play to scene 38 in the film. As a result, whereas the play is dominated by the theme of prejudice against the outsider, in the film the emphasis shifts to the emotionally constricted lives of the four couples who make up the community which Jorgos disrupts—dramatizing their limited horizons, petty jealousies and quarrels, emotional manipulation and exploitation, and the latent fascism that explodes in the beating of Jorgos. Michael Töteberg has pointed out a more subtle shift in the transformation of the play to the screen. The play follows an "escalating structure," climaxing in a series of scenes set in a church which invoke the symbolism of Christ as a sacrificial lamb in preparation for the beating of Jorgos, after which the tension resolves as the characters, in various groupings, comment on that assault. The film, however, eliminates those religious references and proceeds quite differently, its laconic snippets of "the rituals of everyday life" following one another at an even pace.[36]

Fassbinder once summarized the relationships among the four couples at the beginning of the film: "Marie belongs to Erich; Paul sleeps with Helga; Peter lets Elisabeth support him; and Rosy does it with Franz for money."[37] In the film the problematics of these relationships—either added to or considerably expanded from the play—become manifest well before Jorgos arrives on the scene. For example, Marie (Hanna Schygulla) tries to dissuade Erich (Hans Hirschmüller) from his involvement in some sort of illegal activity and lovingly offers him her savings; Paul (Rudolf Waldemar Brem) beats Helga (Lilith Ungerer) for no apparent reason and then gets involved, for money, in a homosexual liaison; Elisabeth (Irm Hermann) constantly reminds Peter (Peter Moland) that she is paying the bills and makes him sleep in a separate bedroom; Rosy (Elga Sorbas) gets upset with Franz (Harry Baer) because he has told the others that he is paying her (she insists that the money was merely a gift); and he wonders if their sexual activity could not be "a little more like love." These eight young people are constantly bickering with one another (often in groups of men and women in temporary alliance against the other sex) and with Gunda (Doris Mattes), another outsider, whose man has recently left her and who is jealous of all the other women. As John Sandford notes, Jorgos is by no means the cause of the troubles that break out after his arrival: "The *Gastarbeiter* [guest worker] acts as a catalyst, unleashing the pent-up jealousies, rivalries, antagonisms, and frustrations of the milieu into which he enters. He then becomes a scapegoat, blamed and punished for problems he has not caused but merely made manifest."[38]

Stylistically, *Katzelmacher* substantially defies mainstream cinematic conventions of gesture, dialogue, mise-en-scène, and camera work. Most of the shots are made straight-on, with the actors grouped formally in a line facing the camera (even in many of the scenes where they sit at a table). There is virtually no camera movement, perhaps primarily because of the heavy camera used in this film.[39] Many of the scenes recur with almost clockwork regularity and only slight variation. For example, the film returns again and again to an overexposed scene alongside their apartment building, with several windows and flower boxes in the background, in front of which two or more of the actors are sitting on or leaning against a railing in groupings that are modified from shot to shot. Another recurring shot is set in the garage courtyard, with various pairs of characters walking toward the camera (which tracks back slowly in the only moving-camera shots of the film) talking about other characters against the lush musical background of Franz Schubert's "Sehnsuchtwalz" (Waltz of Longing). The inside shots are limited to a few locations, mostly the pub and the bleakly furnished apartments of several of the characters (their blank white walls noticeably over-lighted). The actions and speech of all the characters are extraordinarily passive. The language they speak, as in the play, is an artificial version of Bavarian dialect that owes a great deal to the dialogue style in the plays of Marieluise Fleisser. It consists mostly of lower-middle-class "clichés about love, order, and, above all, money, for money comes into most of the conversations and all the relationships," as Sandford notes.[40]

Katzelmacher is the most stylized of Fassbinder's films made before his late period. The formalistic influence of Jean-Marie Straub, with whom Fassbinder was working closely while he was writing the stage version of *Katzelmacher,* is strongly felt here. One German critic noted that the film seemed to him "lifeless and abstract" compared to the play. The filmmaker Wim Wenders found it "gruesome" and "lifeless," the characters acting like marionettes in a photo-novel with black bands over their eyes.[41] In 1982 Fassbinder character-

Katzelmacher, 1969. A static cinematographic style reflects constricted lives. Left to right: Marie (Hanna Schygulla), Erich (Hans Hirschmüller), Paul (Rudolf Waldemar Brem), Helga (Lilith Ungerer), and Peter (Peter Moland). (By permission of the Rainer Werner Fassbinder Foundation, Berlin)

ized *Katzelmacher* as "important" but added that, although it was not "false," it did seem to him in retrospect "a little stubborn, hard-hearted."[42] Many critics, however, have praised the stilted style of the film, in fact finding in that manner the key to its interpretation. "Fassbinder has created a style which fits his content like a glove," wrote a British critic.[43] Anna Kuhn points out that the parallelism and repetition in the visual style capture the "inescapability . . . interchangeability . . . [and] claustrophobic circularity" of the characters' lives.[44] And after seeing the filmed *Katzelmacher* a second time in 1974, five years removed from his experience of the play, Wilhelm Roth said that he found it "more lifelike" than he had at first thought. What he now felt coming through in the nonrealistic, paradigmatic portrayals in the film was the "incredible rage" of these "so coldly and unlovingly depicted characters . . . striking out with their helpless way of speaking, with their blows . . . against the limits (of their consciousness and their self-consciousness)."[45]

Experimental Potpourri

It is possible here only to glance briefly at the remaining six films of Fassbinder's antitheater period, three of which originated in antitheater stage productions. None of them demonstrate the control of theme, tone, and style that are exhibited in the three gangster films and in *Katzelmacher,* perhaps because they did not have such useful models as Fassbinder had found in film noir crime melodramas and in the theatrical work of Straub and Fleisser.

Why Does Herr R. Run Amok? (1969)

Fassbinder's fourth film (made after the first two gangster films and *Katzelmacher*) was *Warum läuft Herr R. Amok?* (*Why Does Herr R. Run Amok?*). Shot in thirteen days in December 1969, this was his first color film (shot on 16 mm stock that was blown up to 35 mm for theatrical projection) and the first of his many films made in collaboration with German television. It was produced for 130,000 DM by the antitheater and Maran Films, commissioned by the SDR television network; it opened in theaters in May 1971 and on the ARD television network in December.

The film was based on an idea Fassbinder had first conceived at about age seventeen.[46] He codirected it with Michael Fengler (the friend who had been camera operator on the short film *Das kleine Chaos* in 1967), and the two were jointly given a directorial award for the project in the 1971 German Film Prize competition. The film tells the depressing story of a technical draftsman, Herr R.

82

(played by Kurt Raab in the lugubrious style that is typical of his many Fassbinder roles), who one day breaks out of his banal petit-bourgeois existence by killing his wife, young son, and a neighbor with a candlestick before hanging himself in his office bathroom. The film's manner contrasts strikingly with the highly stylized *Katzelmacher*. It has the feel of those improvisational dramas of middle-class anomie, such as *Faces,* 1968, that John Cassavetes was making in the United States at about this time, though it is much tighter in structure. Each scene consists of a single long-running shot, often static but sometimes moving or zooming to follow the action; the actors improvised the dialogue and action from an outline script written by Fassbinder and Fengler. Fassbinder said that it was Fengler who was most interested in this improvisational style; he himself found it enjoyable, even though the result was mostly a "disgusting . . . revolting . . . middle-class striptease" that he thought revealed the essentially bourgeois nature of the antitheater actors; and he was disappointed in Dietrich Lohmann's camera work, especially his frequent use of zoom shots, in this largely nondirected film.[47] In any case, Fassbinder would not make another film in such an improvisational style. Still, *Herr R.* does anticipate much of the director's later work both in theme and characterization. As John Sanford points out, it was Fassbinder's first attempt at a type of film for which he would shortly become famous, portrayals of "ordinary people, their frustrations, problems, and tragedies, set in realistically sketched milieux."[48] And the protagonist of *Herr R.,* alienated both in his work life and within his family, is another in what would become a long line of repressed and long-suffering male Fassbinder heroes.

Rio das Mortes (1970)

Fassbinder's next film, *Rio das Mortes* (Portuguese: River of Death), provided decidedly comic relief from the emotional bleakness of *Herr R.* Produced at a cost of 125,000 DM jointly by antitheater-X Films and Janus Film and Television, it was shot on 16 mm color film in January 1970 and first seen publicly on the ARD television network thirteen months later.

The film may be interpreted as a sort of fulfillment of the escapist fantasies of Franz and Günther in *Gods of the Plague,* who were killed by the police before they were able to go fishing off their imaginary island in the south. It was based on a story Volker Schlöndorff shared with Fassbinder.[49] Two pals, Michel (Michael König) and Günther (Günther Kaufmann), come up with the cockeyed idea of searching for buried treasure in Peru along the apparently fictional Rio das Mortes as a means of escaping the limitations of their lives in Munich. Michel is locked into a dull job laying tile and a depressing relationship with his conventional girlfriend, Hanna (Hanna Schygulla), who, like the Schygulla character in *Love Is Colder Than Death,* wants to marry and have children. Günther has just returned from service in the army, which he joined to prove that he, a black man, is a "good German." The two pals scurry around trying to make logistical plans and raise funds for the trip, overcoming various discouragements, including Hanna's resistance. At the end they finally set out on their adventure. As they board their plane Hanna, who has trailed them to the airport intent on stopping them by force, puts down the pistol she had aimed at them, when a car drives across her line of fire.

Rio das Mortes can also be read as a comic allegory of filmmaking. Fassbinder and his group were certainly learning that the business of making movies—like the two friends' expedition to Peru in search of treasure—is a risky collaborative enterprise that flies in the face of practical wisdom, sustained on the one hand by utopian dreams and on the other by persistence in such mundane matters as research, fundraising, and endless drawing up of budgets and schedules. This reading is reinforced by one of the many inside jokes in the film: the friends finally get the funds they need for the trip from a rich patroness, Hanna Axmann-Rezzori, the Bosch heiress who provided funding for *Love Is Colder Than Death,* playing herself.

In general, the film works effectively as a slapdash comedy and satire with an improbably happy ending. Fassbinder said that he really enjoyed making it—adding that even though it was not especially important for his or the antitheater's development, it was a significant step in the direction of making films for wider audiences.[50] The film's comedy consists for the most part in the discrepancies between the heroes' real-world situations and their utopian dream of finding treasure in an exotic land. There are several memorable scenes: the protagonists' fundraising visit to the office of Hanna's uncle, an international business executive, who takes considerable pleasure in unmasking their naive claims to know something about Peru; a soiree at the home of an anthropologist who encourages them to write a government grant proposal for their "expedition" (a scene rich in satire of intellectual-cultural pretentiousness and opportunism); and long-haired Michel's disappointing efforts to raise a substantial sum by selling his sports car to a dealer dressed in a red three-piece suit.

The Coffeehouse (1970)

The next month (February 1970) Fassbinder and his entourage shifted directions again, taping in a Cologne television studio their recent adaptation of the eighteenth-century Italian comedy by Goldoni, *The Coffeehouse,* which had been staged with somewhat different casts in Munich and Bremen. The production was shot on videotape in black and white, mostly in static long and medium shots, consistent with what German playwright Botho Strauss had described as the elegiac, "restrained and serenely spoken dialogue" that Fassbinder's stage production had substituted for the lively, witty speech of the original (see chapter two). The project seems to have had negligible significance for Fassbinder's artistic development. But the bitter resentment expressed by some members of the Munich cast of the play who were replaced in the film by members of the Bremen theater troupe further convinced Fassbinder of the futility of the collectivity ideal.[51] Nevertheless, there were presumably financial benefits for the struggling filmmaking group in this their third collaborative venture with a West German television network, the first of four Fassbinder productions to be shot with video cameras. The film was produced by WDR and premiered on the WDR III network in May 1970.

Whity (1970)

It is hard to imagine a more radical change of theme, style, and production method than the antitheater's move from their restrained, formal studio production of Goldoni's play to their next project, *Whity*.[52] This ambitious film was shot in April 1970 in Almería, Spain, using 35 mm CinemaScope color film stock; it was jointly produced by antitheater-X Films and Atlantis-Films at a cost of 680,000 DM. The production soon became legendary as a self-lacerating experience for the antitheater group, who consumed whatever was left of their communal spirit in sexual intrigues, jealous squabbling, and near-disasters in the production. According to Peter Berling, the production manager, the filming of *Whity* was traumatic for Fassbinder, who was experiencing serious difficulties at the time with his lover Günther Kaufmann, cast in the title role. According to this account, Fassbinder displayed during this time some of his most petulant behavior. There were two fights, during one of which the corpulent Berling floored Fassbinder with "a swift karate chop to the back of his neck," after which the director whispered in his ear, "I love you. Now I know I can finish this film!" Later Fassbinder was beaten by two "hefty stuntmen" after he kicked the female script supervisor in the shins.[53]

The film is an odd blend of high technical values—achieved through impressive use of color, the CinemaScope format, and a subtle sound track—with an utterly improbable melodramatic story and unconvincing acting. The title character is a mulatto servant in the household of a decadent ranching family somewhere in the American Southwest in 1878. The family members are mostly caricatures of American Western types. The father, Ben Nicholson (American B-movie actor Ron Randall), tyrannizes over his two sons by a previous marriage, his sexually rapacious wife Katherine (Katrin Schaake), and the townspeople. One of the sons, Frank (Ulli Lommel), flaunts his homosexuality, his eyebrows shaved and redrawn, dressed sometimes in his stepmother's black underwear and sometimes in a Spanish-style black velvet jacket. The other son, Davy (Harry Baer) is feebleminded. Whity, the illegitimate son of Ben and the family cook (Elaine Baker), obsequiously does the bidding of the members of what he calls "my family," no matter how unreasonable. In a dramatically unconvincing scene, he rescues the pathetic Davy from a beating by his father by baring his own back to the lashes of the old rancher's whip.

For most of the film Whity is treated as an outsider, bearing the brunt of the others' frustrations and inadequacies, somewhat like Katzelmacher in the film of the previous year. And just as that Greek immigrant worker found acceptance and affection from Marie (Hanna Schygulla), so Whity carries on a love affair with the local bar singer and prostitute, Hanna (Schygulla), who inspires him to recognize and resist his oppression. With Hanna's encouragement Whity fulfills the wishes of several members of the family that he kill the others: he guns down all the Nicholsons one after another. Then he and Hanna escape, but hardly to a utopian future. In the final shot they stagger across the desert, drain the last bit of water from a bottle, collapse, struggle to their feet, and dance in silhouette over Kaufmann's singing of "Goodbye My Love, Goodbye."

Whity was coolly received in its premiere at the 1971 Berlin Film Festival and was never put on the market by a commercial film distributor.[54] Critics have generally agreed that it is Fassbinder's least successful film. Nevertheless, it won awards for set design (Kurt Raab) and acting (Hanna Schygulla) in the 1971 German Film Prize competition. And it marks a significant step in Fassbinder's artistic development, exhibiting what Wilhelm Roth describes as "a new, more professional, freer association with the medium of film."[55]

The film is a fascinating, sometimes camp, mélange of self-conscious references to many cinematic traditions. It is particularly reminiscent of two of Fassbinder's favorite Hollywood films. The first is Raoul Walsh's *Band of Angels* (1957), in which Clark Gable plays a Southern slave trader who buys a light-skinned female slave, and Sidney Poitier plays an ex-slave who helps them flee the South during the Civil War. Fassbinder called it "one of the loveliest films I've ever seen" and looked at it along with some other Walsh films before he made *Whity*.[56] The other film recalled here is Josef von Sternberg's stylish *Morocco* (1930), in which a cabaret singer (Marlene Dietrich) shows preference to a simple soldier (Gary Cooper) over other suitors, just as Hanna prefers

Whity in Fassbinder's film.[57] The film also frequently plays with the Hollywood Western genre—for example, in a shot of the father walking across a wide dusty street to pay a visit to the prostitute in the saloon, past "Joe's Dry Goods" store, with desert and mountains in the background. There is even more pointed parody in Fassbinder's self-conscious performance as a cowboy in the saloon, with a lace-front shirt, vest, and ten-gallon hat. In one scene he roughly embraces Hanna and bites her on the neck before thrusting her aside and holding out his glass for more whiskey, which he drinks down in one gulp.

Die Niklashauser Fart (1970)

After venturing into the nineteenth-century American West for *Whity*, Fassbinder returned to southwestern Germany as the geographical setting for his next project, *Die Niklashauser Fart* (Journey to Niklashausen).[58] But the temporal setting of this anachronistic film is anything but clear. Shot on 16 mm color stock in May 1970 in Munich and two other Bavarian locations, the 550,000 DM project was produced by Janus Film and Television on assignment from the WDR television network and first shown over the ARD television network in October 1970.

The film is derived from the life of a fifteenth-century shepherd, Hans Böhm, who claimed that the Virgin Mary had appeared to him in a vision and called him to become a revolutionary preacher. For a few months in 1476 Böhm led a large group of peasants in an uprising in the free city of Niklashausen, asserting their rights to equality in land and goods, against the power of the church and the aristocracy; then he was arrested by the bishop's army and burned at the stake. Rather than merely narrating those historical incidents, Fassbinder set about to "tell something that has to do with us."[59]

The major figures in *Die Niklashauser Fart* are the preacher Hans Böhm (Michael König); a wealthy married woman, Margarethe (Margit Carstensen), whose interest in Böhm is as much sexual as spiritual; "the Black Monk," a somewhat skeptical follower of Böhm, played by Fassbinder in his already-legendary black leather jacket; and Böhm's lover Johanna (Hanna Schygulla), whom the Black Monk persuades to appear before the preacher's discouraged followers as the Virgin Mary herself and whom Böhm later casts aside in favor of his higher calling. The film is an imaginatively constructed and tightly written meditation on Marxist revolution in general, and in its final sequences it reflects both the failed revolutions of 1968 and continuing Third World uprisings. Like Jean-Luc Godard's *Weekend*, 1968, with which it has often been compared, *Die Niklashauser Fart* freely intermingles historical periods, costume styles, and settings; and the dramatic action is frequently interrupted by self-conscious camera techniques, revolutionary speeches (most of them seemingly drawn from contemporary Third-World Marxist struggles), and debates on economic theory. It is the only film directly reflective of contemporary politics that Fassbinder would make until *Mother Küsters Goes to Heaven* in 1975. In spite of its comparative neglect by Fassbinder critics to date, *Die Niklashauser Fart* is a serious and richly ironic film with considerable significance as an example of the director's political ideas and his self-consciousness as a cinema artist at this early point in his career.

Pioniere in Ingolstadt (1970)

In November 1970, shortly before he staged the second of his two theatrical adaptations of Marieluise Fleisser's *Pioniere in Ingolstadt,* Fassbinder directed a 35 mm color film version of the play in collaboration with Janus Film and Television and the ZDF television network, which broadcast it in May 1971. Most critics agree that this is one of his least successful films; he reportedly said that he lost interest in the project while working on it.[60] Like *Whity,* the film combines considerable technical expertise with a largely unconvincing story and style of acting. It both sentimentalizes and brutalizes the taut, ironic tone of the play. "Fleisser's tight and bittersweet original is soon dissolved into tedium and irrelevance."[61] Color and lighting are handled here quite professionally, and there are some instances of subtle camera work. But for the most part the scenes are set up and filmed unimaginatively, frequently in long-running static takes. The film wavers between two quite different styles: the formal, theatrical manner derived from Brecht and Straub and used so successfully in *Katzelmacher,* and the more fluid, realistic style of Hollywood melodrama exhibited in *Whity.*

Hanna Schygulla's performance as the naive servant Berta is the most compelling aspect of the film. One German reviewer praised her "little gestures of love [which give] a very solemn importance to the story of a domestic servant." But Schygulla's effective acting does not quite make Berta's story the "great melodrama of painful love" that this critic claimed it to be.[62] The final scene of the film, in which Berta lugubriously laments her desertion by the soldier who has just made love to her, contrasts sharply with the restrained, ironic ending of Fleisser's *Pioniere,* in which Berta stoically looks at a photograph of herself and her lover (all she has left of the affair) while a new sergeant tells the bridge-building troops that he expects them to be on good behavior on their next assignment.

By the beginning of 1971 Fassbinder's critics were beginning to carp. There was talk that the Wonder Boy of the New German Cinema had burned himself out at the age of twenty-five. Yet before this disappointing adaptation of Fleisser's play, in September 1970, the director had completed an extraordinary self-examination both of himself as a film director and of the antitheater collective, in *Beware of a Holy Whore* (it would not be seen until the August 1971 Vienna Film Festival). And he had discovered, in the Hollywood melo dramas of Douglas Sirk, both inspiration and models for moving beyond the self-indulgent excesses and the stylistic and tonal uncertainties of much of his apprentice work. The much more sure-handed and accessible films he was about to start making would confirm that his was a talent still to be reckoned with

Notes

1. Baer 28.
2. Limmer 16.
3. DIF 9.
4. Müller Int 179.
5. Müller Int 179.
6. Lorenz Let 24 May 1994. Juliane Lorenz here points out that the assessment board held Fassbinder responsible for the antitheater's unpaid taxes, and that he was facing the possibility of going to prison for this debt when he asked his mother for assistance in 1971; working with a tax expert, Liselotte Eder succeeded in getting the assessment board to lower the tax bill to 30,000 DM, plus 10,000 DM in penalties levied against both Fassbinder and Raben. Lorenz points out also that Fassbinder owed at this time 150,000 DM for production services for antitheater films, a debt he was still paying off when she began working for him in 1976. Fassbinder told her that he gave Peer Raben work as music director for most of his films on the assumption that he was continuing to pay off these tax debts. When Lorenz pointed out to Fassbinder that this was not true (after Liselotte Eder showed her the financial records of the antitheater), he showed "how idealistic he was in those days" by responding, "I don't want to believe that Peer doesn't pay." Fassbinder said in 1973 that "one of the tragedies of the antitheater" was Raben's failure to incorporate the antitheater (Brocher Int I).
7. Brocher Int II 28.
8. Töteberg, "Einführung" 21.
9. The name *film noir,* first applied by postwar French critics, derives from the black covers of French crime novels in what was called the *Serie noire*. Classic Hollywood noir gangster films include Howard Hawks's *Scarface* (1932); Fritz Lang's *Scarlet Street* (1945) and *The Big Heat* (1953), John Huston's *The Asphalt Jungle* (1948); Raoul Walsh's *White Heat* (1949); Samuel Fuller's *Pickup on South Street* (1953); and Irving Lerner's

Murder by Contract (1958). Like Lang, Robert Siodmak and Otto Preminger, two other Hollywood directors known for making films of this type, had made films in Germany before fleeing the Nazi regime. Noir gangster films were often imitated and parodied by French New Wave directors, particularly Jean-Paul Melville and Jean-Luc Godard.

10. The films are *White Heat* and *Murder by Contract,* as Töteberg has noted ("Einführung" 9).

11. Limmer Int 67; see also *Anarchy* 3.

12. Thomsen Int 84.

13. Thomsen Int 198.

14. "Postwar German Cinema" 27.

15. In the film, Lommel wears a broad-brimmed hat identical to one worn by Alain Delon in Jean-Paul Melville's French version of the Hollywood gangster film, *Ice-Cold Angel;* this was Lommel's contribution, as Fassbinder had not yet seen the Melville film (Roth/AF 113).

16. Roth/AF 113.

17. *Anarchy* 6.

18. This was a discarded version of a shot in Straub's *Der Bräutigam, die Komödiantin und der Zuhälter.* It was filmed along Landsbergerstrasse, a major Munich thoroughfare in an industrial area, frequented by prostitutes.

19. There is a nod to Straub in Bruno's identification at one point as "Mr. Straub." The film was dedicated to him, along with French directors Eric Rohmer and Claude Chabrol (who had little direct influence on this film), and to "Linio and Cuncho" (corrected by Töteberg to Gringo and Cuncho ["Einführung" 12]), from Damiano Damiani's film *Töte Amigo,* which Fassbinder claimed motivated him to make this his first feature film, as noted in chapter 2.

20. Baer 30.

21. "Einführung" 19.

22. Scherer Int 99.

23. As in this role played by his lover, Günther Kaufmann, Fassbinder in his early films often gave characters their real-life names. Günther's surname in the film is of course an allusion to the filmmaker Volker Schlöndorff, who was married to Margarethe von Trotta, who plays Margarethe in this film.

24. The meeting recalls Franz's pretend-tough frisking of Bruno, followed by an embrace, when Franz first turns up at Joanna's apartment in *Love Is Colder Than Death.*

25. Harry Baer remarks that this and a later "ridiculously expensive" helicopter shot (as the group leaves Joe's home) were motivated in part by the Fassbinder team's desire to show that they could do anything that big-time filmmakers could do (30).

26. This was one of the director's favorite sayings, according to Harry Baer. Juliane Lorenz has pointed out that it derives from a song recorded by the British rock group The Rolling Stones, whose lead singer Mick Jagger often used the slogan (Let 24 May 1994).

27. "Fassbinder's Reality" 88.

28. Several commentators have noted Carla's resemblance to the tie-selling police

informer played by Thelma Ritter in Samuel Fuller's 1952 Hollywood film, *Pickup on South Street.*

29. The commissioner's demand is another echo from Fuller's *Pickup on South Street.*

30. Fassbinder objected to Peer Raben's proposed new version of this well-known song, and instead dubbed in the original Dietrich version (Pflaum and Fassbinder 128). The name of this night club is a reference to one of Fassbinder's favorite films, Max Ophüls's 1955 *Lola Montez,* a stylized account of a nineteenth-century dancer who was once mistress to the composer Franz Liszt and King Ludwig I of Bavaria.

31. "Postwar German Cinema" 25.

32. Fassbinder was absent from the production of *The American Soldier* for considerable time, and Hanna Schygulla was replaced by Elga Sorbas in the important role of Rosa (Töteberg, "Nachwort," *Fassbinders Filme 2* 249). According to Kurt Raab, the film was originally intended as a major vehicle for Günther Kaufmann (in color and CinemaScope, like *Whity*), but Fassbinder changed his mind when difficulties arose in their relationship (157).

33. Thomsen Int 90.

34. Ricky's surname (in a typical Fassbinder insider joke) is that of Hanna Axmann-Rezzori, the Bosche heiress who loaned him money for *Love Is Colder Than Death,* and who had played a type of herself in Fassbinder's *Rio das Mortes.*

35. Töteberg, "Einführung" 18. Thomas Elsaesser writes that Fassbinder was disappointed by the commercial failure of *Katzelmacher* in spite of the prizes it received ("Postwar German Cinema" 24). In the German Film Prize competition it won a Gold Band, an award for the screenplay, and—along with *Love Is Colder Than Death* and *Gods of the Plague*—awards for acting (to the antitheater troupe) and for cinematography (Dietrich Lohmann).

36. Töteberg, "Einführung" 16.

37. Roth/AF 114, 117.

38. Sandford 69.

39. Dietrich Lohmann, the cinematographer for *Katzelmacher,* said that Fassbinder had not planned the static photographic style of the film in advance; he made "a virtue out of necessity" when the camera they arranged to borrow from Bavaria Film Studios proved almost impossible to move because of the heavy sound shield and dolly (Pflaum, *Rainer Werner Fassbinder* 20).

40. Sandford 70. Töteberg characterizes the dialogue of the play and film versions of *Katzelmacher* as an "artificial language" and quotes Fassbinder's description of the primary motif of the film as "petit-bourgeois/proletarian norms . . . the daily monotony of cliché-ridden imaginations shaped by wishful thinking, the morality of affluence, ideas out of the *Bild* newspapers, and popular sentiments" ("Einführung" 16–17). Roth suspected that the "relative popularity" of the film was due to a considerable extent (especially in northern Germany) to its "curious synthetic" Bavarian dialect (AF 117).

41. Roth/AF 116.

42. Steinborn Int 14.

43. Quoted in Eckhardt 87.

44. Kuhn 85.

45. AF 116.

46. Brocher Int I.

47. Brocher Int I.

48. Sandford 70.

49. Fassbinder said that he was fascinated by the story, which Schlöndorff had long contemplated for a film; after Fassbinder requested it, Schlöndorff gave him permission to use it in a film of his own (Brocher Int I).

50. Brocher Int I.

51. Brocher Int I.

52. Apparently no one in the group realized that in English the protagonist's name would normally be spelled "Whitey."

53. Berling, "The Making of *Whity*," Katz 209, 215; see also Katz 45–46. Juliane Lorenz recalled Fassbinder telling about this fight with Berling (Int), which is presumably the inspiration for the beating of the director in *Beware of a Holy Whore*. On the need for skepticism in dealing with Berling's Fassbinder stories, see the entry under his name in the bibliography.

54. *Whity* was shown on German television some time before late summer of 1990, when the author was given access to an off-air copy in Munich.

55. Roth/AF 125.

56. Thomsen Int 82.

57. Roth/AF 126.

58. Juliane Lorenz has pointed out that the film's title uses an archaic spelling of the modern German word *Fahrt* (Let 24 May 1994).

59. Roth/AF 129.

60. Sandford 74.

61. Sandford 74.

62. Benjamin Henrichs, *Fernsehen und Film,* May 1971, 51; quoted in Roth/AF 137.

CHAPTER FOUR

Reconsidering the Holy Whore
Reflection, Reflexivity, and Sirkean Melodrama

Fassbinder's next-to-last antitheater film was *Warnung vor einer heiligen Nutte* (*Beware of a Holy Whore*), shot in September 1970, a few weeks after he completed *The American Soldier*. This was both a self-reflective and a "reflexive" project for the twenty-five-year-old director. That is, he reflected seriously on himself and the team with which he had just completed nine films in sixteen months in a film that is a notable example of reflexive cinema—film that, instead of presuming simply to mirror reality, explicitly calls attention to itself as a narrative medium.

Beware of a Holy Whore was made during a period of major transition, both professional and personal, for the director. Three months later, after shooting *Pioniere in Ingolstadt,* he would take an eight-months respite from filmmaking. This significant pause seems to have been inspired in large part by his discovery of the films of the German-American director Douglas Sirk, which helped him define a new direction for his work. When Fassbinder next went behind the camera, in August 1971, he had decided that he had made enough films "for me and my friends" and began, with considerable success, to reach out for wider audiences through relatively accessible, if provocative, melodramas. Consistent with this shift in artistic direction, early in 1971 Fassbinder dissolved antitheater-X Films, which had never been officially incorporated, and established a new production company, Tango-Films (officially, Tango-Film Rainer Werner Fassbinder), which would produce (or, in one instance, coproduce) nine of his remaining films.

Personal Transitions

During this period Fassbinder's personal life underwent several important changes, all of which affected his film work. In August 1970, during the shooting of *The American Soldier,* he married Ingrid Caven, a diminutive cabaret singer who was a member of the antitheater group. It was a stormy marriage, which officially lasted for two years; they lived together considerably less than that. As Fassbinder often remarked, he and Caven were much better friends after than during their marriage, and she continued to act in his films.

Marriage did not mean that Fassbinder was renouncing his homosexual attachments. The first of the three most intense emotional relationships of his life—all with male lovers—was, however, coming to an end at this time, when his lover Günther Kaufmann became involved with Peer Raben.[1] As noted in the previous chapter, Fassbinder had in recent months given Kaufmann major roles in three films that grapple with themes of love, friendship, and death: *Gods of the Plague, Rio das Mortes,* and *Whity.* After the breakup of their intimate relationship the director continued to cast Kaufmann in his films, mostly in minor parts (though he assigned him a major role as a brothel owner in *Querelle*). Early in 1971 Fassbinder entered into the second of his three most significant gay liaisons, with a Moroccan, El Hedi ben Salem (full name: El Hedi ben Salem m'Barek Mohammed Mustafa), whom he had met at a gay sauna in Paris. Fassbinder was fascinated by Salem's self-reliance in a foreign culture and "his interest in learning new things,"[2] as well as, presumably, by the handsome North African's slim, dark body. The following year Fassbinder made a short-lived attempt to play father to two of Salem's young sons that was, reportedly, nearly disastrous for the boys.[3] Fassbinder broke off this relationship in 1973, after Salem had begun to demonstrate his dangerously violent temper, particularly when drunk.[4] (The third great love affair in Fassbinder's life, with an uneducated German butcher named Armin Meier, will be discussed in chapter seven.)

A final personal transition for the director during this period was the death of his stepfather, Wolff Eder, in September 1971. This event left Fassbinder's mother, Liselotte, time to assist her son in more ways than small acting roles, though she continued to work full-time as a computer programmer and then as a newsletter editor at a research center in Munich. She took responsibility for organizing the financial records of the antitheater and began keeping books and preparing financial reports for the new Tango-Films. She continued this work until Fassbinder began living with Juliana Lorenz in 1978.[5]

Beware of a Holy Whore (1970)

In September 1970, Fassbinder and the antitheater troupe, along with several others, including older American actor Eddie Constantine, gathered in Sorrento, Italy, a picturesque coastal town south of Naples, to film a version of their self-destructive experience making *Whity* four months earlier in Almería, Spain. He called it *Warnung vor einer heiligen Nutte* (*Beware of a Holy Whore*). This was Fassbinder's most expensive film to date, and his first international coproduction. The 1.1 million DM project, shot on 35 mm wide-screen color film, was produced by antitheater-X and Nova International (Rome), and premiered at the Venice Film Festival the following August. It was seen on West German television in January 1972 (NDR III). But because of the cost of rights to the music used in the film, it was not given theatrical release in Germany until June 1992—after Fassbinder's mother had gone to court to stop distribution of a mutilated version of the film reportedly authorized by Wilhelm Rabenbauer (Peer Raben, musical director for most Fassbinder films and production manager—but not producer—of *Beware of a Holy Whore*).[6]

In *Beware of a Holy Whore,* Fassbinder projects images of himself as both tyrannical and abused artist, and as frustrated lover, in a self-conscious, humorous, and finally moving study of the cinema, the holy whore who both inspires and degrades her devotees. The film is also an obituary of the antitheater's ideal of an artistic collective, which in any case had not been viable for some time.

Several central themes of the film are anticipated in its odd opening sequence, a monologue by a thin man with long blond hair standing in a field. The man is Werner Schroeter, a West German filmmaker whom Fassbinder particularly admired.[7] Schroeter tells an anecdote about Walt Disney's cartoon dog Goofy (presumably from a real Disney cartoon), who borrows an outfit from his aunt so he can get a job as a kindergarten teacher. Laughed out of the school by the children, Goofy discards the clothes in a trashcan. They are picked up by a notorious dwarf gangster, Witz-Willi (Silly-Willy), recently escaped from prison, who puts on the clothes and convinces the stupid dog that he is an orphaned little girl. Goofy, delighted that he has found a child to care for after all, brings Willi home and feeds him, amazed at how much the supposed little girl can eat. That night the police raid his home and arrest Willi, revealing his true identity. The confused Goofy can only mutter, "What a shock that must have been for the poor little girl when she discovered that she is a crook"! One can see in Schroeter's monologue (not to make too much of this whimsical opening) an amusing analogue to the illusory character of the cinema, an homage to Fassbinder's gangster films, and an anticipation of the sexual games to come in the film.[8]

The main narrative of the film opens with a long-running scene set in the lobby of a Spanish seaside hotel decorated with deep red draperies and paintings of fighting cocks on black velvet. A German film crew and cast wait for the arrival of their director—as well as for the star, the film stock, and the second payment of their federal subsidy from Bonn. The actors and crew members seem incapable of anything except backbiting, boasting, and sexual intrigue, as they lounge about or lean on the lobby bar drinking Cuba Libres (rum and Coke), while the production manager Sascha (played by Fassbinder) harangues them. Action finally begins with the dramatic arrival of a helicopter bringing the director, Jeff (the Swedish actor Lou Castel) and the star, Eddie (Eddie Constantine, who had played tough American private eye Lemmy Caution in French action thrillers and in Godard's *Alphaville,* 1965).[9] Jeff castigates the production manager for his choice of this location and for the general disarray, and he aggressively takes charge of the group. At the same time, he gets caught up in the complications of his love affair with one of the actors, Ricky (Marquard Bohm). Meanwhile, Eddie and his costar Hanna (Hanna Schygulla) become lovers, keeping largely apart from the emotional chaos that surrounds them.

The tensions implicit in these relationships slowly escalate. As Jeff sets the production crew to work, he referees rivalries among the group; confronts his furious former lover, Irm (Magdalena Montezuma); and engages in alternating rounds of affection, suspicion, and jealousy with his current lover Ricky—who, for his part, is having doubts about his acting ability, is trying to come to terms with his homosexuality, and is longing to return home to his wife. The strain takes its toll on Jeff. He becomes increasingly harried, depressed, and tyrannical. He makes patently insincere marriage proposals to two women in the crew. Nevertheless, he manages sporadically to assert his competence as film director in spite of all these distractions. The tensions come to a head when he slaps a female crew member and is beaten in return by one of the men while the rest of the group watch unconcernedly. This outburst seems to relieve the pressures on everyone, however, and they finally begin shooting. The film they are making, *Patria o Muerte* (Country or Death)—the title of a film Fassbinder evidently had once planned to make himself—is about "state-sanctioned violence," an ironic comment on the emotional and sexual power-games that constitute so much of the "frame" story.[10]

The heavy melodramatic potential of *Beware of a Holy Whore*—both as the story of a sensitive and frustrated artist and as a dramatization of complex interpersonal relationships within the group—is kept in check through the first half of the film by a number of distancing effects, which are often quite amusing. For example, the melodramatic situations are time and again taken to the point of absurdity, as in the opening sequence in the hotel lobby, when the photographer Dieters (Werner Schroeter) passionately kisses Irm, angers her by telling her she needs to brush her teeth, boasts of his recent drug "super-

Beware of a Holy Whore, 1970. Film director Jeff (Lou Castel in RWF's leather jacket) with Eddie Constantine (playing himself) and Hanna (Hanna Schygulla). (By permission of the Rainer Werner Fassbinder Foundation, Berlin)

trip," and discusses his plans to make a killing either by writing a book or making a big dope deal. Another character tries to seduce a member of the Spanish lighting crew through ludicrously glib talk of the workers' struggle and changing "the hearts of the people." Repeatedly, the most painful interpersonal scenes are interrupted by calls for Cuba Libres and by the crashing of empty glasses on the floor and walls. In one odd shot the hotel manager, who has dutifully swept up the results of these tantrums, is shown slumped unconscious over the bar, for no clear reason. As Harry Baer has emphasized, critics who speak of this film only as an expression of the director's deep despair, of his "merciless self-accounting," are ignoring much of its humorous effects. Baer recalls Fassbinder once saying, "I had a great time making this film."[11] It is obvious that he did.

A considerable part of the fun in *Holy Whore* comes from its self-conscious reminders that one is watching a film. This is obvious in the Italian-language street signs, billboards, and automobile license plates in what is supposedly Spain. Similarly, the highly stylized blocking, cinematography, and sound track regularly undermine the illusion of reality. Moreover, the sound track is often pointedly obtruded into the action, with operatic music surging up at moments of emotional tension, and popular songs of the late 1960s (by Elvis Presley, Leonard Cohen, Ray Charles, and Spooky Tooth) played on the jukebox and offering sentimental or ironic commentary on the romantic-sexual intrigues.

Ironic and humorous overtones are achieved also in the many direct and indirect references to Fassbinder and his antitheater group and to other cinematic traditions. One of the main pleasures of the film for early Fassbinder aficionados was to guess which members of "the Group" are represented by which characters in the film. Obviously, Jeff, the director, is standing in for the director of *Holy Whore*. Wearing Fassbinder's well-known black leather jacket, Jeff is alternately bullying and vulnerable and is embattled in present and past love affairs; but he remains professionally competent through it all. There is also pointed irony in Fassbinder's giving himself the part in this film of the tyrannical production manager, Sascha, whose authority is undercut by the director once the latter arrives for the filming. Jeff's unhappy lover Ricky, anxious to get home to his wife, seems to represent Fassbinder's recently departed lover, Günther Kaufmann. Kurt Raab, the most self-pitying and unhappy member of the Fassbinder troupe, is type cast as the bitchy, drunken art director Fred, a role he said he found humiliating.[12] The greatly wronged Irm, who drunkenly accosts Jeff in front of the group, represents (perhaps with considerable exaggeration) the masochistic Irm Hermann, who actually dubbed the speaking parts of the actress playing Irm, Magdalena Montezuma.[13]

There is much more to *Beware of a Holy Whore* than comic stylization, insider jokes, and reflexive game-playing, however. For one thing, as John Sandford points out, the comedy often has dark overtones: "The humor is cruel and crude, laughter at ineptness, disaster, and discomfiture" (74). Beyond that, as the film progresses, its treatment of the director and his relationships with his colleagues becomes increasingly serious. In the process, the film more and more assumes the tone of a thoughtful discourse on the question of leadership within an artistic collective, and on the nature of cinema.

The knowing viewer who may at first smile in recognizing Jeff's unhappy love relationship with Ricky as a version of the Fassbinder-Kaufmann affair is soon likely to empathize with this public dramatization of a painful private relationship. There are many genuinely moving scenes involving the two—as when Jeff sympathetically tries to reassure Ricky about his acting ability, and Ricky in return assures Jeff that he wants most of all to make things easy on the director. Jeff shows considerable pain when Ricky expresses his longing to get back to his factory work and his wife, and later he seems deeply disturbed on hearing that Ricky has told someone that he sleeps with Jeff "only for the money." The painfulness of this recognition is particularly clear (for all the self-conscious allusion to the title of Fassbinder's first film) in an exchange between Jeff and the art director David, which takes place in front of Ricky (but in French, which he cannot understand):

JEFF: Without money, he'll come back to me. Love is colder than death.
DAVID: Not colder, but simpler.
JEFF: No! Much, much colder.

In a later scene Ricky, alone in a car, mutters to himself that he will never find peace again until he knows that Jeff is dead, but then seems to be comforted when Jeff joins him. In return, Ricky reassures the despondent Jeff about the film he is making, which prompts the director to say, "I love you," echoing Ricky's statement to him in their telephone conversation early in the film.

In the course of the film Jeff's character and situation come across increasingly as a serious self-examination and imaginative self-projection on the part of Fassbinder. While he may be exaggerating his tyrannical side here, he would confess in a note to Dirk Bogarde, the star of *Despair,* that only in working with Bogarde on that film in 1977 had he been able to learn how to assert "authority without making fear."[14] On the other hand, *Holy Whore* dramatizes the situation of an ambitious and energetic cinema director being victimized by vampirish coworkers who are utterly dependent on him—who literally suck his blood, as Jeff says at one point. Throughout, the film insists on Jeff's professional competence, in spite of the chaos of his personal life and his frequent irrational outbursts against the cast and crew. His ability to get this bedeviled production under way contrasts pointedly with the ineffectual dreaming of several would-be filmmakers in the group. For example, the floor manager Korbinian (Ulli Lommel), who spends most of his time fetching drinks, talks about making a film in a couple of years and glibly excuses himself for not having done so yet because his wife oppresses him. His efforts to ingratiate himself with Jeff by complimenting him on the artistic quality of his work prompts only an abrupt "Kiss my ass" from the director.

The complex and sympathetic characterization of the director figure, Jeff, is glimpsed in his first few moments after his arrival at the hotel. He makes a quick personal query about the whereabouts of his lover Ricky, and a professional query about his cinematographer. Then he turns ferociously on his production leader Sascha for his choice of this location: "I wanted a palace, and what did you get for me? The most pathetic hole in the world. Are you people a kindergarten? You've got to learn how to make films, you swine." Shortly afterward, in a complex traveling shot, Jeff demonstrates to his cameraman a difficult take he is planning for the next day, painstakingly explaining the dramatic effects he wants. He explains how he wants the camera to follow the assassin (Eddie) entering the palace of a government minister while his wife watches helplessly: "And now we slowly go into a long shot, in which the murder is committed. Perhaps we will pan earlier over to the woman. She is standing in the door, watching. She is completely speechless and quietly moves back. Then a slow pan over to Eddie. This is the moment when the minister is murdered." The cameraman remarks, "That's really nice. But difficult." The next day, as they prepare to start filming, the cameraman asks Jeff again about that shot, commenting that the director had not explained the camera movements exactly. Jeff impatiently exclaims: "Do I have to do it all myself? If you don't decide anything yourself, you'll never have any fun in your work!" The director voices here what many of Fassbinder's more accomplished coworkers have characterized as the most interesting aspect of working with the director: his trust in their ability to collaborate with him creatively, rather than merely follow orders.

For all the self-control and authority that Jeff exhibits as cinematic director, his personal relationships with his colleagues rapidly deteriorate as the film progresses. In a series of short scenes with various members of the group, he becomes increasingly hysterical, firing one actress on the spot, shrieking at the makeup woman to move her table out of his way, and ordering Sascha to send everyone home. In one highly stylized but no less moving scene, a large group of them watch coldly as Jeff writhes on the floor of an elegant bedroom that is part of the set, screaming: "All of you can disappear! You are all swine, exploitative swine! . . . I hate you!" In an even more contrived but equally emotional scene on an outdoor terrace by the sea, a drunken Jeff slaps the production secretary Babs, to whom he earlier proposed an elopement to Peru, and in return is knocked to the floor with a blow to the stomach by another member of the crew, while his coworkers look on dispassionately (most of them piled together in an odd parody of an orgy). Ricky alone comforts him. This beating seems to constitute a kind of purgation for Jeff, although he still has the energy to give a tongue-lashing to his lighting crew and to shatter yet another Cuba Libre glass on the floor, remarking, "When I can no longer smash things up, then I'm dead."

Beware of a Holy Whore concludes on a note of what seems to be serious personal commentary by Fassbinder on his dilemma as a creator of artificial reality who had plenty of difficulties managing the realities of his personal life while at the same time playing the father figure with so many people dependent on him. On the set (a jumble of crisscrossed wires, lighting, cameras, and sound equipment) Jeff, still tipsy, informs a reporter that the film will be about "brutality . . . what else can we make films about?" He hugs Sascha, whom he has regularly berated throughout the film, and falls to the floor with him, mumbling, "I have a friend."

The penultimate shot of Fassbinder's film is Take 47 of *Patria o Muerte,* produced, like *Whity,* by "antitheater-Atlantis," according to the upside-down clapboard. In a pointedly reflexive sequence the viewer now sees the murder scene, which Jeff had earlier walked through with his cameraman, from the point of view of the *Patria* camera (a few changes have been made in the action). Then, in the brief closing scene of Fassbinder's film, Jeff, Hanna, and Eddie are seated facing the camera. Hanna reassures Jeff that his movie is "really nice." Eddie comments enigmatically (in French), "They have found what the others have forgotten—time." And Jeff makes a final despairing comment on his love affair with Ricky, unknowingly echoing the latter's earlier words to himself, as the camera zooms in on his face: "I believe I will be at peace only when I know that he has met his end." Then follows a title card carrying a traditional lament of the artist, from Thomas Mann's *Tonio Kröger* (1903): "I tell you, I'm often dead tired of portraying humanity without participating in it."

As many writers have observed, *Beware of a Holy Whore* is also a swan song for the utopian dream of the artistic collective, living and working together and sharing responsibilities free of repression. Fassbinder often talked about this aspect of the film. It was certainly a film about filmmaking, he said in 1974, "but its real theme is how a group works together. . . . I wasn't sure that it was a new start, but I knew it had to be the end. With that film we buried the *anti-theater,* which was our first dream."[15] "It was a beautiful dream," Fassbinder said in 1974, "which we talked about time and again in the hope that it would come true."[16]

This is also a film about filmmaking in general, a subtle meditation on the cinema in the tradition of Federico Fellini's *8 ½,* which Fassbinder had studied a few years earlier, and Jean-Luc Godard's *Mépris,* 1963 (*Contempt*), in which the French New Wave director whom Fassbinder admired plays assistant director in a film-within-his-film. Like all such reflexive films, Fassbinder's *Holy Whore* challenges the viewer's naive assumptions about storytelling on the screen and engages in the process of "deconstructing narrative," producing "a double movement of celebratory fabulation and demystificatory critique," in Robert Stam's words.[17]

The two stars of the inner film, Eddie and Hanna, seem to epitomize two complementary components of cinematic mythology. Eddie Constantine plays himself, the aging American star of French thriller films. From the moment of his entry into the hotel with the director, Eddie seems an outsider, ordering whiskey rather than Cuba Libres and sitting apart, warily observing the backbiting and scheming of the others with what the script describes as his "murderer's eyes."[18] Fassbinder's leading actress, Hanna Schygulla, also plays herself, the most aloof member of the Fassbinder troupe—or perhaps the director's fantasy of her as movie sex goddess, a shimmering image of fleshy eroticism and almost spiritual beauty in a backless white minidress fit for a Greek goddess. She sides with the self-contained older actor, and they become lovers. The tough old gangster and the goddesslike reincarnation of Marilyn Monroe hover in Olympian calm over the absurd antics of the frustrated director and his minions and tormentors.

At one point their aloof and self-satisfied companionship exacerbates Jeff's frustrations. He observes Eddie respond to someone's glass-throwing tantrum at the bar by stroking Hanna's hand and saying quietly, "Shall we go listen to some music?" Jeff gazes after them, then throws his own glass in their direction, muttering, "And in the future you can kiss my ass!" This gesture seems to suggest the director's frustration at how far short the actual work of making films falls from the ideal the two of them seem to symbolize. In this respect, it is significant that Hanna increasingly becomes Jeff's most faithful supporter (as a sort of cinematic muse who both inspires and comforts him). She is the one who perfectly understands his restrained style of directing and explains to Eddie (who finds Jeff a dilettante) that this is the way Jeff expresses his rare ability to give his actors a sense of freedom. Moreover, she bucks Jeff up at moments when he is most discouraged. When he says despondently that he is going to quit working on this "shitty film," she reassures him, "I think it will be really nice" (to which he immediately agrees). Later, near the end, he remarks to her how "incredibly bourgeois" he feels, and she calmly replies: "Just look at your films. You really do understand a lot about such things."[19]

Douglas Sirk and the German Hollywood-Film

It is clear from the self-reflection in *Beware of a Holy Whore* that at this juncture Fassbinder was taking a critical look both at himself as a film director and at his relationships with members of the group within which he was work-ing. Moreover, as seen in chapter three, in both *Whity* and *Pioniere in Ingolstadt* (made in April and November 1970) he was experimenting substantially with Hollywood-style production values. Thus it seems to have been a stroke of good fortune for the young director that the Munich Film Museum scheduled at the beginning of 1971 a retrospective screening of the Hollywood melodramas of the German-American director Douglas Sirk.[20] Fassbinder saw six of them, including *All That Heaven Allows,* 1955; *Written on the Wind,* 1956; and *Imita-tion of Life,* 1959.

In February 1971 Fassbinder wrote for a film journal an essay on Sirk that would turn out to be a manifesto for much of his own later work.[21] He charac-terized Sirk as a highly cultured man and a consummate craftsman, whose films were motivated by deep human sympathy. Sirk's films, he wrote, are made "by someone who loves people and doesn't despise them as we do."[22] Fassbinder notes approvingly in Sirk's films themes that were already, and would continue to be, central in his own work: "loneliness and fear,"[23] emotional abuse of chil-dren by parents, exploitation within intimate relationships, self-deceptive dreams of individuals feeling pressures to conform to prescribed social roles, and pres-sures on women who think for themselves. Moreover, Sirk was a master of his craft: he knew how to create exactly the decor, gestures, and speech appropriate to his subjects. He understood the essential nature of the medium—that films are made "with people, with light, with flowers, with mirrors, with blood."[24]

Fassbinder was so impressed by Sirk's work that he made a visit to his home in Lugano, Switzerland, early in 1971. A considerable friendship devel-oped between the young Fassbinder and the older director, who was perhaps the most significant of the several older males who seem to have served as father figures to him during his adult life. In 1977 the two of them collaborated on a teaching-production project at the Munich School for Film and Televi-sion.[25] And Fassbinder intended to dedicate to Sirk the film *Kokain,* for which he wrote a script in 1981 but which he did not live to produce.[26]

Fassbinder's encounter with Sirk seems to have substantially helped him move beyond the often eccentric and derivative films of his apprenticeship—with their frequent inside jokes, personal allusions, cross-references, and un-certain stylistic experimentation—to a style of filmmaking that would have much broader audience appeal. In 1974 he characterized the films he made through 1970 as "for the most part films to be thrown away, films that were made in a specific situation for a specific reason, and which therefore, as far as I'm concerned, can subsequently be forgotten." They were "films for my friends, for people who think just like me . . . made in order to learn how to make films.[28] After completing *Pioniere in Ingolstadt* late in 1970 he stopped making films for eight months (a long break indeed for a director so driven to make movies), during which, he said, he "discovered a way to approach autobiography less onanistically, less as an end it itself, and possibly to find out what I could say about myself that would be more universally valid."[29] Sirk's films took away his fear of making "profane" art with broad audience appeal, Fassbinder said.[30]

The older director's substantial influence can be seen in the clarity and restraint of the next film Fassbinder made after their meeting, *The Merchant of Four Seasons,* shot in August 1971. Two years later, in another of his most successful domestic melodramas, *Ali: Fear Eats the Soul,* Fassbinder would refer specifically to Sirk's love story about an older woman and a younger man, *All That Heaven Allows.* But the example of Sirk's films did not inspire Fassbinder merely to reach out for larger audiences. Rather, they seemed to him models of popular films which challenge viewers to think critically about their lives and their society. Fassbinder said in 1980 that only after he had seen Sirk's films, which are "completely direct and unconcealed," did it become clear to him that it is possible to make films in such a way that viewers would notice "a falseness in the way they are narrated."[31] The "falseness" Fassbinder notes in these films is apparently the often-noted alienation-effects of Sirk's elegant artifice, with its subtle critique of the bourgeois life so accurately pictured there. A well-known history of film has summarized these effects:

> On the one hand [Sirk's films] seem sleek depictions of the most tawdry values of materialistic, middle-class life. On the other hand, they seem brutally funny comments on this very tawdriness, on the values of bourgeois life that the characters automatically accept. . . . . We are never quite sure who is kidding whom. . . . Sirk shoots his bourgeois world filtered through reminders of Hollywood's presence. Doorways, partitioning screens, window panes, glass mirrors, plate-glass windows, reflective surfaces . . . dominate Sirk's frames, calling attention to the fact that we look not at life but at a frame.[32]

As Eric Rentschler has written, what Fassbinder learned from Sirk was primarily "how a popular form could be recast to appeal to audience expectations while simultaneously subverting them."[33]

Fassbinder now set himself the goal of making, if not exactly a "German Hollywood-film," then one "very much like Hollywood," a film that is "as entertaining as in Hollywood, and yet that says something about reality"—in the way that Sirk and a few other Hollywood directors he admired managed to do."[34] "The best thing I can think of would be to create a union between something as beautiful and wonderful as Hollywood films and a criticism of the status quo," he told Wilfried Wiegand in 1974. "That's my dream, to make such a German film—beautiful and extravagant and fantastic, and nevertheless able to go against the existing order," such as Alfred Hitchcock's *Suspicion* (1941), "the most drastic film against the bourgeois institution of marriage I know."[35]

Melodrama

Fassbinder's critique of his contemporary society in his later films would be undertaken, like Sirk's, largely through deliberate use of the forms and styles of melodrama, his own propensity for which is evident in many of his earlier films, as has been noted. *Melodrama* is one of those terms (like *romanticism*) that has "been hopelessly debased by popular misuse," as James L. Smith observed in his 1973 book on the topic for the British Critical Idiom series.[36] Smith points out that, for much of this century, critics reacting against the blatant emotionalism, superficial characterization, and predictably moralistic themes of much nineteenth century popular drama and fiction have used the word as "a blanket term of abuse and contempt."[37] His book and several others have led recently to a use of the term with more sympathy and historical specificity. Smith argues that melodrama consists in the resistance of "whole" protagonists to external adversaries, as opposed to the internal conflicts in the "divided" protagonists of tragedy, and that it expresses more than tragedy "the reality of the human condition as we all experience it most of the time," for all the crudeness with which it has often been realized.[38] In his influential 1976 book Peter Brooks recognized in the "mode of excess" characteristic of "the melodramatic imagination" the urge to express more than polite discourse normally allows: the desire to pierce through "to a mythological realm where the imagination can find a habitat for its play with large moral entities [in] a world where what one lives for and by is seen in terms of, and as determined by, the most fundamental psychic relations and cosmic ethical forces."[39]

Film historians have regularly noted how narrative cinema in its early days uncritically imitated the sentimentality and crude theatrics of nineteenth century stage melodrama. Since the early 1970s there has developed, alongside the revaluations of melodrama among literary critics, a substantial historical and theoretical discourse on cinematic melodrama, inspired by theatrical performance studies and by the interest of French "structuralist" and neo-Marxist theorists in "the operation and ideological effectivity of aesthetic form."[40] This reconsideration, which has been led by feminist scholars, has discovered in the "family melodramas" of Sirk and other Hollywood directors of the 1940s and 1950s a highly sophisticated genre in which generational and gender conflicts were played out with considerable subtlety, usually reinforcing—but occasionally subverting—the dominant bourgeois, patriarchal ideologies of postwar America.[41]

The occasional use of melodramatic themes and styles in Fassbinder's antitheater films was noted in chapter three. After his encounter with Sirk, melodrama became Fassbinder's most characteristic mode, and he employed it with considerable flexibility and stylistic variation. "Earlier, when I was starting out, I liked very cool, stylized, calculated films better than what you might call drama," Fassbinder said around 1973. "Later I liked melodramas better."[42] Sirkean melodrama proved much more fruitful for him than the models he had used in most of his apprentice work—film noir and the gangster genre, and the critical folk play. As in Sirk's films, Fassbinderian melodrama is more often than not problematized, checking stock audience responses through various distancing techniques—such as stylized acting, unconventional lighting, sound, and camera work and cinematic self-reflexivity—which regularly prevent our taking them "straight." In 1977 Fassbinder characterized melodramatic films as "correct films," pointing out that instead of following "the American method" of melodrama, which leaves the audience "with emotions and nothing else," he wanted to engender in the spectator "the emotions along with the possibility of reflecting on and analyzing what he is feeling."[43] As Jane Shattuc summarizes the matter, Fassbinder's films consistently "undermine the overt social morality of the melodramatic narrative," a narrative that, as she points out, has traditionally reinforced social presuppositions about bourgeois socioeconomic hegemony as well as patriarchal attitudes about gender.[44]

The mode of melodrama is rarely merely parodied in Fassbinder's films. They take their melodramatic moments seriously, typically enacting "the victory over repression" that Peter Brooks sees as a central component of the melodramatic imagination. Fassbinder's respect for melodrama is indicated in a comment he made about the religious music composed by Peer Raben that is heard at the end of *Chinese Roulette*. He suggests that religious belief is essentially melodramatic, and explains how he was able to project himself imaginatively into the mind of a religious believer even though he personally rejected such belief: "When you're working with the interior of a character you reach a point where you really understand their need for religion. . . . I have to let them keep their own wrong feelings. And I don't believe that melodramatic feelings are laughable—they should be taken absolutely seriously."[45]

The complex legacy of Douglas Sirk—Hollywood-style films with both heart and critical intelligence, melodrama with both emotional power and an ironic edge—would be a major inspiration for Fassbinder as he moved away from the esoteric work of his apprenticeship and the intense self-reflection of *Beware of a Holy Whore* into his maturity as an artist of the popular cinema intent on creating critical versions of "the German-Hollywood film."

Notes

1. Juliane Lorenz has written that Fassbinder thus explained to her the cause of his breakup with Kaufmann (Let 19 June 1993). In her interview with the author, she characterized Kaufmann's relationship with Fassbinder as largely exploitative: "He never loved Rainer. He just realized that Rainer was attracted to him and used it. Günther was never interested in men . . . only in women." She said the director once countered her statement that Kaufmann seemed to her "a very nice person . . . very simple, a sort of 'nature-boy'" by exclaiming "No, he has much more destructive power than you will ever know. . . . I tell you, he has often made me suffer."

2. Lorenz Int.

3. Katz 71.

4. El Hedi ben Salem's last Fassbinder film role was a small part in a scene in *Fox and His Friends,* filmed in Marrakech in 1974. In 1977 he hanged himself in a French prison. Fassbinder apparently learned of this only shortly before his own death (Katz 76). He dedicated his last film, *Querelle,* to his "friendship" with Salem .

5. On this work for Fassbinder, Liselotte Eder commented: "There were so many things to take care of. So I did it—in all innocence! Somebody had to. The others were all interested in making films." She contradicted Katz's claim that she was given "the purse strings" of Tango Films in 1971: "No, no. I wasn't able to do that. . . . [Rainer] was not the sort of person you could do that to." She said that she typed scripts (including *Berlin Alexanderplatz*), kept records and accounts, and prepared tax returns and reports to the Federal Ministry of the Interior on expenditures of subsidy money. Later, she said, Fassbinder told her he didn't like it when people accused him of sending his mother to "put things in order" when they got complicated and shortly thereafter turned such matters over to Juliane Lorenz. (Int)

6. According to an account in Spaich (184–187), the revised version of the film was cut by fifteen minutes and the original music, primarily American pop songs, was replaced by music which Peer Raben had composed for Fassbinder films, often overlapping the dialogue. For a detailed account of this incident, see Töteberg, "Wie man einem Film verstümmelt." The Fassbinder Foundation subsequently purchased the

theatrical music rights, and the film premiered in Berlin on June 2, 1992, as part of the Fassbinder exhibition.

7. *Anarchy* 100–103.

8. Andrew Sarris has observed that, among its many contemporary allusions, *Beware of a Holy Whore* contains "the minimyth of Werner Schroeter, who opens the film with a characteristically androgynous anecdote, and who posts himself in the center of the lobby as part of the Pirandellan decor" ("Can Fassbinder Break the Box-Office Barrier?").

9. Fassbinder had seen Lou Castel with Ulli Lommel in *Töte Amigo* in 1967, the film which inspired him to write *Love Is Colder Than Death,* as noted in chapter 3 (Töteberg, "Einführung" 12).

10. *"Patria o Muerte"* was the well-known slogan of Spanish fascists. Michael Töteberg has described two of Fassbinder's earlier and incomplete treatments of this material. The first, entitled *Patria o Muerte,* outlines a political-thriller set in Latin America, with the title figure Lemmy Caution—the American detective whom Eddie Constantine had often played in French thrillers and in Godard's *Alphaville.* The second is an untitled treatment for a film about a director named Anselmo Fadardi who is preparing to make a film titled *Zéro-Ville,* in which Eddie Constantine is to play an agent named Carry Motion, and in the production of which the director encounters serious problems with the cast similar to those in *Holy Whore* ("Nachwort," *Fassbinders Filme* 2 252).

11. Baer 61–62.

12. Katz 57.

13. Montezuma was Schroeter's favorite actress. Late in the film she plays an odd sequence in a motorboat, which recalls a scene from Schroeter's film *Eika Katappa;* Schroeter actually directed this scene of Fassbinder's film. (Roth/AF 135)

14. Several writers have asserted that Fassbinder exaggerates the negative side of his self-portrait in this film (e.g., Baer 70–71). Fassbinder's note to Bogard is published in Watson, "Bitter Tears" 27. One important word (misspelled by Fassbinder) is erroneously transcribed there ("couldt" as "couldn't"). The relevant portion of the letter reads correctly as follows: "I thank you for the things I couldt [could] learn from you, things I never learned before. I thank you, that you gave me your authority without making fear, because fear makes sick, and normally authority goes together with fear, but you did show me a way how to combine authority with freedom, which I knew so far only theoretically and what [that] is one of the most important ideas for work and life."

15. Thomsen Int 89–90.

16. Wiegand Int 65. In 1973 Fassbinder said that, because of the antitheater troupe's dependence upon him, it had never really been "a group," and noted that in the postmortems of the collective, other members questioned his role but not theirs (Brocher Int I).

17. *Reflexivity* 11. Stam notes the similarity of *Holy Whore* to Godard's *Contempt* in "its Mediterranean setting, its multilingual ambiance, and its subtending metaphor of

prostitution" (108). For further discussion of self-reflexivity in European and American films, beyond Stam's extensive coverage, see Schäfer.

18. *Filme 2,* 210.

19. In contrast to the relationship between Jeff and Hanna in the film, tensions between Fassbinder and Hanna Schygulla during the shooting of *Holy Whore* was so high that he talked of firing her from the cast, which led the others in the group to threaten to quit (Brocher Int I).

20. Douglas Sirk (1900–1987), born Hans-Detlef Sirck, had made several melodramas for UFA before he emigrated to the U.S. in 1937.

21. "Imitation of Life." The essay consists largely of plot summaries and random comments on Sirk's films. Nevertheless, it is important for understanding Fassbinder's appreciation of the older director's work.

22. Ibid. 77. By "we" he meant European filmmakers, Fassbinder explained later (Wiegand Int 72). Fassbinder saw in Sirk's work an insistence upon high artistic standards and a critical approach to American culture that was unusual for Hollywood directors (*Anarchy* 12, 43).

23. Ibid. 86.

24. Ibid. 77.

25. Fassbinder and Sirk worked with students at the Academy in making a short film, *Bourbon Street Blues,* Sirk directing and Fassbinder taking an acting role. In an interview with himself and Sirk published early in 1979, Fassbinder denied his "alleged father-son relationship" with Sirk, pointing out that such relationships "are usually a struggle" (*Anarchy* 43).

26. The dedication to Sirk, in "gratitude and friendship," is written on the cover of Fassbinder's handwritten screenplay for *Kokain* (RWFF Cat 248).

27. Wiegand Int 68.

28. *Med* Int 6.

29. Wiegand Int 76.

30. Sherer Int 97.

31. Limmer Int 91.

32. Mast 312–313.

33. *West German Film* 85.

34. Scherer Int 97.

35. Wiegand Int 82. In 1972 Fassbinder said, "American cinema is the only one I can take seriously, because it's the only one that has really reached an audience," as the prewar German cinema had once done (Thomsen Int 83). He added that the Hollywood narrative style is not "so complicated or artificial [as European film]. Well, of course it's artificial, but not 'artistic'." Fassbinder often expressed his admiration of the unusual ability of Sirk, Hitchcock, and Raoul Walsh to direct films within the capitalistic and industrialized American studio system—maintaining its conventional technical quality and narrative clarity—all the while subtly subverting the conservative and conformist ideologies which Hollywood films have traditionally reinforced.

36. Smith, *Melodrama* 6.
37. Ibid. 7.
38. Ibid. 7–8.
39. Brooks 5, 13.
40. Gledhill 5–6.
41. This reevaluation of film melodrama in the 1970s is summarized in Gledhill's introduction to *Home Is Where the Heart Is,* which reprints a number of important essays on film melodrama. The feminist implications of this work are extended in Jackie Byars's *All That Hollywood Allows.* Fassbinder's appreciation of the critical aspects of Sirkean melodrama apparently played a significant role in what Gledhill has characterized as a "neo-Marxist" revaluation of Sirk's films in the early 1970s (7).
42. Bronner/Brocher Int 181.
43. Sparrow Int 20.
44. Shattuc, "Fassbinder's Confessional Melodrama" 45. In a later article, Shattuc presents Fassbinder's self-conscious use of Sirk as one among many ways in which he drew from American "pop" culture in his films ("*Contra* Brecht" 48–49).
45. Thomsen Int 97.

CHAPTER FIVE

Outsiders and Underdogs
Male Melodramas

Over the next four years Fassbinder certainly fulfilled his intention of making films that would have wide audience appeal as well as a critical edge. The six films considered in this chapter, shot between August 1971 and July 1974, are all emotionally compelling melodramas with male protagonists, mostly from the lower socioeconomic levels, who are struggling to maintain their own integrity within various social structures—in couple relationships, families, and the workplace. All are variations on the long-suffering Franz Biberkopf of Döblin's *Berlin Alexanderplatz* who, in Kaja Silverman's formulation, lack the phallic and social power which the cinema has traditionally ascribed to males.[1] (Chapter six will examine seven melodramas from the early and mid-1970s that deal primarily with women.)

Fassbinder's films of this period reflect his personal history and private concerns, but they do so less obviously than much of his earlier work and some of his more-confessional later films. Moreover, while most of these films document specific living and working conditions within the early Federal Republic, they treat social, economic, and political conditions primarily as background for stories of individual lives, in contrast to the more emphatically historical and political films of his final period.

Stylistically, these films of the early 1970s for the most part follow the conventions of classical Hollywood melodrama: straightforward plotting, clearly defined character motivation, high-key lighting, unobtrusive and eye-level camera placement, seamless editing, and background music reinforcing stock emotional responses. Nevertheless, the smooth flow of this classical narrative style is regularly interrupted in these films. Shots are occasionally held much longer than usual; actors are placed in slightly unnatural positions or deliberately framed in windows or doorways; the music comments ironically on the action. Through such distancing effects as this, Fassbinder hoped, as Brecht had intended in his *Verfremdungseffekt,* to engage the viewer's critical intelligence and to "liberate the mind," as he claimed Sirk's films did.[2]

The Merchant of Four Seasons (1971)

Fassbinder's first film after his eight-month pause in filmmaking was *Händler der vier Jahreszeiten* (*The Merchant of Four Seasons*).[3] It was shot in Munich in eleven days during August 1971, on a budget of 178,000 DM, using 35 mm color film. This modest project turned out to be one of the director's most popular and critically honored films, after its premiere in Paris at the celebrated Cinématheque the following February and its opening in West Germany in March.

The Merchant of Four Seasons is the story of a Munich fruit-seller, Hans Epp (Hans Hirschmüller), whose life is a succession of rejections and failures that ends in suicide. The plot moves ahead in straightforward fashion, occasionally intercut by clearly marked flashbacks. It begins with Hans's return from service in the French Foreign Legion, which he had joined in defiance of his bourgeois mother's hope that he would pursue higher education and a professional career. He takes a job as a police officer but is fired after a sexual encounter with a prostitute in the station house. So he sets himself up as a peddler, hawking fresh fruit from his handcart in apartment-house courtyards. Most of Hans's family scorns him for having taken such demeaning and financially unpromising work. His "great love" Ingrid (Ingrid Caven) turns down his marriage proposal on the same grounds and marries another man (though she later shows romantic and sexual interest in Hans). Apparently on the rebound from this rejection, Hans marries the practical and unsympathetic Irmgard (Irm Hermann), who helps him expand his business. Their marriage soon degenerates into bickering and mutual resentments, exacerbated by his heavy drinking; the bitterness between them climaxes in his brutal beating of her in front of their young daughter.

Irmgard leaves Hans after this beating, but she agrees to take him back when he suffers a heart attack. While her husband is recuperating in the hospital, Irmgard has a one-night sexual encounter with a married man, Karl (Karl Scheydt). Coincidentally, Hans later hires Karl as a helper in the fruit-selling business. Irmgard, presumably uncomfortable with his presence in their lives, tricks Karl into underreporting his receipts by promising him more sex with her in return for some of the money he skims, knowing that Hans is suspiciously watching and will catch him at it. Hans does so, and he fires Karl, to Irmgard's perverse delight. In another coincidence Hans encounters an old friend from the Foreign Legion, Harry (Klaus Löwitsch), and hires him as Karl's replacement. Harry comes to live with Hans and his family and, without intending it, gradually takes over Hans's roles in the household. Hans becomes increasingly depressed and ends his life by literally drinking himself to death in his neighborhood pub. At his burial his disapproving family makes virtually no show of emotion, and Ingrid watches from a distance. In the closing shot of the film, Harry unenthusiastically accepts Irmgard's suggestion that they get married, since it would be convenient for the business and for their personal lives.

This story contains allusions to Fassbinder's personal history, but they are not obvious and for the most part are irrelevant to interpretation of the film. The protagonist is based on the director's favorite uncle (his mother's brother), a man who worked as a fruit-seller, much to the disappointment of his family. Another uncle, who worked for a right-wing "Christian" newspaper, is represented in Hans's uptight brother-in-law Kurt (Kurt Raab in yet another unflattering role), who holds the same kind of position in the film.[4] Hans's mother's desire that he pursue higher education and a respectable bourgeois profession may reflect Fassbinder's mother's hopes for his education when she sent him to a humanistic *Gymnasium*.

The film is a melodramatic study of a character type that one has already begun to see as the typical Fassbinder male protagonist: a frustrated, mostly passive man who internalizes his oppression instead of struggling against it in any effective or sustained way. He is a universal type, according to Fassbinder: his is "a story that almost everyone I know has lived himself. A man wishes that he had made something of his life that he never did. His education, his environment, his circumstances don't admit the fulfillment of his dream."[5] The action of the film stays almost entirely within the domestic sphere—starting with Hans's rejection by his mother, who at the beginning of the film greets him upon his return from French Foreign Legion service in Morocco, where a friend of his has died, with these chilling words: "It's always the same. The best remain out there, and the ones like you return." In several later scenes, the mother sides with her snide son-in-law Kurt in continuing to show her disapproval of Hans's lack of ambition. The only member of the family who shows Hans any sympathy is his sister Anna (Hanna Schygulla), who appears to be a writer or teacher. But she is so caught up in her work on a manuscript that she fails to recognize his desperate need for emotional support when he comes to her late in the film. And her honesty at a climactic family Sunday dinner in the apartment of her sister and brother-in-law, when she accuses her family of having contempt for Hans, is certainly no comfort to her brother, who has internalized their attitude toward him. In fact, that bit of candor from his favorite sister may be just what pushes Hans into deliberately drinking himself to death in the following scene.

Like many of Fassbinder's male protagonists, Hans suffers greatly at the hands of women: his mother, the prostitute at the police station, his "great love," his wife, and even his sympathetic but insensitive sister. Moreover, like Döblin's Franz Biberkopf, Hans is disappointed by the male friends to whom he turns. His pals at the neighborhood pub are always ready to raise a beer with him, but they offer no personal comradeship. His one supposedly true male friend, Harry, has the best of intentions; nevertheless he usurps Hans's role in his family. Hans's daughter turns to Harry rather than her depressed father for help with her schoolwork, and Irmgard increasingly looks on Harry as her real partner in the business. In the suicide scene, all of these male friends sit passively, while Irmgard weeps, as Hans drinks himself to death. He quietly calls them all "swine"—even Harry, though he is only a "really little" swine, who tried to do "what was best for me," Hans admits.

Ingrid, Hans's "great love," seems to embody the protagonist's unattainable dream of unconditional love and acceptance. This significance is reinforced through the visual imagery in which she is presented. Early in the film she calls down to Hans to bring her some of the pears he is selling, peering out

The Merchant of Four Seasons, 1970. Hans Epp (Hans Hirshmüller) drinks himself to death, watched by his wife Irmgard (Irm Hermann), his friend Harry (Klaus Löwitsch), and pub pals. (By permission of the Rainer Werner Fassbinder Foundation, Berlin)

at him from the window of her apartment like a fairy tale princess in her tower. When he comes up she speaks from behind her door, which he dares not enter since Irmgard knows where he has gone. Later, Hans recalls her rejection of his marriage proposal, as she stood in a white dress against a dark background of trees. When he finally takes up her invitation to visit her in her apartment while her husband is out, he is utterly passive in response to her invitation to make love.[6] In the viewer's last glimpse of her, Hans's unattainable love watches from a distance as his casket is lowered into the grave. Dressed in white, she holds a bouquet of roses identical to the one Hans had proffered with his marriage proposal.

The story of Hans Epp is told in this film with a sympathy and a realism that surprised and pleased West German critics and filmgoers. One critic was astounded by "this patience, this exactness, this unmistakable love for what [Fassbinder was] making, showing, telling."[7] All the characters except for Hans's mother and brother-in-law are presented sympathetically—even Irmgard, up to a point. Of the minor characters, the most poignantly and suggestively rendered is Renate, the young daughter of Hans and Irmgard. A stereotypical blonde Bavarian girl, she suffers several severe shocks: her mother slaps her because Hans is late for supper; in her presence, her father viciously beats her mother, and she watches through a door as her mother wildly makes love with Karl. Through most of these events the child remains quiet and self-contained. But she is clearly disturbed, and she gets no comfort when she inquires of her aunt Anna if her depressed father is going to die: "He will live if he wants to" is the reply. In a few quick strokes Fassbinder sketches in a memorable portrait of a helpless child victimized by troubles in the adult world.[8]

For the most part, *The Merchant of Four Seasons* makes effective and restrained use of visual metaphors to enhance its melodrama. As in Sirk's films, characters are often framed by doorways and windows, reinforcing our perception of their circumscribed lives, just as the cryptic dialogue, reminiscent of *Katzelmacher,* underscores their psychological and intellectual limitations. For example, early in the film the emotional distance between Hans and Irmgard is suggested in a shot indicating Hans's view of her across the street, through the window of a bar in which he has gone for a quick drink. The bleakness of the Epps' family life is summed up in a long-held shot of the dining table at which Irmgard and the child wait for Hans to join them for supper. The emptiness of Irmgard's marriage is ironically suggested when she passes in front of a bridal shop and a stylish furniture store after trying in vain to get Hans to come home from a bar.

None of these visual metaphors seems forced. The tact with which they are presented enhances the effectiveness of a highly mannered sequence set in Kurt's apartment, where the family has gathered for Sunday dinner, near the end of the film. Hans sits in silence as his mother and brother-in-law continue their criticism of his failures and then—after Irmgard boasts that they have acquired a second cart and a helper—condescendingly grant that Hans now has "a real business." During this dialogue the camera tracks several times along both sides of the table, momentarily centering each family member in the frame. Then, in a complex, long-running shot, the aloof Anna, seated alone at the far end of the table, accuses her mother, her sister, and Kurt, all seated to her right, of having always looked down on Hans, in spite of their denials. The camera pans left to show all of them as her sister tells Anna that she is "too aggressive." "I'm not aggressive, just frank," replies Anna, lighting a cigarette as the camera pans right to isolate her in the frame again. Then it pans further right to show Hans, Irmgard, and their child, as Hans mumbles his agreement with his family's snobbish put-down of him. A melodramatic zoom-in then reveals the mother rising from the table, defending her son-in-law against Anna's charge that he is either dishonest or as reactionary as the "Christian" newspaper for which he works; she leaves the scene with a headache. While the stylization of this scene is not obtrusive, it is pointed enough to create, at a climactic point in the film, a substantial emotional distance between the viewer and the melodramatic action, inviting critical analysis of the social and personal dynamics among this family group and between it and the larger society.

There are a few points at which *The Merchant of Four Seasons* does not maintain such stylistic tact, however. For example, Hans's melodramatic heart attack and collapse early in the film looks simply ludicrous. An early sequence in which Hans interviews applicants for the job as his helper indulges in comic high jinks reminiscent of *Rio das Mortes,* which seem altogether inappropriate in this movie.[9] And in the scene where Hans drinks himself to death, his flashback to a severe beating he had received at the hands of a Moroccan during his Foreign Legion service, when he begged his tormenter to kill him, seems an unusually heavy-handed dramatization of his present death wish, perhaps deriving from the director's private fantasies.[10]

Although *The Merchant of Four Seasons* focuses primarily on the pathos of Hans Epp's individual case, in a strictly domestic setting, the film implies a general critique of life in early postwar West Germany. It specifically documents the everyday lives of middle-and lower-middle-class Bavarians in the early 1950s in its dreary apartment blocks, tasteless interiors, overstuffed furniture, knickknacks, and cheap religious art (including a wooden crucifix that looks down on Hans and Irmgard's bed), along with some visual details that ironically evoke both the Nazi period and the early 1970s.[11] All these details underscore the self-satisfied bourgeois materialism that reasserted itself in West Germany after the war, and the ways in which the institutions of marriage and the family were implicated in this materialism. For one contemporary West German critic, *The Merchant* was the first film to make the Adenauer era and the Economic Miracle "historically recognizable" and to furnish it with "a leitmotif. better is worse. (That is, the better things are for us, so much the worse for us)."[12]

The film's depressing closing shot, after Hans's funeral, suggests a bleak existence for those who, unlike him, have managed to come to terms with their lives in the Federal Republic. Harry, Irmgard, and her child are seen, through a dirty windshield, sitting almost motionless in a Volkswagen van. Irmgard listlessly summarizes the reasons she and Harry should now marry: "You know the business. I don't want to be alone any more. You get along well with Renate, you like her. I don't know how you feel about me, but . . . I like you a lot. If we get together, that would be best for us all, I think." After a distinct pause, Harry responds simply: "Okay," and the screen fades to black.

After the increasing hostility of the public and press to his work since *Katzelmacher*, Fassbinder must have been buoyed by the positive response to *The Merchant of Four Seasons* from the public and the critics. The film won a Gold Band and acting awards for Irm Hermann and Hans Hirshmüller in the 1972 German Film Prize competition. In Frankfurt, the reviewer Wilfried Wiegand praised the new sympathy for ordinary people he saw in *The Merchant,* which he found "one of the most important German films in years." Fassbinder "makes this film not only *about* these people, but at the same time *for* them." The Munich film critic Hans-Günther Pflaum declared that people who had not liked Fassbinder's film would now have to change their minds. "For me it is the best German film since the war," he wrote.[13]

Variations on a Theme

Four additional Fassbinder melodramas of the early 1970s with male protagonists can be discussed only briefly. Two were made for theatrical release: *Wildwechsel,* 1972 (Wild Game Crossing) and *Angst essen Seele auf,* 1974 (*Ali: Fear Eats the Soul*). The other two were made for television: a five-part "family" miniseries, *Acht Stunden sind kein Tag,* 1972 (Eight Hours Don't Make a Day); and a science-fiction romance, *Welt am Draht,* 1973 (World on the Wire), the only one of these four films not set in a lower-middle-class environment.

Wildwechsel (1972)

The film variously referred to in English as "Jail Bait," "Wild Game," and "Wild Game Crossing," is an adaptation of a play by Fassbinder's contemporary, Bavarian playwright Franz Xaver Kroetz.[14] It was filmed in March 1972 in collaboration with the SFB television network, on which it was first broadcast in January 1973, ten days after its theatrical premiere in Munich.

With a few notable—and controversial—exceptions, Fassbinder's *Wildwechsel* is faithful to Kroetz's text, although its visualization of the bleak 1950s Bavarian petit-bourgeois milieu goes considerably beyond the projected backdrops on a relatively bare stage that Kroetz's text calls for. Both play and film tell the story of a depressing teenage love affair. A sexually precocious girl of fourteen, Hanni (Eva Mattes) feels trapped in her parents' home. Her father (Jörg von Liebenfels), who complains of losing his youth to the Nazi regime and occasionally indulges in fascistoid sentiments, is domineering and occasionally abusive; her mother is passively sympathetic. Hanni has a sexual affair with a nineteen-year-old worker in a chicken processing plant, Franz Biberkopf (Harry Baer).[15] Franz is jailed briefly for seduction of a minor. After his release Franz renews the relationship with Hanni, over her father's increasingly strong objections. Eventually, Hanni induces Franz to gun down her father in the forest. At the end of the film, as Franz morosely waits outside the courtroom during his trial for that murder, Hanni coldly informs him that the baby she has borne them died just after birth, and she claims that she never really loved him.

Like Fassbinder's theatrical and film versions of *Katzelmacher,* Kroetz's play works within the tradition of the Bavarian critical folk play. This tradition is particularly evident in the inarticulateness of the lower-middle-class characters. Lacking an authentic language, they "resort to the clichés and sententious stereotypes of the class above them" or vent their frustrations in "mindless violence," as Sandford puts it.[16] Fassbinder's film characteristically interweaves that distinctly Bavarian theatrical tradition with elements of American popular culture of the 1950s. The film recalls the Natalie Wood-James Dean love affair in *Rebel without a Cause,* 1955, particularly in the portrayal of Franz as a motorcycle-riding "rocker" with a ducktail haircut and in the sentimental teenage American love songs heard on the sound track.

Fassbinder's film shifts much of the sympathy given to Hanni in the play

118

to Franz, another of Fassbinder's vulnerable male protagonists damaged by women (Harry Baer's characterization of Franz here pointedly recalls his portrayal of Franz Biberkopf in *Gods of the Plague*). Some of the additions Fassbinder made to the story—particularly a scene in which Hanni is almost seduced by her father, and another in which she picks up a guest worker while Franz is in prison—led Kroetz to condemn Fassbinder's adaptation as "obscene" and to compel him through court action to cut these and other elements, including a close shot of Franz's (flaccid) penis. But the contested scenes were restored in later theatrical releases. This controversy does a disservice to the film. As many critics have noted, it treats all the characters, including even the oppressive father, with sympathetic understanding and with remarkable stylistic control and poise.[17]

Acht Stunden sind kein Tag (1972)

Fassbinder's television miniseries *Acht Stunden sind kein Tag* (Eight Hours Don't Make a Day) was filmed in 16 mm film format between April and August 1972 for broadcast over the West German Broadcasting Network (WDR) in five episodes (running seven hours, forty minutes altogether), starting in October. It was produced by the network, at a cost of 1,375,000 DM. Fassbinder developed the script though extensive consultations with workers, seeking to dramatize the real concerns of their everyday lives. He wrote three additional episodes that WDR refused to produce.

The series drew from two television genres popular at the time: the "family series," in which the domestic lives of middle-class West Germans were presented in a genial, sympathetic style; and politically provocative, left-oriented "worker-films," many of which the WDR produced in the late 1960s and 1970s. Fassbinder's film shows a group of Cologne factory and office workers, and their friends and relatives, cooperating with each other to make significant changes in their lives, in defiance of industrial and governmental authorities. The central figure in the series, Jochen (Gottfried John), is a young man who works in a machine-tool factory. The five episodes dramatize internal troubles among the workers at this factory, including prejudice against an immigrant worker, as well as a series of conflicts between the workers and the managers. They also explore a number of private and public problems encountered by the other characters: the marital troubles of Jochen's sister Monika (Renate Rolland) and her husband (Kurt Raab); class prejudice against Jochen, as a factory worker, from a friend of his fiancée, Marion (Hanna Schygulla); difficulties encountered by Jochen's grandmother (Luise Ullrich) in getting younger members of

119

the family to accept her love affair with a widower, Gregor (Werner Finck); and efforts by city authorities to close a kindergarten the grandmother has set up in a vacant library building. Most of the characters eventually find satisfactory solutions to their problems, both at work and in their personal lives. As Fassbinder remarked, his primary purpose was to "show that the workers do have means of defending themselves, and that they are most effective in sticking together."[18]

In its modest utopianism—its insistence that ordinary people can solve their private and public problems if they stand up for their rights and work cooperatively—*Acht Stunden sind kein Tag* differs decidedly from the usual Fassbinder film. It is also distinctive for the lack of subtlety in its plotting, characterization, and style. This relative simplicity is consistent with the director's expressed desire to appeal to a wide working-class audience, in what he termed "a kind of folk art."[19] When Harry Baer suggested that a workers' strike scene be filmed in a highly politicized style, with red flags, Fassbinder demurred, saying that he intended "a family series and not a political film." In this, his first television series, he wanted "to let people come along slowly."[20] At this point in his career Fassbinder seems to have conceived of television and theatrical cinema as distinctly different media. He spoke at length in 1973 about the differences between cinema and television audiences and his obligation to reach out to more unsophisticated viewers in his television films, which he said should portray human possibilities more hopefully than theatrical films.[21] In keeping with that strategy, *Acht Stunden* frequently employs heavy-handed melodramatic devices—ominous music, sudden zoom shots, and stylized framing, for example—without the implied irony that often accompanies such techniques in most of his other films. Fassbinder denied that such techniques in this series were intended as parody of the usual style of television melodrama. What may seem parody there "is actually where my taste coincides with that of other TV series writers," he said,[22] in a comment that apparently applies primarily to this particular project.[23]

Certainly, sophisticated filmgoers are likely to find that much of the melodramatic action and style of this television series borders on the ludicrous. But the original television audiences did not. According to Fassbinder, the workers "were able to take the so-called fairy tales" in the series and "rethink them in terms of their own situation, and that's what they did."[24] The programs were well received by viewers, capturing between 41 and 65 percent of the television audience for its various segments (between 55 and 67 percent of viewers described it as "good" or "very good").[25] But it was attacked on various fronts. Mainstream newspaper and magazine critics found it aesthetically unappealing.[26] And its subject matter drew negative criticism from both conservatives and liberals. The former were apparently threatened by the treatment of workers as "not only the objects but also the subjects of history," that is, as people who could take control of their lives in the way that bourgeois protagonists had done in traditional literature.[27] Leftist critics objected to Fassbinder's decision to avoid showing the "lousy, dull everyday lives" of the working class in the documentary style of the typical WDR worker film, so the director concluded.[28] Representatives of West German unions and of industrial works committees (*Betriebsräte*) protested that the series did not accurately portray the significant roles they played in West German industrial management.[29]

Fassbinder brought such matters much more directly into focus in the three additional parts he wrote for the series, which, for reasons that are not entirely clear, were never produced. It may be that the director was not willing to accept "script limitations" from the producers; that was the reason given by WDR executive Günther Rohrback for stopping what some critics thought had become "a political embarrassment for him."[30] Or perhaps Rohrback really did find the scripts unsatisfactory "on dramaturgical grounds," as he also said.[31] Fassbinder speculated once that the series was cut short because its proposed Parts 6 to 8 had become "politically more aggressive."[32] On another occasion, he said that Rohrbach canceled the series because of its implicit criticism of the ineffectualness of trade unions in addressing the human problems of workers.[33]

Welt am Draht (1973)

Five months later Fassbinder shot another 16 mm film for the WDR television network, *Welt am Draht* (World on the Wire), a two-part (197-minute) science-fiction-crime thriller, which in its way is as optimistic as the workers' miniseries, though it is considerably more sophisticated in its narrative structure and its style. Based on a novel by the American journalist and science-fiction writer Daniel F. Galouye (1920–76), the film tells the story of Fred Stiller (Klaus Löwitsch), a researcher in a cybernetics institute who learns that the world in which he lives is merely a computer projection.[34] With such knowledge, he represents a grave threat to the mysterious coalition of political, corporate, and law-enforcement powers that seems to control most of Europe and that pursues Stiller both in West Germany and in France.

Stiller is in some respects another typical Fassbinder male protagonist of the early 1970s melodramas—lonely, troubled, oppressed by powerful forces outside himself. But in its romantic happy ending, his story departs significantly from the usual pattern. For once, love is not colder than death but, rather, the agency of a miraculous escape. After a series of exciting chases, reverses, and close calls Fred is saved by a young woman who has fallen in love with him—Eva (Mascha Rabben), the daughter of a colleague whose death had set Fred off on the path of inquiry into the dangerous knowledge he has gained. Just at the moment when his pursuers seem to have killed him, Eva translates Fred into another dimension of reality where they can enjoy their love in peace.

Mascha Rabben, the female lead in the film, once suggested that she and Klaus Löwitsch were here essentially playing Lauren Bacall and Humphrey Bogart in Howard Hawks's 1946 Hollywood noir gangster film, *The Big Sleep*.[35] *Welt am Draht* is, however, much more pointed than Hawks's film in dramatizing the dangers that independent-minded individuals face from colluding corporate and state officials in a society pervaded by a police-state mentality. The film implies an ominous not-too-distant future for Western society, particularly West Germany. It set the stage for Fassbinder's more direct cinematic treatments of political repression later in the 1970s, after official and unofficial reactions to left-wing terrorism had escalated to disturbing levels.

Stylistically, *Welt am Draht* is an exuberant mixture of surrealistic effects and imitations of Hollywood crime and science-fiction movies. Police detectives wearing 1940s-style fedoras move among futuristic plastic-and-chrome furniture while electronic music alternates with Bach fugues and Chopin love themes, and even Stiller's heartbeat, on the sound track. In a Paris hotel Fred sleeps with a secretary, who admits that she has betrayed him to the authorities, in a fur-covered bed set among classical statues. Later Eva demonstrates to Fred, in a mysterious triple mirror, the possibilities of projecting their consciousnesses into other worlds. Some of these effects are rather far-fetched, giving the film a camp flavor at points. But overall, this is fairly compelling drama, and a substantial treatment of both personal and political themes that are central in Fassbinder's work.

Ali: Fear Eats the Soul (1973)

Since its release in March 1974 *Angst essen Seele auf* (*Ali: Fear Eats the Soul*) has been one of Fassbinder's most popular and admired films. Produced by Fassbinder's Tango-Films, it was shot during the previous September in only fifteen days, on a relatively low budget of 260,000 DM .

The film tells the story of a love affair between an older woman and a younger man that Fassbinder had had in mind at least since 1970, when a hotel chambermaid gave a different version of it in his film *The American Soldier*.[36] Both main characters are social outsiders: Emmi (Brigitta Mira) is a cleaning woman in her sixties, and Ali (El Hedi ben Salem) is a Moroccan immigrant worker at least twenty years her junior.[37] The ungrammatical German title of the film (in so-called Turkish German) ironically underscores the cultural difference between them that the film dramatizes.[38]

The couple meet in an immigrant-worker bar into which Emmi has retreated during a rainstorm. Shortly afterward they marry, in spite of the disapproval of Emmi's children and her prying neighbors. Emmi and Ali are happy together as long as they feel these outside pressures. However, their marriage gradually comes to be accepted by others, for self-serving motives. The neighbor women need Ali to move heavy items, Emmi's daughter and son-in-law (Irm Hermann and Fassbinder) need her to take care of their children, and the neighborhood shopkeeper who had initially refused to sell to them (Walter Sedlmayer) needs their business. This acceptance by others seems to inspire problems in Emmi and Ali's marriage. Emmi shows off Ali's muscles to her friends, treating him like an exotic possession, and he drifts back to his former lover, a barmaid (Barbara Valentin) who knows how to prepare his favorite Mediterranean food, couscous. After Ali melodramatically succumbs to a ruptured stomach ulcer (recalling Hans Epp's heart attack in *The Merchant of Four Seasons*), Emmi joins him at his hospital bed and hears the attending physician utter a bleak prognosis as the film ends.

As in *The Merchant of Four Seasons* and *Acht Stunden sind kein Tag,* both the characterization of the protagonists and the social themes of *Ali* are relatively unambiguous. For example, the film pointedly criticizes the narrowmindedness of those who object to the couple's reversal of the usual "December-May" marriage and, more emphatically, to their prejudice against foreign workers in West Germany, a theme Fassbinder had sounded earlier in *Katzelmacher*. Consistent with this thematic clarity, the film tells its story for the most part in a straightforward, unmannered style. The camera work is relatively unobtrusive, except for a few instances when it subtly underscores thematic points—for example, Emmi's isolation from her disapproving fellow scrubwomen early in the film. Fassbinder said that he took particular care in shooting the film; although he usually went with his first take, he made as many as twenty takes of some shots ("I really wanted to get the maximum out of every moment").[39]

Ali is the most obvious instance of Douglas Sirk's influence on Fassbinder's work, specifically recalling the older director's *All That Heaven Allows* (1955).[40] That film tells the story of Cary, a rich widow apparently in her late forties (Jane Wyman) who represses for some time her romantic attraction for her considerably younger gardener, Ron (Rock Hudson), under pressure both from

Ali: Fear Eats the Soul, 1973. Top: Emmi (Brigitta Mira) reaches out for approval from her fellow scrubwomen. Bottom: Ali (El Hedi ben Salem, on right), plays cards with friends in the pub where he met Emmi. (By permission of the Rainer Werner Fassbinder Foundation, Berlin)

friends in her country-club set and her grown children. But an improbable accident (Ron's fall from a cliff) brings the lovers together for a far-fetched happy ending. Sirk's highly polished film well illustrates the combination of Hollywood aesthetics and social critique that Fassbinder wanted to achieve in his own work. Sirk frequently portrays the closed-mindedness of the widow's friends and children in an ironic style that is not far from what one often sees in Fassbinder. This critique is obvious in several scenes involving Cary's well-to-do friends. A more subtle instance is her children's presentation to their mother of a large television set as a Christmas gift. The emotional emptiness and the bourgeois idcologies behind this gift are implied in a memorable shot in which Cary stares wanly at her reflection in the blank screen of the set.

Fassbinder goes considerably further than Sirk in exposing the faults of the world in which his melodrama is set and in undermining the spectator's expectations of this film genre. This difference can be clearly seen in a comparison of the closing sequences of the two movies. In Sirk's film Cary and the recuperating Ron look out a picture window onto a picture-postcard snowscape featuring a handsome antlered stag, gazing in at them, as romantic music rises. If this is scene is intended as ironic, as some critics argue, it is not clearly so, and the point was apparently lost on many viewers.[41] The irony of Fassbinder's closing scene is much more obvious. One recognizes there many of the trappings of melodrama: Ali lies asleep in his hospital bed, as Emmi talks quietly with the attending physician, against the musical background of a popular song, "A Little Love." But the doctor's remarks to Emmi substantially undercut the emotions usually associated with such a scene in a melodrama, giving no reassurances to Ali and Emmi and making pointed criticism of West German policy toward foreign workers. Stomach ulcers are a common ailment for these workers, the doctor tells Emmi: "It is rather hopeless. They don't let us send them to a sanatorium—we usually operate—and half a year later they have a new ulcer. . . . Good luck in any case." Emmi walks to Ali's bed, touches him lovingly, and then turns to look through a window opening only onto blank grayness—in sharp contrast to the romantic snowscape in the final shot of *All That Heaven Allows*.

Fox and His Friends (1974)

Fassbinder's next "male melodrama," *Faustrecht der Freiheit* (*Fox and His Friends*) portrays a man driven to suicide, like the protagonist of *The Merchant of Four Seasons* three years earlier. This film is set in a gay milieu, with Fassbinder, as Franz Biberkopf, playing the protagonist for the third and final time in one of his own feature films. The character once again fits the pattern of

Döblin's protagonist: a simple, trusting man buffeted by life and exploited by supposed friends. Produced by Tango-Films and shot in 35 mm and in color on a budget of 450,000 DM, the film was based on an anecdote Fassbinder had heard from a man he knew in Berlin.[42]

The film has sometimes been called a morality tale because of its relatively simple and straightforward narrative structure, its stereotypical characterizations, and its pointed theme—condemnation of exploitation in the name of love. In the opening sequence Franz is separated from his lover, Klaus (Karl Scheydt), a carnival barker who introduces him as "Fox, the talking head." Left alone to shift for himself, Franz lets himself be picked up in a public toilet by a wealthy antique collector, Max (Karlheinz Böhm), who introduces him to his circle of sophisticated upper-bourgeois gay friends. Those friends become intensely interested in the crudely mannered, pock-marked proletarian young man once they discover that Franz has won half a million marks in the state lottery.

Franz is attracted to one of Max's friends, the handsome and stylish Eugene (Peter Chatel), who breaks off with his former lover Phillip (Harry Baer) and invites Franz to live with him. Eugen undertakes to improve the tastes of his pathetically unsophisticated lover, using Franz's own money. He supervises Franz's purchase of a new wardrobe and sports car and persuades him to buy a modern penthouse and to equip it with pretentious furnishings, purchased (like the clothes) from friends of Eugen. Finally, Eugen talks Franz into investing 100,000 DM in his family's failing printing business. Franz is soon working there as a laborer in a T-shirt while Eugen, in jacket and tie, plots with his alcoholic father how they can further exploit his lover. Eugen soon tires of this awkward relationship, not least because of the embarrassment Franz's drunken and brazenly lower-class sister (Christiane Maybach) causes him in the presence of his friends at the house-warming party. After getting Franz to sign over ownership of the penthouse to him, Eugen takes Phillip back and locks Franz out.

With the help of his sister, Franz finally comes to understand how badly he has been used, but he does not have the will to do anything about it. He develops psychosomatic chest pains and then commits suicide. In the last scene his dead body is seen lying in the shiny new Munich subway station at Marienplatz, with the empty fatal Valium bottle nearby. The station is weirdly empty except for two young boys who steal his watch and money and even his denim jacket (with "Fox" spelled out in metal nailheads on the back). Along come Max and Klaus, who hurry away from the body after they recognize it in fear of getting involved in a police investigation. It is a bleak ending to another Fassbinder story of personal exploitation disguised as love.

126

Fox and His Friends was one of the first mainline feature films to present the gay milieu frankly and realistically as a natural setting for dramatic action, rather than exploiting it as a subject of exotic interest. Fassbinder emphasized that the film was not about homosexuality but about emotional exploitation and class conflict.[43] The most sexually provocative scene in *Fox* is set in a gay sauna, with a long-running shot of the front midsection of a nude man, in the background of a conversation between Franz and Max. But their dialogue emphasizes the economic exploitation of Franz, as Klaus gives him deliberately misleading information on the financial condition of Eugen's father's firm.

In fact, the film has considerable significance at the political-economical level. There are Marxist overtones in its dramatization of the exploitation of a member of the proletarian class by a pretentiously upper-bourgeois group of friends. Fassbinder characterized the story as "a private struggle between an entrepreneur and a non-entrepreneur who'd like to become an entrepreneur."[44] He later compared the action of the film to a traditional British foxhunt: his "Fox" is "pursued by the rich, cheated, abused, then thrown away."[45] On another occasion he spoke of Eugen's use of the elegant furniture (which he later confesses that he does not even like) as a subtle "instrument of terror" over the lower-class Franz.[46] The theme of bourgeois exploitation is also emphasized in the fact that the boys who steal the dead Franz's money and jacket in the final shot are dressed in prep-school ties and blazers. Like vultures, the next generation of the ruling class is already robbing the proletariat.

Fassbinder's casting of himself in the role of Franz certainly invites consideration of the autobiographical dimensions of the film. On the one hand, the film represents the director's most public and explicit "coming-out" as a homosexual up to that time (he slimmed down considerably for the role), in spite of his insistence that the story could just as well have been set in a heterosexual environment as a gay one. This perception of the film is reinforced by its dedication, "For Armin and all others," referring to Fassbinder's new lover, Armin Meier, whom he had met toward the end of his shooting of the film. Fassbinder's portrayal of Franz may also to be a thinly disguised comment on the director's sense of himself as an outsider in the established German cultural scene, as Wilhelm Roth has argued.[47] Fassbinder once gave a different interpretation to the film, as a comment on his role as film director. While he could identify with Franz "on a moral level," he said, he identified more with Eugen, who exercises such power over Franz. Just as Eugen had taken it upon himself to "educate" Fox, "I also mostly deal with people that I try to educate, though less from year to year"[48]—the last phrase apparently referring to his increasing use of established professionals in his work.

As one early reviewer noted, *Fox* "begins in comedy and ends in melodrama."[49] The comic tone of the first half of the film is established in its light-hearted treatment of Franz's frantic efforts to buy a lottery ticket before sales stop at 5:00 P.M. It continues in its subtle satire of the *haute-bourgeois* pretensions of Franz's new "friends" and in the amusing discrepancies between their effete manners and his crudeness (playing "Chopsticks" on the grand piano in Max's elegant library and making a boyish pistol-shooting gesture when he can think of nothing else to do, for example). The mood of the film becomes more somber, however, after Franz makes a costly mistake in the printing plant. In the next scene, as Franz eats dinner with Eugen's family, Eugen harshly corrects his table manners. Franz crumbles his bread into his soup and then plays a stupid matchstick game with the mother, to the accompaniment of minor-key violin music. Thenceforth the stylization begins to take on more ominous overtones. In a highly mannered scene in a lawyer's office, Franz signs papers, which he obviously does not understand, for his loan to the printing company, while Eugen and his parents look on like vultures. This scene is presented in multiple tracking shots reminiscent of the complex Sunday dinner-table sequence in *The Merchant of Four Seasons*. Even more sinister is the visual imagery of a scene in which Max tries to soothe Franz as he complains that Eugen is abusing him: the cold, abstract forms of a parking garage, seen in repeated traveling shots and a self-consciously high-angle shot. A quite different kind of visual stylization—a mélange of various reds, chiaroscuro lighting, and reflective surfaces—reflects Franz's growing desperation in two scenes in a bar, where he is crudely insulted by two American soldiers to whom he makes a sexual proposition. At the end of the second of these scenes Franz winds up in the arms of the bartender, crying pathetically, "I always have to pay." That is the last time the viewer sees Franz alive.

Two of Fassbinder's most sympathetic German critics found problems in the latter, more melancholy, half of the film. Hans C. Blumenberg thought the characterization was too simplistic and heavy-handed; Hans Günther Pflaum wrote that Fassbinder had not originally intended the film to develop during its shooting from a comedy into a heavy melodrama—the more serious Franz's problems become, he wrote, the more serious Fassbinder's problems with sentimentality.[50] But neither of these readings takes enough account of the film's stylization and its ironic use of the conventions of Hollywood melodrama as artistic strategies. Other negative criticism of *Fox and His Friends* came from members of the gay community who objected to the film as a betrayal by one of their own, assuming that Fassbinder was obliged to portray his fellow gays in a better light. Fassbinder's version of the gay world "degrades us all, and should be roundly denounced," wrote one letter-writer to a gay journal.[51] For similar reasons, the melodramas about women that Fassbinder was also making during the early 1970s—and to which the discussion now turns—were disturbing to many feminist viewers.

Notes

1. "Fassbinder and Lacan" 60, 65–81. Silverman's analysis is based on theories developed by French psychoanalyst Jacques Lacan (1901–1981), well known since the 1970s for his reinterpretation of Freud in terms of structural linguistics. This essay in expanded in Silverman's *Male Subjectivity at the Margins* (125–156).

2. *Anarchy* 84. Fassbinder once agreed with an interviewer that the practice of holding shots longer than usual and moving the camera very slowly in highly emotional scenes produced "a kind of alienation." He said that in such cases the audience "can really see what is happening between the characters involved." (Thomsen Int 83)

3. The title is derived from a French phrase designating a fruit and vegetable vendor, *marchand de quatre saisons* (Roth/AN 140).

4. Liselotte Eder identified these two uncles and challenged Katz's allegation (66) that the Raab character is a "merciless portrayal" of Wolff Eder, a committed Social Democrat (Int).

5. Quoted in Kuhn, 91, n. 10.

6. The lack of bedclothes on the new mattress on which they are lying lends a surreal aura to this depressing scene.

7. Jenny 270.

8. Fassbinder later brought back the young actress who plays the troubled daughter of Hans Epp, Andrea Schober, as the daughter whose mother is sent away from her mother in *Effi Briest* (1972–73) and—in a more complex and disturbing role—as the crippled child in *Chinese Roulette* (1976).

9. In this sequence, Fassbinder cuts from one applicant to the other, with no transitional material. Their comments to their would-be employer are patently absurd: the first applicant says he is in Munich only for a short time in his travels around the world; the second demands a salary of 900 DM a month and blithely totes up his anticipated expenses, which include his girlfriend and a new car; the third seems utterly bored at the prospect of getting a job.

10. The flashback is initiated by Hans's asking Harry if he remembers Morocco in 1947. Harry is one of the two legionnaires who save Hans in the flashback sequence, shooting his Moroccan tormenter just as he is about to kill the bleeding Hans. Since that Moroccan is played by El Hedi ben Salem, one wonders if Fassbinder sacrificed the stylistic restraint which prevailed in the film up to this point in order to give his lover a role, and perhaps even to dramatize a private sadomasochistic fantasy. An analogous private fantasy involving Fassbinder's later lover, Armin Meier, may be a component of

a film-within-a-film sequence in *Despair* in which Meier plays both a murderer and the twin brother he kills (see Watson, "Bitter Tears" 28).

11. See Rentschler, *West German Film* 83.

12. Jenny 271.

13. "Händler."

14. The translation of the title of *Wildwechsel* as "Wild Game Crossing," used by Rentschler (*West German Film* 111), is the closest to the meaning of the German, which refers to a spot (often marked by a sign) where deer or other wild animals may leave the forest to cross a highway—presumably referring to the young peoples' murder of the Hanni's father in a forest.

15. Kroetz had named this character Franz. Naturally, Fassbinder adopted that forename, and he added the surname Biberkopf (though it is barely mentioned in the film).

16. Sandford 77.

17. The elements to which Kroetz objected are in the print of the film in the Munich Film Museum. Fassbinder insisted in "An Open Letter" to Kroetz that everything in the film was in the play (*Abendzeitung* [Munich], 3 December 1973; reprinted in *Kopf* 123–124.) This is not literally true. Still, Kroetz's charges are far-fetched, particularly considering the fact that his play calls for Franz to simulate a bowel movement and to discuss the results (material which the film omits). This was the only Fassbinder film not shown in the 1992 Berlin exhibition and retrospective, since Kroetz demanded 30,000 DM for the rights, according to Liselotte Eder.

18. Thomsen Int 86–7.

19. Röhl Int 238.

20. Baer 103.

21. Thomsen Int 86–87. In Fassbinder's later work, the line between his productions for television and for theatrical release was not so clear at it was in the early 1970s. See chapter 11.

22. Wiegand Int 73.

23. In 1974 Fassbinder said that he was not as interested in making *Acht Stunden* as in pursuing "literary topics or topics that work with cinematic experience." He added that he made *Acht Stunden* because he had "grasped certain societal mechanisms" and had recognized his responsibility "to do something for the audience." (*Anarchy* 155)

24. *Anarchy* 158.

25. Collins and Porter 247. Fassbinder's series was part of a deliberate effort by WDR's director-general from 1961 to 1975, Klaus von Bismarck (nephew of the famous nineteenth century Prussian chancellor Otto von Bismarck) to broadcast dissenting points of view on contemporary social issues. The Collins and Porter essay explains the programming philosophy of Bismarck and the controversies surrounding Fassbinder's and other worker-films produced by WDR in the 1970s. See also Alvarado.

26. Röhl Int 238.

27. Märthesheimer, "Okkupation" 247.

28. Röhl Int 239.

29. Märthesheimer, "Der geordnete Gang" 255.

30. Collins and Porter 247.

31. Roth/AF 149.

32. *Fassbinders Filme 5* 236.

33. Roth/AF 150.

34. *Welt am Draht: Ein utopisch-technischer Roman* (A Utopian-Technical Novel), 1964.

35. Roth/AF 152.

36. In that earlier version, the guest worker murders his wife.

37. Since both Emmi and Ali are given approximately equal attention in this film, it could be grouped with the "women's pictures" in chapter 6. Brigitta Mira won a German Film Prize for this role.

38. When Ali translates for Emmi an Arab proverb, "nothing destroys the soul like fear," he says "Angst essen Seele auf," which she gently corrects to "Angst isst Seele auf."

39. Fassbinder may have repeated so many takes in this film because of Salem's inexperience as an actor.

40. Fassbinder said that he at first intended to do a remake of Sirk's film, set in Germany; it would have starred the famous American actress Lana Turner, but he couldn't afford her (Wiegand Int 67–68).

41. There has recently been considerable disagreement among film scholars on the question of how much irony Sirk intended in such scenes as this.

42. Literally translated, the title is "Fist-right of freedom." It means, approximately, "the law of the jungle." The man in Berlin told Fassbinder that he had once played "Fox the talking head," in a carnival, had won a lottery, and turned the winnings over to his roommate, an architect (Baer 106).

43. Eckhardt 118. Fassbinder made no mention of the film's homosexual milieu when he spoke of it in a 1974 interview before the film was released (*Anarchy* 158). In this respect (among many others) *Fox* differs decidedly from Fassbinder's last film, *Querelle,* in which the protagonist's homosexuality is foregrounded and problematized.

44. *Anarchy* 158.

45. In these later remarks, made in 1982 to an interviewer from an American gay magazine, Fassbinder unconvincingly explained Fox's problems partly in terms of the gay-straight conflict, stating that the film is "about the typical homosexual relationship with heterosexual society," which controls "the money, the system, the power" (Haddad-Garcia Int 53).

46. Eckhardt 117.

47. Roth/AF 164.

48. Eckhardt 116.

49. Jeremias.

50. Blumenberg, "Der Rest sind Tränen"; Pflaum, "Wie fleischfressende Pflanzen."

51. Andrew Britton, "Foxed," *Gay Left,* no. 3, cited by Richard Dyer, "Reading Fassbinder's Sexual Politics" 54.

CHAPTER SIX

"Women's Pictures"

Douglas Sirk's 1955 film *All That Heaven Allows*—that subtext for *Ali: Fear Eats the Soul*—was one of the more recent in a large class of Hollywood movies popular from the 1930s through the 1950s that were variously labeled "weepies," "women's pictures," or "women's films." Featuring such stars as Bette Davis (*Dark Victory,* 1939), Gene Tierney (*The Razor's Edge,* 1946), and Joan Crawford (*Humoresque,* 1946), usually in upper-middle-class roles, this was the one Hollywood genre in which women were regularly given serious attention instead of being relegated to the background as in such male-dominated types as the Western, the war adventure, and the gangster film.

Putting a woman at the center of a film narrative, however, did not usually mean allowing her to venture far from the circumscribed roles traditionally assigned to her gender—as mother, wife, or other supporter of men. Characteristically, these movies were anything but liberating for the female members of the audience. As Molly Haskell points out in her pioneering study of the treatment of women in Hollywood films, *From Reverence to Rape,* "the weepies are founded on a mock-Aristotelian and politically conservative aesthetic whereby women spectators are moved, not by pity and fear but by self-pity and tears, to accept, rather than reject, their lot."[1] In her recent feminist study of the Hollywood "women's picture," Jackie Byars has identified in these films somewhat more resistance on the part of "feminine voices, gazes, and power" to the "dominant (male) voices, gazes, and power," but still finds substantial inequality between male and female roles.[2]

Fassbinder and Women

Many of Fassbinder's films point to that Hollywood tradition of women's pictures, showing women both as victims and resisters of patriarchal social pressures. In the seven feature-length films discussed in this chapter, female protagonists for the most part passively submit to constraints imposed by dominant males. In five later "women's films" that explicitly probe recent German history (discussed in chapter nine), the women are usually more assertive, though in the end most are no more successful than their sisters of the early 1970s melodramas in challenging patriarchal mores.

The strong motif of misogyny in Fassbinder's early gangster films was noted in chapter three, and there is a fairly consistent pattern of abuse of women by oppressed men in the films discussed in chapter five. According to Wolfram Schütte, Fassbinder presented women in his early films as "wicked, inhibited, treacherous, and destructive enemies of man," in contrast to his much more sympathetic treatment of female characters starting with *Effi Briest* in 1974.[3] But that is misleading. As has been seen, Fassbinder's earlier films go to considerable lengths to portray sympathetically women's loneliness and oppression and to dramatize misogyny as an attitude of flawed male characters.

Assertive but ultimately victimized women are presented with considerable empathy in two films that Fassbinder claimed were the "most important" he had ever seen.[4] In Luis Buñuel's *Viridiana,* 1961, a wealthy, naively religious woman is cynically exploited by a group of mostly male beggars she has taken into her home. Jean-Luc Godard's *Vivre sa vie,* 1962 (*My Life to Live*) depicts a married woman who turns to prostitution as a means of achieving a sense of independence and is accidentally and melodramatically killed at the end. (Fassbinder claimed in 1974 that he had seen that movie twenty seven times.) It is significant that, although the women in both these movies are victimized, each asserts herself (according to her lights) vigorously in the face of the limiting expectations society has traditionally placed on women. This is the issue on which Fassbinder's "women's films" have often been criticized by feminists: he is charged with showing women primarily as victims who internalize their oppression rather than try to liberate themselves from it. Fassbinder did not deny that his films did this. But he insisted that such female acceptance of victimization was the result of powerful social forces. "Most women have been brought up to be completely satisfied when these mechanisms of repression take hold. That doesn't mean they don't suffer under them . . . of course they do."[5] Moreover, he maintained that even if women do internalize their oppressions, they still resist them more interestingly than men do. Women are more exciting, he said, because while being oppressed they are also likely to use their oppression as an instrument of "terrorization." Men, on the other hand, are "so simple . . . primitive in their means of expression."[6]

Fassbinder strongly denied the accusation of misogyny sometimes raised against him. "I take women more seriously than most directors do," he objected. "To me women aren't just there to get men going."[7] He elaborated on this topic in several conversations with Christian Braad Thomsen between 1973 and 1977. Directors who "always show them as beautiful, elegant . . . don't like women, don't take them seriously," he said.[8] But he resisted being labeled a supporter of women's liberation, the talk of which often "irritated" him. "The world isn't a case of women against men, but of poor against rich, of repressed against repressors. And there are just as many repressed men as there are repressed women."[9] He said that he tried to portray women honestly, recognizing that they "behave just as despicably as men." It was not for him to say how they should be liberated; each woman must decide that for herself.[10]

The Bitter Tears of Petra von Kant (1972)

Each of three women is seeking her own means of liberation in *Die bitteren Tränen von Petra von Kant* (*The Bitter Tears of Petra von Kant*), which portrays a troubled love affair between a middle-aged upper-class woman and a younger woman from the working class and concludes by focusing ambiguously on the relationship between the older woman and her assistant. Produced by Fassbinder's Tango-Films for theatrical release and shot in January 1972 in 35 mm on a budget of 350,000 DM, the film is an adaptation of Fassbinder's stage play *Petra von Kant,* which had opened seven months earlier in Frankfurt. The film was well received by West German critics and won German Film Prizes for Margit Carstensen's and Eva Mattes's acting and for Michael Ballhaus's photography.

The dialogue and action of the film are drawn almost entirely from the play, with a few important exceptions, particularly in the ending. Like the stage version, the film is enacted entirely on one set, the split-level studio apartment of the protagonist, a successful fashion designer. And it preserves the five-act structure of the play through the use of a fade-out-fade-in at the end of each act. The film's cinematic effects, however, go far beyond what could be achieved in a theater.

The protagonist of the film *The Bitter Tears of Petra von Kant* is a thin, sophisticated, successful fashion designer (Margit Carstensen), once widowed and once divorced, who in her mid-thirties is having her first lesbian affair. She falls desperately in love with a sensuous, ill-educated, and slightly fleshy woman twelve years younger, Karin (Hanna Schygulla), who has no qualms about exploiting Petra's desire for her. Accepting the older woman's affection and financial support with little commitment from her side, Karin moves into Petra's apartment, half-heartedly takes modeling lessons at Petra's expense, and gets started in a career as the featured model in Petra's successful new line of clothes. But she continues to sleep with men, including a black American whose sexual prowess she recounts to Petra in graphic detail. At the end of the third act, when the husband from whom she has been separated returns from Australia, Karin abruptly leaves Petra to her bitter tears of remorse.

The fourth and fifth acts are set six months later, on Petra's thirty-fifth birthday. She is alone and deeply depressed, lugubriously lamenting her lost love as she lies on the carpeted floor (where, significantly, her bed previously stood), drinking gin straight from a bottle and hoping for a call from Karin. The bleak mood is broken only momentarily by her daughter, Gabriele (Eva Mattes), home after a four-month absence at boarding school. The arrivals of Petra's old friend Sidonie von Grassenabb and then of Petra's mother complicate matters considerably as Petra's anguish, reinforced by gin, degenerates into hysterical insults to her daughter, her friend, and her mother, who is shocked to learn that her daughter is in love with "a girl."[11] At the end of the fourth act Petra lies on the floor caressing the birthday present Sidonie has brought her, a large baby doll whose round face and curly blond hair suggest Karin. Then she says pathetically to the woman standing over her (whose feet and legs dominate the foreground of the shot), "I want to die, Mama."

In the brief fifth act Petra awakens later that evening in her bed, which has been inexplicably restored to the main room.[12] Her mother sits beside her, offering cold comfort. Almost without expression, and looking away from Petra, she upbraids her daughter for her irresponsibility toward Gabriele, restates her distaste for the lesbian affair, reaffirms her own loyalty to her dead husband, and utters platitudes about turning to God for consolation. Under the pressure of this domineering, conventional mother, Petra begins to repress her passion for Karin. She confesses that she is still afraid and lonely, but she seems to be gradually recovering from her ordeal. She tells her mother that she now understands that she had never really loved Karin but only wanted to possess her. The telephone rings; it is Karin. Petra seems to be utterly self-possessed as she puts off Karin's suggestion that they meet soon, pointing out that neither tonight or tomorrow is convenient—but someday later they will certainly meet. She signs off bravely, "Best of luck!"[13] Reassuring her mother—and, presumably, herself—Petra tells her that she can safely leave now: "I've calmed down. I'm peaceful again."

Throughout the film the melodrama between Petra and Karin is observed, in absolute silence, by Petra's live-in illustrator, secretary, and servant, Marlene (Irm Hermann). Marlene impassively complies with Petra's often abrasive commands, bringing tea and other refreshments, or typing and working on dress designs in her work area in a corner of the room. In the closing moments of the film, after her mother has left, Petra turns to Marlene and—in what seems to be a sincere gesture of friendship—apologizes for the "many things" she has done to her. She promises that in the future they will work together, and that Marlene will have what she deserves, "freedom and happiness." When Marlene bends and kisses her hand in apparent gratitude, Petra says cordially, "Tell me about your life."

The stage version of *Petra von Kant* ends on this possibly hopeful note, leaving it up to the audience to interpret how the two will follow up Petra's invitation to Marlene to talk about herself, presumably for the first time in her three years' employment. The film adds what seems to be a much more negative conclusion: Marlene walks away from Petra and puts on a record of the American pop group The Platters singing "The Great Pretender." This song—perhaps too obvious in its implied comment on the protagonist—dominates the otherwise wordless final shot of the film. Petra sits on her bed in the semidark bedroom, which is lit only by the light from an adjacent room on the left. In a sequence that nicely balances emotional tension and stylized action, Petra watches in silence as Marlene brings a suitcase, fills it with items she fetches from off-camera right and left, puts on her coat, and walks out without a word, carrying the suitcase and clutching the large baby doll that Sidonie gave Petra. She turns off the light in the next room, and Petra lies down on the bed as the screen fades to black.[14]

As this summary suggests, mise-en-scène plays an especially important role in the film version of *Petra von Kant*. The visual impact of the set and furnishing is rich in symbolic suggestion. Most of the action in the first three acts takes place on or near Petra's bed, in front of a large wall mural that reproduces most of *Midas and Dionysos,* a painting by the French artist Nicolas Poussin (1593–1665). In the mural a corpulent nude bacchante—a female worshipper of the Greek god Dionysus—reclines before King Midas and the nude god, whose genitals are pointed at her, as Midas pleads with Dionysus to free him from the golden touch.[15] In contrast to the classical-baroque style of this mural, the rest of the multilevel studio apartment is a mix of modernist effects, including partially translucent glass panels and plain walls decorated with abstract prints. There are no views outside the apartment, and the closeness of this interior space is reinforced by a virtual webbing of dark, roughly finished wooden framing, railings, and open shelving, which increasingly are used to suggest Petra's emotional entrapment. Fassbinder and his cinematographer, Michael Ballhaus, make the most of the visual possibilities of this confined set, with long-held still shots, ponderously slow pans and traveling shots, and self-conscious framing of such suggestive images as long-necked nude manikins, bright red dress designs, and, time and again, the silent, uncommunicative face of Marlene observing Petra. Adding to the sense of stylization are Petra's and Karin's exotic clothes and Petra's variously colored wigs, which are changed, like her clothes, for each of the five parts of the film. As Wilhelm Roth has written, the film is, in an important sense, "a study of a room, and of the woman who inhabits that room and puts her mark on everything contained therein."[16]

For all its formal stylistics, Fassbinder's *Petra von Kant* is a moving, intimate melodrama. In fact, the contrast between the formalism of the film's decor and cinematographic style and "the primitive anguish" of Petra's suffering gives the film its particular emotional edge, as Penelope Gilliatt has noted.[17] Along the same general lines, Jack Babuscio reads *Petra von Kant* as a notable example of homosexual "camp"—an ironic, highly aestheticized style for which, he argues, "the gay sensibility" has particular affinity "in the service of the serious." He notes how the artificiality of the film underscores its main melodramatic themes: "the interdependence of sex and power, love and suffering, pleasure and pain."[18] Like *Fox and His Friends, The Bitter Tears of Petra von*

The Bitter Tears of Petra von Kant, 1972. A mural from a painting by Poussin serves as backdrop to a love affair between Petra (Margit Carstensen) and Karin (Hanna Schygulla). (By permission of the Rainer Werner Fassbinder Foundation, Berlin)

Kant dramatizes the recurrent Fassbinder theme of love as a means of emotional exploitation in a story of same-sex lovers of different social and economic classes. But in this case the victim is the *haute-bourgeois* Petra, not the lower-class partner. Petra's passion for Karin "is born of capitalism," since Petra believes that "she paid for Karin by giving her the benefit of her greater talent and income."[19] But in the end Petra's investment turns out to have been a distinctly bad one: she is the one who is deserted, not only by Karin but even by her previously abject assistant.

Some feminist writers have criticized *Petra von Kant* for perpetuating insulting stereotypes of lesbian relationships. An extreme instance is the charge by the British filmmaker Caroline Sheldon that Fassbinder's film, no less than the sensationalistic 1968 British film *The Killing of Sister George,* was intent on depicting the lesbian relationship as a "freak show."[20] As in his response to some gay critics of *Fox and His Friends* on similar grounds, Fassbinder emphasized that the central issue of *Petra von Kant* is emotional exploitation, without special reference to the lesbian context.

Petra von Kant seems to be one of the more obviously personal Fassbinder films of the early 1970s, at least in its initial conception. His dedication of the film "to the one who here became Marlene" has invited speculation about its autobiographical references. Fassbinder said in 1976 that the film was relevant to "a particular relationship of mine" with a man who was for a while "like a father, like a child, like a man, like a woman."[21] Four years later he said that, while *Petra von Kant* had begun with an attempt to explore his relationship with Günther Kaufmann, it had gradually absorbed elements of his relationships with Irm Hermann, Peer Raben, and Ursula Strätz and ended up being a story "about women."[22] Another interesting autobiographical angle is to see Petra von Kant as an imaginative projection of Fassbinder as film director. As Ronald Hayman argues, the fashion designer Petra can be interpreted as an imaginative stand-in for the director, trying to buy love by "helping people to dangle their good looks in front of [the] public."[23]

Effi Briest (1972–73)

In September 1972 Fassbinder began shooting what would become one of his most critically honored films: his adaptation of *Effi Briest,* 1895, a venerable novel by the north German writer Theodor Fontane. He called it *Fontane Effi Briest.* Like the novel, Fassbinder's film tells the unhappy story of an upper-class young woman rejected by her stern older husband because of a flirtation with another man, working an interesting variation on the "women's picture" theme of the woman who internalizes her own oppression. Fassbinder's first black-and-white movie since 1970 runs considerably longer than most of his other feature-length films: 141 minutes. It was made in a self-consciously literary style, with considerable care for historical authenticity. The project, budgeted at about 750,000 DM and produced by Tango-Films, was not completed until November 1973 because a leading actor became ill.

Fontane (1819–98), who grew up in the Baltic Sea town of Swinemünde, spent many years as a pharmacist and then as a poet and feuilleton writer before starting a career as a novelist at age fifty-nine. He completed fourteen volumes of fiction before his death twenty years later, much honored as a poetic realist who approached his characters—mostly drawn from his native district of Brandenburg—with both compassion and quietly ironic judgment. *Effi Briest,* one of his most popular novels, was published when he was seventy-six. With a subtle blend of sympathy and detachment, the writer tells the story of a lively and imaginative young woman of an upper-class couple living near Berlin. Her parents arrange her marriage to Geert von Instetten, a politically ambitious aristocrat twenty years her senior who had once courted Effi's mother. Apparently the pressure Effi feels to go along with this inappropriate marriage results from her mother's desire to realize through her daughter a marital option she had turned down (Briest offered more material security at the time) as well as her father's passivity and intimidation by the more successful Instetten. Several times during the engagement period, Effi's mother inquires whether her daughter is really happy in the choice of husband they have made for her, but she does not probe deeply or honestly—even when Effi tells her that she fears this "man of character . . . of principle" whom she is about to marry.[24]

Instetten takes his young bride to his manor house in the Baltic spa town of Kessin. Effi soon becomes bored with their social life, which is limited almost entirely to the few "good" families in the region. She is lonely, and her sleep is troubled by childish fear of a Chinese man buried near the house—a fear that Instetten encourages as a means of control over her. As her husband becomes increasingly involved in Prussian politics Effi is attracted by the attentions of Crampas, a young married military officer. Their horseback rides and picnics on the beach, undertaken with Geert's knowledge and with the family groom as chaperon, develop at length into a surreptitious love affair with passionate letters and secret meetings—and perhaps a sexual consummation, though the novel is coy about that. Effi is far too much the child of her time and culture, and too respectful of her authoritarian and heavily moralistic husband, to be entirely comfortable with this secret affair. So when Geert informs her that they will be

Effi Briest, 1973. Fassbinder's mother, Liselotte Eder, as the protagonist's mother. (By permission of the Rainer Werner Fassbinder Foundation, Berlin)

moving to Berlin, where he will assume an important post in a government ministry, her first words are "Thank God."[25]

Six years later Instetten accidentally finds Crampas's love letters and learns of his wife's affair. Although it troubles him greatly, Geert is driven by the inflexible codes of his social class to challenge Crampas to a duel on the beach at Kessin—he kills him with one shot—and to drive Effi out of his house; he keeps their daughter. Effi's parents at first refuse to let her come home; they are full of pity for her but unwilling to let the stigma of her impropriety damage their reputations. Only when it is clear that Effi is dying—of nothing more than a broken heart, it seems—do they allow her to return home so that they can care for her. Effi, who was initially angry that her husband would take such inhuman retribution for a long-forgotten affair, at length decides that he was right in doing so. She forgives Geert, rationalizing that the social system that has destroyed her young life is both just and natural. At the end of the novel, a month after Effi's death, the parents share their regrets over their daughter's tragedy. The mother, sentimentally noting that Effi's dog Rollo has stopped eating in his grief, asks if they might be guilty in some way: Should they have raised her differently? Was not Effi perhaps too young? Her husband brushes aside the questions in a fashion that is characteristic of him, with a phrase that has become a German cliché for avoiding moral responsibility: "Ach, Luise, lass . . . das ist ein *zu* weites Feld" ("Ah, Luise, let it be . . . that is much too complicated a matter").[26]

It is not hard to see why Fassbinder was attracted to Fontane's famous novel, considering its central themes of emotional exploitation within intimate relationships, reinforced by pressures for conformity to social conventions. In fact, he said that he had initially planned to adapt *Effi Briest* for his first feature-length film in 1969 but had not have sufficient money then to mount the effort.[27] By 1972 he was able to fund the project with earnings from earlier projects and a 250,000 DM federal award for the script.[28]

Fassbinder said he was glad that he could not afford to make the film in 1969. If he had, he would have tried to "adapt the story instead of . . . filming the book."[29] If ever there was a movie unqualifiedly committed to "filming the book," it is *Fontane Effi Briest*. It constantly reminds the viewer that it is a literary adaptation, starting with its reference to the author in its title, *Fontane Effi Briest*. It has a somewhat old-fashioned look not only because it is shot in black and white but also because of the coarse-grained film stock used in the project. Moreover, every word in the film is drawn directly from the novel, usually without omissions within passages. The novel's text is replicated in three different ways: in the dialogue, which is sometimes spoken by the actors and sometimes read by an off-screen narrator (Fassbinder); in narration and "authorial" commentary by that same off-screen voice; and in visual titles between scenes, printed in a German Gothic script.

The acting and cinematography in *Effi Briest* are unusually formal, reinforcing the feel of the movie as an adaptation of an honored novel. The film consists of seventy-seven scenes, many of which are single shots, often with a static camera. Sometimes the characters stand still during the course of the scene; occasionally they do not even talk, remaining totally immobile like figures in an old photograph album while Fassbinder's off-camera voice reads the dialogue or even, in a sort of counterpoint, material from another part of the novel.

The literary character of the film is also suggested in the unusual transitions between shots, in which the first shot fades out to white before the succeeding shot fades in. This device is unconventional, first, because the fade-out-fade-in transition is a traditional cinematic device indicating a significant passage of time between scenes. Its use between virtually all shots in the film, therefore, heightens the viewer's sense of the slow passage of time. These transitions are doubly odd in being mostly fades to and from a white, rather than black, screen. One effect of this unusual transition is that the viewer experiences an optical disturbance at the beginning of each shot as the eye readjusts from brightly lit screen to the darker image that emerges, reminding the viewer of the artificiality of the image. Fassbinder said that these unusual transitions were intended to resemble the page or chapter breaks in a book, to shock the reader into a state of mental alertness, and to simulate the reader's experience of turning a page of a book. Moreover, the heavy use of verbal text in *Effi Briest* lets the images "almost function like blank film, so that even though there are images there you can fill them again with your own imagination and your own emotions."[30]

The film takes from Fontane's novel a motto that underscores its central theme: "Many who have a notion of their possibilities and their needs still accept the prevailing order by their actions, and by doing so, strengthen and confirm it." This passage seems to refer particularly to Effi's frame of mind at the end of the story, when, encouraged by her mother, she gives up her resentment over her treatment by her husband and her parents and even blames herself for the troubles that have come to her. In discussing his film Fassbinder emphasized how the case of Effi can be generalized to a critique of the desire of those holding power in society to exercise hegemony over the minds of those they dominate, convincing them that their exploitation is good for them. He once said that the topic of *Fontane Effi Briest* "isn't a woman but a writer"; it is a film about Fontane's attitude toward his society, whose "failings and weaknesses" he recognizes while still seeing it "as the valid one for him." Fassbinder said that in the film he tried "to bring out somewhat more clearly the whole mechanism of oppression," such as Instetten's efforts to control Effi through her fear of the legendary Chinese man, which were only hinted at in the novel.[31]

Like Fontane, Fassbinder works out this theme in *Effi Briest* primarily through the relationship between Effi and her mother, who is played by Fassbinder's mother, Lilo Pempeit, in the most substantial of her twenty-five roles in her son's films. Like Pempeit's second most important characterization (Sister Gudrun in *In a Year of 13 Moons*), Luise von Briest in *Effi Briest* embodies the archetypal figure of the phallic "bad" mother behind the mask of the ostensibly angelic "good" mother, to use the terminology of the Freudian dichotomy.[32] On the one hand, Luise projects the image of an attractive and caring mother. Her hair is arranged and lit flatteringly; she is dressed in lovely late-nineteenth-century period clothes; many shots emphasize the similarity between her appearance and that of her daughter. The mother's demeanor is reserved and thoughtful, and she exudes apparent sympathy for Effi. On the other hand, Luise's beauty and her elegant costume and manner emphasize her conformity to the expectations of her social class and its patriarchal underpinnings. Thus, when she strolls with Effi through their park early in the film, merely listening to the girl's fears about the up-coming marriage, her smiling passivity constitutes a real threat to her daughter's well-being. As the film nears its close, her apparent sweetness is even more ominous. In a scene reminiscent of the conversation between Petra von Kant and her disapproving mother, Luisa sits by the bedside of her dying daughter, listening approvingly as Effi renounces her quite justified anger at Instetten's treatment of her. She supports her daughter's willing sacrifice of her personal integrity to societal expectations of the good wife, gently reassuring Effi that all her sufferings were indeed her own fault! Thus one sees, in the image of the apparently gentle and caring mother who nevertheless calmly sacrifices her child to her own selfish fantasies and to the conventions of high-bourgeois society, one of the most disturbing, if subtle, of Fassbinder's many exposés of emotional exploitation within intimate relationships.

Women's Melodrama for Television, and a Comic Reprieve

Between 1972 and 1977 Fassbinder filmed five additional melodramas featuring well-to-do female protagonists caught up in painful relationships, primarily with men, all produced in cooperation with West German television networks for broadcast in that medium. Two are largely realistic stories of contemporary married women, shot on 16 mm film: *Martha,* 1973, whose protagonist succumbs to an obsessively controlling husband; and *Fear of Fear,* 1975, in which a woman suffers mysterious attacks of generalized anxiety that presage the darker, more complex, themes of Fassbinder's final period. Three are filmed or videotaped plays set in earlier times: *Bremer Freiheit,* 1972, and *Nora Helmer,* 1973, in which oppressed women break out of their cages in quite different fashions; and *Women in New York,* 1977, a considerably more pessimistic portrait of women playing games prescribed for them by men. A sixth women's picture made in this period, *Wie ein Vogel auf dem Draht* (Like a Bird on the Wire), may be considered comic relief of sorts. It is a camp forty-five-minute television production made in 1974 featuring one of Fassbinder's favorite older actresses and a frequent motherly figure in his films, Brigitta Mira, singing cabaret songs and love ballads.

Martha (1973)

Shot in the summer of 1973, during the last three months of the year-long break in the work on *Effi Briest, Martha* was produced by WDR at a cost of approximately 500,000 DM. It was shown on the ARD television the following May (and given theatrical release in 35 mm in the fall of 1994). It has been called—with some exaggeration, but perceptively—"a 'trivial' horror-version of *Effi Briest.*"[33] The title character (Margit Carstensen) is a tense woman in her middle thirties who works as a librarian and lives with her parents. While she and her father are on vacation in Rome, he dies suddenly; her alcoholic mother blames Martha for his death. Soon Martha moves from her mother's home into what turns out to be a nightmare marriage to a handsome, rich engineer, Helmut Salomon (Karlheinz Böhm).

Helmut sadistically sets out to bring his new wife completely under his psychological control. He forces Martha to give up her job, isolates her in his palatial house, forbids her to socialize, and dictates her musical and reading tastes. Like Effi Briest, Martha is frightened of her husband and turns to another man for comfort, though not for love. At the end of the film Martha is crippled in an automobile accident as she flees in terror from her husband. As Helmut pushes her into the hospital elevator in the wheelchair to which she will be confined for the rest of her life, it is clear that he finally has the control over her he has wanted all along, and he is reassured by the doctor's muttered platitude about the need to accept what God has decided. At many points in the film Martha seems to have internalized her oppression, like Effi Briest. Fassbinder has indicated that that was the impression he intended to give. "Martha is not really oppressed, but educated. And this education is like oppression. . . . If Martha is no longer capable of living on her own at the end of the film, then she has achieved what she really wanted."

In *Martha,* Fassbinder once again balances heavy melodrama with a mannered style. For example, there are a number of mirror shots, a self-conscious 360-degree circling shot around the couple when they first meet, and a stylish traveling shot between wife and husband when Martha delights Helmut by quoting passages from a book on engineering he has forced her to read. In the final scene, the closing elevator doors pointedly symbolize the crippled Martha's bleak future with her sadistic husband. As an American critic wrote after its theatrical release in 1994, "you don't have to agree with its premise—that middle-class marriage equals sadomasochism—to respond to the bravura comic glee with which the director lays it out."[34]

Fear of Fear (1975)

Two years later, in April and May 1975, Fassbinder shot a film that is almost a sequel to *Martha.* Like the earlier film, *Fear of Fear* was produced by WDR, this time on a budget of 375,000 DM; it was first broadcast in July 1975. Fassbinder developed his script from a semiautobiographical account by Asta Scheib, a young housewife from Schweinfurt who later became an established writer. Once again, Margit Carstensen plays a thin, tense upper-middle-class housewife on the edge of insanity; her name is Margot. But there are no clear reasons for her recurrent anxiety attacks, in contrast to the case of Martha, the victim of a controlling husband.

Margot's husband, Kurt (Ulrich Faulhaber), is a decent enough man who is puzzled by and concerned about his wife's neurotic behavior. But he is not particularly sympathetic or attentive, especially since he is studying for an examination of some kind (his behavior is reminiscent of Anna's neglect of her brother's needs in *The Merchant of Four Seasons*). Thus, much of the time Margot is left alone in their spacious, well-furnished apartment, reading or listening to records or looking out the window, dreading the next onset of the inexplicable fear that comes upon her without warning and is signaled to the viewer by wavy subjective images (a traditional Hollywood signifier of losing touch with reality) accompanied by a trilling flute. She tries in vain to explain her condition to her husband, saying on one occasion, "I'm afraid of . . . " (without completing the sentence) and telling him one night in bed, "You seem so far away from me."

The professionals to whom Margo's husband takes her for help all exude confidence and competence, but they disagree on what is troubling her. Her doctor finds nothing organically wrong and prescribes Valium. One psychiatrist tells her husband that she is schizophrenic. Another diagnoses her condition as depression, which the doctors are certain can be cured by medication and by keeping her mind busy. In any case, Margot is almost completely alienated. Her husband neglects her. Her nosy mother-in-law (Brigitta Mira) and sister-in-law, Lore (Irm Hermann), disapprove of what they characterize as her abnormal behavior. Even Margot's four-year-old daughter, Bibi (Constanze Haas) distances herself from her mother. Margot finds some companionship with a crazy neighbor, Bauer (Kurt Raab), and appreciates the little kindnesses offered her by Lore's husband (Armin Meier). She briefly goes along with a sexual liaison with Dr. Merck, the pharmacist at the corner drugstore (Adrian Hoven), in exchange for extra doses of Valium. Ironically, Margot seems to communicate most meaningfully with Edda, her silent roommate in a psychiatric clinic to which she is sent.

When Margot returns home from the clinic, she discovers that Bauer has hanged himself. From her window, in a shot that matches one in which Edda had watched her leave the clinic, she observes his casket being carried to the hearse. Then "normal" activity begins again as people come into and go out of his building. Another brief wavy image suggests that her troubles are not over. Or, perhaps, under medication she will be able to control the symptoms of her anxiety, even though she will apparently never get at the basic causes.

Fear of Fear, made in the spring of 1975, anticipates the final stage of Fassbinder's career in two important ways. Margot's inexplicable fears foreshadow the generalized existential angst of several characters in films of the next two years—including the deeply troubled young male protagonist of *I Only Want You to Love Me* (November–December 1975), the angry and sadistic child of *Chinese Roulette* (April–June 1976), and the subtly insane Hermann Hermann of *Despair* (April–June 1977). A shot late in *Fear of Fear* suggests at least one of the major external factors behind this anxiety: the hostility of West German authorities and the general public toward the political left and their increasingly shrill response to political terrorism—a theme that Fassbinder would take up seriously in several later films. In this shot an armored police car drives by while Margot looks out her window. John Sandford has pointed out its political implications: the image suggests "the wider anxiety gripping this whole society . . . the repression needed to bottle in the frustrations it has created. The armored car is the political equivalent of Margot's Valium: an attempt to quell the symptoms by those who are too shortsighted to cure the illness."[35]

Bremer Freiheit (1972)

The earliest of the three Fassbinder plays featuring women protagonists that were adapted for television broadcast during this period was *Bremer Freiheit* (Bremen Freedom). Premiered in Bremen in December 1971, the play was videotaped in a television studio in Saarbrücken in September 1972 and first broadcast three months later; the television version was produced by Telefilm Saar, on assignment from the SR television network, on a budget of 240,000 DM. *Bremer Freiheit* tells the story of Geesche Gottfried, a Bremen woman who was executed in 1831 after being convicted of multiple poisonings and other crimes. According to the typescript of an interview with the press service *Bremen Special,* Fassbinder consulted contemporary records of the case—though his version departs from them significantly—in his effort to imagine the kinds of coercive pressures that would have led the woman to commit such an "act of freedom."[36]

Fassbinder's play is a darkly comic portrayal of a woman's revenge on a number of people, mostly males, who are trying to control and limit her life. Employing heavy irony and stylization, it compresses the narrative into fifteen relatively short scenes dramatizing Geesche's oppression by her husband, her fiancé, her mother, her father, and a woman friend, among others, whom she disposes of serially by serving them coffee (in one case, tea) laced with poison. Along the way, she murders her two children. The play concludes with her recognition that she will soon die for what she has done. The set for the television production, designed by Kurt Raab, is a largely bare stage with a few pieces of period bourgeois furniture, against a background projected onto a rear screen of water, reeds, and boats, presumably in Bremen harbor.[37] The movement is heavily choreographed, and the actors read their lines in mostly exaggerated fashion, although the acting style of Margit Carstensen, as Geesche, becomes slightly more naturalistic as the production proceeds. After each murder (only two are actually performed onstage) Geesche ritualistically sings parts of a little song about bidding farewell to the strife-filled world and going to heaven, and then genuflects before a crucifix. At the end of the film she states simply, "Now I'm going to die," and sings the song through completely as the lights dim.

Fassbinder's *Bremer Freiheit* may be said to constitute a modest and ironic contribution to the literature of women's liberation. In her frankness, her refusal to be dominated by men, and her mastery of her former husband's saddler business, Geesche anticipates one of Fassbinder's most assertive female protagonists, Maria Braun in the film of that name (who, as will be seen in chapter nine, resists male hegemony, outlives two lovers, and dies with her husband in an explosion of her own making). Like that later film, however, *Bremer Freiheit* concludes by suggesting the futility of women's resistance to their oppression by a patriarchal society. As Roth writes, there is for Geesche "no victory, but a capitulation, an act of desperation. . . . no independence, but only loneliness."[38] And, he might have added, the certainty of her own death.

Nora Helmer (1973)

The female protagonist comes to a better end in Fassbinder's television adaptation of the Norwegian dramatist Henrik Ibsen's well-known 1890 play, *Nora Helmer* (known in English as *A Doll's House*). It was shot in May 1973 in a television studio in Saarbrücken, like *Bremer Freiheit* the previous September, on a budget of about 550,000 DM and was first broadcast the following February. This project is a largely unrestrained exercise in mannered set design and camera technique (five video cameras were used), which Fasbinder would employ for much more effective artistic purposes in such films as *Chinese Roulette* and *Despair*.

Fassbinder's *Nora Helmer* closely follows the text of Ibsen's play, which is thematically similar to *Effi Briest, Martha,* and *Bremer Freiheit.* But the production departs considerably from the naturalistic style in which Ibsen's play has traditionally been presented. The mise-en-scène is a grotesquely exaggerated version of late-nineteenth-century bourgeois home decoration, overloaded with mirrors, draperies, and etched glass doors and partitions. For the most part the costumes are slightly modified period dress. A major exception is Nora's anachronistic light-green chiffon dress, which leaves her midriff and shoulders bare—presumably making an implied statement about her independence.[39] The acting style is stiff and highly choreographed: most lines are delivered in regularly cadenced fashion with a straight-ahead stare and no pretense of naturalism. This restrained acting style sharply contrasts with the highly mobile use of the five cameras within this visually overcharged space, particularly in the employment of mirror shots.

Fassbinder's *Nora Helmer* has been criticized for making the protagonist "a much more self-possessed character from the outset" than is usually the case, a strategy that takes "much of the force out of the final confrontation between Nora and Torvald."[40] It is true that the ending of the film comes as no surprise, but the portrayal of this Nora is nevertheless effective. Margit Carstensen reads her lines in a quiet, low-pitched voice that establishes her as a patient and strong-willed woman and allows for considerable dramatic irony (often underscored through close-ups), since the audience understands the strength of her character long before Torvald does.

Women in New York (1977)

Frauen in New York (*Women in New York*) is a made-for-television film based on Fassbinder's September 1976 staging of *The Women,* a comedy by the American magazine editor, playwright, and Republican politician Clare Boothe Luce, which had a long run on Broadway after it opened in 1936. Fassbinder's film was shot on 16 mm film during seven days in March 1977 at Hamburg's Deutsches Schauspielhaus, where he had presented the play. The project was produced by the NDR television network at a cost of about 320,000 DM and first broadcast in June over the ARD network. The cast of eighteen, playing a total of forty roles, was drawn primarily from the theater's Women's Ensemble but included three Fassbinder regulars—Margit Carstensen, Eva Mattes, and Irm Hermann—and Barbara Sukowa in the first of her several major Fassbinder film performances.

In twelve scenes taking place over more than a year, the play follows a group of wealthy American women as they gossip, backbite, and intrigue in high-fashion clothing boutiques, beauty parlors, reducing salons, and their plush living rooms, bedrooms, and bathrooms. They are attended by hairdressers, saleswomen, manicurists, exercise instructors, servants, and secretaries. Although no men are present, males are the primary subject of the women's conversations and their jealousies (considerably expanding a motif introduced in *The Bitter Tears of Petra von Kant*).

This is a stylish and cynical story of wealthy women who are content with their inferior positions in the privileged world run by their husbands. Nowhere is there heard a note of protest or a desire to assert themselves against male hegemony—an attitude that is consistent with the increasingly resigned, pessimistic mood of much of Fassbinder's late work. The women's antics in this play contrast pointedly with the female resistance offered to patriarchal power in *Bremer Freiheit* and *Nora Helmer*. Self-conscious visual effects underscore the film's cynicism: each scene is shot in one take; the camera is sometimes static for long periods; at times it moves into complicated tracking shots. Particularly memorable visual details include a large fish tank in the foreground of the first scene, which lends an ironical perspective on the women's card game in the background; a scene shot through a water-covered window that two women are washing; and a circle motif that appears in virtually all the scenes, suggesting the entrapment of these women in their privileged but superficial and powerless lives.

Brigitta Mira as Songbird: *Wie ein Vogel auf dem Draht* (1974)

This is an appropriate place to mention what might be called (by stretching descriptive categories considerably) yet another Fassbinder women's film of the mid-1970s, *Wie ein Vogel auf dem Draht* (Like a Bird on the Wire, 1974).[41] Thematically, it has virtually nothing in common with the other films discussed in this chapter—except by contrast—in its portrayal of an older woman who seems utterly self-confident and in control of her situation, and in its light-hearted attitude toward stereotypical female roles and attitudes. This garishly styled forty-four-minute television program, shot in July 1974, is a mixture of broad satire and gay camp. It was produced by WDR for 150,000 DM and first broadcast over the ARD network in May 1975.

The program was a showcase for one of Fassbinder's favorite older stage performers, Brigitta Mira, who often played motherly roles in his films. Announcing itself as a film about "the disgusting and lugubrious nature" of the Adenauer era, the program features parodic renditions of American love ballads and other show-business tunes, as well as German cabaret favorites, by the good-natured chanteuse, dressed in elegant costumes. In one scene Mira sits astride a BMW motorcycle wearing a satin dress and a feather boa. In another, the plain-looking scrubwoman of *Ali: Fear Eats the Soul,* glamorous now in a glittering evening gown, wanders through a futuristic gymnasium filled with plexiglass and chrome bars, ogling muscular male bodybuilders in jeweled briefs as she belts out "Diamonds Are a Girl's Best Friend." Some of the skits in this show were so offensive that they had to be cut before the broadcast on ARD; Fassbinder was amused by the controversy.[42]

But this tongue-in-cheek television production provided only temporary comic relief in an artistic career that was on the verge of a major crisis, during which Fassbinder would emerge into his complex final phase as a cinema artist. His films of the early 1970s—relatively straightforward and largely private melodramas showing men and women trapped within oppressive social structures—would soon be replaced by much more complexly textured films exploring not only the internal crises of deeply divided protagonists but also the troubled history of Germany, from the Weimar Republic through "the third generation" of terrorists in the Federal Republic of the later 1970s.

Notes

1. Haskell 155.
2. *All That Hollywood Allows* 6. For additional feminist studies of Hollywood "women's films" see Doane; Gledhill; Kaplan, *Women and Film;* and Kuhn, *Women's Pictures.*
3. Schütte, "Respekt für sein "Cheynne autumn.'"
4. Wiegand Int 61.
5. Thomsen 91.
6. Thomsen 89. See also *Anarchy* 67.
7. *Anarchy* 20.
8. Thomsen 96.
9. Ibid. 85.
10. Ibid. 92.
11. Sidonie von Grassenabb is the name of a somewhat cynical older friend of the young protagonist in Theodor Fontane's novel *Effi Briest,* which Fassbinder began filming nine months after making *Petra.*
12. The bed seems now be in its original position, although in this fifth act the camera is never placed in a position to show the large wall mural which serves as its symbolic backdrop in the first three acts.
13. This is a significant change from the play, in which Petra agrees to meet Karin the next day at "the Tschang," presumably an oriental restaurant.
14. Whether or not Marlene's enigmatic departure from Petra is an act of freedom is not clear. John Sandford sees it as an act of rebellion in which she takes "the freedom that only she can give herself' (76). Fassbinder characterized such an interpretation as "wildly optimistic, even utopian," alleging that Marlene is "going in search of another slave-existence" (Thomsen Int 84).
15. Lynne Kirby has identified the painting and has ingeniously (and convincingly) interpreted it as "a sort of play-within-a-play that choreographs the themes of perversion, joy and/in suffering, ambivalence, unstable identity, and dissimulation" (9).
16. Roth/AF 141.
17. Gilliatt 94.
18. Babuscio 49–50. See also Susan Sontag, "Notes on Camp."
19. Gilliatt 95.
20. Dyer, *Gays and Film* 13–14. Sheldon also contrasts the action of the film, in the "totally hermetic" atmosphere of Petra von Kant's apartment, to Fox's "involvement in the world of gay men . . . in a multitude of milieux"—finding this difference evidence that "male gay film makers are not more sympathetic to lesbians than straight ones" (14).
21. Müller Int 184.
22. Limmer Int 74. Baer wrote that he had heard much of the dialogue between Petra and Karin in conversations between Fassbinder and Kaufmann (96). Fassbinder

frequently cast Irm Hermann, the actress who plays the enigmatic Marlene, in demeaning roles reflecting what appears to have been her often masochistic behavior in their personal relationship. In a panel discussion at the Babylon Theater during the Fassbinder retrospective in Berlin during the summer of 1992, Irm Hermann said that it had taken her many years to outgrow this kind of behavior.

23. Hayman 62.

24. Fontane, *Effi Briest,* ed. Keitel and Nürnberger (1989) 35. 25. Ibid. 182.

26. Literally, "too wide a field" (295–96).

27. Thomsen Int 87.

28. In proposing this project during a period of increasing concern in the Federal Republic over left-wing terrorism, Fassbinder was presumably aware that federal and state film funding agencies were more interested in supporting adaptations of recognized literary masterpieces than films offering critical comment on contemporary events.

29. Thomsen Int 87.

30. *Anarchy* 151, 157.

31. *Anarchy* 149–50.

32. See Kaplan, *Motherhood* 45–46.

33. Roth/AF 156.

34. Holden. See also Buchka, "Geschichte."

35. Sandford 89.

36. The interview is in the Fassbinder Foundation archives. Peter Iden has compared Fassbinder's version of the Geesche Gottfried story with an 1844 theater piece, *Maria Magdalene,* by German writer Friedrich Hebbel (1813–63): "where Hebbel leaves off (with doubts, questioning the old order) Fassbinder begins" (McC 21–2). There is no evidence that Fassbinder knew Hebbel's play.

37. The theatrical set, designed by Wilfried Minks, was "a cross, swimming in a sea of thick blood, into which the expensive furniture half-threatens to sink . . . surrounded at the sides by . . . seagulls in a blue sky" (Hellmuth Karasek, *Theater heute,* Jan. 1972, quoted in Roth/AF 214).

38. Roth/AF 214.

39. On the other hand, there is no obvious explanation for the tight dress into which the buxom Barbara Valentin, playing Mrs. Linde, is only partially stuffed, or for her ludicrously overpowered face.

40. Sandford 85.

41. The title is presumably derived from American poet-songwriter Leonard Cohen's 1969 song, "Bird on the Wire."

42. Spaich 54.

CHAPTER SEVEN

Art out of Crisis
The Emergence of "Late" Fassbinder

While there are considerable differences among the Fassbinder films made in the first half of the 1970s, virtually all of them are relatively accessible treatments of sympathetic protagonists caught up in essentially private crises. Most make only indirect reference, if at all, to the director's personal concerns or to the specific political and historical contexts in which they are set. Moreover, most of them stay within the general stylistic parameters of classical Hollywood melodrama, though they often subvert the conventions of that genre through subtle distancing effects.

In contrast, Fassbinder's later films exhibit, with sometimes extraordinary virtuosity, what Wolfram Schütte has described as "an increasingly complex system of multiple esthetic codes,"[1] as well as a marked increase in psychological intensity and in autobiographical reference. Moreover, they deal much more explicitly with history and politics—of their time, as well as earlier periods—than any of the director's films that preceded them. In short, the final, seven-year phase of the brief career of Rainer Werner Fassbinder is the period of his most complex achievements as an extremely personal film artist whose work also deeply engages the political and historical realities of modern Germany.

While it is important to avoid attributing Fassbinder's artistic output reductively to conditions in his private and public worlds, as some biographers have done, many of the films of this late period—particularly several made between 1975 and 1979—are explicitly engaged with major crises in both of those spheres. This chapter summarizes those historical and personal crises and discusses seven Fassbinder films made during this period that seem to reflect, and reflect on, them with particular intensity. Other films of Fassbinder's final period will be examined in the following chapters: his very personal adaptation of Vladimir Nabokov's novel *Despair* (chapter eight); a group of melodramas about women that constitute a sort of history of modern Germany (chapter nine); another unusually personal project, and his most ambitious film, the fifteen and one-half hour adaptation of Alfred Döblin's novel, *Berlin Alexanderplatz* (chapter ten); and his last film, *Querelle,* an adaptation of Jean Genet's exploration of male sexuality (chapter eleven).

Fassbinder's Purgatory

The most traumatic phase of Fassbinder's short adult life seems to have commenced about the beginning of 1975 and to have continued through mid-1978. Wolfram Schütte, to whom the director talked at length during this period, has characterized it as Fassbinder's "Purgatory, a far-reaching identity crisis."[2] Fassbinder's comment to Christian Braad Thomsen in 1975 sets the tone of this period in his life: "When I meet people in the streets and in railway stations, see their faces and their lives, it fills me with despair. I often want to scream out loud."[3] Over the next several years he often spoke of leaving West Germany, of suffering psychosomatic illness, of possibly committing suicide, and of his need for psychotherapy and of filmmaking as a substitute. Moreover, it was during these years that he began to use cocaine, which would figure largely in his accidental death in 1982.[4]

Paradoxically, there were many signs by the middle of the 1970s that Fassbinder was beginning to achieve substantial success both as both a popular and a critical filmmaker. Although his films won no German Film Prizes from 1975 through 1977, he had by then gained relatively easy access to funds from German television networks as well as private producers, increasingly through international arrangements. He told Wolfgang Limmer that starting in 1972 he had been able to count on earning enough income from his films that he could at least avoid losing money on them.[5] By mid-decade he had added a number of established German actors to his repertory company, and he began to sign on top international stars for individual films and to receive considerable recognition abroad.

Trouble at the TAT and the Anti-Semitism Controversy

A major ingredient of Fassbinder's mid-1970s crisis was his unhappy experience, starting in the fall of 1974, as director of the Theater am Turm (Theater by the Tower [TAT]), a small, publicly subsidized avant-garde theater in Frankfurt am Main, West Germany's leading center of industry and finance. Those difficulties at the TAT had been anticipated two years earlier during his brief appointment as director of the Bochum city theater, where he had had a falling-out with Peter Zadek, its respected artistic manager.[6] Fassbinder reportedly felt constrained by the "built-in limitations" of the theater at Bochum, from which his exit had been "rather violent."[7]

His experience at the TAT in Frankfurt was much more traumatic. By the early 1970s its reputation as one of the country's most prestigious experimental theaters—known particularly for its commitment to *Mitbestimmung* (collective decision-making by directors, actors, and technicians) had fallen on hard times. In the view of Karlheinz Braun, literary agent for Fassbinder's theater work at the time, the TAT had virtually self-destructed through "endless discussions and internal disagreements." Fassbinder was invited to take over the theater by the head of the city's department of culture, Hilmar Hoffmann, who thought that it would be "a terrific achievement . . . a sensation" to bring such a star as Fassbinder in to restore the TAT to its former glory.[8]

Fassbinder projected ambitious artistic goals for himself at the TAT. If he had realized them according to the plans he submitted to Hoffmann, his future career would have been substantially different from what actually eventuated. He planned to revive the ideal of the artistic collective, hoping to work with a group of people he knew in order "to gain an understanding of ourselves and our environment, to share this with the audience, and to develop ourselves further along with the audience." They would perform plays from the world theatrical repertory, as well as works more directly related to contemporary experience. The theme chosen for the first year was "group psychology." There would be a play based on Émile Zola's 1885 novel *Germinal,* along with adaptations of works by Shakespeare, the Russian playwright Maksim Gorky, and the nineteenth-century French comedy writer Georges Feydeaux. There would also be "a play about Frankfurt" and another, authored by the ensemble, using the materials of psychoanalysis.[9] Fassbinder said at this time that he intended to cut back drastically on his production of films during his tenure at the TAT to only two a year, one for television and one for cinema theaters.[10] "The whole thing began . . . with unbelievable vigor that was the product of pure energy and enthusiasm," recalled Karlheinz Braun, emphasizing that the director seemed seriously committed to reviving the radically participatory tradition of the TAT.

But Fassbinder's work in Frankfurt quickly turned into what many have called "the TAT fiasco." Ronald Hayman asserts on the basis of conversations with several people involved that Fassbinder was neither seriously committed to the democratic goals of the project nor ready "to shoulder the responsibility of running a theater."[11] Braun concluded that the primary problem was the lack of organization, an aspect of the project in which Fassbinder had little interest and that he left up to others, resulting in chaos.[12] In April 1975 the theater critic Peter Iden wrote that the ensemble had almost fallen apart amid talk that Fassbinder was "finding himself." There were public quarrels between Fassbinder and the management, and reports of drunkenness on the stage and brawling in the aisles during performances.[13] This episode ended early in 1975, a few months after it had begun, when Frankfurt authorities fired Fassbinder and the rest of the TAT ensemble.[14]

The most direct cause of Fassbinder's abrupt departure from his position at the TAT was his "play about Frankfurt," *Der Müll, die Stadt und der Tod* (*Garbage, the City, and Death*), which had been inspired in part by Gerhard Zwerenz's 1973 novel *Die Erde ist unbewohnbar wie der Mond* (The Earth Is Uninhabitable Like the Moon).[15] This play operates somewhat in the Brechtian manner, making use of cynical aphorisms and mock-romantic songs and opera parody, for example. It is thematically much bleaker than any of Brecht's work however. It is more reminiscent of Fassbinder's earlier plays *Pre-paradise Sorry Now*, 1969, and *Blut am Hals der Katze*, 1971 *(Blood on the Cat's Neck)*, though it is even more pessimistic than those sardonic theater pieces.

The central characters of *Garbage, the City, and Death* are an embittered pimp named Franz B. (yet another variation on Döblin's Franz Biberkopf) and his wife Roma, a sickly prostitute on whom Franz depends for his meager existence. Her father, Müller, is an unreconstructed fascist and a transvestite. One of her customers is a cynical Jewish real estate developer, who profits from carrying out the will of the city's power brokers to turn the run-down West End into a district of high-rise condominiums and corporate skyscrapers. He is taken with Roma's quiet sensitivity to him and rewards her with bank accounts, houses, and cars, to the consternation of Franz ("I loved you in the crap, the filth. My feelings can't quite cut it in the high life.")[16] Franz informs Roma that he has fallen in love with a man and deserts her. He is next seen as the masochistic victim of a homosexual orgy ("I thank you. Degrade me again and again." [183]). In despair, Roma persuades her rich patron to strangle her. At the play's end, the chief of police, who is in league with Roma's patron, murders an informer who has identified Roma's killer, and the hapless Franz is brought in to serve as "just the murderer we need to make things work out."

This is a deeply disturbing play. Its dense text recapitulates in extreme form the recurrent Fassbinder themes of public corruption and emotional exploitation. It would take a broad-minded audience indeed not to be offended by its crude dialogue and the bitter outlook it offers on life in the financial center of the Federal Republic. Fassbinder's intention to present this shocking distillation of his darkest themes as one of the first productions in his new appointment as director at the TAT might be interpreted as evidence of how seriously he intended to go about that work, as well as of the naïveté of his faith in the willingness of bourgeois theatrical audiences to accompany him in the exploration of his bleakest imaginings.

Such considerations were not cited in the cancellation of the play, however. Rather, city officials were responding to complaints that the play was anti-Semitic in its portrayal of the Roma's patron, the real estate developer, who is identified only as "The Rich Jew."[17] At one point a character who is an admitted Nazi expresses regret that "the Jew" who "drinks our blood" had not remained "where he came from" or that he had not been killed in the Holocaust. He expresses the latter idea in a shockingly offensive pun: "Sie haben vergessen, ihn zu vergasen" (they forgot to gas him [88]).[18]

In 1976, about a year after Fassbinder left the TAT, the controversy was renewed with the publication of his play by Suhrkamp Press. A well-known critic, Helmut Schmitz, published on 12 March a harshly negative review of the play in a leading left-liberal newspaper, the *Frankfurter Rundschau*.[19] A week later Joachim Fest, a senior editor of that paper's crosstown rival, the conservative *Frankfurther Allgemeine Zeitung* (*FAZ*), vehemently attacked the play as an example of what he called "left-wing anti-Semitism."[20] The Suhrkamp publishing house withdrew the volume in which it was to appear. Less controversial, surprisingly, was the release that year of a film version of the play under the title *Schatten der Engel* (Shadow of Angels). It was directed by a friend of Fassbinder's, Daniel Schmid, and produced by Michael Fengler's Albatross Productions with Fassbinder in the male lead role (here named Raoul). Critics found it "cold and sober, though not anti-Semitic."[21]

Fassbinder strongly denied the charges of anti-Semitism directed at him during the controversy over his play, claiming that his critics were unwilling to acknowledge that corrupt business interests in the Federal Republic were hiding behind the postwar taboo against German criticism of Jews in order to enrich themselves while making the cities unlivable for humans. He charged his attackers with engaging in deceptive and condescending "philosemitism.[22] (Fassbinder was still thinking of directing a performance of the play as late as 1978. The most controversial of several later attempts to stage it occurred in 1985, when a group of Frankfurt Jews, under the banner "Subsidized anti-Semitism," occupied the stage on opening night and stopped the performance).[23]

It seems likely that the TAT arrangement would have soon unraveled, even without the conflict over alleged anti-Semitism. Hayman concludes that Fassbinder lacked the patience for sustained work in the theater, preferring the intensity and speed of filmmaking.[24] Two years after this episode, Fassbinder said that his tenure at the TAT had come to a premature end because he was "an anti-authoritarian type" who could not stand "compulsion" as a result of a trauma during his school days.[25] In 1975 he remarked that the theater seemed to him to have little relevance to "the direct situation of human beings" and that he found it "boring" to interpret on the stage "literary models for the contemporary situation."[26] There may be some rationalization in that statement; on the other hand, it may help explain why Fassbinder's recent theatrical work had been relatively dissatisfying for him and for his audiences.

In any case, Fassbinder and his group moved quickly back into filmmaking, producing a controversial political movie, *Mother Küsters Goes to Heaven,* in February and March 1975, as well as three more complete films and part of a fourth before the end of the year. During the remainder of his life he directed only one more stage production, *Women in New York* (September 1976). However, he did at various times during his last years make indefinite plans for several other theater projects.[27] And in June 1981 he directed *Theater in Trance,* a forty-five-minute television documentary (shot on 16 mm film) featuring brief segments of performances by unconventional theater groups from around the world, including the Squat Theater from New York and The Kipper Kids from California, in a festival in Cologne. On the sound track Fassbinder reads from Antonin Artaud's *The Theater and Its Double,* 1938.

The Terrorist Crisis

Beyond the personal and professional frustrations of his experience at the TAT and its fallout, Fassbinder, like many other West German intellectuals and artists of his time, was increasingly disturbed by the reactions of the West German people and government to the left-wing political terrorism of the 1970s, reactions in which he and many others thought they saw only thinly disguised fascistic tendencies.

After their failure to win workers and older leftists to their side in 1968, some of the most committed and most alienated members of Fassbinder's generation had considerably raised the stakes in their revolutionary struggle with government and corporate powers. They bombed military bases, bars, and other places frequented by U.S. service personnel, and kidnapped and murdered public officials. Between 1970 and 1978 more than two dozen people were killed and more than ninety injured in terrorist actions in West Germany.[28] Most of these actions were the work of a group calling itself "The Red Army Faction" (RAF), which was also known as the "Baader-Meinhof Gang" after its two most important leaders, both dropouts from the cultured West German middle class: the charismatic Andreas Baader and the brilliant journalist and political theoretician Ulrike Meinhof. Although he did not agree with their methods, Fassbinder was acquainted with at least two members of this "first generation" of West German political terrorists and had considerable sympathy for their ideological positions.[29]

158

The general population in the Federal Republic was increasingly alarmed over the terrorist actions, and the government response escalated to levels many found ominous. A conservative backlash had been developing for some years in West Germany, starting with the Emergency Degrees of 1968, limiting basic individual rights. Loyalty checks had been instituted in 1972 to root out alleged leftist subversives from government bureaucracies and public school faculties. By 1975 West German security police had put more than thirty members of the RAF in prison. Several of their leaders were housed in a new high-security addition to Stammheim prison near Stuttgart; a new generation of terrorists tried to force their release through new acts of violence. The government reacted with ever stronger measures, urged on by public alarm and the shrill rhetoric of the right-wing press. Leftist writers and artists were highly suspect; filmmakers found it increasingly difficult to find public subsidies for projects with contemporary political relevance. To many, the government's response to terrorism was as dangerous as the disease. For example, the respected weekly *Die Zeit* warned that the reactionary climate inspired by the terrorist threat would undermine "our whole way of life."[30]

Tensions reached a critical point on 5 September 1977 when terrorists kidnapped Hanns-Martin Schleyer, a leading West German industrialist and former Nazi SS officer, after killing his bodyguards. They demanded the release of Andreas Baader and ten other imprisoned terrorists, along with a large ransom. The government refused. On 13 October four Palestinian terrorists hijacked a Lufthansa jet with eighty-six passengers aboard and murdered the pilot before the plane landed in Mogadishu, Somalia. West German antiterrorist police stormed the plane in Mogadishu, killing three of the hijackers and freeing the hostages. In response, Schleyer was murdered by his captors. Five days later, RAF leaders Andreas Baader, Gudrun Ensslin, and Jan-Carl Raspe mysteriously died in Stammheim prison. Some have speculated that they killed themselves in a coordinated suicide with guns smuggled into prison by their attorneys.[31] But a great many West Germans, including Fassbinder, were convinced that the Stammheim deaths were state murders committed in retaliation for the killing of Schleyer.

Left-Wing Melancholy and the Possibility of Exile

Amid the dangerous political tensions of the Federal Republic in the later 1970s, Fassbinder found himself with a deep ambivalence about his homeland. While he never lost the personal sense of himself as a German filmmaker, for several years he felt increasingly alienated within his own country and talked often about moving away—perhaps to Paris, more likely to New York. In 1977 he said that he felt that Nazism was returning to his homeland "in new forms" and that he had to "go into exile" to continue to exist.[32] About the same time he remarked that he would prefer to be "a streetsweeper in Mexico than a film-maker in Germany."[33] But Fassbinder apparently felt strong ties to his home-land even when he was most unhappy living there. In 1974 he had remarked, "I find it hard to speak of Germany, there's still too much I don't know; I am German and would prefer to work here."[34] Three years later he said that both the German language and his childhood were important factors keeping him in the country.[35] In any case, as he noted in 1978, it would have been difficult for Fassbinder to emigrate, considering the number of film projects he always had underway.[36] By 1980 he was able to say that he had given up the idea of exile because state repression, supported by popular conformity, had passed: "The climate here is quite different from what it was five years ago."[37] Shortly before his death, Fassbinder emphasized his commitment to remain essentially a Ger-man filmmaker: "I think there is a world to explore within Germany, within our culture of today . . . and as American filmmakers explore the American experi-ence, I explore German experiences."[38]

Fassbinder seems never to have identified himself with specific partisan movements or parties in his homeland. He said in 1977 that he would not char-acterize himself as a West German "leftist," considering how "depressingly ineffectual" the various "splinter groups" were at the time.[39] Although he some-times suggested that his films constituted a substitute for political involvement, they rarely focus directly on contemporary political crises in the Federal Re-public. As early as 1969 he said that his films were not directly involved in public controversies; their aim was rather to promote "private revolution."[40] Six years later, in response to a question about the pessimism of his films, he observed that "revolution doesn't belong on the cinema screen, but outside, in the world." Films should show people "how things can go wrong . . . warn them that that's the way things *will* go if they don't change their lives."[41]

For the most part, Fassbinder's films express little hope for positive change in the social and political worlds they depict. They are characteristically domi-nated by what has been called the kind of "left-wing melancholy" that follows a failed revolution—they are "post-revolutionary" and therefore "utopian."[42] In 1977 Fassbinder said that he still believed in "the importance of commitment" as implied in *Acht Stunden sind kein Tag:* "as long as I live I will do whatever I can." But he added an almost metaphysical qualification: "All the values one has, and the fear and the pain linked to them, are ultimately quite unimportant when set against higher values. You have to understand that everything is unimportant before you can become *really* committed, because then it becomes a fearless commitment."[43]

Only two of the feature-length films of Fassbinder's final period directly addressed the tense political conditions in the Federal Republic during the 1970s. One is *Mother Küsters Goes to Heaven* (1975), which portrays the exploitation of a naive older widow by her children, the sensationalist press, German Communists, and leftist terrorists. The second is *The Third Generation,* a dark comedy about the absurd antics of the most recent generation of terrorists, filmed in the winter of 1978 79. Those two films chronologically bracket four intensely personal films. Nevertheless, Fassbinder's attitudes on contemporary political conditions are certainly implied in almost all of his late films and are made explicit in his contribution to the collaborative project *Deutschland im Herbst* (*Germany in Autumn*), made a few weeks after the deaths of the terrorists in Stammheim prison.

Mother Küsters Goes to Heaven (1975)

The first of Fassbinder's two feature-length film treatments of contemporary West German political issues was *Mutter Küsters Fahrt zum Himmel* (*Mother Küsters Goes to Heaven*). Produced by his Tango-Films for about 750,000 DM, it was filmed in 35 mm in February and March 1975 in Frankfurt. Although the film deals explicitly with the tense political environment in which it is set, it might also be grouped with the "women's films" discussed in the previous chapter. Moreover, it anticipates the "women's history" films of his final period, discussed in chapter nine. Like most of those earlier and later films it is largely naturalistic in style, and it generates considerable viewer empathy for the female protagonist, Emma Küsters (Brigitta Mira), a naive elderly woman whose personal tragedy is exploited by everyone in whom she places her trust.

At the beginning of the film Emma's husband kills his supervisor and then himself in a protest against threatened mass layoffs at the factory where he works. Afterward, Emma is rejected or deceived everywhere she turns for comfort or assistance. The factory management denies her a pension. Her son (Armin Meier) and his wife (Irm Hermann) shun her. Her daughter Corinne, a cabaret singer (Ingrid Caven), exploits the family tragedy to promote her career. A reporter (Gottfried John) wins Emma's confidence and induces her to tell the story of her married life, which he sensationalizes in a story portraying her husband as a violent drunk who oppressed his family. An older upper-middle-class couple, the Tillmans (Margit Carstensen and Karlheinz Böhm), who publish a communist newspaper, cultivate her in order to showcase her at a party meeting, then drop her. Seeking solace from an apparently sympathetic anarchist, she accompanies him and some terrorist friends of his to the office of the newspaper that had published the defamatory article. The terrorists surprise her by pulling out guns, taking hostages, and demanding release of all political prisoners in West Germany.

Fassbinder made two endings for the film. In the first, Emma accompanies the terrorists and their hostages to the airport, from which the terrorists expect to flee the country; there she is killed in a crossfire between police and terrorists, as the viewer is informed by a written title over the final freeze-frame shot of her daughter Corinne melodramatically clasping her body. Late in 1975 Fassbinder made a happier (if apparently ironic) ending for American distribution of the film: the newspaper staff members simply ignore the terrorists and leave, the terrorists depart when they realize that there will be no press coverage, and Mother Küsters goes home with a kindly night watchman. Fassbinder claimed to prefer the second ending, which he characterized as "gentler" and "more effective emotionally," to the first, which he found "more intellectual, more clinical."[44]

The film was not well received by many leftists, who denounced its representation of communists as bourgeois exploiters of the old working-class woman, as well as its ridicule of the terrorists. The Berlin Film Festival turned it down for fear of political reprisals. *Mother Küsters* almost invites leftist criticism in its explicit evocation of a well-known 1929 German film, *Mutter Krausens Fahrt ins Glück* (Mother Krausen's Journey to Happiness), directed by Piel Jutzi. Jutzi's film, which hewed strictly to the leftist line, had been widely acclaimed among revolutionary West German students after its revival in the late 1960s. In that film Mother Krausen commits suicide because of her desperate poverty, which is exacerbated by her son's drinking; but her daughter falls in love with a young Marxist and joins him in revolutionary activities that transcend the private tragedy of her mother's death.[45]

The Third Generation (1978–79)

In 1974 Fassbinder said that although he would like to make a film about those members of the Generation of '68 who had turned to terrorism, he could not do so because he did not know how to portray their "strength," their "great intellectual potential," and their "over-sensitive despair," and he did not really

know what their alternatives were.[46] He never did make a film about those idealistic revolutionaries who so troubled his imagination. His only feature-length
film dealing substantially with West German terrorists is *Die dritte Generation*
(*The Third Generation*), a black comedy about some who were active at the end
of the 1970s and who, according to Fassbinder, knew little of what had motivated their forebears of his generation.[47] The 35 mm film was shot in Berlin in
the winter of 1978–79, which is when its action takes place; it was produced by
Tango-Films for approximately 800,000 DM.

In its archly critical approach to its subject, *The Third Generation* considerably extends the sardonic portrait of ineffectual anarchist-terrorists seen at
the end of *Mother Küsters*. A small group of come-lately West German terrorists has gone underground after one of their number has been shot by the police.
It is Carnival season, and they make much ado about their costumes and masks
as they rehearse their new roles. They spend most of their time watching television, playing Monopoly(!), and engaging in personal intrigues before kidnapping the owner of an American electronics company, P. J. Lurz (Eddie
Constantine), without realizing that he has set up this kidnapping through his
former secretary, Susanne Gast (Hanna Schygulla), who had joined the group,
and another double agent in the group, August Brem (Volker Spengler).[48] Lenz's
motive is to increase his company's computer sales to the West German security police, which have fallen off with the recent decrease in terrorist activity. In
the closing scene, still dressed in their carnival costumes, the terrorists rehearse
with Lenz a videotaped message they plan to send out to the press in which he
declares that he is "a prisoner of the people." Lenz's ironic smile reminds the
viewer that it was he who arranged all this in the first place. The scene underscores what Fassbinder said was his main point in the film: "It's precisely those
people who don't have any reasons, any motivation, any despair, any utopia, who
can easily be used by others. . . . In the last analysis terrorism is an idea generated
by capitalism to justify better defense measures to safeguard capitalism."[49]

The film is largely naturalistic, though there are a number of stylized and
reflexive elements. In a manner reminiscent of Godard, Fassbinder divided it
into distinct sections, marked by graffiti intertitles photographed in West Berlin toilets; the terrorists' Carnival costumes recall the revelers from Michelangelo
Antonioni's *Blow-Up,* 1966; and Fassbinder noted his film's indebtedness to
films by Orson Welles, Michael Curtiz, and Luchino Visconti.[50] There are also
allusions to Fassbinder's early gangster films and the American and French
traditions they draw on in the man's overcoat and fedora that Hanna Schygulla
wears; a brightly colored Korean jacket looks like the one worn by Harry Baer

in *Wildwechsel*. The soundtrack is harshly obtrusive, especially the constant radio and television programs and news reports (on the Iranian revolution, for example.)

Fassbinder's difficulty in seeking funding for this explicit treatment of the sensitive subject of terrorism fueled his conviction that German film and television producers and funding agencies were unduly cautious in dealing with controversial current issues—in contrast to the Italians, the French, and even the Americans.[51] Both the WDR television network and the Berlin Senate withdrew their initial commitments to support the film after shooting had begun. But Fassbinder had, he said, the "courage, or . . . the craziness" to complete the project on borrowed money.[52]

Portraits of the *Autor* as Mad Plagiarist and as Gift-Giver: *Satan's Brew* and *I Only Want You to Love Me* (1975–76)

Between the two largely political movies *Mother Küsterss Goes to Heaven,* 1975, and *The Third Generation,* 1978–1979, Fassbinder made five emphatically personal films that reflect and comment on various aspects of his mid-1970s crisis. Between October 1975 and February 1976 he worked on two of them simultaneously: *Satansbraten* (*Satan's Brew*) and *Ich will doch nur, dass Ihr mich liebt* (*I Only Want You to Love Me*); the second was filmed during a pause in shooting of the first. Together they can be interpreted as an imaginative self-portrait of the artist in crisis, projecting extreme versions of opposite sides of himself in altogether different styles. It has already been seen how Fassbinder presented contrasting images of himself as both abused and abusive artist in *Beware of the Holy Whore,* 1970, at another major juncture in his career just before a significant pause in his filmmaking. This pair of films, made during what seems to have been the most intense part of his mid-1970s crisis, when he once again cut back substantially on his rate of film production, explores the director's bipolar personality in more extreme ways.

The first of the two films to get underway was *Satan's Brew,* filmed during two weeks in October 1975 and two weeks in the following January and February. It was produced by Michael Fengler's Albatros Productions in cooperation with Trio-Film Duisburg.[53] It is a crudely overplayed comedy about a megalomaniacal, tyrannical, and fraudulent poet named Walter Kranz (Kurt Raab). A self-appointed muse of the revolution of 1968, Kranz has run out of inspiration and is troubled by debts, a plain and practical wife with a fatal stomach illness (Helen Vita), and a demented brother, Ernst (Volker Spengler), whose chief obsession is torturing and killing flies. It is only when Walter simultaneously reaches orgasm and murders his mistress that he is suddenly freed from writer's block. He writes a poem and reads it triumphantly to his adoring mother (Brigitta Mira). But his wife discovers that it is plagiarized from a poem by the celebrated gay aesthete and poet Stefan George (1868–1933), "The Albatross" (itself a version of a poem by the nineteenth-century French symbolist poet Charles Baudelaire).[54] In response to this revelation Kranz convinces himself that he is, in fact, Stefan George. Supported financially by a female admirer with grotesquely thick glasses and warts (Margit Carstensen), he sets up a poetic circle of young male admirers. Later he robs his parents of their burial money; he also steals money from a prostitute, for which he is brutally beaten by one of her patrons. After he threatens to tell the police that it was his demented brother Ernst who murdered Walter's first mistress, Ernst shoots him. That seems to be the end of Walter Kranz. But the bullets turn out to be blanks, and the irrepressible artist rises to his feet, covered with stage blood, to romp wildly with an investigating policewoman who is clad only in a raincoat and to beat up his hapless brother.

Everything about this film seems calculated to defy good taste, hearkening back to some of Fassbinder's most farcical Action-Theater and antitheater stage productions. The melodramatic gestures are grossly overplayed. Much of the dialogue is coarsely shouted. The sex scenes are crudely drawn, the humor sophomoric. The conflicts among the characters are dramatized in a blend of slapstick and parody of Antonin Artaud's "Theater of Cruelty," which is quoted at beginning of the film. Peer Raben's vaguely romantic music track, imitating Schubert, Brahms, and Schumann,[55] works more often than not as a parodic counterpoint to the action.

Much of the comedy in the film works at the expense of Walter's pretensions as an artist. The central joke is that his supposed masterpiece is plagiarized. His response, to convince himself that he is the poet from whom he has stolen the poem, pushes the idea of self-deception to absurd lengths. The motif of plagiarism particularly connects this film with Fassbinder's personal history: he had recently been accused of taking ideas for his film *Martha* without acknowledgment from a story by Cornell Woolrich, and there were also suspicious similarities between *I Only Want You to Love Me* and a recent West German television play.[56]

Several critics have seen *Satan's Brew* as a thinly disguised cry of deep distress on the part of Fassbinder at a time of crisis in his personal and professional lives, less than a year after the "TAT fiasco." Wilfried Wiegand wrote of an undertone of "almost hatred of humanity, which breaks through . . . demolishing all the boundaries of good taste and narrative culture."[57] Fassbinder himself claimed that the film expressed personal "despair," arising out of "very private things—needs, obsessions, wishes."[58] He also ambiguously characterized the film as "a comedy about myself as seen from the outside, a comedy about what I would be if I were like that and what I perhaps am, but don't believe I am."[59]

The protagonist of *Satan's Brew* kills his mistress, robs his parents, and ignores his wife as she is dying, among other offenses. By contrast, the central character in the film made during an interruption in the making of that film, *I Only Want You to Love Me,* is vulnerable, abused, and exploited. It is only on an irrational impulse that he fatally strikes out at a person who momentarily symbolizes parental oppression. Shot in 16 mm, the film was produced in November and December 1975 by Bavaria Studios for WDR television on a budget of about 800,000 DM and was first broadcast the following March on the ARD television network. Fassbinder gathered an entirely new company of actors for this project (except for Armin Meier in a minor role); they included Vitus Zeplichal, who resembled the adolescent Rainer in appearance, in the lead role. The film is based on a real-life case history of a young man in prison for murder, published in a book Fassbinder had known for some years.[60]

As a child the protagonist, Peter (Zeplichal), internalizes his parents' insistence that he constantly prove himself a "good boy" to win their grudging love. His mother (Ernie Mangold) scolds him for his dirty fingernails and beats him with a coathanger when he brings her a bouquet of flowers he has stolen. As a young man he becomes a bricklayer and builds a house for his parents—a gift they hardly acknowledge—and he gives his wife, Erika (Elke Aberle), clothes and jewelry and buys furniture that they cannot afford. When he learns that the bailiff is coming to reclaim the furniture, he asks plaintively: "What am I to do? I only want you to love me." He tries to earn more by working overtime, but his boss takes advantage of him. Erika urges him to borrow money from his parents, but he cannot bring himself to do so. He takes a second job and falls ever more deeply into depression. One day he observes an innkeeper, who looks somewhat like his father, rudely accosting a young man. Suddenly all the exploitation he has so passively absorbed during his life is transformed into rage, and he strikes out at the innkeeper, accidentally killing him. Sent to prison for ten years, he agrees to a divorce from Erika, in consideration of her needs. The ending is sudden and bleak. The psychiatrist asks: "Are you glad to be alive?" The only answer is a freeze frame of Peter's pained face, and quiet music.

Peter has much in common with Hanns Epp in *The Merchant of Four Seasons,* who also feels rejected by his bourgeois parents, takes a working-class job, and becomes progressively more depressed as he internalizes others' abuse of him. In a manner similar to that earlier film, the characterization, plotting, and visual manner of *I Only Want You to Love Me* lend a somewhat fairy-tale to its basically realistic style (an opening credit announces it as "a fairy tale about obligations"). This slightly overdone realism is, in fact, similar to the style of most of Fassbinder's melodramas of the early 1970s (in striking contrast to *Satan's Brew*). As Roth says, *I Only Want You to Love Me* is a "simple step-by-step narrative" appropriate for television.[61]

Unlike *Satan's Brew*, *I Only Want You to Love Me* can easily be appreciated without reference to its *Autor*. But when these two films on which Fassbinder worked simultaneously are considered as a pair, the story of Peter invites interpretation as an imaginary projection of the vulnerable side of the director's personality. Among other things, it may be read as Fassbinder's fantasy about his problematic childhood, in which lack of parental attention is imagined as abuse and systematic exploitation, and the absent father assumes the form of an innkeeper abusing a leather-jacketed youth—a substitute father figure that the victimized child must kill. In a somewhat different autobiographical interpretation of the film, several writers have made a connection between Peter's constant gift-giving as a means of buying love—building a house for his parents, buying flowers and furniture for his wife—and the adult Fassbinder's own penchant for buying expensive gifts for his lovers and footing the bill for expensive meals and trips with his friends and colleagues.[62] Fassbinder told an interviewer in 1975 that Peter was a "yes man" who learned early from his parents that "feelings are for sale," either directly through gifts or through conformity to others' expectations. He claimed that *I Only Want You to Love Me* was a quite personal project, conceived as a means of self-examination after the TAT experience. Fassbinder said that he intended the film as a means of considering "what I have up to now let myself in for."[63]

Deadly Games: *Chinese Roulette* (1976)

Four months after completing *I Only Want You to Love Me*, Fassbinder began shooting a film that substantially extends the theme of the wounded child who strikes back at a parental figure. But in *Chinesisches Roulette (Chinese Roulette)* the revenge for perceived parental abuse is psychological, not physical, and it is taken not in an outburst of blind rage but with chilling calculation. This tense psychodrama, made in Fassbinder's most highly mannered cinematic style, also explores the relationships among a married couple and their two lovers.

Chinese Roulette was Fassbinder's first international coproduction and his first film to top one million marks in cost (1.1 million DM). It was produced by Michael Fengler's Albatross Productions (Munich), Les Films du Losange (Paris), and (unofficially) Tango-Films.[64] In the logistical arrangements he made for shooting, Fassbinder revived once again the idea of the artistic collective. For about seven weeks (April–June 1976) he virtually shut himself up with a number of his regular team-members as well as a German actor (Alexander Allerson) and two well-known French actors (Macha Mèril and Anna Karina, the first wife and leading lady of Jean-Luc Godard) in the small castle at Stöckach in Unterfranken that belonged to his cinematographer, Michael Ballhaus, and in which the film is set.

Fassbinder intensified the interpersonal relationships among the production team by involving both cast and crew regularly in the "truth game" of the film's title, which is played at the child's instigation in the climactic scene. The game pits two teams against each other; one of them tries to guess which of its own members the other team has secretly selected by asking questions such as what animal, or coin, or writer the person most resembles. Fassbinder was pleased with the effects these unusual arrangements had on the cast and crew: "The film took place in an atmosphere that I found the most positive in which I have ever shot a film," he said. Playing the truth game among themselves "affected our personal relationships a lot, and it effected our work."[65] The psychological intensity of the project for the participants was heightened by Fassbinder's insistence that night sequences actually be filmed at night.[66] At the center of the film is a precocious, secretive crippled girl, Angela (Andrea Schober), who is troubled by what she perceives as her successful parents' resentment of her handicap—resentment that she believes led to the extramarital affairs of her father, Gerhard, (Alexander Allerson), an executive in a publishing house, with a beautiful Frenchwoman, Irena (Anna Karina), and of her mother, Ariane (Margit Carstensen), with her husband's handsome secretary, Kolbe (Ulli Lommel). Angela vengefully arranges for both parents to meet their lovers at her family's country estate on the same weekend. After the initial shock, the two couples relax somewhat, as sophisticates who can be casual about extramarital affairs. But then Angela arrives unexpectedly, with her crutches, her collection of dolls, and her mute governess, Traunitz (Macha Mèril), and begins to tighten the psychological screws. The drama culminates on the second evening in a game of Chinese Roulette that she directs. Angela's primary purpose seems to be to get back at her mother, who has scarcely been able to disguise her hatred for her daughter.

The spectator suspects from early in the game that Ariana is the person selected by Angela's team, but that is not certain until the end; most of their responses could be applied to other members of the mother's team. Gerhard makes flattering comparisons; the mute governess's responses, interpreted from hand signs by Angela, are insulting; and Angela's answers are vicious. When the question is posed, "What role would this person have played in the Third Reich?" Angela responds, "Commandant at Bergen-Belsen" (a Nazi death camp). The housekeeper, Kast (Brigitta Mira), who has masochistically endured the child's animosity for two days, volunteers that she must be the subject. The others on her team agree. But Angela bursts out with devilish glee: "Wrong. She is the most harmless one. It's you, mother." In response, Ariane aims a gun at her child. But she fires it at the governess, Traunitz, who seems to have been encouraging Angela's hatred of Ariane, wounding her in the neck. In the ambiguous conclusion of the film a religious procession passes in front of the castle at night, praying to the Virgin Mary for mercy "in this valley of tears." A gunshot is heard, and the image on the screen freezes under a title taken from the marriage ceremony: "Are you willing to enter into marriage and remain faithful to one another until death do you part?" One can only guess who has shot whom and for what motives, as Fassbinder said he intended.[67]

While the film is in large part a child's fantasy of revenge, it is also a complex analysis of marriage and other emotional relationships among adults. Ironically, Angela's parents are drawn closer together during the weekend. At supper they recall amusing sexual anecdotes from their past as their lovers watch in uncomfortable silence, and the next morning they share a bathroom. Gerhard declares his love for Ariane at two tense points, once after she almost strikes her daughter and again after the shooting. The film also explores the relationships between the two women and the two men. As Fassbinder has said, "In this film the women are stronger than the men."[68] Ariane and Irene seem to find it easy to express their admiration for each other, often touching and occasionally kissing. In contrast, the two men behave much more like adolescent male rivals; their major mutual activity is a game of chess, during which they talk guardedly about male-female relationships. Once they start to embrace, in imitation of the two women, then break it off self-consciously with a joke.

Chinese Roulette is primarily a tense psychological drama within a small circle of intimates. But broader social and political themes are also suggested. For example, criticism of socioeconomic class differences is implied through the long-suffering housekeeper Kast and her embittered son Gabriel (Volker Spengler), a frustrated artist working as general handyman and valet. The film teases the viewer with other enigmatic political implications. The mute governess, Traunitz, may be, as John Sandford notes, "the last, dispossessed scion of an old family whose ancestral seat is this very mansion,"[69] which is identified late in the film as "Castle Traunitz."[70] Moreover, an odd conversation between Gerhard and Kast about the murder of one "Ali ben Basset" in Paris suggests that they may have once been involved in some political intrigue. But none of these hints are followed up.

This is one of Fassbinder's most visually stylized films. Along with *Despair,* made a year later, *Chinese Roulette* marks the high point of the director's use of images reflected in mirrors or seen through translucent materials—here primarily the plexiglass cabinets in the dining room, around and through which the camera restlessly moves and peers. In addition, the actors are often framed in odd fashion or seen from unusual angles, or hold their poses unnaturally long. The game sequence is highly choreographed, both in the acting and in the camera work. In general, as Anna Kuhn points out, *Chinese Roulette* recalls *Petra von Kant* in its stylized use of a spatially confined area to dramatize

Chinese Roulette, 1976. Gerhard (Alexander Allerson—right) and his wife's lover (Ulli Lommel), seen through a plexiglass cabinet. (By permission of the Rainer Werner Fassbinder Foundation, Berlin)

"intense personal interactions and emotional power plays."[71] The music track contributes to the stylization. For example, tense interpersonal confrontations are underscored by minor-key music that hints at parody of horror films or melodrama, or by cheerful waltz music in ironic counterpoint to the action.

Chinese Roulette was coolly received in West Germany. Kuhn notes that it "did little to ingratiate Fassbinder with the German public; the critics, while lauding Fassbinder as a *metteur en scène,* rejected the film on the basis of its cold intellectualism."[72] Many of the reviewers did not do justice to the sophisticated entertainment this intricate and elegant cinematic-psychological game constitutes, but the influential American critic Andrew Sarris is said to have devoted an entire university course to it (Katz 113).[73]

Public Crisis as Private Anguish: *Germany in Autumn* (1977)

Chinese Roulette, made in the spring of 1976, was followed by two more intense psychodramas, both adaptations of novels set in the latter days of the Weimar Republic (*Bolwieser* [October–December 1976] and *Despair* [April–June 1977], discussed in subsequent chapters), and a highly mannered adaptation of the cynical stage play *Women in New York* (March 1977). Fassbinder's next project was a 26-minute contribution to a 134-minute collaborative film titled *Deutschland in Herbst* (*Germany in Autumn*) made after the deaths of the RAF terrorists in Stammheim prison in October 1977. One of the most direct self-revelations ever made by a cinema director, the film makes emphatically clear the connection between the director's personal anxiety and political conditions in the Federal Republic at this time.

Germany in Autumn is a complex comment on the contemporary political crisis by a group of West German filmmakers and writers, expressing their dismay at the reactionary mood of the West German populace and officials in response to the terrorist threat and suggesting the root causes in German history. Shot in 35 mm and produced by the Filmverlag der Autoren and two film companies at a cost of approximately 450,000 DM, the film mixes traditional documentary and cinema-verité styles in constructing both realistic and surreal narratives. The collaborating directors included, besides Fassbinder, such politically engaged writers and filmmakers as Heinrich Böll, Volker Schlöndorff, and Alexander Kluge, who provides the voice-over commentary throughout.[74] The filmmakers' purpose was not "to add to the hundred thousand theories the first correct one," as five of those involved (including Fassbinder) wrote in a manifesto, but rather to counteract the "imageless verbal usages of the news media" in reporting the events of the fall of 1977 by "trying to hold onto memory in the form of subjective momentary impressions."[75]

In the words of James Franklin, *Germany in Autumn* "tears away what the filmmakers believed to be the romanticized mask of modern West Germany, strips away the facade of a supposedly liberal, peaceful, and prosperous capitalist democracy to reveal a dangerously resurgent fascism," with many direct and indirect references to the failed revolution of the 1960s as well as the Third Reich.[76] Schlöndorff's section, made in documentary style, contrasts the funeral of Hanns-Martin Schleyer, the German industrialist murdered by terrorists, with the burial of the three terrorists who had died in Stammheim prison. The former is a solemn ceremony attended by thousands of well-dressed public officials, business executives, and respectable upper-bourgeoisie, with all the trappings of state power and Roman Catholic tradition. By contrast, the terrorists are unceremoniously buried in plain wooden caskets in an open field, attended by about a thousand mostly young, obviously antiestablishment types, guarded and observed by large numbers of police and reporters. Another particularly effective episode, based on an actual incident, shows a West German television commission debating at length the "distancing text" for a planned production of Sophocles' *Antigone,* fearful that the broadcast of this classic play will be interpreted as politically subversive.

Fassbinder's segment of *Germany in Autumn* was shot by Michael Ballhaus in what looks to be a largely cinema-verité style in six days in October, shortly after the Stammheim deaths.[77] The setting is the director's dark brown Munich apartment, an almost totally enclosed environment that seems to have symbolized his state of mind at the time. The segment opens with an interview in which Fassbinder speaks of the need for marriages to go through periods of crisis before stabilizing, implying the possibility that the Federal Republic might be able to emerge from its present crisis in healthier condition. Then the film goes on, by means of two intercut sequences, to make it clear that this process will not be an easy one.

In the first sequence Fassbinder enacts his personal response to the news of the Stammheim deaths, mostly in scenes with his lover, Armin Meier, who voices the reactionary response of many West Germans to the current crisis. This part of the film dramatizes both Fassbinder's distress over those public events and his frustration at the present state of his relationship with Meier. In the second sequence Fassbinder questions his mother, in an increasingly tense dialogue at his kitchen table, about her earlier reactions to the recent events, seeming to push her at last into voicing a longing for authoritarian rule in Germany.

Early in the film Fassbinder engages in several distressed telephone conversations about recent events. During one of these he sits naked on the floor holding his genitals like a baby, while confessing his fear over what government authorities might do to their critics in these paranoid times. At other times he vomits into a toilet bowl, stares at himself in a mirror, and leans his head against a wall despairingly. His desperation and fear are also suggested when he places an order over the telephone for a taxi delivery of cocaine; later he cuts the white powder on a mirror and snorts it; shortly afterwards, hearing sirens outside, he frantically collects drugs from several locations in his apartment, rinses out his mouth, flushes the toilet, and cringes in the hallway as footsteps are heard outside his door.

Fassbinder's interactions with Armin Meier vividly dramatize several aspects of their troubled relationship, as well as the director's private pain in response to the public crisis.[78] Their views on the Mogadishu incident are radically different. Early on, Meier exclaims, "I'd blow up the whole plane. The others in prison should be shot or hanged. If they don't obey the law, then the state needn't either"—to which Fassbinder can only respond, "Oh my God, Armin." They go through various rituals of sadomasochism and love. Rainer rudely gives orders to Armin, who obligingly brings drinks and waits on him at the table. They fight. They go to bed. After the drug-raid scare, Armin says, "It's your fault," and Rainer screams back, "You little shit!" Rainer throws out an acquaintance Armin has brought home. Then he weeps uncontrollably, and Armin tries to comfort him as they fall to floor.

Intercut with this tense drama with his lover is a discussion between Fassbinder and his mother on the current political crisis and its implications for democracy (Liselotte Eder is credited in this film by her real name, not her usual screen name, Lilo Pempeit). This sequence is conducted in the fashion of an interview by the son as they sit at his kitchen table; it was edited into six brief segments that are inserted at various points into the sequence with Armin Meier.[79] The discussion is not completely spontaneous, as some interpretations suggest; nor does it seem completely planned. As Liselotte Eder has explained, she agreed to repeat for the film some comments on the terrorist crisis that she had made earlier and then regretted.[80] Later comments by Fassbinder support this viewer's sense that the conversation goes beyond what she might have expected.[81]

Initially, the mother says that she would prefer not to talk about the government's crackdown on leftists because such talk is dangerous at this time, as it was during the Nazi regime. Her son presses her, politely at first, and she asks, "Who can talk about it? I don't know, maybe [the writer Heinrich] Böll."

After all, she says, Germans are not really democratic; maybe these issues should be explored in the press—to which the son, now aroused, says, "Nonsense!" He presses her harder, accusing her of foregoing her responsibility as a citizen in a democratic society. He recalls her having told him that the authorities should shoot one terrorist in prison for every murder committed by terrorists on the outside and asks, "Was that democratic?" She responds that in such situations democracy may not be able to act effectively. He presses her aggressively, demanding, "Answer me please!" as she patiently pleads for understanding. He points out that the state gives ordinary murderers the right to a fair trial and demands to know how she could have such retrograde ideas about terrorists, who had reasons, whether good or bad, for killing. "Can't you understand that?" he shouts. His mother then backs away from the argument by stating that democracy is the lesser evil among possible political systems. As the Fassbinder episode of *Germany in Austria* comes to a close, she smiles and says: "The best would be some kind of authoritarian leader, who is really good and kind and orderly." Thus Fassbinder, playing Fassbinder, seems to be pushing his mother into voicing a sentiment that sums up what most disturbs him about his homeland: that the real nature of the West Germans' characteristic concern for order and propriety is a deep mistrust of democracy, a fear of challenging the status quo, and a nostalgic longing for authoritarian rule, which had so monstrously expressed itself in recent German history.

While Fassbinder's contribution to *Germany in Autumn* gives the general impression that it observes the cinema-verité principle of recording pure spontaneity, this is by no means entirely the case. This is most obvious in the inter-cutting of the two sequences. And within each sequence the film maintains a balance between spontaneous and deliberately staged action—for example, in such details as the reflection of the director's face in the mirror on which he cuts the cocaine and his self-conscious gestures of despair.[82] Still, for all its unobtrusive artifice, the film seems to be an extraordinarily candid self-revelation, which for many critics makes it the most compelling segment of *Germany in Autumn*. Wilhelm Roth wrote that it illustrates well "the feeling of power-lessness experienced by a left wing intellectual. It is not the political discussions that give this half hour its importance, but the brutality and honesty with which Fassbinder deals with himself as a man and a director."[83] And Ruth McCormick has pointed out that in this film, as well as in his other two major confessional films, *Beware of a Holy Whore* and *Satan's Brew,* the director admits his own responsibility for perpetuating systems of domination that his films condemn, dramatizing himself as "a quasi-oppressor." "As painful as it may be to look now at the scene there with Armin Meier, after his suicide," she writes, *Germany in Autumn* "adds to our feeling that [Fassbinder] is trying very hard to be honest about himself, as well as about the human condition."[84]

Trauerarbeit for Armin: *In a Year of 13 Moons* (1978)

Fassbinder's contribution to *Germany in Autumn* seems to be an unusually candid revelation of his state of mind at a moment of intense crisis for him, both privately and as a member of the disillusioned Generation of '68 as the Federal Republic underwent its most trying test as a democracy. This project seems to be a good example of the way in which the director's filmmaking served as a substitute for psychoanalysis, as he sometimes claimed. The following year he said that making his part of the collaborative film had helped him move beyond his worry about what might happen to him as a leftist during the terrorist fright: "Nothing can get to me after that film; it took care of a lot of my fear."[85]

But Fassbinder's Purgatory was not over yet. His troubled relationship with Armin Meier, with whom he had lived for four years, was about to come to a painful conclusion. Meier was the handsome product of a Nazi breeding experiment whom the director first met in the late spring of 1974 in the Deutsche Eiche, a Munich restaurant popular with gays. Armin had had a traumatic childhood and adolescence: at the end of the war his mother had given the infant over to the care of nuns in a convent; he had been kept nearly illiterate and later was sexually abused for years by a country doctor for whom he worked as a domestic.[86] Fassbinder began this improbable love affair with the most romantic hopes. According to Kurt Raab, he thought Armin resembled James Dean,[87] the star of Nicholas Ray's popular film about a disaffected young leather-jacketed American, *Rebel without a Cause,* 1955, who had died young in an automobile accident. In retrospect, it is not surprising that such a relationship would have gone bad, as this one soon did. If the scenes they share in *Germany in Autumn* can be taken as evidence, the two men were worlds apart in their political attitudes and understanding, and by the fall of 1977 their relationship had become a contradictory mix of recrimination, abuse, and brief reconciliations.[88] In a pained farewell letter to Meier dated 2 May 1978 Fassbinder wrote that despite "all the love that is there somewhere" their friendship lacked "a very patient interest in who the other person really is, and what one must contribute to make it more of a friendship than nothing at all."[89] A few weeks after the letter was sent, Fassbinder's mother discovered Meier's partially decomposed body in the Munich apartment he shared with Fassbinder, who was out of the city. Many commentators have treated his death as a suicide from an overdose of the sleeping pills found near the body; but the death certificate did not state this, and others, including Fassbinder, his mother, and Juliane Lorenz, have disputed the suicide theory.[90] In any case, many friends of Armin's accused Rainer of cruelly using and casting off his lover and blamed him for the death. According to Harry Baer, in the gossip at the Deutsche Eiche the director was held to be a "murderous swine."[91] Fassbinder stayed away from Meier's funeral, for which his mother made the arrangements. As he explained later, while he was not willing to play into the expectations of "the entire subculture" on that occasion, he had mourned Meier's death for an entire year.[92]

After Armin Meier's death Fassbinder spent two weeks with friends in Cologne and three weeks at Volker Spengler's home in Frankfurt am Main "doing nothing"; then, in one night, he wrote a brief treatment for his next film, intended as a tribute to this relationship.[93] He shot the film in July and August[94] and titled it *In einem Jahr mit 13 Monden* (*In a Year of 13 Moons*), explaining in the opening titles that 1978 was both a "year of the moon," in which emotional people suffer from "intense depressions," and a year of thirteen new moons, in which they often encounter "inevitable personal catastrophes."[95] While the film does not directly deal with Armin Meier, it significantly refers to his life, and to Fassbinder's as well. It is clearly a memorial to their ruined relationship, a *Trauerarbeit* (work of sorrow). Fassbinder took personal control of more aspects of the production than in any other feature-length film he ever made, functioning as scriptwriter, cinematographer, art designer, and—at least officially—editor.[96] The 35 mm wide-screen project was produced by the director's Tango-Films at a cost of about 700,000 DM. Fassbinder said in 1981 that he had three options after Armin's death: to become a farmer in Paraguay; to lose interest in working, which for him would have "a kind of mental sickness"; or to make a film, "which for me was the simplest." But the film would be much more than a record of his "feelings about [Armin's] suicide," his "pain and sadness." It would "go much beyond that, to say much more than I could say about Armin."[97]

In a Year of 13 Moons is Fassbinder's bleakest, most complex, and arguably most cinematically interesting feature-length dramatization of the themes of emotional exploitation and neglect, which are explored here explicitly in terms of sexual orientation and gender roles. The film recounts the last five days in the life of Elvira Weishaupt (Volker Spengler), a transsexual living in Frankfurt. In the opening moments of the film Elvira is beaten by a group of Czech guest workers; shortly afterward she is beaten again and deserted by her lover, Christian (Karl Scheydt), a failed actor whom she has supported through prostitution. Elvira is befriended by a kindly prostitute, Zora (Ingrid Caven), to whom Elvira tells part of her life story as they visit the beef processing plant in which she worked when she was a man named Erwin. Elvira tells Zora about her previous marriage to Irene (Elisabeth Trissenaar) and about their daughter, Marie-Ann (Eva Mattes), both of whom still love her. She also explains the sex-change operation she underwent some years earlier—pointlessly, since the man she had loved (as the male Erwin), who had casually suggested the operation, cared nothing for her, and she had not really wanted to become a female. Elvira and Zora visit a convent, where the mother superior, Sister Gudrun, explains how the boy Erwin, left at the convent during the war as an illegitimate baby, had his hopes of adoption dashed when his mother refused to ask her husband, who had not known of the child, to sign the release papers.

At the request of Erwin's former wife, Irene, Elvira seeks out the man for whom she had the sex-change operation, Anton Saitz (Gottfried John).[98] Irene wants Elvira to apologize to Saitz for having spoken of their relationship in a magazine interview, for which Irene fears that Saitz might seek revenge through their daughter. Saitz is a Jewish survivor of the Nazi extermination camp at Bergen-Belsen who has become a successful real-estate developer in Frankfurt.

In a Year of 13 Moons, 1978. Irene (Elisabeth Trissenaar) embraces her former husband, Irwin (after a sex-change operation now named Elvira, played by Volker Spengler). (By permission of New Yorker Films, courtesy Museum of Modern Art/Film Stills Archive, New York)

The narrative now proceeds in an almost surreal series of non sequiturs. As Elvira waits in a hallway of Saitz's sleek glass-and-steel office building, she watches a victim of Saitz's ruthless financial manipulations hang himself. When she finally gets to see Saitz, he can hardly remember this former companion who had undergone a sex change on his account, and he is not at all distressed about the magazine interview. But he does go to Elvira's apartment for a cup of coffee, and within a few minutes he is having sex with the prostitute Zora. After this, the increasingly despondent Elvira cuts her hair, dresses in male clothes, and visits Irene and their daughter, hoping to pick up their old life again. But, as Irene says, "It's too late now." Elvira has no more success in getting help from the journalist to whom she gave the interview; it is late, and he has to take a trip the next day. So she goes home and dies, perhaps by suicide (although there is no evidence of that in the film) or perhaps only of a "broken heart" as Fassbinder once explained it.[99] All the major figures in her life, including, unaccountably, Sister Gudrun, show up shortly afterward to commiserate briefly over her unhappy life and death.

As this summary makes clear, the bare plot of the film is highly unlikely, and the action is extremely melodramatic. Still, the narrative is compelling, working more at metaphorical and symbolic levels than as straightforward drama and both recapitulating and exploring further the themes of many earlier Fassbinder films. Visually and aurally, this is a thick-textured film, with many embedded narratives. In one of the most memorable and disturbing sequences Elvira explains her past life to Zora—including her efforts to boost her lover Christoph's self-image as an actor, quoting lengthy passages from Goethe's verse play *Torquato Tasso,* 1790, which they had rehearsed. This scene is played against the background of cattle being slaughtered and butchered in the processing plant where Erwin had worked (Armin Meier had once worked in a slaughterhouse). The film makes frequent use of television, often at high volume, as a narrative and symbolic counterpoint to the main action—as when Elvira switches a blaring television set from a videotape of herself and Christoph to a news report about the Chilean dictator Augusto Pinochet, to an interview with Fassbinder, to a French movie.

A particularly rich instance of what Roth has called the "polyphonic visions and narrations" of *13 Moons*[100] is the sequence at the convent Elvira visits with Zora to rediscover her repressed childhood as the boy Erwin, who lived there until the age of fourteen. That early part of Elvira/Erwin's story is the most significant material in the film drawn directly from the life of Armin Meier, whose mother had abandoned him at a convent. The mother superior, Sister Gudrun, is played by Fassbinder's mother in her second-most-substantial role in her son's films (she is credited in the film as Liselotte Pempeit, not Lilo

Pempeit, her ususal screen name). Sister Gudrun greets Elvira with a subtle mixture of apparent affection and recrimination: "Erwin Weishaupt, little Erwin. I remember you. I remember very well, because I used to try to love you. Are you unhappy?" Sister Gudrun begins to walk ceremoniously around the courtyard of the cloister, recounting in a quiet monologue against a background of somber violin music the pathetic story of little Erwin, rejected by his mother and sorely disappointed in his hopes for adoptive parents. The painful ordeal of love ostensibly offered but in reality withheld, so central to Fassbinder's conception of the dangers inherent in all emotional intimacy, is suggested in several ways during this short scene: (1) in the manner in which Sister Gudrun's monologue completely takes over the discourse, silencing Elvira/Erwin; (2) in the concentration of the camera almost solely on Sister Gudrun, ignoring Elvira until she is finally shown collapsed on the ground; (3) in Sister Gudrun's vivid representation of Erwin's mother's refusal to allow the boy to be adopted (the voice of the "bad" mother being heard through the story being told by the ostensibly "good" mother); and finally (4) in Sister Gudrun's startling condemnation of "Little Erwin" in her own voice at the conclusion of her monologue: "Erwin lived like this, in a virtual hell, for a long time. And worse, he . . . learned to thoroughly enjoy the horrors of this hell instead of being destroyed by them" (28). In this complex sequence Fassbinder, behind the camera, directs his mother (dressed in nun's habit, no less) speaking lines that seem, among other things, the artist-son's fantasy of the maternal voice chiding him for rejecting her love and unashamedly and unrepentantly enjoying himself by turning his troubled life into cinematic images. Moreover, as in his mother's portrayal of Effi Briest's mother (discussed in chapter six), one sees in this sequence the appearance of sweetness and nurturing spirit disguising cold rejection.[101]

This intensely personal film also carries considerable significance at the public level. It recalls *Garbage, the City, and Death* and *Shadows of Angels* in presenting Frankfurt am Main as a symbol of unfeeling commercial exploitation of human beings in the Federal Republic. In Anton Saitz one sees the former Nazi victim now turned oppressor—though he is presented much less provocatively than is "the rich Jew" in *Garbage, the City, and Death* and its filmed adaptation.

Together with his episode of *Germany in Autumn, In a Year of 13 Moons* seems to have carried Fassbinder out of the purgatorial crisis that had begun for him at mid-decade. Although his future life was by no means free of serious private complications, after completing *13 Moons* in August 1978 he virtually stopped talking about exile and focused his attention on a number of major projects rooted in German history and tradition, moving away from the self-absorption and the involvement with contemporary political issues that marked his work during the three years that began in 1975. Shortly after Armin Meier's death, he settled into a relatively calm domestic relationship with Juliane Lorenz, who had been editing his films since 1976, and who would remain his intimate companion for the rest of his life. Fassbinder continued to have homosexual liaisons in these last years, but not so frequently as before, according to Lorenz.[102] And though one or more of them may have been stressful, none of them seems to have had the intensity of his love affairs with Günther Kaufmann, El Hedi ben Salem, and Armin Meier. Shortly before his death Fassbinder spoke to an interviewer with a kind of resignation about his failure to experience "an equal love relationship between two men." He pointed out that "two or three times" in the past, relationships into which he had entered incautiously and "euphorically" had ended "in disaster."[103] It may be that his emotional distance from those relationships made it possible for Fassbinder, in *Berlin Alexanderplatz* and *Querelle,* to explore his complex sexual identity with a directness not seen in the earlier films—not even in *In a Year of 13 Moons.*

Notes

1. Jansen and Schütte 66.
2. Jansen and Schütte 69.
3. Thomsen Int 93.
4. There are varying accounts of Fassbinder's use of cocaine during his later years. He seems to be calling attention to it himself when, playing himself in *Germany in August* (1977), he cuts and sniffs a white powder. Harry Baer reported that Fassbinder increased his drug use about the time of *Despair,* made in the spring of 1977 (116). Richard Roud, director of the New York Film Festival, wrote that in the later years of his life Fassbinder routinely offered cocaine to him and other guests during the Berlin Film Festival (289). Katz describes Fassbinder's use of drugs during his later years in lurid detail (113 ff.). His major sources, insofar as they are identified, seem to be Peter Berling (whose exploitative fascination with Fassbinder scandal is discussed in chapter 11, note 95 and in the bibliography), and interviews with Michael Fengler (the producer of *Chinese Roulette* and *Maria Braun*), who had had a serious falling-out with Fassbinder over the latter project. It is difficult to separate fact from mythologizing in Katz's glib, sensationalist book. In correspondence with the author, Juliane Lorenz, Fassbinder's intimate companion for the last four years of his life, maintains that Katz distorted her comments to him about Fassbinder's drug use to emphasize its problematic nature. She stressed that the Fassbinder she knew was not the habitual drug abuser that Katz's book portrays. She confirmed its report that Fassbinder stopped using cocaine during the 154-day shooting of *Berlin Alexanderplatz* (1979–80). She denied that he began using it again during the shooting of the Epilogue of that film, which Katz reports as a surmise

by Fassbinder's former assistant director Renate Leiffer (173). Lorenz wrote that Fassbinder also stopped using cocaine while he was shooting *Lola* and *Veronika Voss* (April-May and November-December 1981), but that he used it "a few days during *Querelle* [March 1982] and after the shooting of it." (Let 22 June 1993) Lorenz told a *Cahiers du cinéma* interviewer in 1993 that she had naively thought she was succeeding, in long conversations with Fassbinder, to convince him to get along without cocaine. She added that nonetheless one should "relativize the importance" of this use. It was not surprising, she said, considering the fatigue and stress in his life, and the frequent drug use by his associates. She emphasized that Fassbinder was using only cocaine and sedatives during the time she lived with him (in what he realized was "a vicious circle"), and not heroine, as was sometimes reported. ("Je ferai" 66)

5. Limmer Int 138.

6. See Raab 190–200; Baer 60.

7. Iden 14; Jansen and Schütte 18.

8. Braun. Karlheinz Braun was founder of the Verlag der Autoren (the publisher of Fassbinder's plays and film scripts). In this interview Braun assumes some of the blame for this unhappy episode, recalling that he had suggested to Hoffman that Fassbinder be invited as director of the TAT. This interview is cited in the following paragraph.

9. *Kopf* 124.

10. Med Int.

11. Hayman 51.

12. Braun. Robert Katz characteristically portrays the TAT episode in the most cynical terms, drawing primarily from Peter Chatel (an actor-director in the Fassbinder entourage who played a central role in working out arrangements in Frankfurt), who claimed that Fassbinder was never serious about the undertaking and that the ostensibly democratic planning sessions in the theater were nothing more than rituals designed to disguise the director's authoritarianism (88–89). This analysis takes no account of Fassbinder's stated intentions, cited above. In her interview with Braun, Juliane Lorenz suggests that since one of Fassbinder's codirectors at the TAT, Roland Petri, was responsible for organization, Fassbinder should not have received so much blame for the problems there.

13. Hayman 51.

14. According to an account by Peter Chatel, one of the actors in Fassbinder's TAT ensemble, Fassbinder persuaded all the members of the company except him to turn in their three-year contracts with the TAT when their planned production of *Garbage, the City, and Death* ran into trouble (Katz 95–97). Juliane Lorenz writes, on the other hand, that during their rehearsals for the play, Fassbinder was informed that Frankfurt officials "decided to fire the whole TAT-ensemble," an account that she says was confirmed by (among others) Volker Spengler, a major TAT actor who thereafter played important roles in several Fassbinder films (Let 24 May 1994).

15. Fassbinder's play is not, as has often been reported, an adaptation of Zwerenz's novel. A detailed comparison, showing substantial differences between the two works,

181

was prepared in 1987 as part of court proceedings instituted the previous year against the Verlag der Autoren by Gerhard Zwerenz in order to determine if the charges of anti-Semitism made against the play could be applied to his book (Lorenz Let 24 June 1994). Critics have disagreed over whether or not Zwerenz's novel has anti-Semitic overtones (Markovitz et al 7–8, 26). In the spring of 1976 the Film Subsidy Board denied funding for a film version of the novel Fassbinder wanted to make—which would have been much closer to the book than his play—on the grounds that it would "injure moral or religious feelings" (Rentschler, *West German Film* 147–8).

16. *Rainer Werner Fassbinder: Plays,* tr. Denis Calandra 179. This is the source of further English-language quotations from the play.

17. The corresponding character in Zwerenz's novel is named Abraham Mauerstamm. The character is listed in the 1976 Suhrkamp Press edition of Fassbinder's play as "Der reiche Jude" (Fassbinder, *Stücke 3* 92), but as "A., genannt Der reiche Jude" (A, called The Rich Jew [58]), in the 1980 Verlag der Autoren edition—consistent with Fassbinder's intentions, according to Braun. It should be noted that virtually all the other characters in the play are given type-names (Miss Violet, The Little Prince, The Dwarf, Marie-Antoinette), stereotypical German names (Herr Müller, Frau Müller, Müller II and "Kraus, Peter") or names with ironic overtones—such as the prostitute named Fraulein Tau (dew), and the Jew-hater named Hans von Gluck, presumably alluding a Grimm brothers' fairy tale, "Hans im Glück" (Hans in Luck).

18. Fassbinder's former wife Ingrid Caven said in 1993 that Fassbinder's dispute with the management of the TAT had turned on his refusal to put a Nazi armband on the character who speaks the line about gassing, on the grounds that "it's not Nazis but ordinary people who say things like that today" (61). In 1982 Fassbinder said that he was writing a book about the TAT experience (Steinborn Int 14).

19. Markovits et al 8.

20. Lichtenstein 50–55. A few years before his attack on Fassbinder's play, Fest had written a controversial biography of Hitler, which Andrei Markovits has described as "rather apologetic" (Markovits et al 8). Fassbinder characterized the book as "terribly reactionary and actually an attempt of a bourgeois citizen to relieve himself of his guilt" (*Anarchy* 230).

21. Markovits et al 8.

22. *Anarchy* 119–23. A sympathetic account of this controversy appears in the 1982 Fassbinder memoir written by Gerhard Zwerenz, whose novel had in part inspired the play; his memoir presents the director as a scapegoat for German guilt over the Holocaust, describing his disappointment at the TAT as the beginning of the director's "long, lonesome death" (7). Fassbinder had met the former East German writer in 1974 and collaborated with him on several projects.

The issue of anti-Semitism was also raised when the general manager of the WDR television network and a government film financing agency in 1977 turned down Fassbinder's proposal to make a ten-part television miniseries based on the 1855 German novel *Soll und Haben* (*Debit and Credit*) by Gustav Freytag (1816–95). Fassbinder said that his film would have explicitly confronted the anti-Semitic sentiments of the book (*Anarchy* 115). See also Thomsen Int 95.

23. Markovits et al 9. For analysis of the complex political implications of various attempts to stage the play in the Federal Republic, see Markovits et al 4–6, 19–20, and Kaes, *From Hitler to Heimat* 90–97. Juliane Lorenz and Karlheinz Braun discuss Fassbinder's interest in restaging the play in Braun.

24. Hayman 53.

25. Fischer Int 17.

26. Bayer.

27. Among Fassbinder's unrealized theatrical projects were collaborations with Gerhard Zwerenz and Peer Raben on an opera and on a play, *Fädra* (Phaedra), based on the ancient Greek legend often dramatized since Euripides' classical Greek tragedy, *Hippolytus* (Zwerenz 153). The latter project has interesting psychological implications: instead of having the queen, Phaedra, destroy herself and her stepson Hippolytus because of her illicit love for him, Fassbinder intended to have King Theseus and Hippolytus agree to share Phaedra; but she refuses, out of vanity, and leaves the father and son, who "love each other." (Limmer Int 60; see also Töteberg, "Theaterarbeit" 164)

28. Dornberg 18.

29. Juliane Lorenz has written that Fassbinder told her he once met Baader (who, she writes, "was everywhere around in Munich and Berlin at the beginning"), and that the only other terrorist he knew was Horst Söhnlein, through his work at the Action-Theater in 1967 and 1968 (Let 24 May 1994). According to Harry Baer, Fassbinder failed once to respond to a message from the radical underground that Ulrike Meinhof wanted to talk with him, but he reconsidered after she was arrested and her film *Bambule* was barred from television. Baer said that Fassbinder tried in vain to get WDR to broadcast it, "to show what moved this woman" (133–34).

30. Dornberg 18–20. See also Phillips 51.

31. Dornberg 19. The previous year Ulrike Meinhof had died in prison; her death was also officially held to be a suicide.

32. Thomsen Int 101.

33. *Anarchy* 141. The next year, Fassbinder cited the suppression of his proposed television series on Freytag's novel *Debit and Credit* as a justification for his need to emigrate in order to maintain his integrity as an artist (Jansen Int/"Exile" 13).

34. Scherer Int 97.

35. *Anarchy* 16.

36. *Anarchy* 22.

37. Limmer Int 136.

38. Haddad-Garcia Int 54.

39. *Anarchy* 18; see also Baer 243–44.

40. Farber Int 475.

41. Thomsen Int 93.

42. Dyer, "Reading Fassbinder's Sexual Politics" 55; Wiegand 512

43. Thomsen 97. Ruth McCormick confusingly translates Wiegand's statement that this postrevolutionary feeling of alienation "does not belong to Fassbinder's 'discoveries'" (since it was shared by many in his generation) as: "does not figure in Fassbinder's 'world'" (McC 51; Jansen and Schütte 59). While not denying the "left-wing melancholy" of the 1970s, Eric Rentschler challenges the charge (made by British critic Raymond Durgnat, among others) that West German filmmakers of this period had no interest in taking on subjects of historical relevance (*West German Film* 158–164).

44. Thomsen Int 77.

45. Micheu.

46. Thomsen Int 91.

47. According to Fassbinder, the three generations were (1) sensitive idealists from the Generation of '68 who hoped to make revolutionary changes nonviolently, but who were driven nearly insane in their "almost pathological despair at their own helplessness"; (2) the Baader-Meinhof generation, whose defense of the first generation was "slandered . . . as fundamentally criminal," so that they were virtually driven to move "from legality to armed struggle to total illegality"; and (3) the present group, whose action "derives its meaning from nothing more than the activity itself . . . undertaken . . . without any sense of perspective." (*Anarchy* 125, 131–132)

48. The name of the character played by Eddie Constantine was changed during dubbing to P. J. Lurz from Peter Lenz (the name designated in the screenplay), which the distributor and the coproducer Theo Hinz thought was too close to the name of a Berlin policeman kidnapped two years earlier, Peter Lorenz (Lorenz Let 24 May 1994).

49. *Anarchy* 37.

50. Fassbinder said that *The Third Generation* was indebted to Orson Welles's *Touch of Evil,* Michael Curtiz's *Flamingo Road,* and Luchino Visconti's *Conversation Piece* (*Anarchy* 133).

51. *Anarchy* 128–31.

52. *Anarchy* 36; see also Zwerenz 97. According to Harry Baer, *The Third Generation* was finally paid off only with profits from Fassbinder's final film *Querelle* (136), but Juliane Lorenz has written that all the debts for the film were paid off by the sale of foreign rights, except for some lab costs (Let 24 May 1994).

53. Fassbinder's Tango-Films was an unofficial producer of the film (Lorenz Let 24 May 1994).

54. On Stefan George as an exemplar of a German tradition of male homosexuality, see Dyer *Now You See It* 22.

55. Pflaum and Fassbinder 126.

56. Woolrich (also known as William Irish, 1903–68) was a reclusive Hollywood writer, whose film scripts included *Rear Window* (dir. Alfred Hitchcock, 1954) and *The Bride Wore Black* (dir. François Truffaut, 1967). Harry Baer, who identifies the Woolrich story as "For the Rest of Her Life," concludes that it was quite possible that Fassbinder, with his extraordinary memory for specific details, might have inadvertently plagiarized Woolrich's story (127). Fassbinder said in 1981 that he wasn't sure whether or not he

plagiarized from Woolrich in *Martha* (Limmer Int 93). Hans-Günther Pflaum found the resemblance between *I Only Want You to Love Me* and a play on the ZDF television network several years earlier closer than Fassbinder admitted (Pflaum and Fassbinder 12–13). The housekeeper's son in *Chinese Roulette* (1976) is also accused of plagiarism.

57. Quoted in Roth/AF, 174–75; see also Pflaum and Fassbinder 11.

58. Jansen Int 113–115.

59. Limmer Int 94.

60. Roth/AF 173.

61. Ehrhard and Antes.

62. However, Juliane Lorenz has written that although Fassbinder "really liked to give presents," this was not for him a neurotic means of earning love (Let 24 May 1994).

63. Bayer.

64. According to Juliane Lorenz, Fassbinder did not want to identify Tango-Films as a producer of *Chinese Roulette* because "the board of taxes was trying to get more from him than they should" (Let 24 May 1994).

65. Filmverlag der Autoren press kit. Cited hereafter as press kit.

66. Pflaum and Fassbinder 55.

67 Pflaum and Fassbinder 17.

68. Press kit.

69. Sandford 96.

70. Gerhard identifies the castle as "Schloss Traunitz" when he telephones the police after the governess is shot; Angela had once referred to her as "von Traunitz" during the game of Chinese Roulette.

71. Kuhn 106.

72. Kuhn 107.

73. In the press kit, Fassbinder asked, "Why not? Why shouldn't I make a film that aims for artificiality, for an extreme art-form?"

74. This project recalls a 1966 French film, *Loin de Vietnam* (Far from Vietnam) in which Jean-Luc Godard, Alain Resnais, and Agnès Varda, among others, collaborated in a protest against the Vietnam War (Franklin 50).

75. Rentschler, *West German Film* 132.

76. Franklin 49.

77. Fassbinder regretted that all segments of the film were not made quickly and spontaneously, as his and Kluge's were, but he was not unhappy with overall outcome (*Anarchy* 137).

78. Fassbinder's and Meier's nudity in several scenes contributes to the film's aura of candor.

79. The conversation is published in *Anarchie* 214–218.

80. Liselotte Eder told the author that in her distress after the killing of Hanns-Martin Schleyer she told her son that the government ought to "kill one imprisoned terrorist in Stammheim every time the hijackers in Mogadishu killed one of the passengers. . . . It was only a momentary idea, and I was ashamed of it. But I was also surprised to

hear how many people were talking the same nonsense." About two weeks later, she agreed to Fassbinder's request that she "say those things again for a film he was making."

81. During this sequence, Fassbinder refers to earlier comments his mother has made. In an April 1978 interview, he implies that there was considerable spontaneity in the scene, stating that he had gone "rather far" in talking with "the woman." He also indicates considerable understanding of his mother's point of view, saying that for neither of them was mere "knowledge" enough to be able to live "another [kind of] life inside this system" (*Anarchie* 228).

82. Eric Rentschler wonders if anything in this film "was left to coincidence"— including the dictation of passages from *Berlin Alexanderplatz* (which are particularly apt for this context) and "the mother's smirk" as she delivers her final line about the need for an authoritarian leader. He also points out the difference between the image Fassbinder portrays of himself here as "a subject so overwhelmed that he cannot actively respond" and the Fassbinder who actually made the film (*West German Film* 192–3, 199, 202 n. 23).

83. Roth/AN 191.

84. McCormick, "Fassbinder's Reality" 81, 94.

85. *Anarchy* 137.

86. Spaich 210; Katz 85.

87. Kurt Raab 217.

88. Fassbinder said in an interview published in April 1978: "For three and a half years I've been living with Armin Meier, and that's a particularly difficult relationship" (*Anarchy* 20). Moments earlier he had told the interviewer: "I have pretty much the same relationship with men and with women. When needs become compulsions, when something that was once fun degenerates into a demand, I always react aggressively and negatively." Juliane Lorenz said that Meier was "a very warm person, but . . . in no way an intellectual partner for Rainer. He was like a child that Rainer loved. . . . Rainer wanted to give him so much. . . . He wanted to give him the opportunity of working in film . . . offered him a lot of possibilities. But Armin wasn't interested. . . . The few times I saw them together . . . I thought, 'My God, why do they suffer so much?'" (Int)

89. Liselotte Eder gave to the author a copy of the following passage from Fassbinder's letter to Armin Meier (here published for the first time, translated from the German); she said the police found the letter in Armin and Rainer's apartment and later gave it to her:

> And—in short—our friendship began with impatience, toying with feelings, child-less, thoughtless injuries. It went down the drain. It has gotten to that stage again. It hasn't changed enough—despite all the love that is there somewhere. What is lacking is a very, very patient interest in who the other person really is, and what one must contribute to it to make it more of a friendship than nothing at all. . . . Never in my life, never before, have I wished so often that I were gone, dead, definitely gone, gone, gone, as in this last year. . . . Armin, you wouldn't want to live with me the kind

of life I want to live. And I won't be able to live it, so long as we somehow still have anything to do with one another. . . . However sad this letter might be, the reality, call it my reality, if you wish, is still sadder, more desperate, than the words I could find for it.

In their interviews with the author, both Liselotte Eder and Juliane Lorenz challenged Kurt Raab's charge that Fassbinder "perversely made the letter too complicated for Armin to understand" (Hayman 76), asserting that its complexities reflected the author's genuine disturbance at breaking off this relationship.

90. Fassbinder's comments on the cause of Meier's death are ambiguous. He said in 1981 that, although he first thought it was a suicide, he didn't still believe that. If it were true, he said, he would indeed have guilt feelings about having lived with someone three years and not having been able to make it possible for him to have fun (Limmer Int 96). Later in that interview he commented that he had apparently been much more important for Armin than he had thought (129). Liselotte Eder challenged the suicide theory, pointing out that the official police report did not conclude that it was suicide (Int). Juliane Lorenz has written that her knowledge of Meier convinced her that his death was accidental (Let 24 May 1994).

91. Baer 122.

92. Baer 228. Baer writes here that the only time he observed Fassbinder weep was when he reproached him for not attending Meier's funeral.

93. Lorenz Let 24 May 1994.

94. Fassbinder's nineteen-page treatment, written largely in chronological order, was published in 1978 and is reprinted in *Anarchy* 177–195. According to Spaich, Fassbinder worked directly from this treatment when he shot the film (211).

95. This and all other quotations from the film are from Joyce Rheuban's translation of the continuity script, published in *October* 21 (Summer 1982): 5–50.

96. Juliane Lorenz has written that she cut *13 Moons* largely on her own, though she was pleased that Fassbinder accepted her offer that he take full credit for the editing "because I thought it was very important for him at that time." Fassbinder had at first refused her offer to help him with the film, since "he *wanted* to do everything himself." Later a friend who was assisting with the film suggested that she come to Frankfurt to help out. When she did, Fassbinder showed her the rushes, and together they began editing it. After an hour, she told Fassbinder that she would assist him in the job, to which he laughingly replied: "I will be back tomorrow and see what you've done." She edited the film in six days—during which time Fassbinder was rehearsing the role of Iago in a production of Shakespeare's *Othello*. "The film was perfectly directed; it was not difficult to cut." (Let 24 May 1994)

97. Limmer 95–96. Juliane Lorenz said that Fassbinder told her in 1978, "If I had not shot that [film], I would be dead" ("Je ferai" 66).

98. This name is spelled incorrectly as "Seitz" in the Jansen and Schütte filmography. Saitz's bodyguard (Günther Kaufmann) spells out his name with words for Elvira when

she first enters his office, using "Auschwitz" for "a," as Juliane Lorenz has pointed out (Let 3 June 1994).

99. Roth/AF 198.

100. Roth 199.

101. This analysis is indebted to Robert Burgoyne's reading of the convent scene (in "Narrative and Sexual Excess" 56–57).

102. Lorenz Int.

103. *Anarchy* 71.

CHAPTER EIGHT

Rewriting Nabokov
The Stoppard/Fassbinder *Despair*

In the midst of the crisis described in the previous chapter Fassbinder made his second film (after *Chinese Roulette*) intended for the international art film market: *Despair—Eine Reise ins Licht* (*Despair* [A Journey into the Light]). This ambitious undertaking was an adaptation of an early novel by the well-known Russian-American writer Vladimir Nabokov. It was the first of three Fassbinder films to be shot in English and the first to be made from a screenplay by someone other than himself—it was written by the celebrated British playwright Tom Stoppard, best known for his *Rosencrantz and Guildenstern Are Dead,* 1967. For the starring roles Fassbinder recruited two internationally-acclaimed actors, Dirk Bogarde (British) and Andrea Ferréol (French). And as art director he hired Rolf Zehetbauer, the Academy Award-winning designer of *Cabaret,* a 1972 Hollywood musical film set in Weimar-era Berlin. A joint German-French production, the 35 mm *Despair* was funded at six million marks, making it by far Fassbinder's most expensive project up to this time.

Although the film had a disappointing opening at Cannes in the spring of 1978, Fassbinder has ranked it among his best work.[1] It won three German Film Prizes in 1978—for direction, cinematography (Michael Ballhaus), and for Zehetbauer's set design. And it has come under substantial and sympathetic scrutiny from critics.[2] But for all the critical attention given *Despair,* surprisingly little notice has been taken of its personal relevance for the director, except for brief mention of the topic in two German reviews.[3] As suggested there, Fassbinder's adaptation of Nabokov's novel was for him a means of exploring deeply subjective issues in the midst of the most intense crisis of his life and of the Federal Republic. Taking considerable liberties with the screenplay (to the consternation of Tom Stoppard) and directing Dirk Bogarde in what many consider the most compelling performance of his career, Fassbinder transformed the protagonist of Nabokov's novel from a clever, perhaps mad, but in any case despicable, murderer-as-author into a largely sympathetic existential-absurdist hero driven insane largely by forces outside himself. He is another in a long line of imaginative self-projections by one of the most self-dramatizing auteurs in cinema history.

Writer's Block

Fassbinder began work on *Despair,* apparently, in the summer of 1976. Earlier that year he had told an interviewer that he was thinking of taking a trip, or going into psychotherapy, or writing a novel.[4] He told another that to remove himself from the "hysterical togetherness" of his life he would go away by himself to Paris or New York for six months to write the novel, which would be about a hypochondriac who recovers from apparent paralysis of his arm through intense self-analysis and probing of his memories. The director claimed that he saw the project as a means of examining his own life, particularly to find out whether he could work alone.[5] The working title was "Journey into the Interior of the Soul, or, Journey into the Interior of Fear."[6]

But Fassbinder did not go away that August, and the novel was never written. Instead, he stayed in Germany and started to write a film script about a person with a more subtle and more pervasive paralysis. It was to be based on Nabokov's *Despair,* 1937, a novel he had come across a few years earlier in a used-book-and-record store.[7] He seems to have read the book largely as a reflection of his distressed state of mind at the time; he described its subject as that "point [in everyone's life] when not only the mind but the body too understands that it's 'all over.'" He saw its protagonist, Hermann Karlovich, as someone who rejects the possibility of living "a life which consists only of repeats" but who, instead of committing suicide, "openly decides to go insane."[8] Fassbinder's personal identification with the novel's protagonist is elaborated in three brief quasi-philosophical texts he wrote about the time he was working on *Despair.*[9]

Perhaps his subjective investment in the novel made it difficult for Fassbinder to find the aesthetic distance he needed for turning it into a screenplay. In any case, he soon found it impossible to write anything that suited him. The book seemed to him "rather difficult and complicated to adapt to film." Hoping to avoid an excessively serious tone, and thinking that no German screenwriter would be able to "make something light and loose and funny" from such "tragic" material,[10] he turned to the British playwright Tom Stoppard—that master of absurdity and the three-level pun, who had recently worked on the script for Joseph Losey's film *The Romantic Englishwoman,* 1975.

Nabokov's *Despair:* Artist Manqué as Monster

Nabokov's novel is a highly reflexive and parodic first-person narrative purportedly written in 1931 by one Hermann Karlovich, an upper-class Russian with inflated pretensions as an author, who has been living for a decade in Berlin, where he owns a chocolate factory. The witty and haughty Hermann barely disguises the discomfort he feels in his present circumstances. His chocolate business is threatened by the Wall Street crash and by the tense politics of the late Weimar Republic. And he is tied to an empty-headed wife, Lydia, who stuffs herself with his chocolates and carries on under his nose a love affair with her indolent and self-satisfied cousin Ardalion, a painter of sorts. Presumably as a result of these conditions, Hermann has begun to experience psychic "dissociation" when he makes love to his wife, or contemplates it. But it appears that all his problems may be over when he discovers his apparent identical twin in the person of a tramp, Felix ("the happy one"). He insures his life, dresses Felix in his clothes, and murders him, planning to start a new life in the South with the insurance money and his wife (away from her cousin). There are two hitches, however. Hermann really does not resemble Felix; and Hermann has carelessly left Felix's walking stick, with his name engraved on the handle, at the scene of the murder. This evidence identifies the victim as well as the murderer, who is passing himself off as Felix. Thus Hermann's supposedly perfect crime, in which "the murderer is the victim," ends up a shambles.

Initially, the reader of *Despair* is likely to be won over by the literary sophistication of its protagonist-author. Hermann's story is a clever, teasing account of the recent and continuing events in his life, full of self-conscious allusions to, and pastiches of, nineteenth-and twentieth-century European writers—Aleksandr Pushkin, Charles Baudelaire, Walter Pater, Oscar Wilde, James Joyce, and especially Fyodor Dostoyevsky (whom he calls "Dusty"), among others.[11] Up to a point the reader is also led to empathize with Hermann as a victim of a peculiarly modernist neurosis, to sympathize with the consternation of this fine-tuned sensibility condemned to endure the banalities of the modern world, and even to share his superior laughter at the stupidity and vulgarity of the two people closest to him—his wife, Lydia, and her paramour cousin, Ardalion. However, the attentive reader whom Nabokov assumes here, as elsewhere in his fiction, soon becomes suspicious of Hermann's presentation of himself and begins to see him increasingly as an utterly unreliable narrator.[12] Early on, one suspects Hermann's sanity, given all his talk about "dissociations," as well as the nervous jerkiness of his style, his unexpected outbursts against the reader, and his obtuseness about Lydia's unfaithfulness to him, which is obvious to the reader. More important, it becomes increasingly clear from Felix's reactions that Hermann is quite mistaken about their being identical.

The reader gradually senses also that Hermann is a liar and that the truth about him consists largely in what he has distorted or suppressed. Hermann's most outrageous lie is the claim that his cold-blooded murder of Felix is the ultimate creative act of a supremely gifted artist, inspired by the miracle of his encounter with his double. In truth, the killing seems to be motivated by nothing more than Hermann's wish to escape his frustrations in Berlin and set up a new life with the insurance money in "a remote abode of work and pure delight," in the words from Pushkin he quotes to Lydia.[13] One begins to suspect, in fact, that Hermann is by no means insane, but rather a supremely clever liar and murderer trying to pass as a madman.

In any case, Hermann is a monstrous narcissist who appropriates those closest to him as instruments of his ego—his wife, Lydia, no less than his supposed double, Felix. And the "despair" he so dramatically announces for the title of his narrative[14] is inspired by nothing more profound than the discovery that his perfect crime has been spoiled by his absentmindedness. Like many another Nabokov novel, *Despair* is thus a morality tale disguised as parodic comedy. Nabokov himself suggests this quality of the novel in one of the comments in his ironic 1965 foreword that can probably be taken seriously. He asserts that both Hermann Karlovich and Humbert Humbert of his best-known novel, *Lolita* (1955), whom Hermann anticipates in important ways, are "neurotic scoundrels" who deserve to be damned, the author asserts. But while Humbert will be permitted to wander once a year in "a green lane in Paradise . . . Hell shall never parole Hermann."[15]

The Stoppard Screenplay: Straight Plotting, Absurdist Ironies

Fassbinder's film adaptation of *Despair* substantially transforms the narrative apparatus as well as the tone of Nabokov's novel, converting the increasingly suspect and finally abhorrent Hermann into a patiently suffering, basically decent if a bit supercilious man driven to madness before the viewer's eyes by forces outside his control—indeed, into the sort of person Hermann Karlovich seems to want the reader of his novel to believe that he is.

Stoppard's screenplay proved useful to the director in this process. It takes a basically sympathetic approach to Hermann as a prototypical victim of modernist angst, though this sympathy is qualified by an ironic touch that is often ambiguous about Hermann's moral character.[16] The script substantially alters the narrative structure of the novel—eliminating most of the impressionistic, erratic narration in the book, arranging the plot into a largely chronological account, and providing clear continuity for most episodes. It makes no pretense of carrying over from the novel the illusion of first-person narration, although some of Hermann's more memorable asides to the reader are turned into witty dialogue.

Stoppard initially imagined that Hermann and Felix would be played by the same actor, but Fassbinder dissuaded him.[17] He gave the role of Hermann to Dirk Bogarde and that of the supposed double to Klaus Löwitch—an actor who can hardly be mistaken for Dirk Bogarde, even cleaned up and dressed in Hermann's suit. Unlike the reader of the novel, then, the viewer of the film is clearly aware of Hermann's delusion from his first meeting with Felix, which occurs —significantly, in a hall of mirrors—about forty minutes into the film.[18] Because of Stoppard's straightforward plotting up to that point, this fateful meeting seems to be only one in a series of events beyond Hermann's control that have been driving him toward his tragic fate.

The increased sympathy for the protagonist that such restructuring of the plot generates is reinforced by the emphasis in the screenplay on the increasingly disturbed political situation—the looming Nazi threat—as a significant source of psychic pressure on Hermann. Political conditions in late-Weimar Berlin are scarcely mentioned in the novel, which, of course, did not have the benefit of postwar hindsight.[19] In the script, and even more in the film, they constitute a particularly ominous component of the environment threatening Hermann's sanity.

The author of *Rosencrantz and Guildenstern Are Dead* could hardly have been expected, however, to reduce Nabokov's clever, witty, reflexive novel into a traditional realistic film script. As Fassbinder apparently anticipated, the screenplay is written in Stoppard's characteristically ironic-absurdist style, if not merely "light and loose and funny." Stoppard changed the name of the protagonist from Hermann Karlovich to Hermann Hermann—recalling, for the knowing viewer, Humbert Humbert of *Lolita*. Moreover, the screenplay is rich in puns and other wordplay, some derived from the novel, many original, and it preserves some of the book's many literary allusions. Finally, although the screenplay eliminates the novel's substantial reflexivity as a written narrative-in-progress, it does include interesting analogues to the novel's literary self-consciousness in several instances of cinematic reflexivity. These include an episode in a movie theater where Hermann, Lydia, and Ardalion watch a silent crime melodrama; Hermann's repeated remark to a foreman in his factory (played by Armin Meier, who also plays the twin brother in the crime film) that he has seen him in the movies; Hermann's initial claim to Felix that he is a film actor in need of a double; and Hermann's imagined "coming-out" speech as a movie actor, at the end (all of these elements except the second are inspired by Nabokov's text). Thus, while the script Stoppard gave Fassbinder was relatively straightforward in structure, and more sympathetic to the protagonist than the novel, it was still a highly contrived and witty piece of writing that preserved and even enhanced many of the comic ironies of the literary original.

Screenplay to Film: Darker Ironies

Stoppard's screenplay seems to have served Fassbinder well as an instrument for transforming Nabokov's novel into a compelling psychodrama with complex historical resonances. Fassbinder told producer Peter Märthesheimer that he planned to "direct the film from just the script . . . very quickly and fast paced, something like a boulevard comedy." That is not at all what happened, however.[20] The director had already persuaded Stoppard to make some changes during their several script meetings.[21] And Bogarde, who was present at at least one of those meetings, guessed that Fassbinder had already made up his mind to take considerable liberties with whatever script emerged.[22] Fassbinder later indicated that this had in fact been his intention. "I tried to forget the script and return to the novel, which has that darkness and strangeness which wasn't in the script. . . . The better the material [in the script] the better chance there is of the director creating his own fantasies."[23]

The completed film largely follows the narrative structure of Stoppard's script. But Fassbinder added substantial dramatic material and visual effects, all of which display Hermann Hermann's existential angst a great deal more somberly than Stoppard had imagined. And he cut out a good bit of continuity material, as well as elements in the script not directly related to the protagonist's psychic crisis—mostly in the editing, it seems.[24] It is not clear how much of the filmed material was cut by the original editor, Reginald Beck (the favorite cutter of British director Joseph Losey, who had often worked on Bogarde films), and how much by Fassbinder and Juliane Lorenz, who edited the film after Beck left the project in July 1977. According to Lorenz, she and Fassbinder cut the film from two hours, forty-five minutes to slightly under two hours, in two stages—the second time against Fassbinder's better judgment, under strong pressure from the producers, Bavaria Studios.[25]

Much of the material that was cut from the scripted film must have seemed to distract from the intended concentration on Hermann's tormented consciousness. In addition, a lot of Stoppard's wordplay was left out.[26] A good bit of subplot material, most of it adapted by Stoppard from the novel, was also cut.[27] The most unfortunate casualty of the cutting room was the elimination of a conversation in a restaurant among Hermann, Ardalion (Volker Spengler), and

Ardalion's Russian artist friend, Perebrodov (Gottfried John), who in the completed film is barely glimpsed in a panning shot. The spectator thus can have little idea of Perebrodov's identity when he shows up later at Hermann's flat, hoping to sell him painted cigarette boxes, and hence cannot understand the significance of Hermann's hysterical laughter when he recognizes Perebrodov after mistaking him for Felix.

With distracting subplot elements removed and the major dramatic scenes stripped of conventional transitional material, the film leads the viewer to share in Hermann's deepening identity confusion and his increasingly insane obsession with his double as his means of escape from his private hell. Fassbinder enhanced this process by shooting a good bit of additional dramatic material, and through many complex visual effects not called for in the screenplay. Especially important for rendering the protagonist's divided consciousness are the mirrors and other reflective and opaque surfaces in the Hermanns' apartment, and the broken glass partitions in a shadowy restaurant where Hermann and Felix meet.

The choice of Dirk Bogarde to play the role of Hermann, to which Fassbinder and Stoppard agreed early on, was critical to the intense and sympathetic emphasis on Hermann's psychic torment in the film. Bogarde's previous screen personae, both as a dapper romantic lead in British comedies and in his recent roles as tormented victims of erotic love and modern history, respectively, in Visconti's *Death in Venice,* 1971, and *The Damned,* 1969, made him an obvious choice for the protagonist of *Despair.*[28] Time and again in Fassbinder's films, the camera lingers in close-up as Bogarde's expressive face registers painful emotions with the greatest subtlety. One recalls, for instance, his enigmatic gaze through his secretary's glass enclosure, recalling the house of mirrors in the preceding scene; his ironic glance in response to his wife's vacuous comments on contemporary politics; or his intent staring at the sleeping Felix in their hotel room after Felix has agreed to act as Hermann's double (instead of going to sleep himself, as the script called for).

Hermann's growing madness is also substantially augmented by frequent allusions in the film to the imminent Third Reich. It often seems as if Hermann is oppressed by the post-Holocaust significance of events in 1930–31. Some suggestions along these lines are made in the screenplay, but Fassbinder greatly expanded on them. Early in the film, for example, shortly after walking past an image of Hitler on a Nazi political poster in a chocolate factory in Homburg, Hermann stares at candy human figures piled alongside a conveyor belt, which resemble corpses in future newsreels showing Nazi concentration camps (the script emphasizes their resemblance to Hermann). Later, Hermann sits in an

Despair, 1977. Hermann Hermann (Dirk Bogarde), holding his life insurance policy, listens to his wife, Lydia (Andrea Ferréol), discuss politics with the insurance agent (Bernhard Wicki) in the Hermanns' art deco apartment. (Courtesy Museum of Modern Art/Film Stills Archive, New York)

outdoor restaurant, a canted shot indicating his disturbed mental state. As the script indicates, he witnesses a group of Nazi thugs throwing bricks at a Jewish shop. Fassbinder adds two elements to the scene that strengthen the suggestion that Hermann's madness is somehow implicated in the coming historical insanity: a dogcatcher locks the gate on his truck and drives away, the dogs looking anxiously through the wire grating as if they were Holocaust victims heading to their doom; and two Hasidic Jews play at chess, weirdly oblivious to the brick-throwing, as much of the world would later be to the Nazi murders of the Jews.

Finally, Fassbinder's treatment emphasizes, far more than the novel or the screenplay does, Hermann's frustrated erotic relationship with the wife. As in the book and the script, Fassbinder's Hermann frequently ridicules Lydia's stupidity and bad taste. But the film suggests an intensity in his sexual desire that is absent in those earlier versions of the story: he hides his face in Lydia's breasts after a nightmare, ogles her as she sprays her underarms, fantasizes her kissing his boots, and caresses her silk-clad thigh through leather gloves as she drives him to work. Who can say exactly why he strips her and throws her to the floor as he makes up the outrageous story of the supposed twin brother whom he must murder? Moreover, in the film, but not in the screenplay, it is clear that Hermann is deeply disturbed by Lydia's open flirtation with Ardalion—for example, in a long-held close-up shot when he enters his flat to find them together (the script calls for him to be in the flat with the two of them for this entire scene), or his ponderous look out a restaurant window into the snow after a conversation with Lydia and Ardalion that reminds him of their intimacy.

Denouement: Hermann in Hell

Fassbinder's radical departure from Nabokov's novel in his conception and presentation of Hermann is most obvious in the concluding sequence of the film, which is based on the final chapter of the novel. Nabokov's Hermann Karlovich had not intended to write that eleventh chapter of his book; chapter ten was to be the conclusion of his tale of the perfect crime as a perfect work of art, which he had begun writing a week earlier "to explain to the world all the depth of my masterpiece."[29] But Hermann abruptly breaks off the chapter and begins another, for he has just read in a newspaper that the police have found an object that can identify the victim, and, therefore, the murderer who has assumed his identity. Impossible, Hermann tells the reader. Nevertheless, he goes back through his manuscript to see if he can find a clue. He spots it in his mention of Felix's walking stick, left at the scene of the murder. The disastrous truth is instantly clear. "The whole of [his] masterpiece" has been destroyed through "a blunder . . . of the very grossest, drollest, tritest nature" on his part.[30] "I smiled the smile of the condemned," he writes (in language straining hard, but unsuccessfully now, to carry the reader with it), "and in a blunt pencil that screamed with pain wrote swiftly and boldly on the first page of my work, 'Despair.'"[31] In a daze, Hermann goes to pick up his mail, which he regrets, since he finds there a letter from his wife's cousin and paramour, Ardalion, that condemns him for his murder of Felix and his mistreatment of Lydia. Ardalion calls him "a blackguard and bully" who never cared for anyone else, "a great grisly wild boar with putrid tusks."[32] For all its grotesque overstatement, this is a condemnation that the attentive reader is prepared by this point in the novel to accept as essentially true.

The final pages of Nabokov's novel take the form of a moment-by-moment diary as Hermann waits in his hotel room for the inevitable arrival of the police, looking down at the crowd beginning to gather outside the hotel. He concludes his story by contemplating the possibility of escaping after making "a little speech" through the window, advising the crowd below that "a famous film actor" who is playing an "arch-criminal" in a German film will now leave the hotel. "You are asked to prevent [the police] from grabbing him. This is part of the plot. . . . I want a clean getaway. That's all. Thank you. I'm coming out now."[33] In its irony and subtle reflexivity, this final paragraph of Hermann's narrative is amusing, to be sure. But it is also the last pathetic gesture of a morally repulsive character.[34]

In contrast, the final sequence of Fassbinder's film brings the story of his long-suffering protagonist to what can only be called a tragic conclusion. Hermann Hermann is viewed here with reverential awe, as he completes his lonely and heroic "journey into the light" of an almost sublime madness. This attitude is consistent with Fassbinder's comment that Hermann's insanity is a sort of "utopia" that he has had "the courage to recognize and to open [him]self up to."[35] The full German title of the film (Despair—A Journey into the Light) is vividly reinforced in the lighting of this scene, both in the horizontal rays from the window shutters that seem to entrap Hermann as he lies in bed at first and in the blinding light he blinks at when he throws open the shutters. He stares in amazement at Ardalion, who absurdly turns up in the village to which Hermann has escaped, not to issue the novel's moralistic judgment on the protagonist but as a tormenting demon in Hermann Hermann's private Inferno, as Hermann recalls his devilish laughter from an earlier scene.[36]

Hermann gazes in silence. In this somber treatment of the hero in extremis, Fassbinder ruled out the suggestion in Stoppard's screenplay of loud, anguished screams. The only sound in the room is the quiet drip of water onto a broken dish (recalling a close-up of broken eggshells in the opening shot of the film) in front of a cracked mirror, imaging Hermann's psychic disintegration and the relentless pressure of external forces on him. Fassbinder also discards Stoppard's idea of having Hermann shout his "coming out" speech from the window. Rather, he speaks his last mad fantasy quietly to his captors as he leaves his lodgings. Bogarde's tone of voice, his tearful eyes, and his wan smile invite the viewer to interpret the complex cinematic reflexivity of his final words—"I'm coming out now. Don't look at the camera. I'm coming out"—with an utterly sympathetic understanding of the tragic absurdity of Hermann's life, of the extent to which for him "not only the mind but the body too understands that it's 'all over,'" to use Fassbinder's formula for the theme of the film. Thus, Fassbinder's

Hermann Hermann may be said, without too much exaggeration, to have fulfilled the ironic forecast Nabokov made in the 1965 foreword to the novel that
someday someone would claim his Hermann as "the father of existentialism."[37]

Fassbinder's somber treatment of Hermann was altogether different from
what Stoppard had in mind when he scripted what he considered his "first real
film . . . part of my real output like the plays," as he wrote Bogarde (10 December 1977):

> Clearly Rainer and I were after two completely different things. This is true
> from the first words, where my lighthearted compendium of Russian clichés
> (wolves, samovars etc) was spoken without apparent irony to the last [the
> final scene, when the protagonist answers the police officer who comes into
> his room asking, "Hermann Hermann?"] where my "Yes and no" came out
> as "Yes (immense tragic pause) No." . . . . The crux of it is that I wanted to
> write the script because it was Nabokov's book, and Fassbinder wanted to
> film the story *despite* its being Nabokov's book.[38]

It is hard to imagine Fassbinder making a film of the sort Stoppard had in
mind at this point in his career. In any case, as has been seen, he certainly did
not undertake his adaptation of *Despair* in the spirit of cool, detached irony.
The Hermann Hermann that emerges from his transformation of Stoppard's
script seems clearly to be an imaginative projection of the director's subjective
state at a time of intense crisis in his personal and public lives. Fassbinder, in
his mid-1970s Purgatory, seems to have fantasized here a tragic Hermann
Hermann as a kind of double of himself: a divided persona who hides his inner
vulnerability behind a sardonic wit, self-conscious stylization, and cruelty to
others; who is both fascinated and disturbed by the presence of his doppelgänger
(one recalls particularly his ambivalence at the time over Armin Meier, who
plays a fascinating double role as twin brothers in a film within this film); who
is stirred by erotic longings even while feeling betrayed and keeping up the
pretense of insouciance; and who is oppressed by ominous and apparently ines-
capable historical forces over which he had no control.[39]

Asked by interviewers how *Despair* could be a real German film, given its
screenplay by a British playwright, Fassbinder responded that he had made
"quite clear" stipulations about it. He added: "Germany of 1930 is not so strange
to me. And the situation this man experiences is not so strange to me. What I
really wanted to do was to film my needs and my impulses."[40] As in two other
adaptations of major novels discussed in later chapters—his subjective treatment of Alfred Döblin's *Berlin Alexanderplatz* (the novel he said enabled him

to accept his homosexuality) and his highly ritualized reworking of Jean Genet's *Querelle*—Fassbinder turned Nabokov's novel to his own quite personal artistic purposes. In the process, he disregarded a great deal in the light, ironic script he hired Tom Stoppard to write for him, creating during the shooting and editing of the film precisely those heavy and intensely introspective effects he had feared a German scriptwriter would produce.

A major ingredient in Fassbinder's intensely personal interpretation of Nabokov's novel was the close, if largely unspoken, relationship he developed with Dirk Bogarde, who seems to have served at this time as one of the more significant father figures in his life. On the last day of shooting Fassbinder told an interviewer that his work with Bogarde had been a "very strong" help in his artistic development. In the final three days, particularly, "things happened to me that really no one else could have made possible."[41] That evening, Fassbinder slipped a handwritten note under Bogarde's door. In halting English, he expressed his gratitude for the opportunity of working with the older man, from whom he thought he had at last learned how to assert "authority without fear." He apologized for not being able to "speak about the things, which happen in my head." "More than likely there is more despair than anything else. But . . . life is timeless and end is endless." And he emphasized what an intensely personal undertaking their collaboration had been for him (as the other evidence adduced here makes clear): "I thank you for the Hermann you made possible for me, and I hope, it will be *our* Hermann like his madness is a little bit our madness."[42]

Notes

1. *Anarchy* 10.
2. Of particular interest is Elsaesser's "Murder, Merger, Suicide," which argues among other things that the complex cinematic codes of *Despair* constitute a "critique of realist narrative and didactic fiction," including Fassbinder's own melodrama of the early 1970s (41).
3. Pflaum, "Reise ins Land des Wahnsinns"; Schütte, "Ich—was ist das?"
4. Müller Int 186.
5. Schütte Int 77–79.
6. Zwerenz 104.
7. Fassbinder said in 1977 that when he had first seen a copy of *Despair* four years earlier he wondered why he had not already known of it, bought it for 50 *Pfennige,* and immediately decided to base a film on it (Jauch Int 27). Elsewhere, he claimed that he found the title *Verzweiflung* (despair) "a nice word, since I can identify with it, and I

really like Nabokov" ("Ponkie" Int). Nabokov's novel was first written in Russian and published in 1934. In 1937 he published his own translation of the novel into English, which he substantially revised for a new edition in 1965—serialized in *Playboy* (December–February 1965–66) and published in book form by Putnam (1965). The first German edition of the novel appeared in 1972. Stoppard has confirmed in a letter to the author that his script was based on the 1965 G. P. Putnam edition (London). The edition cited here is a reprint of that edition (New York: Viking Penguin, 1981).

8. Thomsen Int 99.

9. *Anarchy* 173–76.

10. Jauch Int.

11. Many of these allusions are identified in Stuart, 116.

12. On Nabokov's assumed reader, see Stuart 49–50.

13. Nabokov translates the Pushkin quotation in his 1965 foreword (11).

14. Nabokov 169.

15. Ibid. 11. Seymour Chatman argues that Humbert Humbert of *Lolita,* for all his unsavoriness, his sarcasm, and his admitted errors, is "reliable": "we feel that he is doing his best to tell us what in fact happened" (*Story and Discourse* 234). Just the opposite is true of Herman Karlovich.

16. This analysis of Stoppard's script is based on two largely complete shooting scripts used during the filming by assistant director Harry Baer. One is in English; the other is a German translation.

17. Stoppard-Bogarde Letters, 1 November 1976 and 9 March 1977; Thomsen Int 99.

18. Hermann encounters Felix on the fourth page of the novel (16).

19. In his 1965 revision of the novel, Nabokov included many additional hints about Hermann's madness, increased the sexual explicitness, and added Hermann's imagined "coming out" speech at the end, noted below (among other changes); but he refrained from reinterpreting the political events of the late Weimar period from a postwar perspective (Grayson 61–82).

20. Märthesheimer wrote that he could "see what Fassbinder was up to at night after the first day of shooting" ("Letter to the Editor" 188; this is also the source of the previous quotation).

21. Thomsen Int 99.

22. Bogarde describes a script-revision session at his home in the French countryside. "Mr. Stoppard feverishly re-wrote passages and then read them, eagerly, aloud, while Fassbinder shrugged from time to time, showing a marked indifference to what was going on." After half an hour Bogarde realized that Fassbinder "would make his *own* version of 'Despair,' when the time came, and do exactly what he wanted. Which is precisely what he did." (*Orderly Man* 259).

23. Thomsen Int 99–100. According to Stoppard, Fassbinder ignored a number of changes the screenwriter recommended in a letter he sent him in April 1977, about the time shooting began (Letter to Bogard, 10 December 1978).

24. The markings on Harry Baer's copy of the script suggest that virtually all of Stoppard's screenplay was shot.

25. The editing of *Despair* has a complex and somewhat confused history. Juliane Lorenz (coeditor of the film with Fassbinder) has given the following account of it in a letter to the author (1 September 1991), an interview with the author (10 June 1992), and in her interview with journalist Hans C. Blumenberg (30 May 1991, to be published in *Rainer Werner Fassbinder: Leben und Werk*): Reginald Beck made the first cut of *Despair* (to two hours, forty-five minutes) while the film was still being shot, with Lorenz as first assistant editor. One evening early in July 1977, Fassbinder saw part of this cut; not satisfied with its rhythm, he asked Lorenz to help him reedit the film to show to the producers the next day (Beck had not been willing to work in the editing room after 5:00 P.M.). Fassbinder and Lorenz worked all night at two editing tables, hardly speaking, but understanding each other very well. By 10:00 A.M. the next day they had recut the film, shortening it to about two hours, fifteen minutes. ("It was one of the most exciting nights I have ever spent in a cutting room. . . . That night I learned what it means 'to be an editor'!") The next morning, Beck (who had told Lorenz that he was not impressed with Fassbinder's work as a director) saw what had happened and left the project voluntarily. When the producers brought up the need to hire a new editor, Fassbinder replied that Lorenz would take over the job. Later that month, the producers insisted that the film be cut another twenty minutes, threatening to cut off further funding of Fassbinder projects if he didn't cooperate. Fassbinder reluctantly agreed. "We found a way to cut it without changing the structure." Cuts made during those editing sessions in July included a conversation among Hermann, Ardalion, and the Russian painter Perebrodov in the Russian restaurant scene; material from some other interior scenes and from a sequence at the train station (the sequence—in which, according to the script, Hermann and Lydia say goodbye to a drunken Ardalion, brought to the station by Perebrodov, as he leaves on his journey to Switzerland); some "atmosphere shots"; and a scene in which Lydia makes love to Klaus Löwitch (Felix), thinking he is Hermann. Lorenz wrote that Fassbinder wanted to restore the later cuts and reissue the film. She said that she hopes to do so herself.

Lorenz disputes Dirk Bogarde's assertion that Fassbinder mutilated the film between the time he saw a black-and-white print in Paris at a dubbing session, in September 13, 1977, and its premiere at Cannes the following May (Letter to the author, 21 May 1991). Bogarde wrote Fassbinder on September 24, 1977 that he had done "a fantastic job with the editing. God knows what it would have been like if it had been left to Reggie Beck . . . who is brilliant for some people but not for you" (Watson "Bitter Tears" 27). But he thought the print shown in Canes was "a mess." "Scenes were transposed, cut, eliminated, and all, or nearly all, of Andrea [Ferréol]'s performance [as Lydia] was ruined. The comedy, and there had been valuable comedy, had gone. So too had many other splendid 'set pieces'. I was pretty shattered. . . . Having witnessed the ruin of what had been, in my opinion, my very best performance, I left the screen for 13 years. (Letter to the author, 21 May 1991). However, Lorenz has insisted that Bogarde could have seen in

Paris only the final cut of the film—in black and white, and without music and some other effects—and that it was never cut further after the end of July 1977 (Let 1 Sept. 1991).

Credit given to Reginald Beck (misspelled "Bech") for additional editing "for the American version" of *Despair* in several editions of Jansen and Schütte was dropped in the most recent edition. According to Lorenz, there was no additional editing of the film for its American distribution (Let 1 Sept. 1991).

26. Bogarde wrote that Stoppard's puns "meant absolutely zilch" to Fassbinder, and he had to explain them in detail: "No easy matter. He would consider in silence, sucking on his moustache, and then say, 'It's schoolboy stuff, right?' and throw them out. . . . If anything in the script became too complicated he'd say 'Another Stoppard "pun." God! The English!'" (Letter 5 February 1991).

27. These excisions include Felix's theft of Hermann's silver pen; a scene at the public library, where muddle-headed Lydia goes to find a phone number she has scribbled in a book; and much business with Ardalion. Stoppard wrote that he was interested in adding to the script "something for Ardalion," since "there is some unease about the way Ardalion is introduced as an important character and is then allowed to drift out of the story," and that Fassbinder did not object (Letter to Bogarde 1 November 1976).

28. Amy Lawrence's paper makes clear the appropriateness of Bogarde for his role in *Despair*. Stoppard wrote that both he and Fassbinder wanted Bogarde for the part (Letter to Bogarde 17 December 1976). Bogarde recalled Stoppard calling to inquire if he would be interested, understanding that he was not making any more films. Bogarde answered, "I'm not making any more crap," and thought, "Stoppard, Nabokov, Fassbinder. . . . Not a bad package . . . . The old surge of excitement welled up again: after all it *was* my job, and those three names were not easily dismissed. . . . The fascination of working with Fassbinder was overwhelming" (*Orderly Man* 248).

29. Nabokov, 159–62.

30. Ibid. 169.

31. Ibid. 169.

32. Ibid. 171.

33. Ibid. 176.

34. Surprisingly, several Nabokov critics have written that Hermann actually makes this speech; he only considers it.

35. *Anarchy* 176. Fassbinder said that in *Despair* he was seeking not only to express his own "need to come closer to a utopia" but also to inspire viewers to begin to look for their own (Jauch Int 27).

36. That earlier scene took place in the Russian restaurant, in which one wall was painted (presumably by Ardalion) with a mural of a scene very similar to the one Ardalion is now painting again. Part of Hermann's present horror presumably consists in the recognition that he has unknowingly made his way to this very spot.

37. Nabokov 10.

38. While admitting that the film had some "secondary virtues" ("decor, camerawork,

composition of frames") Stoppard wrote in this 10 December 1977 letter to Bogarde that he found the film "boring, slow, pretentious, humourless and difficult to comprehend." He said he had urged Fassbinder "to keep the playing light, dry and quick," and warned him that playing it "weightily with introspective pauses, etc." would be "disastrous as well as excessive in length," requiring cutting "at the expense of its shape and clarity."

39. On Armin Meier's roles in the film, see chapter 5, n. 10.

40. Jauch Int.

41. Jauch Int.

42. Watson, "Bitter Tears" 27.

CHAPTER NINE

The "Women's Picture" as History

Fassbinder credited his stepfather, the politically liberal journalist Wolff Eder, with first helping him to understand the continuity of modern Germany's problematic history, particularly the deep roots of Nazism. He complained about the West Germans' repression of their recent history, particularly filmmakers' avoidance of the Holocaust as a subject. He noted in 1982 that "only recently has anyone begun to explore in film the stories of any German Jews during the war. . . . The average German prefers not to remember."[1] Furthermore, although he sympathized with the revolutionary utopianism of those members of his generation who had turned their political disillusionment to terrorism, he criticized their impatience and lack of historical consciousness: "They thought the revolution must happen tomorrow and because it hasn't they've flipped out. You have to reckon in centuries, but they thought only in decades."[2] Fassbinder said that his generation in particular had "learned so little about German history that we . . . have to do quite of bit of catching up on basic information."[3]

Fassbinder's interest in the political and cultural history of his homeland showed itself in many of the projects previously discussed. *Effi Briest* makes clear how the social codes of late-nineteenth-century Prussia oppressed even the members of its most privileged class. His planned adaptation of Gustav Freytag's novel *Debit and Credit* would have emphasized the roots of fascism in mid-nineteenth-century Germany. Political tensions in the immediate pre-Nazi period lend an ominous aura to *Despair*. The conditions of everyday life in the early Federal Republic are documented in many of the early films. The revolutionary fervor of the late 1960s is portrayed in *Die Niklashauser Fart*. And the more recent political history of the Federal Republic is depicted in *Mother Küsters Goes to Heaven* and *The Third Generation*.

This chapter focuses on five films of Fassbinder's final period which, taken together, constitute a sustained effort to come to terms with the history of Weimar-era and wartime Germany and of the Federal Republic. But Fassbinder was not seeking here to make "historical" films in the ordinary sense of the term; his aim was more personal. As he said in 1974, he was interested in what he could understand from history "about my possibilities and impossibilities, my hopes and utopian dreams."[4] Appropriately enough, he employed the genre of the melodramatic "women's picture" as the vehicle of these personalized historical-cultural explorations.

The earliest of these films, both in its historical setting and its time of production, is *Bolwieser, 1976–77* (*The Stationmaster's Wife*), which takes place late in the Weimar Republic era. *Lili Marleen,* 1980, is set primarily during World War II. Fassbinder designated the other three films his "BRD Trilogy," referring to the Bundesrepublik Deutschland (Federal Republic of Germany). *Die Ehe der Maria Braun,* 1978 (*The Marriage of Maria Braun*) begins in 1943, during the war, but quickly shifts to the immediate postwar period, ending on 4 July 1954. *Die Sehnsucht der Veronika Voss,* 1982 (*Veronika Voss*) covers several weeks in 1955, ending on Easter Sunday; *Lola,* 1981, is set in 1957 and 1958. (The five films are discussed below in the order of their making, not of the historical periods they depict.)

As several critics have suggested, these five films can be seen as attempts to deal with the terrorist crisis of the late 1970s—in a less direct way than in *The Third Generation.* That is, they are investigations into the historical sources of both the despair of the idealist revolutionaries-turned-terrorists and the government's authoritarian reaction against the terrorists and those who sympathized with them. In setting these historical investigations within the framework of the traditional women's melodrama, in which even the most assertive women are usually subdued by the powers of patriarchal society, Fassbinder seems to some critics to have been making a gesture of political despair, born of "left-wing melancholy," over the direction of West German politics in the late 1970s and the early 1980s. Ann Kaplan, for example, argues that *Lola* and *Veronika Voss* "reflect an increasing cynicism about German society . . . as if [Fassbinder] had lost the sense of dialectical movement."[5]

The Stationmaster's Wife (1976–77)

Set in a small town in Bavaria in the 1920s, *Bolwieser* (*The Stationmaster's Wife*) tells the story of an officious railroad-station manager and the wife who dominates and cuckolds him. Beyond this private melodrama, the film bears historical significance as a realistic portrayal of German life shortly before the onset of the Nazi era. At 1.8 million DM, this was Fassbinder's most costly project to date. It was produced by Bavaria Studios for the ZDF television network, shot on 16 mm film late in 1976, and first broadcast the following July as a two-part television series, running 201 minutes. After the television version was completed, Fassbinder cut a 112-minute theatrical version of the film, which was blown up to 35 mm wide-screen format and given theatrical release on the first anniversary of his death.[6]

The film is based on a 1931 novel, *Bolwieser: Roman eines Ehemannes* (Bolwieser: The Novel of a Husband), by the Bavarian writer Oskar Maria Graf (1894–1967). Wilhelm Roth notes that the longer television version is faithful to the novel, presenting detailed portraits of "a gallery of George Grosz-like German philistines of the Bavarian variety" alongside the narrative of the stationmaster and his wife, while the theatrical version focuses on the Bolwiesers' relationship.[7] Both versions sympathetically present the husband, Xaver Bolwieser, as a variation of the Franz Biberkopf type: betrayed, abused, and finally beaten down. He is played effectively by Kurt Raab, once again cast as a dependent, self-pitying masochist, in his final Fassbinder role. In his position as a railway stationmaster, Bolwieser is at first impressive in his military-looking uniform, and he commands the respect of his subordinates. But his stature is increasingly undermined through his dependence on his wife, Hanni (Elisabeth Trissenaar), whom he cannot satisfy sexually. She betrays him in love affairs with two townsmen, in whose businesses she invests her own money. To put a stop to rumors about her first affair, Hanni and her lover Merkl (Bernard Helfrich), a handsome butcher, file a slander suit; they win it, partly on the basis of Bolwieser's false testimony. When Hanni abandons Merkl for her hairdresser, Schafftaler (Udo Kier), the jealous Merkl successfully sues Xaver Bolwieser for perjury in the slander trial, and the hapless husband is sentenced to four years in prison, during which he agrees to Hanni's petition for divorce.

Bolwieser's plight at the end, after his release from prison, is presented poignantly in both versions. In the television version he emerges a broken man and wanders the countryside, eventually going to work for an old ferryman (Gerhard Zwerenz), whose place he takes after the old man's death. The closing credits appear over a long-held shot of a lovely winter landscape as the former stationmaster ferries two passengers across the partially frozen river.[8] The less sentimental theatrical version eliminates this "reconciliation between [Bolwieser] and nature."[9] In its concluding shot Bolwieser, after agreeing to his wife's request for a divorce, is escorted through a long dreary hallway back to his cell, into which he gradually disappears.

In spite of the film's considerable attention to Xaver Bolwieser's pathetic story, the viewer is also led to empathize substantially with his wife, Hanni, who is perhaps the most independent of all the female protagonists of Fassbinder's historical melodramas.[10] Hanni's control over her fate is suggested with particular force in one highly choreographed scene, in which her smiling face, seen in a classic profile, fills the right side of the frame, while she watches

The Stationmaster's Wife, 1976. The stationmaster Xaver Bolwieser (Kurt Raab) tries to make contact with his wife, Hanni (Elisabeth Trissenaar). (By permission of New Yorker Films, courtesy Museum of Modern Art/Film Stills Archive, New York)

the suave Merkl wield a phallic cue stick as he defeats her husband in a game of billiards. Hanni's future after her easy divorce from Xaver—as one can imagine it on the basis of what the film shows of her—looks promising. She seems to have the capacity to rise above the level of the small-town paramours and provincial mores that have limited her life up to now.

The Stationmaster's Wife is a specifically rendered period piece which, as John Sandford writes, "evokes perfectly the atmosphere of provincial life in pre-war Bavaria."[11] Moreover, in lording it over his inferiors at the train station like a martinet, Bolwieser represents the type of the authoritarian petty official who would soon find a place in the Nazi bureaucracy or armed forces. His fall from a position of responsibility within the quasi-military railroad system is marked by his exchange of the imposing stationmaster's uniform for nondescript prison garb. Near the end of the film a swastika is glimpsed, and Bolwieser's jealous, snooping, subordinate at the station is already wearing an S.A. uniform.

BRD 1: The Marriage of Maria Braun (1978)

The historical implications are emphasized more pointedly, and the assertive female character is put into a more central role, in the second of Fassbinder's "women's history" films, Die Ehe der Maria Braun (The Marriage of Maria Braun), though Maria Braun does not fare as well in the end as what can be imagined for Hanni Bolwieser. This first part of Fassbinder's "BRD trilogy" depicts the successful business career of a clever, attractive, and strong-willed West German woman during the years immediately after World War II. It is both a moving personal melodrama and a parable of the postwar West German Economic Miracle, combining Hollywood-style melodrama on the theme of a tough but vulnerable woman making it in a man's world with an implied critical commentary on that world.

Maria Braun was one of Fassbinder's most successful films. It won him popular and critical acclaim both in West Germany and abroad, establishing him as a major figure on the international film scene. While his big-budget international collaboration Despair was unenthusiastically received at the Cannes Film Festival in May 1978, Fassbinder's private screening of Maria Braun there was a stunning success.[12] The movie was quickly sold for distribution in the United States, where it was the final attraction at the New York Film Festival in 1979 and ran for more than a year at its first-run house. In West Germany the film opened in March 1979, just after the weekly magazine Stern had begun running a serialized novelistic version of the movie written by Gerhard Zwerenz and illustrated with photographs from the film—a marketing strategy that perhaps contributed to the considerable commercial success of the movie in West Germany.[13] Audiences were enthusiastic, and critics praised Fassbinder's return to "realism" and "humanism" after the "self-centered eccentricity" of Satan's Brew and In a Year of 13 Moons and "the self-consciously 'artistic' trappings" of Chinese Roulette and Despair.[14] In the 1979 German Film Prize competition Maria Braun received a Silver Band and won awards for direction, acting (Hanna Schygulla and Gisela Uhlen), and set design (Norbert Scherer and Helga Ballhaus). At the Berlin Film Festival that year the film won the second-place

Silver Bear, and Hanna Schygulla won the best-actress award for her leading role after her four-year absence from Fassbinder's entourage.

Fassbinder had abruptly undertaken the production of *Maria Braun* during a five-month break before the scheduled start of shooting for *Berlin Alexanderplatz*. Harry Baer says that *Maria Braun* was begun under the most "unfavorable and chaotic omens" of any Fassbinder film; he reports that *Alexanderplatz* producer Michael Fengler objected to the director's dissipating his efforts on what seemed such a minor project. Moreover, according to Baer, Fassbinder was taking "more stimulants than were good for him or the work," and the atmosphere surrounding the production was "at point zero." Juliane Lorenz attributes much of the blame for Fassbinder's difficulties at this time to Fengler.[15] However the blame for this turmoil should be assigned, its intensity makes it all the more remarkable that *Maria Braun,* filmed during thirty-five days from January to March 1978, should have turned out to be such a brilliant artistic and popular success. (Fengler's Albatross Productions did coproduce the film—a 35 mm wide-screen project budgeted at slightly under two million marks—along with the WDR television network and another German company, Trio-Films.)

Fassbinder had dictated a treatment for the film under the title "Die Ehren unserer Eltern" (The Marriages of Our Parents) that would have resulted in a picture eight hours long. He turned this treatment over for rewriting to Peter Märthesheimer, an editor at Bavaria Studios with whom he had worked on previous projects, and Pea Fröhlich, a psychologist.[16] They reduced it to a screenplay of approximately two hours, which Fassbinder approved, praising them for giving him "a dramatic concept or corset which doesn't constrict but rather frees me."[17]

The marriage of Maria Braun is an unusual one, to say the least. Barely consummated, it consists primarily in separation. In the complex opening sequence of the film an exploding Allied bomb interrupts the wedding of a young German woman, Maria (Hanna Schygulla), and a German soldier, Hermann Braun (Klaus Löwitsch), in a marriage registry office. In the tumult of flying papers, antiaircraft fire, and crying babies that follows, the couple manages to get the marriage certificate stamped and signed. The next day Hermann is shipped off to the Eastern Front. After the war Maria waits in vain for Hermann's return and eventually engages in a love affair with a black American soldier, Bill (George Byrd), by whom she becomes pregnant. When Hermann does return he surprises Maria and Bill in their bedroom, and in the ensuing scuffle between the two men Maria unintentionally kills Bill when she hits him over the head with a bottle. Hermann assumes the blame, however, and goes to prison for the killing. After having miscarried her child, Maria meets Oswald (Ivan

210

Desny), a French industrialist working in Germany, who hires her as his private secretary and soon promotes her to a major management position in the firm. Oswald falls in love with Maria, and she begins sleeping with him, but she always keeps her emotional distance, reminding him, as she had Bill, that her heart belongs to her absent husband.

Maria's growing material success is revealed through her stylish clothes and the large home that she purchases. But her good fortune is accompanied by increasing loneliness and problems in her relationships with her mother and with Oswald, who, unknown to her, is suffering from a fatal liver disease. Oswald secretly signs a contract with Hermann in prison, promising to leave him a large share of his estate if Hermann will leave the country after his release from prison, allowing Oswald to have Maria as his own until his death. After Oswald dies, Hermann returns. In the closing minutes of the film, Maria excitedly prepares for a long-delayed night of love with her husband, as he listens passively to a radio broadcast of the 1954 world soccer championship game between West Germany and Hungary. They are interrupted by Oswald's accountant, Senkenberg (Hark Bohm) and a female notary (Christine Hopf de Loup), who reads the dead man's will, revealing to Maria for the first time the extent to which her life has been controlled by her husband and her lover. Shortly thereafter, Maria lights a cigarette after having left open a gas jet on the kitchen

The Marriage of Maria Braun, 1978. Maria (Hanna Schygulla) tries to arouse her husband (Klaus Löwitsch). (By permission of New Yorker Films, courtesy of the Museum of Modern Art/Film Stills Archive, New York)

stove, and the film ends with a violent explosion that destroys Maria's house along with (presumably) both Maria and Hermann. As a French critic has written, this is "one of the best endings in cinema: a film which comes to an end because *everything blows up.*"[18] Whether the explosion was accidental or intended is up to the viewer to decide.

At one level *Maria Braun* can be read as an extension of Fassbinder's earlier work in the tradition of the melodramatic "women's picture." Like many of its Hollywood antecedents—but in a distinctly West German setting—the film dramatizes the short-lived success of a self-sufficient woman who moves into traditionally male roles and is eventually victimized by male hegemony and by the romantic ideology of love and marriage. A quick succession of scenes early in the film shows Maria's rise from the position of a wife helplessly waiting for the return of her husband (carrying a sign with his picture on her back) amid the rubble of war to that of an assertive and successful manager in an international business firm. By standing up to an American soldier who has made a joke at her expense she gets two packs of cigarettes, which she exchanges for a piece of her mother's jewelry, which she trades for a black dress, which gets her work as a dance hostess at a bar catering to American soldiers, where she takes up with Bill, from whom she learns English. She quickly masters the language of the victorious nation that is beginning to assert such economic and cultural power over her homeland. This ability allows her to impress the non-English-speaking Oswald, at the time of their first encounter on a train, by putting down an American soldier (Günther Kaufmann) who has insulted them. Shortly thereafter she secures a major position in Oswald's firm by negotiating a deal with some American businessmen.

The personal unhappiness that accompanies Maria's business success is emphasized in several sequences rich in melodramatic style. There are several arguments with her unpretentious mother (Gisela Uhlen), who is happily living with her genial and apparently ne'er-do-well lover, Wetzel (Günther Lamprecht). By contrast, Maria's affection for Oswald modulates into an almost sadistic pleasure in tormenting him.[19] Her isolation and anomie are graphically suggested in juxtaposed sequences near the end of the film, after Oswald's death. In the first, set in an elegant restaurant with wood paneling and stained-glass windows, Maria sits alone at a large table attended by an entourage of stiff waiters, who comically come to life when she gets up and vomits against a wall. The camera then tracks backward to show a couple in the foreground in an erotic embrace, a surreal reminder of what Maria has been missing. The following shot reveals Maria in her new house, still wearing the hat she had on in the restaurant, in a drunken stupor at a table cluttered with empty bottles and glasses.

She is only momentarily aroused from this despondency by the unexpected return of her husband, Hermann, which is followed quickly by the reading of Oswald's will and her resulting disillusionment.

The private melodrama of Maria Braun evokes pointedly public themes. From the portrait of Hitler that is blown apart in the opening shot to the sequence of postwar West German chancellors under the final credits, the film insistently reminds the viewer of its changing historical contexts.[20] This effect is accomplished in large part through the historical accuracy of the sets and changing hair and dress styles, and in such realistic details as the Germans' desperate need for firewood and the smokers' craving for cigarettes after the war. Historical verisimilitude is also achieved in the complex sound track, especially the ever-present radio broadcasts: the monotonous reading of names of missing persons, classical symphonies and American swing-band music, contradictory speeches by Chancellor Adenauer on German rearmament, and the conclusion of West Germany's first world championship in soccer. Another notable aural motif is the increasingly obvious and grating sound of jackhammers (recalling the antiaircraft guns of the opening sequence) as the new Germany rebuilds itself from the ruins of the Third Reich.

The film works particularly as a parable of the West German Economic Miracle as seen by its leftist critics. In this interpretation Maria's professional success, exploitation of her relationships with men, and separation from her mother symbolize the new nation's ruthless pursuit of economic prosperity and neglect of its important socialist tradition, in cooperation with hegemonic American capitalism and Cold War militarism—all the while repressing its recent Nazi past. A comment on the film by Fassbinder reinforces a reading of the film as an allegory of West German moral irresponsibility and prostitution of its professed values: "Is Germany any different? Some in Germany believe that because of our defeat in the war we are redeemed, and that old cruelties cannot happen again, that now we are rich and happy, and we have America to protect us, so when something goes wrong, it is America's fault, not ours. Maria Braun knows success comes faster to the one who prostitutes herself or himself."[21]

Stylistically, *The Marriage of Maria Braun* maintains an effective balance between Hollywood realism and cinematic mannerism. There are plenty of self-conscious mirror shots, along with unusual camera placements and movements and expressionistic lighting. Their total effect, as Anton Kaes has argued, is to keep the discerning viewer from simple identification with the narrative as factual history, to emphasize the nature of the film as a fictional construction of the past, undertaken as a means of understanding the historical conditions of West Germany in the late 1970s.[22] But these stylized effects are used much more subtly in *Maria Braun* than in such recent Fassbinder films as *Chinese Roulette* and *Despair*—or in the avant-garde work of many of his fellow New German Filmmakers. As Kaes observes, *Maria Braun* is "a far cry from the digressive post-modernist filmic discourse of such contemporaries as Kluge, Syberberg, and Schroeter. Fassbinder likes to tell a good story."[23]

Fassbinder's ability to blend private with public themes, and realism with stylization, is well illustrated in the complex final scene of *The Marriage of Maria Braun*. The last seven minutes of the lives of Maria and Hermann Brown converge here with the last seven minutes of Herbert Zimmermann's famous broadcast of the West Germans' victory over Hungary in the July 1954 soccer world championship, which seemed to many to solidify the Federal Republic's place among the postwar world powers. At the level of private melodrama, Fassbinder's ending is much more ambiguous than what the script suggested, never making clear whether the explosion that ends Maria's marriage was intentional or not and, if it was intentional, what her motives might have been in striking the fatal match. The screenplay called for Maria to kill herself and Hermann by driving her car off a cliff in a gesture of desperation (recalling the conclusion of François Truffaut's 1962 film *Jules and Jim*). In writing this ending, the scriptwriters were going along with what they understood to be Fassbinder's conception of Maria's motives at this point. The protagonist was consciously ending her own and Hermann's lives, Peter Märthesheimer said, both because of Hermann's contract with Oswald and because Maria realizes, now that she is actually with Hermann, "that her idea of love didn't correspond with the reality of this love."[24]

In the film, Maria's motives are not nearly so clear as that. Early in the final scene, after lighting a cigarette at her gas range, she blows out the flame in what seems an act of pure absentmindedness that is perhaps attributable to her excitement over Hermann's recent arrival. But there are several suggestions that she is acting deliberately when she subsequently strikes a match in the gas-filled kitchen. Maria has seemed troubled by the reading of Oswald's will, and particularly by his tribute there to Hermann, which shuts her out of a traditional male compact. After hearing of Hermann's "humility," his capability of "appreciating great love in others," and even his right, as one who has served others, "to be a leader as few have been," Maria smiles mechanically at her husband and leaves the room, claiming a headache. In the bathroom she holds her wrist under water as if contemplating suicide, until Hermann shouts that Senkenberg is leaving. Maria returns downstairs, takes a cigarette from a pack on the table, and holds it casually as Hermann reassures her that he has given her everything: "All the money. I don't care about it." Maria replies: "I have given you everything too. My whole life." Then she asks Hermann for a match, which she takes to the kitchen and strikes as her husband, presumably just now aware of the gas, screams "No, no!" But for all those hints of suicidal motivation on Maria's part, the business with the cigarette and match seems so uncontrived that the ensuing explosion can easily be interpreted as an accident. This ambivalence is an essential part of the experience of the film, a classic instance of Fassbinder's often-stated desire to stimulate the imagination of the spectator.

Whatever Maria's motives in lighting her last cigarette may have been, the blast that concludes *The Marriage of Maria Braun*, like the story which leads up to it, carries both private and public symbolic significance. At the private level it can be seen as an explosion of the romantic ideology of marriage that Maria has so persistently asserted. As Joyce Rheuban argues, the film ironically subverts the melodramatic axioms of the sentimental Hollywood "women's film," in which strong women are temporarily allowed to assert themselves in traditionally male roles but willingly agree to return to their subordinate roles after their men return from war or other enterprises.[25] At the public level the concluding explosion emphasizes "the hollow victory of the economic miracle" associated with Maria Braun.[26] It also points to the Germans' historical use of military violence as an instrument of national policy, as well as the continuing violence in the terrorism of the late 1970s and the state's reaction to it. Thus there is more than a little irony in the hysterical shouting of sports announcer Herbert Zimmermann as Maria Braun's house goes up in smoke and flames: "Time's up! Time's up! . . . Germany is World Champion!"

Lili Marleen (1980)

Before returning to his "women's history" in July 1980 Fassbinder completed three additional major projects. Two have been discussed already: his complex tribute to his dead lover Armin Meier, *In a Year of 13 Moons;* and his sardonic portrait of late 1970s terrorists, *The Third Generation.* The third project was the ambitious fourteen-part adaptation of Döblin's *Berlin Alexanderplatz,* shot between June 1979 and April 1980, which is the subject of chapter ten.

During the latter months of the *Alexanderplatz* project Fassbinder engaged in complicated negotiations for the rights to make a film based on the autobiography of a German singer named Lale Anderson, who had become famous during World War II for her cabaret song about a soldier who longs to rejoin his sweetheart.[27] When it was broadcast each night for several years over Radio Prague in Nazi-occupied Czechoslovakia, that plaintive song, "Lili Marleen," had momentarily stilled the guns on both sides of the battle lines.

The initial script for the film was written by Manfred Purzer, a conservative film lobbyist and writer for whom Fassbinder had a strong dislike.[28] The project was to be financed by an older German producer, Luggi Waldleitner, who had invited Hanna Schygulla to take the leading role in the film after seeing her in *The Marriage of Maria Braun;* she agreed only on condition that Fassbinder direct, whereupon Waldleitner offered the film to Fassbinder, who accepted.[29] The fact that Waldleitner was known as a political reactionary caused many on the left to complain that Fassbinder had crassly sold out to commercial interests in his pursuit of the "German Hollywood-Film."[30] The 35 mm, wide-screen *Lili Marleen* certainly follows the tradition of the Hollywood "blockbuster" film. Its ten-million-mark budget was almost double that of *Despair.* International stars Giancarlo Giannini and Mel Ferrer (celebrated Italian and American actors, respectively) headed up a cast with many Fassbinder regulars, including the now-famous Hanna Schygulla as Willie Bunterberg, the Lale Anderson character. The high technical standards of the film were widely noted; they reflected the talents of art director Rolf Zehetbaur and of cinematographer Xaver Schwarzenberger, who had joined the Fassbinder team with *Berlin Alexanderplatz* the previous year. "Light and shadow have never been handled more expertly in a color film," wrote one German critic, who also praised Peer Raben's rich orchestral variations (with echoes of Mahler) on the theme song throughout the film.[31]

Lili Marleen is the story of a frustrated love affair between Willie Bunterberg, a German cabaret singer, and Robert Mendelsohn (Giannini), the son of a wealthy Jewish family that is engaged in helping fellow Jews escape from Nazi Germany. Robert's father (Ferrer) considers Willie a liability in this effort, and he arranges to have her prevented from returning to Switzerland after a visit to Germany. A Nazi bureaucrat, Henkel (Karl-Heinz von Hassel), helps Willie find work in Germany and arranges for her to record the little song that becomes such a hit with the troops on both sides of the war, and even with Hitler. Willie is persuaded by friends of Robert's in the Resistance to assist them in smuggling filmed evidence of a Nazi concentration camp into neutral Switzerland, but after Robert is captured by the Nazis his father arranges for him to be released in exchange for the film. Now in disfavor with the Nazi regime, and her song banned, Willie tries unsuccessfully to commit suicide. Her friends start a rumor that she has been killed in a concentration camp; a public protest follows, and the Nazis are forced to deny the rumor and to rehabilitate Willie at a spectacular concert, where she performs her trademark song once again. As the show ends, a radio announcer reports the end of the war.

Willie makes her way to Zurich hoping to rejoin Robert. Finding him in a concert hall, where he is conducting a symphony orchestra, she learns that he is married and leaves, broken-hearted.

The protagonist of *Lili Marleen* is much less perceptive of the realities of her world, and much less forceful in asserting herself within it, than Maria Braun. The success of Willie Bunterberg's song, which is the primary ingredient of her successful career, is really just a happy accident. Like the protagonist of Fassbinder's later *Veronika Voss,* Willie plays the traditional role of the female show-business star, that staple of "women's picture" melodrama created and controlled by men. Moreover, she seems utterly naive about the political realities of the Nazi regime she serves. When Robert objects to her role in that regime, she answers innocently, "It's only a song." When she first enters a magnificent apartment which Hitler has given her, she dances around like a child, narcissistically gazing at herself in a mirror. Even her brief cooperation with the Resistance comes about only at the urging of her lover's friends.

Lili Marleen dramatizes some of the political and historical realities to which Willie is so largely blind, including the war itself. There are several big-production battlefield sequences in which, during the singing of Willie's song, the big guns briefly go silent and enemy soldiers greet each other across the lines. And there are vivid portrayals of the pain and the intrigues that inevitably accompany war. Most important, the film suggests the extent to which the Third Reich depended on public spectacle, through the mass media of radio and film, as well as gigantic rallies and parades, as a means of keeping its suffering soldiers and citizens committed to the war effort.

Keeping in mind this theme of Nazi spectacle in *Lili Marleen* may be helpful in dealing with some problematic aspects of the film. On the whole, the treatment of both private melodrama and historical themes is considerably more heavy-handed here than in *Maria Braun.* For example, the battle scenes, for all their apparently expensive production values, seem contrived, repetitious, and unduly drawn out, and the concluding scene looks almost like a parody of Hollywood melodrama. How is one to take these effects? Popular response to *Lili Marleen* has been positive, and the first American reviews of the film were, according to Eric Rentschler, "relatively warm" in noting its resemblance to Hollywood musicals of the 1940s and to Douglas Sirk's love stories of the next decade (while failing to notice the film's indebtedness to the Nazi-era UFA *Revuefilm*).[32] Some critics have accused Fassbinder of superficially and cynically blending in *Lili Marleen* the tradition of Hollywood romantic melodrama with the perverse glamour of the Third Reich (which a number of West German films of the late 1970s exploited).[33] But others have read the kitschlike quality of *Lili Marleen* as a deliberate alienation effect. In this interpretation the film parodies the conventions of such popular cinematic genres as war adventure, women's melodrama, and show-business movies, thereby stimulating the viewer's critical understanding of the illusory nature of the mass media, particularly as instruments of state power. The enormous, brightly lighted door that Willie enters on her way to an audience with Hitler seems an obvious example of such contrived excess. So too is Willie's final stage show, after she has been "rehabilitated" by the Nazis. In a shimmering silver-lamé dress and turban she descends a massive staircase with a giant Nazi flag in the background, accompanied by a female chorus in quaint village costumes.[34]

Fassbinder anticipated that critics would accuse him of being fascinated by the ritualistic aesthetic of the Nazis in *Lili Marleen*. He said he did indeed intend to show in the film that for many Germans the Führer was "something fabulous . . . something grandiose." But he insisted that his purpose had been to treat that theme as no one had yet done, "to make the Third Reich transparent" by portraying "details of its own self-revelation."[35] Thomas Elsaesser has elaborated the ideas implicit in Fassbinder's remarks, arguing that the film is a sophisticated deconstruction of Nazi spectacle, as well as of the genre of melodrama, particularly in its highlighting of coincidence, "turning fortuity into a surreal gag." He concludes that the film offers itself ironically as an artifact in the commodity culture of international capitalism, of which fascism is "the constant shadow."[36]

Fassbinder's explanation and Elsaesser's analysis are fascinating, but they do not fully account for what seem to this viewer to be serious problems in the film. Many sequences in *Lili Marleen* come across merely as awkward and heavy-handed, by no means up to the standards of subtlety that Fassbinder achieved in his other films of this period. Several writers have reported that the director gave this project considerably less than his usual attention. Harry Baer, for example, has written that the director's overly ambitious schedule of work on the complex sound mixing of *Berlin Alexanderplatz,* which was continuing during the shooting of *Lili Marleen,* made it difficult for him to maintain in the latter project the balance he intended between fascination with the spectacle and horror at the reality of the Third Reich.[37] It seems likely that such time pressures contributed to Fassbinder's lack of success in modifying what he characterized as the simplistic "allotment of good and evil" in Manfred Purzer's original script.[38] Another difficulty with *Lili Marleen* is that it was shot in English, in anticipation of American distribution, and then dubbed in German— not very effectively at some points. Whatever the reasons, Fassbinder's most extensive treatment of the Third Reich, in what might have been the centerpiece of his projected "women's history of Germany," is a disappointment, for all its moving melodrama, stunning technical effects, and hints of complex reflexivity.

BRD 3: Lola (1981)

Six months after completing the filming of *Lili Marleen,* Fassbinder had another "women's history" project before the camera. *Lola,* which was shot during April and May 1981, was conceived as number three in the Bundesrepublik Deutschland trilogy. It is set in the small Bavarian city of Coburg in 1957 and 1958. This 35 mm wide-screen film was another well-financed project (budgeted at 3.5 million DM), backed by two independent German production companies and the WDR television network. For the second time, Fassbinder worked from a screenplay by Peter Märtesheimer and Pea Frölich.

Lola, the woman at the center of this film, is a descendant of the showgirl Lola Lola in Josef von Sternberg's *Der blaue Engel,* 1930 (*The Blue Angel*), one of the most famous films of the German golden age, which starred Marlene Dietrich and Emil Jannings. In Sternberg's film the sexy, self-possessed singer Lola Lola is the feature attraction of a tawdry traveling show playing in a small-town cabaret called The Blue Angel. An officious teacher at the local high school, Professor Unrat, follows some of his students to the night club, where he becomes infatuated with Lola. Disgraced in his colleagues' eyes, Unrat gives up his teaching position to marry Lola and travels with her troupe, selling picture postcards of her to members of the audience and even performing on stage a humiliating self-parody as a clown imitating a rooster.

Although its setting, characterization, plot, style, and theme are quite different, Fassbinder's *Lola* substantially plays off against its well-known predecessor in its account of sleazy collusion between businessmen and public officials in the Federal Republic, effected through cynical exploitation of love. The character inspired by Professor Unrat is von Bohm (Armin Mueller-Stahl), a conscientious building commissioner newly appointed to Coburg. He is at first unaware of the widespread corruption emanating from a wealthy building contractor, Schuckert (Mario Adorf), who has all the local officials in his pocket and owns the town's most popular brothel, the Villa Fink. The star singer-stripper at the brothel is Lola (Barbara Sukowa), Schuckert's mistress. Ignorant of her connection with Schuckert and his brothel, von Bohm falls in love with Lola, whom he has met in a library and made love to in a hayloft. Lola is touched by his gentlemanly manners toward her and the illusion of innocence they give her. After Lola has broken off the relationship, von Bohm discovers her at Villa Fink, performing a striptease. This disillusioning experience inspires him to renew his attack on local corruption with a vengeance. But the wily contractor convinces Lola to agree to marry von Bohm, who still loves her. Once he is engaged to Lola, von Bohm drops his resistance to local political-economic corruption, and everyone seems happy, including Lola, to whom Schuckert has made a gift of the brothel. Lola now finds herself with a devoted and at least outwardly respectable husband, as well as a corrupt and generous lover to whom she can quietly turn when the fancy strikes her.

As a private melodrama centered on a female protagonist, the film presents Lola as another ambitious but vulnerable female trying to succeed in a patriarchal bourgeois society, somewhat like Maria Braun. More obviously than Maria, Lola uses sex appeal to get ahead. She aspires to the status of a respectable middle-class wife and seems pleased at her success in achieving it at the end. If she has any serious reservations about Schuckert's plan to virtually sell her to the unwary von Bohm, she does not show it, and she seems to be content at the end with a facsimile of domestic bliss contrived by her cynical lover.

At a more public level the film implies that criminal collusion between business interests and supine public officials is an essential ingredient in the much-heralded West German Economic Miracle. It was a time of "the moral apathy of self-seeking advancement and pleasure," as one critic has written, presided over by the grandfather Adenauer, whose election slogan "no experiments" dominates the mood of the film, and whose portrait is seen at its beginning and end.[39] The demonstrations for peace and for freedom for blacks in South Africa that are occasionally glimpsed in the film seem marginal indeed in such a morally apathetic society.

The style of *Lola* is considerably more naturalistic and emotionally engaging than the "cold *Lili-Marleen*-collage," as Fassbinder's previous film has been described by one German critic.[40] Still, it self-consciously employs a number of cinematic effects, including a mobile camera, which often peeks through windows and doors, and a fairly obtrusive soundtrack, which makes use of various musical styles and radio broadcasts heralding the accomplishments of the new Germany. The most notable stylistic effect in *Lola* is its unusual use of color, achieved through pastel filters. For example, in one scene, Lola is bathed in pink, von Bohm in blue. Some critics have dismissed these effects as mere kitsch, but others have pointed out their appropriateness in combining subtle critiques of the genre of melodrama and of the superficiality with which public corruption was covered over during the Economic Miracle.[41] The film was well received in West Germany, receiving a Silver Band and awards for acting (Barbara Sukowa and Armin Mueller-Stahl) in the German Film Prize competition for 1982.

BRD 2: Veronika Voss (1981)

Fassbinder's next-to-last film, *Die Sehnsucht der Veronika Voss* ([The Longing of] *Veronika Voss*), designated as the second in his Bundesrepublik Deutschland series, is set in 1955, between *The Marriage of Maria Braun* and *Lola*. Produced by Fassbinder's Tango-Films and three other West German companies on a budget of 2.6 million marks, it was shot on 35 mm black-and-white wide-screen stock in November and December 1981. This highly crafted and emotionally compelling film is one of Fassbinder's most impressive cinematic achievements, and it won him, at last, the first-prize Golden Bear at the 1982 Berlin Film Festival.

The film is based on the life of Sybille Schmitz, a Nazi-era film star whose career collapsed after the war. Divorced by her husband after she had become an alcoholic, Schmitz was put under the care of a neurologist who deliberately addicted her to morphine and then led her to take her own life though an overdose of sleeping pills, after the former star had signed her property over to her. The screenplay, by Peter Märthesheimer and Pea Fröhlich, was freely adapted from a treatment Fassbinder had written out by hand in May 1981.[42]

Veronika Voss is vintage Fassbinder in several important ways. It is one of the most moving of his many melodramatic accounts of psychological exploitation and frustrated love. As a film about drug addiction, it may also have served the director as a means of exploring imaginatively the potential dangers of his own drug use. It is certainly a disturbing commentary on official corruption in the Federal Republic, as represented by the neurologist and a public-health officer who cooperates with her in her deadly plot to destroy the former star for personal gain. It is also a brilliant reflexive tribute to the medium of film—specifically to several American and German cinematic traditions—as well as a subtle critique of the illusionary power of film as a mass medium with great potential for social control and self-deception.

The film dramatizes the involvement of Robert Krohn (Hilmar Thate), a Munich sportswriter with a penchant for composing poems, in the troubled life of former film star Veronika Voss (Rosel Zech).[43] Although he is living with another woman, Henrietta (Cornelia Froboess), Robert is fascinated by the fading actress, curious about her odd behavior, and increasingly protective of her. Apparently in love with Veronika, he sleeps with her one night, at her invitation, and with Henrietta's knowledge. He soon discovers that the actress is living as a virtual captive in the apartment-office of her charming and ostensibly caring neurologist, Dr. Katz (Annemarie Düringer), who has deliberately addicted Veronika to morphine. Robert learns of other victims of Dr. Katz, particularly an elderly man who is a survivor of the Nazi death camp at Treblinka in Poland. After much effort, Veronika finally secures a small role in a movie. But during the shooting she breaks down in a terrifying drug-withdrawal attack (she had earlier refused her regular shot of morphine during a quarrel with Dr. Katz). Robert, who witnesses this scene, decides to intervene to save Veronika. But he gets nowhere. When he charges into Dr. Katz's office and accuses her of abusing the actress, he gets only stern remonstrances on his behavior from the smiling neurologist. He seeks out the public-health officer in charge of regulating narcotics, Dr. Edel (Eric Schumann).[44] Edel, who is in league with Dr. Katz, assures Robert that the neurologist has done nothing wrong. But Robert persists

Veronika Voss, 1981. Fassbinder and his film editor and companion Juliane Lorenz (in the role of the film producer's secretary) on the set during a pause in shooting. (By permission of the Rainer Werner Fassbinder Foundation, Berlin)

in his investigation. He persuades his amazingly patient girlfriend Henrietta to visit Dr. Katz, posing as a rich divorcée with vague internal pains. The plan seems to work perfectly: after only a few minutes' conversation, the doctor gives her a prescription for morphine. Henrietta happily calls Robert with this news, fantasizing that their relationship can now be restored by their mutual efforts to save the former movie star ("We'll tell each other all we know about each other. I love you"). Unfortunately, the telephone booth from which she calls is visible from Dr. Katz's window, and moments later Henrietta is killed by a speeding car.

The viewer can guess who ordered this murder, as well as whose hands then replace the morphine prescription in Henrietta's purse with a prescription for a legal sedative. This exchange undercuts Robert's charges when he brings the police to Dr. Katz's office in the next scene, his frustration now approaching Kafkaesque madness. The police tell him that his friend's death was an accident, and Dr. Katz assures them that Robert is in shock. At this moment Veronika appears in the doorway of her bedroom, exuding a self confidence reminiscent of her former status as a movie icon. She identifies herself to the star-struck police officer and declares that Robert is merely a reporter who had presumptuously tried to become her friend. But after Robert leaves with the police she breaks down in tears in the arms of Dr. Katz, who appears quite satisfied at Veronika's performance. Katz and Edel now conclude that Robert's snooping is getting dangerous and that it is time for Venonika, like their other victims before her, to "disappear, permanently" by her own hands. They plan a grand farewell party, after which they will leave her locked in her room alone for the Easter weekend with no access to morphine but more than enough sleeping pills for her to commit suicide. In the film star's villa, many of her present and past associates, including Robert, gather for the glittering evening-dress-and-candlelight party. In a husky voice reminiscent of Marlene Dietrich's, Veronika sings "Memories Are Made of This," accompanied by Dr. Edel on the piano. She tells a reporter that she will make her next big movie in Hollywood, and later, lying on her bed, talks to the disillusioned and despondent Robert. "Why did you come after all that happened?" she asks. "Did something happen?" he asks quietly. The deadly Dr. Katz looks like the epitome of feminine gentleness, as she sits on a corner of the bed in a white blouse with a large bow at the neck and smiles in satisfaction.

In ironic counterpoint, these scenes from Veronika's farewell party are inserted as flashbacks into a scene set three days later in her celllike bedroom. It is Easter Sunday morning. Veronika awakens in her bed as church bells toll outside. On her radio the pope's Easter blessing from the Vatican alternates with American country music broadcast over the U.S. armed forces' network.

Dr. Katz, dressed for traveling, enters and sits on the side of the bed in a chilling ritual of deadly control cynically masquerading as love.[45] Veronika fatalistically murmurs, "You gave me a lot of happiness." The doctor pats Veronika's hands with her gloved hand and reminds her sweetly, "I sold it to you." Then she kisses her victim on the forehead. Veronika says, "Now I belong to you. All I have to give you is my death," repeating a line from her an old movie of hers that she was watching in the opening sequence of the film. "You'll be alone now," says the doctor, as she walks out of the room, locking the door behind her. "Yes, I'll sleep," responds Veronika. But she awakens shortly in desperate need of a morphine fix. She tries to force open the locked door, curls up in a corner like a trapped animal, and finally reaches for the sleeping pills conveniently provided in her bedside table.[46] Later, in the newspaper office, Robert reads the account of the death he was unable to prevent: "UFA Star Took Overdose of Sleeping Pills." A colleague suggests that he might want to write a second article based on his research, but he demurs: "No, it's not much of a newspaper story." In the final sequence of the film Robert peers into the window of Veronika's villa, which Dr. Katz has inherited, as the neurologist and her friends enjoy a meal. He walks away, throws his black mourning armband onto the hood of the doctor's car, and gets into a waiting taxi, telling the driver to take him to a Munich soccer stadium. He has had his fill of movie stars.

Like the other films discussed in this chapter, *Veronika Voss* presents a moving personal melodrama about a woman trying to make her mark in a world dominated by men. Rosel Zech's performance as the increasingly desperate fading star has been widely praised for its virtuosity and emotional power, comparable to Gloria Swanson's famous role as Norma Desmond in *Sunset Boulevard,* Billy Wilder's 1950 film about an alcoholic former Hollywood star—against which Fassbinder's film plays in complex ways. In addition, *Veronika Voss* reworks memorably his perennial theme of emotional exploitation in intimate relationships. Not only is Veronika victimized by Dr. Katz and Dr. Edel; Robert is exploited by Veronika, and Henrietta by Robert.

In considering the role of the reporter Robert Krohn, one can see how *Veronika Voss* works both as a tribute to the Hollywood crime-film genre and as a critique of official corruption in the Federal Republic. Robert is a type of the honest reporter or private investigator in many an American film noir crime melodrama, drawn into dangerous waters by a fascinating woman, doggedly pursuing the truth but frustrated and disillusioned by corrupt officials who should be helping him, and ultimately betrayed by the woman. (The sequence in which Henrietta is run over by an automobile at night, not particularly convincing as naturalistic filming, looks like a deliberate imitation of such film noir dramas.) The honest and caring sportswriter does not have a chance against the combined powers of Drs. Katz and Edel, those chillingly efficient representatives of the professional class and government bureaucracy in the new Federal Republic of Germany (whose economic reconstruction is at one point invoked by the sound of the jackhammers that are so prevalent in *Maria Braun*). Moreover, Veronika Voss's addiction to morphine becomes, as Donna Hoffmeister has pointed out, "a metaphor for what Theodor Adorno called 'the administered society,' since society's representatives, the doctor, nurse, and health inspector, victimize the very people whom they are supposed to protect."[47] This motif is emphasized in the elegant self-confidence with which Katz and Edel reassure Robert and the police that their suspicions are entirely unfounded. It is epitomized in Dr. Edel's statement to Robert that even if the medical system does allow Dr. Katz to provide her patients with enough pills to kill themselves, ultimately it is the patients' fault if they do.

The role of the United States as champion and major supporter of the Economic Miracle, which tolerates—perhaps requires—such criminal collusion among those who wielded power in West Germany, is ironically suggested in the role of the enigmatic black American soldier (Günther Kaufmann) who

Veronika Voss, 1981. Veronika (Rosel Zech) hopefully discusses an upcoming film role, telephoning from Dr. Katz's office; in the background, a U.S. soldier (Günther Kaufmann) prepares packets of drugs. (Courtesy of the Museum of Modern Art/Film Stills Archive, New York)

hangs around in Dr. Katz's office-apartment in slovenly fashion. Virtually silent throughout the film, he spends most of his time assembling packages of drugs (presumably for illegal distribution to GIs) while listening to raucous American music on Armed Forces Radio.

At a more general level of significance, *Veronika Voss* is Fassbinder's most sustained reflexive meditation on the cinema since *Beware of a Holy Whore* a decade earlier. This exquisitely photographed black-and-white film (his first since *Fontane Effi Briest,* completed in 1974) celebrates the medium and its historical traditions in many ways. Old-fashioned wipes and irises are used as transitional devices throughout. Both the newsroom where Robert works and Dr. Katz's office are often seen in flickering light (attributable to a ceiling fan and a many-faceted mirror-ball, respectively), recalling flickering early movies. Moreover, as has been seen, the film alludes substantially to the Hollywood genres of women's pictures and crime dramas. It is also, as Roth writes, "a grandiose imitation" of the UFA melodramas in which Sybille Schmitz had starred, delicately balanced between art and kitsch.[48] Those earlier German films specifically are recalled in a shot early in *Veronika Voss* where Fassbinder is seen sitting behind the protagonist as they watch one of her old movies. The viewer is pointedly reminded of the cinematic apparatus by the bright lights of a filmmaking scene that Veronika recalls early on, as well as in a later episode in which she collapses during the filming of *Blue Sky,* a melodrama in which she has finally landed a part. Many in the audience would have recognized the unusually patient film director in the latter scene as the prominent theatrical director Peter Zadek, Fassbinder's former antagonist from his brief tenure as a theatrical director in Bochum, more recently a respected friend.[49]

Veronika Voss continues the characteristic Fassbinder techniques of shooting through doorways, windows, and curtains and into mirrors and other reflective surfaces, this time in a comparatively unobtrusive manner. More noticeable is the chilling all-white interior of Dr. Katz's office, shot in slight overexposure. The sound track is even more obtrusive, with quiet background music (including variations on a theme from *Berlin Alexanderplatz* and zither music reminiscent of the Carol Reed–Orson Welles film *The Third Man,* 1949) interrupted at tense moments by organ bursts and the roll of kettle drums, and the blaring sound of the American Armed Forces Radio broadcast almost overpowering many scenes.

The total effect of this cinematic reflexivity and self-consciousness is to establish a critical distance between the viewer and the melodramatic story, reinforcing the theme of the illusionary quality of cinema. In this reading of the film, Veronika Voss's use of morphine takes on more than the personal and political significance noted above. As Robert Reimer has written, *Veronika Voss* points to the "link between the narcotic effect of drug addiction and the escapist pleasure of film viewing. . . . affecting the subconscious and producing its own form of dependency on a ritual which helps one dream and forget."[50] The most obvious victim of this deception is the fading star herself, who has succumbed to the illusion of herself as an ageless icon of popular culture. It is this extreme and finally pathetic longing for the security and happiness she had once seemed to have as a movie star to which the *Sehnsucht* (longing) in the German title of the film presumable refers. Ironically, Veronika seems to be aware of the illusory nature of this longing. She tells Robert early in the film, after she has asked the waiter to turn down the lights and bring candles, "Light and shadows are what films are all about." Later she recalls an argument with her ex-husband over her request to put on a record and replace the electric lighting with candles, in which she had admitted, "When I play a woman who wants to please all men, I need music and lights." The film's most impressive portrayal of Veronika Voss's knowing victimization by the magic of the movies occurs in the elaborate going-away party staged by Drs. Katz and Edel near the end. In spite of the glittering candles, glass, and jewelry, Veronika must know that this occasion is a send-off to her death. Yet she can still say glibly to a reporter: "Art needs freedom. How else can it liberate people?"[51] As this richly textured scene makes clear, Fassbinder's most appreciative meditation on the artistic medium to which he dedicated his short life is also a revelation of the destructive power of the cinema over those who uncritically accept its escapist myths.

Notes

1. Haddad-Garcia Int 50.
2. Thomsen Int 91.
3. *Anarchy* 45.
4. Wiegand Int 78.
5. Kaplan 60.
6. Lorenz Let 7 April 1994.
7. Roth/AF 182.
8. This account follows John Sandford's description of the conclusion of the television version of the film (97), which the author was unable to see.
9. Roth/AF 182.
10. According to Roth, Hanni is a more assertive character in the theatrical film than in the television version (AF/182).
11. Sandford 97.

12. Fassbinder had previously asked Juliane Lorenz to bring a print of *Maria Braun* with her when she drove to Cannes; he did not have "the idea of flying-in" the film after the premiere of *Despair*, as Katz reports (Lorenz Let 30 May 1994; Katz 138).

13. Kaes, *From Hitler to Heimat* 81; Rheuban 3.

14. Rheuban 4, 211. *13 Moons* had opened in November 1978, although it was made after *Maria Braun*.

15. Baer 156–57. Katz, citing and quoting Michael Fengler and Peter Berling, presents Fassbinder during and shortly after the shooting of *Maria Braun* as almost completely victimized by his drug use and extremely abusive of Michael Fengler (128–135). Lorenz describes Fassbinder's difficulties with Fengler as deriving from Fengler's mishandling of funds and his decision to bring in Trio-Films as coproducer of *Maria Braun* after shooting had begun, without informing Fassbinder; these actions "may have driven Rainer more into his drug problem." She also challenges Katz's report that early in 1978 Fassbinder, "to protect his interests [in the developing conflict with Fengler] summoned Peter Berling from Rome . . . to be hired as executive producer of *Berlin Alexanderplatz*" (129). She writes that *Alexanderplatz* "was at that time only in early preparation, and Peter Berling, as usual, again tried to get his hands into it, but Rainer never wanted him in this project" (Let 30 May 1994). As it turned out, the shooting of that film did not begin until June 1979, as a production of Bavaria Studios.

16. Rheuban 163. Anton Kaes identifies both Märthesheimer and Fröhlich as professional scriptwriters and adds that Fassbinder turned to them after he couldn't get financing for the project ("History, fiction, memory" 278). Märthesheimer writes that this was his first screenplay ("A Letter to the Editor" 188). Märthesheimer had been responsible at WDR for Fassbinder's *Nicklashauser Fart* in 1970 and had originated the idea for *Acht Stunden sind kein Tag,* which was produced by WDR in 1972 (Lorenz Let 30 May 1994).

17. Baer 157. The changes Fassbinder made from the script during the shooting of *Maria Braun* are described in Reuban 164–180, 188.

18. Nevers 57.

19. One of the major changes Fassbinder made during shooting was to replace the sentimental relationship between Maria and Oswald in the Märthesheimer-Fröhlich script (which portrayed them at times almost as father and daughter) with a more cynical, even sadomasochistic, relationship between the increasingly independent Maria and her older lover (Rheuban, 163–4, 186).

20. The series includes Konrad Adenauer, Ludwig Ehrhard, Kurt George Kiesinger, and Helmut Schmidt. Omitted is Willy Brandt, whom Fassbinder once called "a symbol of the reform movement" in spite of such regressive policies as the antiterrorist legislation (Rheuban 191).

21. Haddad-Garcia Int 52.

22. Kaes, "History, Fiction, Memory."

23. Ibid. 279.

24. Rheuban 187–188.

25. Rheuban 7–15.

26. Rheuban 20.

27. Anderson, *Der Himmel hat viele Farben: Leben mit einem Lied* [Heaven has Many Colors: Life with a Song], 1974.

28. In 1975, Purzer had been largely responsible for the decision of the government-funded Film Subsidy Board not to support Fassbinder's planned film version of Gerhard Zwerenz's novel *Die Erde ist unbewohnbar wie der Mond* (Spaich 98, 323).

29. Spaich 98, 323.

30. See Baer (161–65). In 1980 Fassbinder justified this collaboration with Waldleitner, saying that the older producer (who had actively defended the interests of commercial filmmakers against the advocates of Young and New German Cinema) was "just crazy about movies." He added that, like Visconti, he had "more leeway" working with right-wing financiers than with leftists (*Anarchy* 57, 61).

31. Roth/AF 212.

32. Rentschler *West German Film* 82. The film was "the number one box-office hit in Germany," according to Annette Insdorf (126).

33. Insdorf found Fassbinder's film "the most insidious of the recent cinematic revisions of the Nazi era" (26).

34. An ironic reading of such effects in the film is encouraged by several instances of pointed reflexivity. One of these is a self-conscious cameo appearance by Fassbinder as the writer and famous anti-Nazi Resistance leader, Günther Weisenborn. The other, one of the most far-fetched instances of self-referentiality in Fassbinder's films, has Henkel tell Willie the story of a murder dramatized in *Berlin Alexanderplatz* as they walk by the forest in which Fassbinder had filmed that episode a few months earlier.

35. Limmer Int 91.

36. Elsaesser *"Lili Marleen"* 121, 139, 119. See also his "Filming Fascism" and Bathric, "Inscribing History."

37. Baer 168. Baer is credited as "artistic co-worker" on both of these films. Juliane Lorenz, Fassbinder's coeditor on both films, has recalled that under the pressure of the sound editing for *Alexanderplatz* she was initially unclear about the editing rhythm of *Lili Marleen;* at first she had trouble understanding the "inner harmony" of *Lili Marleen.* In what she said was her only crisis as an editor for Fassbinder, she left for ten days' respite before returning (following a call from him) to complete the editing on *Lili Marleen,* which he approved with the comment: "Now you've found the rhythm again. Very nice." (Interview/Richter 59–61)

38. Spaich 323.

39. Faletti 82. The Adenauer election slogan is identified in Roth/KF 252.

40. Roth/KF 249.

41. Stanley Kaufmann characterizes *Lola* as a Sirkean "magazine film."

42. The film considerably simplifies the convoluted story Fassbinder tells in that treatment ("Sybille Schmitz"). Fassbinder once said that he had thought of casting Schmitz as the mother of Petra von Kant, in his 1972 film, before he realized that she was dead. Since "no one knew anything exactly about her fate," he investigated it, with some difficulty, he recalled. (Notes to "Sybille Schmitz" 100—quoting from an interview

with Angie Dullinger, *Abendzeitung* [Munich], 12 December 1981). Juliane Lorenz undertook a substantial amount of the research on Sybille Schmitz for Fassbinder (Interview with Hoffmeister). Schmitz had starring roles in a number of "those escapist melodramas, modeled on Hollywood cinema of the thirties and early forties which Goebbels promoted alongside his outright propaganda films" (Hoffmeister, "Drugs as Metaphor"). One of Schmitz's best-remembered roles was as Leone in the 1932 film, *Vampyr* (directed in France by the Danish director Carl-Theodor Dreyer). See also Jenkins.

43. In Fassbinder's scenario, the male lead is a police reporter. Hilmar Thate reports that Fassbinder spontaneously decided to add the poetic dimension to Krohn's character to encourage him to accept the part (52).

44. German *edel:* noble.

45. Like the bedroom scene at the farewell party for Veronika, this is reminiscent of those scenes in *Effi Briest* and *Petra von Kant* where smiling mothers sit at the bedside of daughters they have, respectively, destroyed and rejected.

46. In a shot edited out of this sequence, Veronika holds up to the window a sign asking for help, at which a mongoloid child stares uncomprehendingly. The film's editor Juliane Lorenz recalled that, after long discussion, Fassbinder decided that "in her state, there was no longer a question of Veronika looking for help" ("Je ferai" 67).

47. Hoffmeister, "Drugs as Metaphor."

48. Roth/KF 258–59.

49. *The Marriage of Maria Braun* was dedicated to Zadek.

50. Reimer 101.

51. Jenkins interprets Veronika's addiction to the cinematic image of herself—"reducing herself to a fetishized object before the camera's gaze"—as a means of "self-negation" (1297).

CHAPTER TEN

Desire and History
Berlin Alexanderplatz

Two scenes in Fassbinder's segment of *Germany in Autumn,* made in October 1977, show the director holding a paperback book and dictating into a tape recorder. The book is a well-known German novel set in a working-class district of Berlin in the last years of the Weimar Republic, Alfred Döblin's *Berlin Alexanderplatz: Die Geschichte vom Franz Biberkopf,* 1929 (*Berlin Alexanderplatz: The Story of Franz Biberkopf*), which Fassbinder said had profoundly affected him since he first read it as an adolescent. In 1930 German director Phil Jutzi had adapted the novel into a feature-length film starring Heinrich George.[1] Fassbinder's adaptation of the book as a television miniseries, filmed in 1979 and 1980, went far beyond that precedent, turning the novel into his cinematic magnum opus, with a running time of fifteen hours and twenty-one minutes. It was shot in 16 mm format for presentation as a fourteen-part series on German television starting in December 1980, after its initial theatrical screening at the Venice Film Festival in late August and early September. Fassbinder's *Berlin Alexanderplatz* is a moving melodrama that reworks many private themes running through the director's previous work, at the same time that it substantially explores the public history of the late Weimar Republic and—by implication—of Germany in the Nazi period and later.

At a cost of thirteen million marks, *Berlin Alexanderplatz* was the most expensive of Fassbinder's films and the most costly West German television production undertaken up to that time—but not unusually expensive considering the running time, as Fassbinder pointed out.[2] The project was originally scheduled for shooting in June 1978. During the previous fall and winter the director worked on the screenplay with extraordinary intensity, compared even with his usual fast pace. He claimed that he dictated the script for a hundred hours at a time, with twenty-four-hour breaks for sleeping—certainly not "a healthy way of writing," he admitted, but efficient.[3] The start of production was delayed for a year, however, because of disagreements between Fassbinder and the then-producer, Michael Fengler. By the time filming started in June 1979 the television rights had been purchased by the Munich production studio Bavaria Atelier, which produced the film in collaboration with the WDR television network and the Italian Television Network (RAI).[4]

Once underway, the shooting went unusually well. During its 154-day schedule, ending in April 1980, Fassbinder reportedly stopped using cocaine. He exercised a disciplined control over the project at which many participants marveled; remained calm when his lead actor, Günther Lamprecht, complained publicly of his lack of direction; organized bowling and soccer competitions for the large cast and crew; and regularly stopped filming early on Fridays so that his coworkers could be with their families on weekends.[5]

Döblin's *Berlin Alexanderplatz*

The novel *Berlin Alexanderplatz: The Story of Franz Biberkopf* was the best-known work of the prolific, controversial, and honored Berlin writer and psychiatrist Alfred Döblin (1878–1957). Set in the tense last years of the depression-ridden Weimar Republic, shortly before the Nazi ascendancy, the book recounts the tribulations of its protagonist and other denizens of the east Berlin working-class district around Alexanderplatz, where Döblin practiced psychiatry for many years.[6]

At the beginning of the novel Franz Biberkopf, a former transport worker and pimp, is released from a four-year prison term for the fatal beating of his girlfriend, Ida. Trusting in the goodness of the world and his own luck and determined to stay out of trouble with the law, he tries without much success to support himself in a series of petty jobs selling neckties, shoelaces, and the Nazi newspaper *Völkischer Beobachter*. To shore up his wounded ego he gets involved with several women. He is betrayed by two close male friends in whom he has naively placed his trust. One of them, the enigmatic Reinhold, is a member of a gang of warehouse thieves who draw Franz unknowingly into their criminal activity. Franz loses an arm when Reinhold pushes him from a getaway car into the path of a following automobile as they flee from a burglary. Later Reinhold murders Franz's "one true love," Mieze, after luring her into a forest. After that betrayal Biberkopf, in an apparently catatonic state, is admitted to a psychiatric hospital, where he experiences terrifying nightmares. He eventually recovers and reenters the world, severely chastened, and takes a job as assistant doorman of a factory. In the concluding pages of the novel Franz admits his vanity in thinking that he could survive completely on his own. And while he recognizes at last his need for society, he is highly skeptical of the mass movements that ominously threaten the latter days of the Weimar Republic.

Although there is plenty of melodramatic material in this narrative, Döblin's *Berlin Alexanderplatz* regularly shifts its focus away from Biberkopf's personal story to its social context. This technique is consistent with the author's rejection of the "bourgeois realism" of the modern psychological novel and "the cult of great personalities" that obliterates "the whole world with its multitude of dimensions."[7] In an essay written in 1924 the philosophically leftwing Döblin spoke of the twentieth century as the "naturalistic age," interpreting such collective enterprises as science, technology, and even nationalistic imperialism as stages in a developmental process analogous to biological growth. He saw the modern metropolis not as hostile to humanity, as the Romantics had alleged, but as the appropriate setting for human beings at their present state of development. "The new spirit makes of the cities its body and instrument. . . . Only the collective being Man as a whole represents the superior species Man."[8]

Accordingly, the personal narrative of Franz Biberkopf in *Berlin Alexanderplatz* is often overshadowed by a montage of documents and narratives depicting the heterogeneous life of the city, such as vignettes of the denizens of Alexanderplatz, streetcar schedules, stock-market and weather reports, and advertising slogans. The book is thus analogous to the collages of dadaist and cubist artists of the time that were often composed of fragments of objects drawn from ordinary life—particularly the work of Kurt Schwitters, which was well known in Berlin since his 1918 exhibition at the Sturm Gallery, with which Döblin was closely connected.[9] In its wide-ranging documentation of the life of the city, *Berlin Alexanderplatz* also recalls James Joyce's famous novel of Dublin, *Ulysses,* 1922, which Döblin reviewed while he was writing *Alexanderplatz,* though a more apt comparison would be with Walter Ruttmann's 1927 documentary film, *Berlin, the Symphony of a Great City.*[10] Döblin himself spoke of his "kinostyle," a "multitude of visions" that passes by with conciseness and precision.[11]

The reader is further distanced from Franz Biberkopf's personal story by the novel's intrusive narrative techniques. Each of its eight "books" begins with an ironic, often enigmatic motto. The chapter headings are variously childish ("Gallop-a-Trot . . . little Horsey starts trotting again" [205]), mock-epic ("Third Conquest of Berlin" [324]), and moralistic ("Ill-gotten Gain thrives" [293]), to mention only a few of their rhetorical styles. And the narrator almost constantly intrudes on the reader's attention, abruptly shifting the point of view and altering the tone—which is at various times cocky, reassuring, sardonic, and prophetic—to undercut the emotional tension of the story at its most melodramatic moments.

Fassbinder Reading Döblin

Those alienating effects did not prevent Fassbinder from making a strong personal identification with the two main characters in Döblin's novel. In an essay written about the time he was completing his work on *Berlin Alexanderplatz,* the director said that he had read Döblin's book first at age fourteen or fifteen, and again at nineteen. Had he set it aside at the first reading, when he became bored after the first two hundred pages, he wrote, his life would have been different "in many, perhaps more crucial respects than I can even say" than it had been with Döblin's novel "embedded in my mind, my flesh, my body as a whole, and my soul."[12]

Fassbinder's subjective reading of Döblin's novel seems to have been focused primarily on the relationship between Franz and Reinhold, which begins only about midway in the book. He said that he saw the book primarily as the story of two men "whose little bit of life on this earth is ruined because they don't have the opportunity to get up the courage even to recognize, let alone admit, that they like each other in an unusual way, love each other somehow, that something mysterious ties them to each other more closely than is generally considered suitable for men" (161). Fassbinder stressed that he did not see the relationship between Biberkopf and Reinhold as sexual but rather as "nothing more or less than a pure love that society can't touch." Nevertheless, reading the novel released his "tormenting fears" about his "homosexual longings" and helped him avoid becoming "completely and utterly sick, dishonest, desperate" (162). After his second reading, at age nineteen, Fassbinder realized that "a huge part" of himself consisted of things in the novel, that he had "unconsciously turned Döblin's imaginings" into his own life (162).[13]

The influence of Döblin's novel can be seen in many of Fassbinder's films before *Berlin Alexanderplatz,* most of whose protagonists are named Franz (some with the surname Biberkopf), one of whom is played by the director.[14] Fassbinder claimed that the protagonist of Döblin's novel was behind his conception of all his characters who "mess up their lives" because "they don't dare to admit to their needs and desires" and want "to believe, beyond all possible and conceivable limits, that people can be good."[15] He seems also to have been fascinated by Reinhold, the supposed friend who so torments Biberkopf, whom he wanted to play in a cinema version of the novel which he hoped to make. Fassbinder told Harry Baer that he really wanted to "know who this Reinhold is . . . how he gets his power over Biberkopf."[16] Presumably the director saw in Franz and Reinhold the masochistic and sadistic sides of human nature and was drawn to them as means of imaginatively exploring opposing tendencies in his own personality.[17]

From "Berlin Alexanderplatz" to "The Story of Franz Biberkopf"

Given his unusually personal interest in the novel, it should not be surprising that Fassbinder's fourteen-part *Berlin Alexanderplatz* transformed Döblin's mostly ironic and stylistically experimental treatment of life in the modern metropolis into an emotionally charged melodrama that is his most sustained exercise in cinematic naturalism. Except for its surrealistic epilogue, which will be discussed separately, the film works within the general conventions of Hollywood melodrama, though its complex visual and aural textures mark it as distinctly European in style. In contrast to the regular interruptions of the main narrative by documentary materials in the novel, the film focuses intently on "The Story of Franz Biberkopf." It develops the subjective aspects of Franz's life in a moving narrative that draws the viewer into a strong emotional involvement—perhaps more than Fassbinder anticipated.[18] This effect is accomplished to a considerable degree through the compelling performance of Günter Lamprecht as Franz (for whom Fassbinder's minimal direction seems to have been exactly right). Viewer identification and empathy are also inspired through the complex but—except for the epilogue—subdued cinematic effects achieved by the director and the cinematographer, Xaver Schwarzenberger: dark shadows and coloring suggestive of Dutch baroque portraits and interiors, as well as of German Expressionist paintings and films; fluid and unobtrusive camera work; and frequent use of expressive close-ups. Peer Raben's complex musical track regularly returns to its poignant romantic theme to inspire emotional release after episodes of the most intense stress. Moreover, the voice-over commentary taken from the novel, which is spoken quietly by Fassbinder himself, more often than not adds a sympathetic tone to the film narrative, in contrast to the usually alienating effect of the intrusive narrating voice in the novel.

Virtually all of the characters are more sympathetically developed in the film than in the novel, and several important new figures are added. As in Döblin's text, the women in the film suffer shocking abuse, from Franz's virtual rape of Ida's sister Minna (Karin Baal) early in the film to Reinhold's murder of Mieze near the end. Even when they are not being so obviously mistreated, women in the film serve as "functions of male fantasies, the go-between for men who cannot express their love for each other directly," as Eric Rentschler has observed.[19] Nevertheless, as in his early gangster films that so reek of misogyny, Fassbinder's *Berlin Alexanderplatz* humanizes its women and treats their relationships with men quite seriously—much more so than the novel does. Thus, Döblin's crudely caricatured "fat Lina," Biberkopf's first live-in woman after his release from prison, is transformed in the performance of Elizabeth Trissenaar (Hanni in *The Stationmaster's Wife*) into an appealing and spirited lover. A small episode early in the novel,[20] in which the just-released Biberkopf is threatened with expulsion from Berlin before he takes up with Lina, is delayed in the film until *after* he has become Lina's lover and is turned melodramatically into a major crisis in their relationship (II).[21] The almost invisible landlady in the novel is given a major role in the film as the sympathetic Mrs. Bast (Brigitta Mira). The character of Franz's good friend and former lover, the high-class prostitute Eva (Hanna Schygulla), is developed in brief but highly suggestive episodes in each of the first four parts of the film—all prior to the point at which she is introduced in the novel—and the later entanglement of her life with Biberkopf's is much more emotionally intense than in the book. Finally, while the novel's attitude toward Biberkopf's "one true love" Mieze never rises far above the condescension implied in the reference to "the pale little whore [Eva] had picked up in Invalidenstrasse,"[22] Fassbinder's Mieze is both an evanescent symbol of innocence and self-sacrificing loyalty and a complex character in her own right.[23] Barbara Sukowa's performance in the role was a major step in her development into an international star.

Most of the Biberkopf's male friends undergo similarly sympathetic development in their translation from the novel to the film. For example, Döblin's brisk and cryptic treatment of Otto Lüders in Book Three is turned in the film into a ponderous and moving drama of sexual rivalry and betrayal (III). Franz's friend from the old days, Meck, who listens to Franz's troubles, provides patient advice, and helps draw him into the gang of thieves, is made in the film to feel remorse for having involved Franz again in a life of crime. Building on that character change, Fassbinder substitutes Meck (Franz Buchrieser) for a minor figure in the novel as the person who arranges Reinhold's deadly tryst with Mieze at a forest resort (XII). And the film introduces an important new male character, Baumann (Gerhard Zwerenz), the patient, sympathetic landlord of an apartment house in which Franz goes through a period of drunken depression after his betrayal by Lüders (Hark Bohm).[24]

The film emphasizes what Fassbinder said he considered "the actual theme" of the novel,[25] the sadomasochistic relationship between Biberkopf and Reinhold (Gottfried John), stressing its homoerotic nature more than might be expected

Berlin Alexanderplatz. Franz Biberkopf (Günther Lamprecht) introduces Mieze (Barbara Sukowa) to the owner of his neighborhood pub (Claus Holm). (Courtesy Museum of Modern Art/Film Stills Archive, New York).

from the director's comments in his essay on Döblin's novel. For example, whereas the novel devotes only one terse paragraph to the first meeting of Biberkopf and Reinhold—when Franz "felt tremendously attracted to him"[26]— the film turns that paragraph into a ponderous and sexually suggestive scene, dwelling on the two men's faces in intimate close-ups (V). During most of the rest of Part V, the film transforms Döblin's hurried, ironic treatment of their agreement for Franz to take Reinhold's castoff women ("Spirited White Slavery") into a tense drama with convoluted sexual significance, in which restless camera work and dramatic lighting are reinforced by electronic background music. For example, a straightforward discussion of their exchange of women at a table in the bar in the novel becomes in the film an intimate meeting of the two men in a dark toilet lit periodically by the ominous flashing of a neon sign outside the window.

In both novel and film Reinhold becomes increasingly disturbed by Biberkopf's naive efforts to "cure" him of his misogyny. As part of this campaign Franz invites his friend home so that he can secretly observe his domestic bliss with Mieze. But his intentions go horribly awry. When Mieze confesses that she has become infatuated with the nephew of her main patron, Franz beats her furiously as Reinhold secretly watches. The complex psychosexual matters going on here—Franz's taking out on Mieze the frustrations of his masochistic relationship with Reinhold—are implied in Döblin's treatment, but they taken much more seriously in the film. Döblin treats this episode almost comically; Fassbinder turns it into heavy melodrama. The vicious beating of Mieze is almost unbearably drawn out, punctuated with visual flashbacks to Franz's earlier killing of his girlfriend Ida (Barbara Valentin),[27] and climaxing in Mieze's blood-curdling scream when she discovers Reinhold's presence.

Döblin's treatment of the lovers' reconciliation after that beating of Mieze is terse and crudely comic; Fassbinder's is pure romance (XI). He brings the sympathetic Eva in to try, with Mrs. Bast, to repair the damage to Mieze's face and then to lead Mieze downstairs to tell Franz she forgives him. The lovers then take a romantic excursion to the nearby Freienwalde holiday resort, which, as in the novel, will be the setting of Mieze's murder by Reinhold. Fassbinder's film makes use of this location twice before the murder, however, with important dramatic effects. In Part VIII, Freienwalde had been the setting for an earlier reconciliation of Franz and Mieze after a quarrel. There were romantic sequences in a rowboat on the lake and in the brightly lighted forest, where they played hide-and-seek. Now, in Part XI, after the beating of Mieze, the two return and go for a walk again in the forest, its dark shadows and heavy mist penetrated by the evening sunlight. At the site of their former games Mieze dances about girlishly, throws herself on her back at Franz's feet, and then slides into his arms. As Part XI ends, the camera slowly pulls back to a long shot of the contented couple nestled at the foot of the trees as romantic theme music comes up.

In Part XII the film greatly intensifies the dramatic impact of the climactic episode of the novel, the murder in Book Seven of Mieze by Reinhold in that forest at Freienwalde. For one thing, it treats this event as a single episode, building steadily to a compelling climax, whereas in the novel the action is spread over two separate visits of Reinhold and Mieze to Freienwalde. Most important, the film presents Mieze—torn between her love for Franz and a combined attraction and repulsion for Reinhold—in a much less critical light than the novel does. In large part by revealing Mieze's calculating private thoughts in this episode, Döblin's text reinforces the suggestion made earlier that she is merely a scheming whore. The film's spectator, however, given no access to Mieze's thoughts, is led by the imagery and melodramatic situation to construct an entirely sympathetic version of the frail girl in the thin dress fleeing her pursuer through the forest.

Fassbinder's exploitation of the melodramatic potential of Mieze's murder is most vividly seen in his use of the forest imagery so graphically established in the two earlier episodes he invented for the film—imagery that seems pointedly to recall illustrations of German fairy tales, the forest paintings of the German romantic painter Caspar David Friedrich (1774–1840), and Fritz Lang's famous 1924 film treatment of ancient Germanic mythology, *Die Nibelungen*.[28] Döblin's evocation of the forest during the murder episode is variously silly and pretentious. The film treats it in much more dramatically compelling fashion, as the scene of earlier reconciliation and love-play becomes a setting for betrayal and death. Slow-cut tracking shots record the gradual transformation of the scene from sun-dappled to fog-shrouded as the drama between the confused, defenseless young woman and her killer reaches its climax. On the sound track the tremulous flute theme, over an ominous electronic background, reinforces the terror and pathos of the action. The frightful fairy tale concludes in a long-held shot of the body of Mieze lying on the floor of the dark forest, recalling precisely the shot of the happy lovers in that same forest at the conclusion of Part XI.

Thus, in the first thirteen parts of the film Fassbinder turns Döblin's stylistically experimental story of Franz Biberkopf and epic of the modern city into a naturalistic melodrama of love and betrayal, thematically recapitulating many of his earlier films. The final image of the dead Mieze in Freienwalde forest epitomizes the highly emotional treatment here of the theme of the destructive potential of sexuality, which Döblin's novel treats largely with irony. Fassbinder seems to have interpreted Döblin's book largely with reference to his own desires and fearful fantasies, seeing in Biberkopf and Reinhold the human potential both for utopian love and mutual torment. He said that *Berlin Alexanderplatz* represented his own "particular reading of Döblin," and that to attempt to make an "objective" version of a novel, even if that were possible, "would certainly result in something pretty sterile."[29]

Fascism as Frustrated Desire

As in the director's "women's history" films, *Berlin Alexanderplatz* makes use of private melodrama to suggest political themes—particularly, in this film, to show how the frustration of national desire during the interwar period led to the abominations of the Nazi era. Döblin's plentiful documentation of public life in late-Weimar Berlin is briefly recapitulated in the film through a fast-cut montage that appears underneath the opening titles of each of the fourteen parts. The images suggest the despair and desperation of Depression-era Germans: unemployed workers, protest demonstrations, and begging children, for example.[30] Life in those difficult times is also documented in the film proper, as in the realistically rendered accounts of Franz's frustrated efforts to gain some measure of financial security, and in his shoddy apartments. However, the concrete particulars of the teeming life around Alexanderplatz, to which the novel returns in detail time and again, are limited in the film to a few episodes staged in outdoor studio sets of Alexanderplatz and streets nearby (most of the movie is set indoors).[31]

The film renders the public life of the Alexanderplatz most vividly in Part II, "How Is One to Live If One Doesn't Want to Die?" At one point Franz is seen hawking pre-tied neckties ("for proletarians") on a street corner, in a complex outdoor city sequence dramatizing the mechanized press of people and machines, the disparities between haves and have-nots, and the ordinariness of anti-Semitic talk, among other things. Later in Part II a scene in "The New World," a dance hall reeking with gemütlichkeit and 1920s Berlin escapism, catches the raucous tone of Döblin's impressionistic original, though it moderates the novel's more extreme sardonic qualities and adds a quiet sequence in the middle in which Biberkopf stares thoughtfully out of a window at barren streets and tracks, worrying about "the world." The film also gives more sympathetic and prolonged exposure than the novel does to a sentimentally chauvinistic and drunken old soldier (Klaus Höhner) who recruits Franz to sell the Nazi newspaper *Völkische Beobachter* after testing whether or not he is a "true German."

As he was writing the novel in 1928 and 1929 Döblin obviously could not have anticipated the unthinkable directions in which such sentimental nationalism would take the German people over the next two decades. But the final pages of his novel are ominous enough in their anticipation of imminent war:

Keep awake, eyes front, attention, a thousand belong together, and he who won't watch out, is fit to flay and flout.

240

The drums roll behind him. Marching, marching. We tramp to war with iron tread, a hundred minstrels march ahead, red of night and red of day, deathward leads the way.[32]

Considering Fassbinder's explicit anticipation of the coming Nazi regime in his adaptations of those two other late Weimar-era novels, *The Stationmaster's Wife* and *Despair,* it is not surprising that the most pointed political references in the film are its representations of the insurgent fascism of the period, viewed through postwar eyes. This treatment transforms the novel's vague premonitions of coming disaster into explicit anticipations of the Third Reich. Much of this foreshadowing occurs in Part II. There is a pointed reference here to the coming Holocaust in Franz's encounter in a subway station with a sausage-seller who asks him if the Nazi newspaper he is peddling is "against the Jews," and Franz responds defensively: "I have nothing against Jews, but I am for order. Everybody realizes that we must have order, right?" The sausage-seller then reads off a few offensive headlines from the newspapers tacked on to the display board and wanders off, turning back to wish Frank good luck, times being what they are, and adding, "I'm Jewish, you know, but no hard feelings . . . good luck," as Franz gazes at him guiltily.

In that scene Franz also runs into Dreske (Axel Bauer), his former socialist comrade-in-arms in the Great War, and some of Dreske's friends. The film transforms what in the novel is good-natured joking about the Nazi armband Franz is wearing into a bitter confrontation between Biberkopf and Dreske, with heavily choreographed movements and close-ups of Franz's armband over minor-key music. When Franz encounters them in a pub that evening, Dreske and his friends sing the socialist hymn, the "Internationale," and then sarcastically invite Franz to sing for them. He responds with a bitter poem and a song about comrades killed in war, then abruptly switches to a heartfelt rendition of "The Watch on the Rhine," a sentimental favorite of the Nazis. With that, one of Dreske's men overturns Biberkopf's table. In the scuffle that ensues Franz goes into a paroxysm of anger and self-justification, accusing Dreske and his comrades, in a speech drawn directly from the novel, of being naive "blood-spillers" with no understanding of work and the need for order in society. In the midst of this speech Franz recalls his killing of Ida, controls the impulse to "do something, grab a throat," and mutters to himself, "we must have quiet, nothing but quiet," as a musical clock against which he has bumped plays the melody of the German national anthem, "Deutschland über alles."

In this episode Fassbinder pointedly dramatizes the connection between frustrated desire and violence in the sociohistorical context of the late Weimar period, suggesting how the despair and frustration of the lower bourgeoisie fed the fires of the Third Reich. For the most part (his occasional violent treatment of women being the major exception), Franz Biberkopf comes across in the film as humble, agreeable, and forgiving, in spite of his economic and emotional frustrations. One sees here how quickly he can turn aggressor when cornered. Fassbinder's sympathetic treatment of Franz in this scene implies his understanding of how such a man, in such circumstances, could have been seduced by Hitler's promises, just as he had sympathetically presented Hanni's proto-Nazi father in *Wildwechsel*.[33] The scene also suggests the potential dangers in the middle-class desire for peace and order, which, as seemed clear to Fassbinder and many other West Germans in the 1970s, could easily be transmuted into neofascist repression when threatened.[34]

The Epilogue: "My Dream of Franz Biberkopf's Dream"

The disturbing metaphors of violence erupting out of frustrated desire become much more explicit in Part 14, the largely surrealistic epilogue to *Berlin Alexanderplatz*. This long final section of the film (111 minutes running time) is based on the concluding Book Nine of the novel. Fassbinder titled it both "My Dream of Franz Biberkopf's Dream" and "On the Death of a Child and the Birth of a Useful Man."[35] The epilogue was filmed after the rest of the shooting had been completed and the cast and most of the crew had been given a two-week break to allow Fassbinder to withdraw to Frankfurt am Main to complete his planning for it.[36]

The epilogue of the film generally follows the structure of Book Nine of the novel. It presents the "real-life" episodes in fairly conventional cinematic fashion. However, in its dramatization of Franz Biberkopf's nightmares and hallucinations, which are presented by Döblin with comparative restraint, the film conjures up lurid, surrealistic imagery similar to the allegorical depictions of sexual and political themes in Pier Paolo Pasolini's *Salò,* 1975 (*The 120 Days of Sodom*) and the West German director Hans-Jürgen Syberberg's *Hitler, ein Film aus Deutschland,* 1977 (*Our Hitler*). Not since *Die Niklashauser Fart* in 1970 had Fassbinder engaged in such freewheeling and heavy-handed cinematic symbolism.

The final book of Döblin's novel picks up Franz Biberkopf's story shortly after he is arrested as a suspect in the murder of Mieze. He falls into a stupor and is committed to a psychiatric hospital. His refusal to eat brings on terrifying dreams and hallucinations drawn from his past experiences. He imagines that he is being tormented by the Whore of Babylon from the Book of Revelations and taunted by Death for having resisted his allurements for so long. At the conclusion of this wrenching experience Franz abjectly admits: "I'm not a human being, I'm just a beast, a monster." The narrator concludes: "Thus died, in that evening hour, Franz Biberkopf, erstwhile transport-worker, burglar, pimp, murderer. Another man lay in the bed, and that other one has the same papers as Franz, he looks like Franz. . . . Let's call him Franz Karl Biberkopf."[37] The doctors conclude that he is recovering, and the police begin questioning him again. Meanwhile, Reinhold has gone to prison under an assumed name for a minor theft he committed to avoid arrest for killing Mieze. But after his cellmate reveals his true identity to the authorities, Reinhold is brought to trial for Mieze's murder. Biberkopf says little when called to testify, since he feels "a curious devotion" toward Reinhold, if not pity;[38] his testimony is the main reason that Reinhold receives a ten-year sentence for homicide while temporarily insane, instead of hanging. Franz, exonerated of Mieze's murder, is given a new job as assistant doorman in a factory. The narrator then announces abruptly, "I have nothing further to report about his life." Nevertheless, the novel continues for a few more pages. Biberkopf's life is summarized metaphorically as a blind rush down a dark street. When he finally reaches his goal, "his head all bunged up, almost at his wit's end," he opens his eyes and in the light of a lamp is able to read "the name of the street."[39] Thus subdued and chastened, understanding at last the nature of his environment, Franz warily accommodates himself to his "dear Fatherland" and takes up his servile job as a cog in the wheels of industry.

Fassbinder took modest liberties in adapting the "real-life" material in this last section of the novel for the epilogue of his film. The most literally rendered portions are set in the hospital, where Franz resists attempted force-feeding and doctors argue about his case in their conference room. The scene in which Reinhold confesses his love to his cellmate, Konrad (Raul Gimenez), and speaks of his murder of Mieze is also adapted in straightforward fashion, but with several significant changes. The film makes explicit the homoerotic nature of the men's relationship, which is only implied in the novel, through several medium-close shots in which Reinhold and Konrad, both nude, caress and kiss. And it emphasizes the Fassbinderian theme of exploitation in intimate relationships by implying that after these tender moments Konrad deliberately betrays Reinhold for a one-thousand-mark reward (in the novel Konrad is guilty only of carelessly mentioning Reinhold's confession to a friend, who goes to the police with the information).

In adapting the nightmares and hallucinations that Biberkopf experiences in the novel's final chapter Fassbinder let his imagination run riot, creating a phantasmagoria that utterly overpowers the "realistic" portions of this part of his film. This material constitutes approximately four-fifths of the film's epilogue, whereas in the final section of the novel it makes up barely half the text and is securely anchored in the naturalistic narrative. Döblin's novel is the source for virtually all the dialogue and voice-over commentary here, and many of the surrealistic scenes are at least suggested by other details in the book. But Fassbinder's epilogue goes far beyond its literary source in its complex montage of dramatic and cinematic horror-show effects with heavy symbolic overtones. The action takes place in a variety of settings, some surreal, but many of them recognizable from earlier in film although they have been wrecked for these episodes. The dense sound track begins with organ music and church bells and modulates at various times into American folk and rock lyrics, operatic arias and choruses, symphonic music, electronic vibrations, heartbeats, and bloodcurdling screams, among other effects.

Most of these scenes represent aspects of Franz's former personal relationships in nightmare style. Virtually all of his friends, lovers, and associates are reassembled, either to torment or to try in vain to comfort him. In the initial sequence Franz wanders in a cemetery in a Berlin red-light district that he had earlier visited. He is observed by a constantly circling camera and watched over by a pair of angels, Terah (Margit Carstensen) and Sarug (Helmut Griem), who comment ironically on his imperfections and his need to suffer. Franz tenderly picks up Mieze's body, which is lying in a patch of trees, and when she disappears from his arms he frantically digs for her in the dirt like a dog. At one point Franz kneels in a cellar drinking milk from a saucer like a cat, surrounded by swarming mice (Döblin's Franz dreams of scampering with mice in a field). When he crawls through a hole that has opened in the wall he finds himself in a Salvation Army assembly hall, where Mieze is excitedly making love to Reinhold, though she insists that she was forced to do it. The figure of Death comes to him in the person of his kindly landlord Baumann, who blackens Franz's face with mud. In the forest at Freienwalde, Franz shoots Reinhold, whose corpse turns into Mieze's and then disappears. Once again he digs with his hands to find her body, but when he peers into the hole he sees another of his former lovers, Cilly (Annemarie Düringer), looking up at him accusingly from a bloody room in a slaughterhouse and singing a Franz Schubert song about death. In later sequences in that slaughterhouse, which are almost too painful to watch, Reinhold swings an ax at a pile of naked bodies on the floor, and Franz and Mieze are moved around like animal carcasses being prepared for butchering. A woman's scream continues interminably throughout this scene as the two guardian angels look on from a doorway, chanting, "swing, hack, swing, hack." Beside them, in dark glasses and a broad-brimmed hat, stands Rainer Werner Fassbinder, observing his protagonist's nightmare at its most excruciating point, without the slightest indication of emotion.

Not surprisingly, Reinhold turns up frequently in the epilogue—as Franz's tormenter, as a smiling would-be friend, and once as a Christ figure, wearing a crown of thorns (accompanied by "The Blue Danube Waltz" on the sound track). Near the end of the film the sadomasochistic relationship of Reinhold and Franz is emphasized as they prepare for a boxing match before a yelling crowd (which is filmed with a 180-degree panning camera and back-projected), preparations that conclude abruptly when Franz draws the resisting Reinhold to him for a passionate embrace and a mouth-to-mouth kiss. The death of the old Franz takes place in a surreal setting whose improbable mix of ingredients includes a classical statue, a nude couple caressing on a sandy beach, and grazing sheep. As a group of Franz's intimates prays fervently, he is crucified on a huge cross, and the image of an atomic explosion appears in the background. The two guardian angels stack bodies on the beach as a big-band version of "In the Mood" on the soundtrack modulates into a choral version of "Silent Night."

That bomb blast in the crucifixion scene appears to be a rather forced effort to link Franz Biberkopf's private nightmares to the general fear of nuclear annihilation in the postwar world. Other symbolic elements, however, connect the director's "dream of Franz Biberkopf's dream" more specifically to the history of late-Weimar and Nazi Germany, underscoring the motif of personal frustrations developing into the mass violence of the Third Reich. Brown-shirted soldiers turn up unaccountably at several points, and once the chanting of "Sieg Heil" is heard. The Jewish sausage-seller returns, now wearing the Nazi armband "with pride." Franz, also with the Nazi armband, sings "The Watch on the Rhine" again. Most significantly, those chilling slaughterhouse scenes evoke newsreel images of the deadly "shower rooms" of the Nazi death camps and the victims' bodies stacked like so much dead meat.

Toward its end the epilogue of *Berlin Alexanderplatz* returns to its earlier naturalistic style, showing Franz's testimony at Reinhold's trial and his final meeting with Eva in the neighborhood pub. The film concludes with several shots of Franz in his new position as "assistant door-man in a medium-sized factory." The film's treatment of that final section, however, constitutes a significant departure from the guardedly hopeful outlook for Franz Biberkopf with which Döblin's book concludes. In its final pages the novel emphasizes that after the loss of Mieze and his terrifying encounter with his memories and his subconscious in the hospital, Franz Biberkopf undergoes a virtual rebirth. Giving up his arrogant struggle against fate as an isolated individual, he guardedly accepts his place as a member of society, finally understanding the importance of allying himself with the people around him. But he will not be stampeded into any kind of mass action. He "watches coolly" the military parades that pass his door and vows not to join them. "I first figure out everything, and only if everything's quite O.K. and suits me, I'll take action."[40] The novel then moves to a puzzling conclusion. The narrator makes an enigmatic, rhyming summary statement: "Biberkopf is a humble workman. We know what we know, the price we paid was not low."[41] That comment is followed by what appears to be a romantic call to battle:

> The way leads to freedom. . . . The old world must crumble. Awake, wind of dawn!
> And get in step, and right and left and right and left: marching on, we tramp to war with iron tread . . . one stands fast, another's killed, one rushes past, another's voice is stilled, drrum, brrumm, drrumm!

Some critics have read this ambiguous ending of Döblin's *Berlin Alexanderplatz* as an indication that Franz has lost his admirable old spirit of defiant independence and is now prepared to accept not only menial work in the service of capitalism but also obedient service in the coming war. But David Dollenmayer, citing Hans-Peter Bayerdörfer, has argued persuasively that such a pessimistic reading misses the central, if admittedly somewhat obscurely presented, point of the novel's conclusion. According to Dollenmayer, Franz has learned that he must give up his "aggressively individualistic battle" against fate, including his frustrated hopes for utopian male friendship with Reinhold and utopian love with Mieze, and seek solidarity with his fellowman. But that does not mean that he is ready to embrace "the false solidarity created by force and legitimized by the idea of fate" and represented by the Whore of Babylon, who was, after all, driven away by Death in Franz's nightmares. Dollenmayer interprets that marching song (printed in italics in the German text, in boldface in the English) as the final refrain of a "street ballad" that the narrator has sung at various points throughout the novel and that the reader should understand as an ironic reference to "the false collective of war" that is one of many forces threatening the world in which the new Franz is prepared to live.[42] This last point is certainly indicated in Franz's caution in expressing his newfound need for becoming a member of collective society: "Everywhere about me my battle is being fought, and I must be beware, before I know I'm in the thick of it. . . . The words come rolling up to us, we must be careful not to get run over. . . . I'll watch, and use the eyes o' mine."

Fassbinder's conclusion presents a considerably more pessimistic view of Franz Biberkopf and his future in Germany than the novel, in Dollenmayer's interpretation, does. The film ends with a brief, quiet sequence in which Biberkopf in his doorman's uniform, apparently in the executive parking garage of a factory, admires and polishes the shiny new automobiles. He mutters to himself, in alternation with Fassbinder's voice-over commentary—the words of both drawn from the closing pages of novel. But Fassbinder leaves out of this scene virtually all of Biberkopf's reservations about going along with the wishes of mass society. Without those reservations, the film implies that Franz will soon join the Nazi parade. It concludes with two passages from the novel: the ominous marching song ("The drums roll behind him. . . . We tramp to war with iron tread") and the ambiguous rhyme ("Biberkopf is a humble workman. We know what we know, the price we paid was not low.")[43] As Wolfgang Limmer has noted, the ending of Fassbinder's film suggests that Franz Biberkopf has been destroyed in the process of becoming a good German citizen.[44] Fassbinder himself once speculated that Franz Biberkopf would probably vote for the Nazis.[45]

Fassbinder's neglect of the slightly hopeful elements in Döblin's ending seems to be another indication of what was defined earlier as his postrevolutionary melancholy. More specifically, the ending of his film can be read as a lament for Franz's lost anarchistic and utopian spirit and perhaps for his own. As Fassbinder put it, Franz Biberkopf is a person with an extraordinary belief in the goodness of human kind, who believes that people are naturally anarchistic; he is destroyed by the fact that he is "an anarchistic figure among purely social creatures."[46] This characterization is in large part true of the many earlier embodiments of Franz Biberkopf in Fassbinder's films, whether so named or not. Fassbinder once said that he had made Berlin Alexanderplatz for all the people "who are forced to do many things that they really don't want to do."[47] Like Hans Epp's "one true love" in The Merchant of Four Seasons, Mieze in this film seems to symbolize all those utopian desires that the world will not allow one to fulfill. Thus it is appropriate that the melancholy conclusion of Berlin Alexanderplatz is followed by a reprise of the murder of Mieze by Reinhold in Freienwalde under the closing credits.[48]

Evaluations

The premiere of Fassbinder's long-awaited version of Döblin's novel at the Venice Film Festival, over several days in late August and early September 1980, was well received by many critics, who found it a masterful literary adaptation and summation of his previous work. The response to *Berlin Alexanderplatz* was not nearly so positive, however, when it was first shown on West German television in fourteen programs from mid-October through December 1980. To the director's consternation, network executives decided that the series was inappropriate for family viewing and scheduled it for late-evening showing, rather than the prime-time slot that he had understood would be scheduled (after he had, at the insistence of the network, canceled a dream sequence dramatizing the Oedipal myth of patricide and mother-incest that he had written for Part X).[49]

Many viewers complained that much of the film was too dark to see on the small screen. This effect seems to have been intended, according to Christian Braad Thomsen, who writes that Fassbinder and cinematographer Xaver Schwarzenberger deliberately abandoned the bright lighting and predominant use of close-ups characteristic of most television productions for lighting and shooting techniques reminiscent of German Expressionist films of the 1920s: deep-focus shots, and high-contrast lighting that often leaves a large part of the

---

Translation of RWF's notes to sketches for theatrical film version of *Berlin Alexanderplatz* (facing page):

Upper left corner: *Pension*: boarding house
Reading left to right (some words illegible):

Row 1—Franz comes forward. The old man. Franz winks. Franz walks toward Lina, camera pans with him.
Row 2—Franz knocks on door, Fränze comes out of kitchen, Franz enters the room. Franz/Fränze. Lina/Meck. Franz exits right.
Row 3—Lina/Meck. Franz in front of mirror, combs his hair, then Franz turns left. Fränze comes into kitchen, turns left. Franz smokes cigarette at the window, then goes forward to the left, camera on Meck.
Row 4—Franz shuts door, goes to the kitchen, Fränze and Bast come out. Franz/Ede, pan to right, traveling shot to left [?].
Row 5—Franz/Bast. Franz/Ede. Franz out, right. Camera on Fränze [?].

Berlin Alexanderplatz. Fassbinder's sketches for a planned theatrical film adaptation of Alfred Döblin's novel; translation on 248. (By permission of the Rainer Werner Fassbinder Foundation, Berlin)

frame and of individual faces in shadow.[50] Fassbinder defended his lighting style in *Berlin Alexanderplatz*, pointing out its similarities to the paintings of Rembrandt and the films of Alfred Hitchcock, and lamented the fact that West German television viewers had been conditioned to expect in television movies the "aesthetic and narrative technique" of the evening news programs.[51]

Attacks on the substance of the film—particularly its frank treatment of sex and its irreverent use of Christian symbols in the epilogue—were led by the right-wing Springer publishing enterprise, which engaged in a vicious anti-Fassbinder campaign after his name topped the list of fifty-two writers who vowed not to do any more work for the Springer publications.[52] The Springer daily paper *Bild* called the film "an orgy of stupid talk," and its Sunday edition *Welt am Sonntag* termed it the most expensive and most celebrated flop on German television.[53] Another writer, perhaps unduly influenced by the epilogue, described the series as a "pornographic bloodbath."[54] Fassbinder was surprised and disappointed by this negative response to his magnum opus in his homeland. Before the film premiered on television he had expressed confidence that it would not cause the kind of uproar that Döblin's novel had at *its* first appearance. While he admitted that the "very idiosyncratic film language" of the epilogue would be likely to stir up controversy, he believed that in the rest of the film he had been careful enough to avoid shocking the sensibilities of the television audience.[55]

In spite of the initial response to the televised *Berlin Alexanderplatz* in the Federal Republic, the film had what one scholar has termed "a resoundingly successful commercial release in American arthouses," and in 1984 it was broadcast again on West German television.[56] Most critics agree that the film is the director's most awesome and moving artistic achievement. Wolfram Schütte characterized it as "the most comprehensive, epically varied compendium" of Fassbinder's portrayals of humanity, of mankind's "feelings and thoughts, wishes and depressions," in a "simultaneously intimate and monumental fresco" that remains the director's most personal "Summa."[57]

Still, the epilogue remains a problem, and even the director had reservations about it, as noted above. Many viewers (including this writer) have found that its extravagant cinematic effects do a disservice to Fassbinder's most ambitious and long-considered film. While almost every one of its scenes makes sense as a surrealistic rendering of Franz's private nightmares and hallucinations, their total effect overwhelms the viewer's credibility and patience. Only the convincing performance of Günther Lamprecht as Franz Biberkopf saves most of them from ludicrousness.[58]

Fassbinder did not live to realize his plans for a feature-length theatrical film version of *Berlin Alexanderplatz*. In 1980 he anticipated that he would be able to make the film, perhaps within five years, even if he were unable to obtain the rights from Michael Fengler.[59] The film was to be reshot, with a completely new cast, including the French stars Gerard Depardieu (as Franz Biberkopf), Isabelle Adjani (as Mieze), Jeanne Moreau, and Andrea Ferréol, with Fassbinder himself in the role of Reinhold.[60] Fassbinder said that after he completed the screenplay for the television series, it had taken him three months to think through the cinematic version, for which he had subsequently completed a script and some sketches of shots. That version would have more "shock effects" and not be "nearly so epic in style," nor "so positive" in its characterization of Franz Biberkopf as the television series had been, he said.[61]

Notes

1. Fassbinder wrote in 1980 that he had found Jutzi's adaptation "quite a good film" although in making it the director had "completely forgotten Döblin's novel" (*Anarchy* 162).

2. *Anarchy* 63.

3. *Anarchy* 53.

4. Juliane Lorenz writes that, after having been impressed by the professionalism of Bavaria Studios, with whom he had made *Despair,* Fassbinder became increasingly distrustful of Michael Fengler, who he thought had betrayed him as coproducer of *Maria Braun.* He forced Fengler to sell the production rights of the television version of *Berlin Alexanderplatz* to Bavaria. At this point, "for the first time in his life, Rainer had a realistic view of his companions of the early days"—including Fengler, Peter Berling, and Hanns Eckelkamp (whose Trio Films had coproduced *Satan's Brew* and *Maria Braun*), she summarizes. (Lorenz Let 30 May 1994)

5. Zwerenz 146; Baer 142, 150. Lamprecht discusses Fassbinder's direction of him in an interview with Harry Baer in Fassbinder and Baer, *Der Film Berlin Alexanderplatz* 566–572.

6. Alexanderplatz is located near the center of the city, a mile or two east of the famous Brandenburg Gate. English quotations from Döblin's novel are from the Jolas translation.

7. Quoted in Kort 44–46; see also Dollenmayer, 56 ff. The second half of the full title of the novel, *The Story of Franz Biberkopf,* was added only at the insistence of the publisher (Dollenmayer 66).

8. Dollenmayer 60.

9. Hayman 121. Döblin cut and pasted some of these documentary materials, collage-fashion, onto his manuscript (Kort 103–104).

10. Fassbinder professed lack of interest in the argument whether Döblin's novel had been influenced by *Ulysses;* he said he had not noticed "any sort of stylistic break" in the novel (*Anarchy* 53).

11. Kort 47 n. 16. See also Dollenmayer 21, 69, 73–74.

12. "The Cities of Humanity" 160. This essay is the source of the quotations in the following two paragraphs.

13. Fassbinder characterized the novel as homoerotic, but not sexual, having to do primarily with the possibility of love that was not forced or exploitable (Limmer Int 76).

14. Versions of the Franz Biberkopf character in Fassbinder's earlier films ("RWF" = those played by Fassbinder) include Franz in *Love Is Colder Than Death* (RWF), Jorgos in *Katzelmacher* (RWF), Franz in *Gods of the Plague,* Michel in *Rio das Mortes,* Whity, Franz in *The American Soldier,* Hans in *The Merchant of Four Seasons,* Franz in *Wildwechsel,* Ali in *Fear Eats the Soul,* Franz in *Fox and His Friends* (RWF), and Peter in *I Only Want You to Love Me.* Franz Biberkopf is also recalled in the first part of the pseudonym "Franz Walsch" which the director used to credit himself as film editor.

15. *Anarchy* 22, 47.

16. Baer 120.

17. Juliane Lorenz has emphasized that Fassbinder was equally fascinated with Mieze, the lost object of Franz's desire (discussed below). She points out that he often spoke to her about "the three personalities, Franz, Reinhold, and Mieze." (Let 30 May 1994).

18. Fassbinder said that he hoped that the film's stylization—limited though it is— would keep viewers from "drowning in the story" (*Anarchy* 52).

19. "Terms of dismemberment" 317. Rentschler notes that the film's treatment of women "invariably provokes extreme discomfort during showings and occasions vehement discussion afterwards" (309).

20. Döblin 44–45.

21. Roman numerals are used in this chapter to designate the fourteen parts of the film.

22. Döblin 444.

23. *Mieze* is a slang word, meaning "pussycat," used often in German as a condescending term for a young woman, like *chick* in American English.

24. Fassbinder said he created the character Baumann out of "scraps of narration coming out of the subconscious" and thought of him as Franz's "alter ego [who] knows more about life than he's willing to admit to himself" (*Anarchy* 54). The character is based on several dialogues with unidentified interlocutors which Biberkopf imagines, in a section of the novel titled "Biberkopf in a Stupor" (161–164). The assignment of the role of Baumann to Gerhard Zwerenz underscores the significance to Fassbinder of his friendship and collaboration with the former East German writer.

25. *Anarchy* 160.

26. Döblin 234.

27. The killing of Ida is recapitulated many times in the film, but given only brief, ironic treatment at the one point in the novel where it is treated in significant detail (122–128).

28. Juliane Lorenz recalls that, as she was editing the scene of Mieze's murder in the forest, Fassbinder called her to ask how it looked. "It reminds me of Fritz Lang's *Die Nibelungen*," she said. He responded, "Wonderful. That's exactly what I wanted." (Lorenz Let 30 May 1994).

29. *Anarchy* 65.

30. These images are reproduced in Fassbinder and Baer, *Der Film Berlin Alexanderplatz* 22–25.

31. Hans Günther Pflaum asserts that, since the costs involved in constructing many of the outdoor scenes depicted in the novel would have been prohibitive, Fassbinder "transferred the events inside—into the inner lives of the characters as well as to spatial interiors, thereby evoking a constantly growing feeling of narrowness and claustrophobia; even outside of prison the characters are prisoners" (*Rainer Werner Fassbinder: Bilder und Dokumente* 70).

32. Doblin 634.

33. *Anarchy* 65. Fassbinder said that in *Berlin Alexanderplatz* he tried to represent faithfully Döblin's prewar point of view, and "not to work in the Third Reich like a good little academic" (*Anarchy* 54). But many details in the film suggest a decidedly postwar perspective, similar to that noted in *Despair* in chapter 8.

34. Fassbinder said in 1980 that he was trying in the film to show how the German people are "predisposed" to be led into fascism, and pointed out continuing evidence of this in the recent demands for "peace, order, and discipline" in the Federal Republic (*Anarchy* 46). For an analysis of the blending of political and personal themes in *Berlin Alexanderplatz* as a drama of "the body," see Rentschler, "Terms of dismemberment" 311–317.

35. The first title appears with other credits in the opening shot; the second appears after the sixth scene.

36. According to Harry Baer, "we regarded this part really as a new film, but with the same actors and relationships that we had all built up. For Fassbinder, it was a kind of outgrowth of what went before—to find himself a little bit, something like that" (interview). In his book Baer recalls Fassbinder's discussions of his desire to create visual effects for the epilogue in styles ranging from Hieronymus Bosch (the late medieval Dutch painter of surreal scenes of corrupt sensuality) to Caspar David Friedrich, whose possible influence on the forest imagery in the film is noted earlier in this chapter (Baer 152–53).

37. Döblin 617, 624.

38. Ibid. 630.

39. Ibid. 632.

40. Ibid. 632–34. As Dollenmayer has pointed out, many Döblin critics have failed

to observe that Franz holds himself back from the mass rush towards war (88–91). Dollenmayer also reports here that Döblin admitted to being unsatisfied with the conclusion of the novel, and he notes that the author never realized his hope to write a sequel in which Franz would step out of his passivity into the role of "the active man."

41. "Wir wissen, was wir wissen, wir habens teuer bezahlen müssen" (501).

42. Dollenmayer 86–90.

43. Fassbinder reads the first passage in voice-over; the second is printed on a title-card.

44. Limmer 39.

45. *Anarchy* 65.

46. Quoted in Spaich 223.

47. *Anarchie* 170.

48. In this reading, the replay of Reinhold's murder of Mieze is not the "gratuitous flashback" it seems to Rentschler ("Terms of dismemberment" 311).

49. See Thomsen, *Rainer Werner Fassbinder* 320. Part One of the series was initially broadcast over the WDR television network at 9:05 P.M., Parts Two through Thirteen at 9:30, and the epilogue at 11:30.

50. *Rainer Werner Fassbinder* 322.

51. *Anarchy* 64.

52. *Anarchy* 62.

53. Limmer 40.

54. DIF 36.

55. *Anarchy* 49–50. Fassbinder said that he thought everything except the epilogue was "really fine, exciting, and enlightening"; he had expected, even hoped for, a controversy, but not against the film itself (Limmer Int 59).

56. Rentschler, "Terms of dismemberment" 305.

57. "Sein Name: Ein Ära" 72.

58. Christian Braad Thomsen found these attempts to render Franz's inner states of mind "empty effects, a drama of the soul turned into papiermaché." Thomsen bases his criticism on the assumption that film can render mental states only externally (*Rainer Werner Fassbinder* 323–44.) However, the problem in these hallucinatory sequences would seem to be attributable more to questionable artistic strategies than to limitations of the cinematic medium.

59. Fengler's Albatros Productions had coproduced *Maria Braun* and originally had the rights to both the television and the theatrical versions of *Berlin Alexanderplatz* (*Anarchy* 56). According to Katz, Fengler was determined never to give up his rights to the cinema version of Döblin's novel, in his anger over being forced by Fassbinder to sell his production rights to the television version to Bavaria Studios after their falling-out over *Maria Braun* (134). Harry Baer said in 1992 that he was certain Fassbinder would have made the film by then had he lived; he also recalled that Fassbinder had once considered shooting the film version of *Alexanderplatz* at night, with a second cast

(of "great actors") while making the television version during the day: "That was our first idea, and it was ridiculous, because nobody can work twenty-four hours a day" (interview).

60. Katz 131.

61. *Anarchy* 53, 50. Fassbinder dictated a screenplay for a theatrical version of *Berlin Alexanderplatz* to a tape recorder in 1977 (RWFF Catalogue 262).

CHAPTER ELEVEN

New Directions (Perhaps) and Conclusions

Querelle, Fassbinder's last film, was shot in March 1982, about three months before his death. Its significant differences from most of his previous work tease one to speculate about the thematic and stylistic directions his work might have taken had he lived longer. *Querelle* explores once again the theme of exploitation in intimate relationships, which is so prominent in the earlier films, but it treats gay sexuality much more explicitly than any of those had. Moreover, the film's stylized set and other formalized qualities suggest a movement away from the predominantly naturalistic manner of most of Fassbinder's films since 1970.

After discussing that final Fassbinder film, this study concludes with a brief consideration of some of the director's unfinished work; a retrospective look at thematic and stylistic patterns running through his films; and a review of the private and professional personalities of this extraordinary cinematic artist.

Querelle (1982)

Fassbinder's final film announces itself as "a film about Jean Genet's *Querelle de Brest,*" a 1953 French novel that Fassbinder had known for many years.[1] Genet (1910–86) was an abandoned illegitimate child raised by foster parents, a brilliant student who ran away from school after winning first place in state exams, a petty thief who spent much of the first half of his life in reformatories and prisons, a vagabond, a homosexual prostitute, and the author of a number of other celebrated literary works besides *Querelle*—including *Notre-Dame des Fleurs,* 1944 (*Our Lady of the Flowers*), a novel based on his life as a thief and hustler in the bohemian Montmartre section of Paris, and the plays *Le Balcon,* 1956 (*The Balcony*) and *Les Nègres,* 1958 (*The Blacks*). Genet was a notable exemplar of that venerable French tradition of *poètes maudites* (accursed poets).[2] An essential part of his legend was his homosexuality—which he considered, and treated in his writing as, a perversion. He remained homophobic throughout his life, and in his treatment of homosexuality in his writing he brings to bear "the weight of Christian morality without which [his] mythology would have been impossible."[3] As Richard Dyer has written, Genet's name evokes "a set of symbols for the homosexual existence and a reference point for argument about what homosexual existence is or should be."[4] Genet's novel introduces its enigmatic protagonist, the sailor Querelle, as both a "figure comparable to the Angel of the Apocalypse" and a boy "whose soul is evident in his eyes, but who has been metamorphosed into an alligator."[5] Genet portrays Querelle's struggles with his identity as a homosexual in a lurid melodrama of erotic longing, betrayal, and murder, transforming a "third-class . . . tale about a criminal" into an "astonishing mythology," as Fassbinder described the book.[6] As he did in the poetic treatment of dirty toenails and other body parts in his 1950 short film, *Un Chant d'amour* (A Song of Love), Genet in *Querelle* "borrows the conventions of what is beautiful and sacred in order to make the criminal and male beautiful and sacred too."[7]

As a highly stylized filming of the highlights of Genet's novel, Fassbinder's *Querelle* in some ways recalls his adaptation of Fontane's *Effi Briest*. Both films are highly mannered homages to well-known (if altogether different) novels, and both seem to assume in the viewer a knowledge of the literary text. Furthermore, just as Fassbinder emphasized his intention to make a quite personal adaptation of Döblin's *Berlin Alexanderplatz,* he made clear that in *Querelle* he wanted to portray his "own fantasy" of the book rather than make "a *substitute* for literature" or create a "congenial" translation from one medium to another.[8]

Fassbinder's film closely follows the book's plot and characterizations, and it draws from the novel for much of its dialogue and for its frequent narration and commentary, both in voice-over (by Hilmar Thate in the German version of the film) and on white title cards. The title character is a handsome young sailor (Brad Davis), a member of the crew of a warship docked at the French seaport of Brest. Querelle gradually becomes aware that his commanding officer, Lieutenant Seblon (Franco Nero), harbors a secret passion for him. The young sailor has smuggled on board a package of opium, which he arranges to sell to Nono (Günther Kaufmann), a black man who is one of the owners of the harbor's chief brothel, La Féria. The other owner of the brothel is Nono's wife, the fading beauty Madame Lysiane (Jeanne Moreau), who has for some time been consorting with Querelle's brother, Robert (Hanno Pöschl). Nono does not mind, since his primary sexual interest is in young sailors. Querelle persuades a shipmate, Vic (Dieter Schidor), to help him smuggle the opium past the customs guards, after which he cold-bloodedly murders Vic. Then he goes to La Féria and rolls dice with Nono for the privilege of going to bed with

Lysiane. Querelle deliberately loses, knowing this means that he will have to submit to anal intercourse with Nono. Never having been buggered before, he finds the experience not unpleasant, but he resists the conclusion that he is homosexual. He convinces the authorities that Vic was murdered by a stonemason, Gil Turko (Pöschl, without a mustache), who is hiding out in an abandoned prison after killing a man who accused him of being homosexual. Querelle finds Gil in his hideaway, almost gets him to admit to killing Vic, and does persuade Gil to rob Lieutenant Seblon, to obtain money for Gil's escape. Querelle helps Gil disguise himself with a moustache, which makes him look exactly like Querelle's brother Robert (since both characters are played by the same actor). In the process of these complicated machinations Querelle becomes more and more infatuated with Gil. At one point they kiss passionately, and Querelle mutters, "I never loved a boy before. You're the first one." This feeling does not, however, prevent Querelle from betraying Gil shortly thereafter to the police, who arrest him and charge him with both murders.

Meanwhile, Madame Lysiane, resentful of the intensity of Robert's and Querelle's fraternal bond, has been trying to seduce Querelle. Soon Querelle is in her bed, to take revenge on his brother, he claims. At the conclusion of the film Querelle seems to have found his true love in Lieutenant Seblon, before whom the young sailor has for some time been flaunting his half-naked body. One night Seblon rescues the drunken Querelle from a brawl and carries him into La Féria, as Querelle melodramatically and drunkenly mutters, "I've been totally conquered. I have feelings of autumn, fine mortal wounds in me," and says that he will never find peace until Seblon "takes" him and holds him afterwards across his thighs, like a *Pietà* "coddling a dead Jesus." In the brothel Seblon mistakenly identifies Robert as "the guy who shot me," and Lysiane upbraids Querelle for having left her alone. Querelle crudely rejects her appeal by revealing that he is her husband Nono's "boyfriend, his piece of ass," to which she replies, weeping, "You've destroyed me. You're not a human." Querelle follows Lieutenant Seblon out of La Féria as the narrator intones a passage from the novel: "Querelle's inner harmony was indestructible because it was sealed in that heaven of heavens where beauty unites with beauty." In the closing scene Lysiane deals tarot cards to a stunned and teary-eyed Robert, assuring him, "You haven't got a brother"—apparently trying both to reassure him and to compensate for her own disappointment in not having Querelle for herself. In a mirror over the sofa Querelle, bathed in blue light, can be seen enigmatically staring at them.[9]

Fassbinder's last film significantly extends his earlier treatments of the themes of male affection, rivalry, and betrayal and the mutual attraction of sadist and masochist. *Querelle* goes further than any earlier Fassbinder work in focusing on the relationship between brothers, as it dramatizes the affection, longing, and power struggles between Querelle and Robert. (The ambiguity of that fraternal relationship is made more complex by having the actor who plays Robert also play Gil, whom Querelle both loves and betrays).[10] This complex relationship is played out in a world from which women are missing—except for the aging madame, Lysiane, who repeatedly sings what may be the central theme of the film: "each man kills the thing he loves."[11]

The title character of the film can be seen as a variation on the sadistic personality embodied in Reinhold of *Berlin Alexanderplatz*. Yet at times Querelle also seems a Franz Biberkopf type, unsatisfied in his longings, melodramatically presenting himself at the end as a crucified Christ. In its concluding moments—with its voice-over invocation of "that heaven of heaven where beauty unites with beauty"—the film seems to be suggesting a kind of mystical bond between Querelle and Seblon, one that might fulfill the utopian potential that Fassbinder said he saw in the relationship between Franz Biberkopf and Reinhold. But homosexuality is explicitly foregrounded and problematized in *Querelle* to a much greater extent than in *Berlin Alexanderplatz* or in the two earlier Fassbinder films set, respectively, in lesbian and gay contexts, *The Bitter Tears of Petra von Kant* and *Fox and His Friends*. The emotional entanglements of *Querelle* are intrinsically determined by their homoerotic nature.

As in the novel, Querelle in the film comes to accept his homosexuality only after anguished self-questioning and intense psychosexual struggles with other characters. In all of this he is presented as sexually both passive and aggressive. As Richard Dyer has written, he seems to embody both machismo and the feminine: his muscles, body hair, and sweat contrast with Lieutenant Seblon's clean, neat uniform, his clean-shaven, pretty face with the rough appearance of the other sailors. Thus "he is available as both . . . fucker and fuckee"—the opposing poles of the sexual power dynamics Dyer sees at work in the film.[12] James Roy MacBean is disturbed by the extent to which the film emphasizes Querelle's sexually aggressive side, presenting phallic sexuality as a weapon of brutal, even deadly, power over other males. "In *Querelle*, Fassbinder, after Genet, can even present murder as an act one commits simply in order to be more of a man." MacBean sees here a "morbid fascination" with "sadistic sexual violence" reminiscent of Pier Paolo Pasolini's *Salò*.[13]

Harry Baer reports that Fassbinder had difficulties dealing with the complex erotic themes of the novel as he was writing the screenplay: "He groped his way through the different layers of the text, trying to decide how to handle the sexuality."[14] The film seems to have been for Fassbinder an occasion of exploring imaginatively—and critically—those aggressive aspects of homoerotic sexuality that apparently both fascinated and troubled him. In an interview shortly before his death, he talked at length of his ambivalence about the possibly fascistic aspects of Genet's *Querelle de Brest* and of his guarded fascination with sadomasochism. He pointed out the difficulty he had had in determining the "fine line" separating the "corny" from the "fascistoid" in adapting the novel and in making clear that the apparent "glorification of violence" in the novel applies only to the particular society with which Genet was dealing—a society in which "if you don't function perfectly . . . you have to become a traitor, a murderer, you have to become violent."[15] He admitted to a fascination with violence, but only to the extent that it is "steerable and predictable"—and an interest in sadomasochistic sex so long as it is "controllable in every respect."[16]

Fassbinder approached these complex and apparently quite personal themes in *Querelle* in an unusually formal manner. The most striking aspect of the film, compared with his earlier ones, is Rolf Zehetbaur's enclosed and nearly surrealistic set, bathed in contrasting orange and blue light (extending significantly the lighting effects of *Lola*). Alongside a dock with large and explicitly phallic posts, a small portion of a ship is visible; scenes are played on its confined deck and in the commander's cabin. Close by are a small grassy area (where Querelle murders Vic) and an abandoned underground jail in which Gil hides out. Most of the action takes place in the dark bordello, which is filled with mirrors, semitransparent curtains, and frosted glass panels in Art Nouveau design, some decorated with copies of classical Greek homosexual pornography. Harry Baer has pointed out the similarities between the style of *Querelle* as "an artistically presented dream-fabric-reality" and the set designs of such favorite films of Fassbinder's as Josef von Sternberg's *Morocco,* 1930; Douglas Sirk's German films *Zu neuen Ufern,* 1937 (*To New Shores*), and *La Habañera,* 1937; and Michael Curtiz's *Flamingo Road,* 1949.[17]

Other aspects of *Querelle* are similarly nonnaturalistic. The acting is reminiscent of much of Fassbinder's early theater work and some of his early films, such as *Katzelmacher* and *Effi Briest.* Movements and gestures are often highly choreographed, particularly in a fight between Querelle and Robert. The intonation of dialogue is flat, and many of the voices are obviously dubbed.[18] The characters often hardly interact with one another. As Candide Carrassco has noted, the dynamism in the film "comes essentially from a shifting from one character to another, from one image to the next . . . from mirror reflection to object seen."[19] The camera moves slowly, frequently in long pans and tracking shots, often shooting through the patterned glass of the brothel doors and windows. The music track—in which Fassbinder and Juliane Lorenz had consider-

Querelle (1982). Bordello owner Madame Lysiane (Jeanne Moreau) and Querelle (Brad Davis) dance against a background of Art Nouveau etchings on glass, through which Querelle's would-be lover Lieutenant Seblon (Franco Nero) peers. (Courtesy Museum of Modern Art/Film Stills Archive, New York)

ably more of a hand than the credit to Peer Raben indicates—progresses generally from ominous to lyrical, corresponding somewhat to Querelle's gradual acceptance of his homosexuality.[20] Early on it is dominated by minor-key chorale voices, later by the sounds of a Handel concerto (Opus 7, Number 4, in D Minor, adagio) and symphonic music, with kettledrums at some tense moments. Near the end more upbeat orchestral tunes are heard, sometimes even with tinkling bells that are reminiscent of the lighter moments in *Berlin Alexanderplatz,* as the film moves toward what seems to be, at least for Querelle, a happy ending.[21]

Several critics have concluded that Fassbinder's cinematic treatment does not measure up to the poetic effects of Genet's writing. James Roy MacBean, for example, was not only disturbed by the violent phallocentricity of the film but was also disappointed with its overall artistic effect, finding it "garish, precious to the point of being silly, violent, and, mostly, boring." While that condemnation seems excessive, the film does leave this viewer unsatisfied. Not the least of its problems is that it makes little effort to provide cinematic analogues for the narrator's explanation and commentary and the internal monologue, both of which clarify the characters' motives in the novel. It is not surprising that the cinematographer Xaver Schwartzenberger would say that this was the only Fassbinder film he shot that he did not understand.[22]

Querelle is unique among Fassbinder's films in its explicit foregrounding of male homosexuality—as both problematic and potentially liberating. Moreover, it suggests that at the time of his death the filmmaker may have been intending to renew the exploration of deeply personal psychosexual themes, which he had largely left alone for the previous two years. And in its quite original use of a self-enclosed, theatrical set with expressionistic lighting and unusually formal acting, Fassbinder's final film suggests that he might have intended to move into new levels of stylization. Unfortunately, one can only speculate about such matters.

Unfinished Business

Several films left in the planning stage at Fassbinder's death constitute a reminder—if any is needed—of the broad range of his intellectual and esthetic interests and the fertility of his artistic imagination. One of the most interesting projects was a planned adaptation of *Cocaina* (Cocaine), a 1922 novel by Pitigrilli (pseudonym of the Italian writer Dino Segre [1893–1975]). *Kokain* was to be produced by Horst Wendlandt's Rialto Films in color and CinemaScope and dedicated to Douglas Sirk. Fassbinder began making plans for this project early in 1980, as he was completing the shooting for *Berlin Alexanderplatz,* and he wrote a script for it in February 1981. But the shooting of *Kokain* was deferred in favor of several more fully developed projects, and the director died before he could complete it.[23]

Fassbinder's plans for *Kokain* reinforce the possibility that in *Querelle* can be seen the beginnings of what might have been a distinct movement toward even more complex stylistics in Fassbinder's work. They also indicate a new approach to internalized portrayal of consciousness. In a preliminary treatment he wrote that the film would dramatize the experience of cocaine intoxication (although he would not argue for or against its use, recognizing that a cocaine user may intentionally choose a short life of intense experience rather than a long and boring one). He said that he intended to film a flashback, during a "fever-dream between life and death," of a man who has deliberately taken an overdose of cocaine. This would have been a surrealistic sequence, making use of "marvellously crazy costumes . . . necessary overplaying" and visual suggestions of ice and frost to convey what Fassbinder called the cocaine's user's sense of freezing of the brain—"freeing one's thoughts of anything inessential, and thereby liberating the essential, the imagination, concentration, and so on." Fassbinder said that "although no other films "could really compare" with what he had in mind, his idea for *Cocaine* was suggested in Fellini's fantasy version of his childhood, *Amarcord,* 1974; in Pasolini's *Salò;* and in the epilogue to his own *Berlin Alexanderplatz.*[24]

As was noted in the introduction, at his death Fassbinder had several film projects well underway. One was *Rosa L.,* based on the life and the murder in 1918 of the German communist leader Rosa Luxemburg.[25] In 1982 Fassbinder also wrote a scenario for a film about three detectives-turned-rock musicians, *Ich bin das Glück dieser Erde* (I Am the Happiness of This World).[26] Among his other plans was a film tentatively titled *Hurra, wir leben noch* (Hurrah, We're Still Alive), based on a 1978 novel by the popular and prolific Austrian-Swiss writer Johannes Mario Simmel (1924–).[27] Another anticipated project was a remake of *Possessed,* a 1947 Hollywood study of a woman with subtle mental problems starring Joan Crawford (according to Robert Katz, Fassbinder wanted him to write the screenplay[28]). Fassbinder's continuing interest in confronting contemporary political issues is evident in his joining several other German directors late in 1981 to make plans for a collaborative film, *War and Peace,* "about the desire for peace and the fear of war in the world." It was to include material on a peace march in Bonn and a meeting between East and West German Chancellors Erich Honecker and Helmut Schmidt.[29]

The Films in Review: Despair and the Utopian Imagination

It is no easy task to summarize the work of such a complex and productive filmmaker as Rainer Werner Fassbinder only thirteen years after his death. Perhaps the most obvious aspect of his legacy is the extraordinary variety in his portrayals of life in modern Germany. As Wolfram Schütte has written, Fassbinder's films constitute a gallery of human types and social settings as diversified as *The Human Comedy* of the nineteenth-century French novelist Honoré de Balzac.[30] They contain highly specific and usually sympathetic studies of characters drawn from many socioeconomic and existential situations— from the depressed and inarticulate petty criminals of the early gangster films set in postwar Munich to the suave, angst-ridden, but cold-blooded murderer

Hermann Hermann in the late-Weimar Berlin of *Despair;* from the suburban housewife Martha, driven to the verge of insanity by her smug husband, to the fading movie star Veronica Voss, driven to suicide by her all-controlling doctor; from the upper-class professional Petra von Kant, tormented in her stylish apartment by the working-class Karin, to the naval lieutenant Seblon, musing in his cabin over his secret passion for the sailor Querelle.

Running through virtually all of these films is what Fassbinder called his constant theme, "the manipulability, the exploitability of feelings inside the systems that we live in,"[31] along with the irrepressible hope of escape. Time after time one encounters there characters flailing about in the "vicious circles" in which they are trapped, "in the utopian hope of finding a way out at the weakest point," as Thomas Elsaesser has put it.[32] Their utopian impulses assume a variety of forms: Franz's and Günther's dream of going to a Mediterranean island in *Gods of the Plague;* Hans Epp's longing for his "true love," and his unexpected encounter with his comrade from the Foreign Legion in *The Merchant of Four Seasons;* Hermann Hermann's "deliberate" escape into madness; Veronika Voss's fantasy of regaining her status as a movie star. But virtually all of those and the other utopian dreams enacted in Fassbinder's films are illusory, and in most cases the characters seem to be ignorant of that fact, or else they are unwilling to do what is necessary to change their private lives or to challenge the outer forces that oppress them.

Not surprisingly, many critics on the left have complained that these films are unduly pessimistic, that they reinforce political passivity. Fassbinder's response was that he intended to criticize what is wrong in personal relationships and in public life so as to inspire in viewers the hope of something better. He often suggested that he wanted to stir more substantial and intelligent utopian hopes in his viewers than the ineffectual fantasies of the characters in his films. He said the viewer is the one who must "complete the film."[33] He wanted his films to stimulate the "anarchy of the imagination," inspiring his viewers not to accept the limitations of their lives as inevitable.[34] He argued that his films exposed "certain mechanisms" in human relations that people need to understand to improve their lives. "When I show people, on the screen, the ways that things can go wrong, my aim is to warn them that that's the way things *will* go if they don't change their lives."[35] As in any other art, the first obligation of film is to entertain, he said. But that should be done in ways that leave the viewer "no stupider" and should "give the moviegoer the courage to continue expressing things, taking a position on them."[36] Even while admitting that he saw little hope of improving life in the contemporary world, Fassbinder insisted that "the more depressing a film is, the more it forces the viewer to look for a Utopia."[37]

The Fassbinder Styles

In his efforts to stir the imaginations and the utopian hopes of his viewers, Fassbinder employed a wide range of distancing strategies, which are reminiscent variously of Bertolt Brecht's theatrical "alienation effects," the reflexive self-consciousness in the films of Jean-Luc Godard, and the more subtle ironies in Douglas Sirk's Hollywood melodramas, among other antecedents. Recent criticism of Fassbinder's films, inspired to a considerable extent by gay film theory, has begun to emphasize the playfully ironic or "camp" quality of Fassbinder's alienation effects—particularly in what Jane Shattuc has called his "oddly self-conscious camp glorification" of Sirkean melodrama.[38] As Shattuc makes clear, however, camp and other distancing effects in Fassbinder's films amount to more than stylistic game-playing. More often than not, Fassbinder's self-conscious distancing strategies have the effect of jarring the viewer into both critical introspection and radical questioning of social mores.[39]

Alienation effects take many forms in Fassbinder's films. Sometimes they are quirky stylistic ploys, such as a ludicrous surge of symphonic or organ music at a point of great emotional intensity, eccentric framing, self-conscious mirror shots, or shots that run an unusually long time.[40] Frequently, distancing is a matter of acting style. Camille Nevers has described the characteristic facial expression of the Fassbinder protagonist, from his earliest films to his latest, as "an indefinable expression or mask . . . an anxious impassivity" that reveals "neither complete indifference nor complete despair, which never tolerates our pity and especially doesn't let us 'judge'" the characters.[41] Similar effects are often achieved through nonnaturalistic dialogue, most obviously in what the director once called the "Fassbinder-talk" of his earlier work (which he later said had made those films virtually "inaccessible"). But it is no less significant, he said, in the "very foreshortened, and also very stylized" language of the later films, which, together with "the structure of the camera movements and the images," constitutes "a beautiful and precise, but still very alien language."[42] Finally, many of the films inspire a critical distance in the audience by subverting the viewers' expectations of established film genres—for example, his early use of the gangster film as a model for intensive character studies, or his refusal to end his films with the kinds of closure characteristic of both Hollywood melodrama and politically correct leftist films.

Beyond noting the prevalence of such varied alienation devices, it is difficult to generalize about the aesthetics of these films. Any attempt to define a "Fassbinder style" must take account of effects as diverse as the largely unscripted cinema-verité manner of *Why Does Herr R. Run Amok?,* evocations of American and French film noir in the gangster films, the self-conscious cinematic reflexivity of *Beware of a Holy Whore;* the realistic effects of such early-1970s melodramas as *The Merchant of Four Seasons* and *Ali: Fear Eats the Soul;* the almost static camera work and tightly restrained acting of *Katzelmacher* and *Fontane Effi Briest* (two films that are worlds apart in most other respects); the self-conscious cinematography and dramatization of interior space in *The Bitter Tears of Petra von Kant* and *Chinese Roulette;* the brilliant combination of literary and cinematic effects in *Effi Briest* and *Despair;* the multilayered visual and aural textures of *The Marriage of Maria Braun, In a Year of 13 Moons, The Third Generation,* and *Berlin Alexanderplatz;* the evocative black-and-white effects of *Veronika Voss;* and the nonnaturalistic color in *Lola* and *Querelle.*

Some general patterns of stylistic development during Fassbinder's brief career can, however, be defined. One is a movement away from the static quality of much of the early work to a more fluid manner. An important factor at the beginning was the limited nature of his material resources (most obviously in the still shots made in *Katzelmacher* with a virtually unmovable camera), what Tony Rayns has called the "startling poverty of means" available to him during the apprentice period.[43] As Rayns emphasizes, however, the restrained style of this and many of Fassbinder's other apprentice films was also largely the result of deliberate artistic choice, owing a great deal to the aesthetics of Jean-Marie Straub, to the team's previous work in the antitheater, and to the films of Jean-Luc Godard. That Straub-Godard aesthetic often reasserts itself in the films Fassbinder made after he gained access to substantial resources and began to incorporate Hollywood production values into his work—from the stylized dinner-table scene at the end of *The Merchant of Four Seasons* to the choreographed movement and elliptical dialogue of *Querelle.*

Fassbinder's cinematic use of space changed gradually but decidedly over the course of his career, reflecting increasingly internalized exploration of character. Many of the apprentice films, as well as the melodramas of the early 1970s, depict the entrapment of characters within social collectives—whether criminal gangs, marriages, families, or workplace groups. These outer constraints on the lives of individuals are often suggested by the use of confining interior or exterior spaces or framing through doorways and windows. The later films generally dramatize more subtle forms of psychological entrapment deriving from the protagonists' inner conflicts. These states of mind are characteristically suggested in shots through glass or opaque materials, such as the plexiglass cabinets in *Chinese Roulette* and the etched glass walls of *Despair,* or in a variety of complex mirror shots, a technique that Douglas Sirk often employed and that came to constitute Fassbinder's trademark cinematic mannerism.[44]

The development of Fassbinder's visual style was to a considerable degree a function of his collaboration with his three chief cinematographers, Dietrich Lohmann, Michael Ballhaus, and Xaver Schwarzenberger. The films shot by Lohmann mostly make use of formal, restrained camera work. (Lohmann shot Fassbinder's first five feature-length films, as well as *The American Soldier, Pioniere in Ingolstadt, The Merchant of Four Seasons, Acht Stunden sind kein Tag,* and *Wildwechsel,* and he shared cinematography duties on *Bremen Coffee* and *Effi Briest*). Fassbinder developed a more expansive visual style in collaboration with his second major cameraman, Michael Ballhaus, who was a nephew of the famous German-French director Max Ophüls.[45] As Tony Rayns has noted, Ballhaus shared with Fassbinder "a determination to meet Hollywood discourse, in all its 'affirmative' expansiveness and syntactic density, on its own terms. . . [to] use social, cultural and cinematic conventions for their distinctiveness rather than their banality. . . to *equal* Hollywood, not to emulate it."[46] Even while he was continuing to work regularly with Lohmann, Fassbinder brought Ballhaus in to shoot several films (*Whity, Holy Whore, Petra von Kant, Welt am Draht,* and *Martha*) that employ color and make use of much more active camera movement and more varied visual textures than Lohmann's films generally did. Starting in 1974, Ballhaus was cinematographer for many Fassbinder films shot in a variety of complex styles: *Fox and His Friends, Mother Küsters Goes to Heaven, I Only Want You to Love Me, Satan's Brew* (with Jürge Jürges), *Chinese Roulette, Bolwieser, Frauen in New York, Despair,* Fassbinder's segment of *Germany in Autumn,* and *The Marriage of Maria Braun;* he subsequently became one of the most sought-after cinematographers in Hollywood.[47] Xaver Schwarzenberger, an Austrian who had shot more than thirty documentary films for Austrian and Bavarian television, joined the Fassbinder team in 1979 as cinematographer for *Berlin Alexanderplatz* and shot Fassbinder's four remaining feature films. Fassbinder said in 1982 that Schwarzenberger's greater interest in color helped him learn in his later films "to paint with the camera," to experiment with "artistic" as well as "natural" color.[48]

Fassbinder's stylistic development significantly reflects other artistic collaborations as well. Kurt Raab, a member of the team since the Action Theater days, served as art director for most of the films until 1976. Juliane Lorenz has asserted that Raab served more as a "set designer" than "art director": "He didn't create rooms. He just arranged things within pre-existing rooms or other spaces, organized things as Rainer wanted him to."[49] For his second film aimed at the international art-house market, *Despair,* 1977, Fassbinder hired the well-known art director Rolf Zehetbauer, who had won one of the eight American Academy Awards given to Bob Fosse's 1972 film *Cabaret.* The complex, highly charged visual effects of three of Fassbinder's later films—*Lili Marleen, Veronika Voss,* and *Querelle*—doubtless reflect Zehetbauer's talent and experience. Another important artistic collaborator was the costume designer Barbara Baum, who worked for Fassbinder first on *Nora Helmer* (his first film crediting a costume designer) and later on six other projects that made notable use of period costumes: *Effi Briest, The Marriage of Maria Braun, Berlin Alexanderplatz, Lili Marleen, Lola,* and *Veronika Voss*—as well as *Querelle.*[50]

Fassbinder was directly involved as editor—or, in varying degrees, as coeditor—in the cutting of fourteen of his feature-length films: seven from his earliest through *Beware of a Holy Whore,* 1970, and seven starting again with *Bolwieser,* 1976.[51] Moreover, it has often been pointed out that others involved in editing his films—chiefly Thea Eymèsz and Juliane Lorenz—had less responsibility than film editors generally have, since the director shot his films with such clear ideas about the final form he wanted them to take. Fassbinder often emphasized that he was not one to shoot a variety of takes and leave it to cutters to decide among them. But he was more dependent on the taste and judgment of his editors and coeditors than has often been acknowledged, as Hans-Günther Pflaum has pointed out.[52] His concern to find cutters who could intuitively understand his intended rhythm is clear in the editing history of *Despair* (discussed in chapter eight). Thea Eymèsz, who edited most of Fassbinder's films from 1970 through 1976, has described how she sensed the need for slightly delaying the running time of most of his shots and how she was able to understand what Fassbinder wanted without discussing it with him.[53] Juliane Lorenz, who was assistant editor for *Chinese Roulette* and *Bolwieser* and editor or coeditor with Fassbinder on his later films, has also emphasized her intuitive sense of Fassbinder's intentions for editing and the amount of freedom the director gave her to realize them.[54]

Another significant factor in the aesthetics of many Fassbinder films, particularly during his earlier years, was whether or not they were intended initially for television broadcast. This consideration seems to have figured often in the choice of subject matter as well. In 1973 Fassbinder told Christian Braad Thomsen that films made for the large and relatively unsophisticated television audience should express an "aesthetics of hope," while theatrical films, whose audiences are "people like you and me," an "aesthetics of pessimism." Four years later he said that television is properly used only "when you show things which go straight to the viewers—talk directly to the family sitting in front of the screen," understanding that the easily distracted television viewers must be led to see things that they do not want to see "because it's excitingly made."[55] These comments may partially explain why a number of Fassbinder's relatively naturalistic personal case studies (such as *The Merchant of Four Seasons, Wildwechsel, Martha, Fear of Fear, I Only Want You to Love Me, Bolwieser,* and even *Berlin Alexanderplatz*) were made for television. But those films certainly are not thematically "optimistic." Perhaps Fassbinder's 1973 statement that television films should express hope reflects the fact that he had just completed his five-part miniseries about the working and private lives of contemporary West Germans, *Acht Stunden sind kein Tag*—which is by far the most optimistic of his films.

In any case, it is clear that Fassbinder had little interest in video as a medium of film production. Thirteen of his movies were produced on 16 mm film, twenty-six on 35 mm film. Only four were shot on videotape: three filmed versions of plays and the Brigitta Mira "entertainment."[56] In 1982, Fassbinder recalled Godard's return to film after experimenting in the video medium, and he challenged the claims of the American directors Francis Ford Coppola and George Lucas that they could create a new film-language with video technology. He said that magnetic tape was useful only as a means of distributing films through television broadcast.[57]

Understanding Rainer Werner Fassbinder: A Personal Retrospect

Studies of Fassbinder's films inevitably have to face the challenge of dealing appropriately with their autobiographical dimensions. Perhaps more than any other major postwar director, Fassbinder points in his films to his personal history—particularly his unusual childhood, his sexual ambivalence, and his intimate relationships as an adult—as well as to his public roles as disillusioned child of the Generation of '68, nonconformist intellectual, and extraordinarily productive film artist. As Günther Rohrbach, an executive producer who supervised several Fassbinder projects at WDR and later at Bavaria Studios, summarized the matter in his obituary of the director, Fassbinder was "Germany's most famous director, the only one whose name almost everybody knew," an artist who in pursuing his intention to become a legend became "part of his art."[58] But Fassbinder's films are by no means merely autobiographical. Their personal references are more often than not imaginative projections, fantasizing or implicitly commenting on the private and public lives of the *Autor* in much more complex (and often more humorous) ways than some commentators have suggested.[59]

Not the least of the difficulties in dealing with the autobiographical nature of Fassbinder's films are the apparent contradictions in his personality, which many people have spoken and written about. For example, Ingrid Caven, to whom Fassbinder was briefly married in the early 1970s and with whom he remained a close friend for some years after that, once said, "You never know with Fassbinder whether his hand will strike you or caress you."[60] Hans Günther Pflaum, after observing Fassbinder at work on three films in 1976, found him to be "as much the Bavarian bully in shirtsleeves as the wounded, vulnerable prodigy; he deals out blows as if he wanted to observe how vulnerable other people are and to see if they take him seriously enough to be actually hurt by him."[61] Harry Baer, Fassbinder's friend and coworker on many projects, was convinced that the director saw important aspects of himself in both the masochistic Franz Biberkopf and the sadistic Reinhold of *Berlin Alexanderplatz*. In his later years Fassbinder frequently spoke of his personality as "manic-depressive." That was the term he used when he explained to Wolfgang Limmer how his creative urges often helped him recover from the spells of gloom that inexplicably came upon him: "I get so sad that I just don't know what my life is all about. On the other hand, sometimes I'm sitting around with people who don't particularly turn me on. Then I entertain the whole table, simply because I enjoy telling stories. Then I get happy without knowing why."[62]

The Danish filmmaker and writer Christian Braad Thomsen, to whom Fassbinder gave a series of revealing interviews from 1970 to 1980, concluded that the secret to Fassbinder's personality was its "bi-polar" nature. Thomsen emphasizes Fassbinder's fascination with Freud's picture of Moses in his *Moses and Monotheism* (1939) as a composite of a fanatical, authoritarian Egyptian priest who converted the Jews to his monotheistic religion and led them out of Egypt, and a kindly Jewish shepherd who took over leadership of the fleeing tribe after they had killed that priest. Thomsen connects Fassbinder's interest in Freud's Moses with the contradictions he observed in the director's personality: "He was tender and cynical, he was gentle and brutal, he was sacrificing and egocentric, he was ruthlessly dictatorial and nonetheless dreamt always of working in groups and collectives."[63]

Thomsen provides a helpful metaphor for understanding some of the contrasting aspects of Fassbinder's personality when he emphasizes the director's childlike qualities, which coexisted with his intellectual sophistication, professional self-confidence, decisiveness, and assertiveness: "His films are *Kinderfilme,* films seen through the eyes of the child. They treat naively the most complicated problem situation, without evading taboos or conflicts."[64] One can see similarly childlike qualities in the sometimes surprising candor of

Fassbinder's self-revelations in interviews, in his neglect of his health, and in the lack of caution with which he threw himself into many of his most controversial creative projects, forgetting or refusing to worry about how they might be received by critics and the general public.[65] Moreover, there is a little-boy quality to Fassbinder's reputed shyness in large groups outside his own entourage and with strangers, particularly well-known artists.[66] Margit Carstensen, who played lead roles in several Fassbinder films, said she had to take the initiative with him to get to know him.[67] There are numerous stories recounting his hesitancy to meet celebrities, such as the French actress Jeanne Moreau (who played in *Querelle*) and the American artist and filmmaker Andy Warhol.[68]

There is also a certain childlike quality in the romantic, utopian idea of love that Fassbinder sometimes expressed, even while fully acknowledging its difficulties: "Love is certainly the greatest thing there is. But we shouldn't put too much strain on it."[69] Most of Fassbinder's comments about intimate ties are bleakly pessimistic, but he seems never to have given up hope for utopian outcomes. In 1973, discussing difficulties he was having in his current close relationship (presumably with El Hedi ben Salem), he said he wished that he could live without such ties, seeing the need to be fixated on a single person as "a relic out of the past" that in his case inevitably lead to mutual dependency. Still, he said that he felt that it was important not to repress his feelings, and he remained hopeful that something good would eventually result. "I think that by going through extreme situations involving despair and pain . . . you can arrive at a new spontaneity. That seems to offer a better chance of achieving a new naiveté of experience than repression."[70]

Certainly, one of the more significant aspects of Fassbinder's bipolar personality was his complex sexual orientation. Critics and biographers have largely presented him as unambiguously homosexual, which is how he represented himself for the most part in conversations with interviewers. He spoke of having "no problems, sexually speaking . . . no complexes and no inhibitions," since he had decided early on "not to make a big deal about sleeping with men."[71] "Coming out" had never been "a problem" for him, he said, perhaps because in his adolescence it seemed nonsense to make an issue over such a matter. "When I had this feeling that I was gay, I immediately told everybody."[72] Fassbinder's most intense emotional relationships were with three male lovers—Günther Kaufmann, El Hedi ben Salem, and Armin Meier. Yet he had female lovers at several different times during his adult life. He was married for a short time to Ingrid Caven. And for the last four years of his life, after Meier's death, he lived with his film editor, Juliane Lorenz, who asserted in an interview with the author that in her experience Fassbinder was an enthusiastic and satisfying heterosexual lover, and that he wanted to marry her and have a child with her.[73] On another occasion she summarized him as "an exceptional individual with a multiform sexuality."[74]

Near the end of his life, Fassbinder talked at length with Wolfgang Limmer about his sexual nature. He resisted Limmer's suggestion that his was "the classic case of the homosexual," with a distant father and mother, and particularly a mother who did not serve the usual "mirror-function" (as defined by Lacanian psychology). Fassbinder suggested that this kind of analysis is simplistic. He agreed that homosexuality "certainly is a social phenomenon and not inborn," derived from childhood experience, adding that the unusual conditions in postwar society led to something "genuinely new" in familial constellations.[75] But he emphasized that he did not "look for mirror images" in his intimate relationships (which Limmer characterized as an essential component of homosexuality). Perhaps, Fassbinder concluded, one could say that in his friendships with both male and females he was searching for his alter ego. "But that's not something that I can concisely say here and now—perhaps in ten years."[76]

Fassbinder was sometimes criticized by gays and lesbians for projecting unappealing images of homosexuals in his films and by gay activists for not being more actively engaged in their political efforts. He often asserted, with reference both to his films and his personal life, that gender or sexual orientation was relatively unimportant to the nature of intimate relationships: "The same mechanisms of oppression are at work in gay relationships as in others," he said.[77] He insisted that *The Bitter Tears of Petra von Kant* and *Fox and His Friends* were films about exploitation within relationships that only incidentally occurred in gay and lesbian contexts.[78]

Considering all of this, as well as the intense sympathy with which most of his films present both male and female perpetrators and victims of emotional exploitation in intimate relationships (both heterosexual and homosexual), it seems appropriate to think of the creative side of Fassbinder's nature, at least, as largely androgynous. But this conclusion is by no means intended to support Peter Berling's glib assertion, in his 1992 book on the director, that Fassbinder "was not gay, did not become gay, but wanted to become gay"—that his homosexual lifestyle was purely "a willful act" motivated by the desire to challenge bourgeois social norms.[79]

Fassbinder's personality resists easy summary not only because of its bipolar nature, but also because he seems to have matured considerably during his brief adult life—a possibility that most biographical accounts have ignored. During and after what has been described above as the purgatorial crisis that began for him at about age thirty, Fassbinder's interviews demonstrate a self-reflective, even philosophical, interest in the emotional power games in which he had earlier indulged so recklessly and sometimes quite viciously (if some of the more shocking parts of the legend can be believed). Speaking in 1976 about the many-sided "game of dependency," he remarked that before 1973 he was "not very self-critical about this."[80] In 1977 he speculated about the mutual dependencies involved in sadism and masochism, emphasizing that "self-knowledge is essential."[81] Future assessments of Fassbinder's personality will need to consider such comments from him more thoughtfully than has yet been done. They will also need to pay attention to the testimony of those who worked with the director during his later years.

Fassbinder at Work

There was apparently a great deal beyond the director's ability to keep them regularly employed that inspired regulars in the Fassbinder group to stick with him in project after strenuous project and that enticed many internationally known actors and other film artists to respond to his call. A number of people have spoken or written about the excitement and appeal of Fassbinder's artistic discipline (even in his most self-absorbed projects), his excitement in collaborative work, the freedom he granted those colleagues in whom he had confidence to discover and develop their own abilities, his power of intuitive communication, and his willingness to learn from his mistakes. Fassbinder could be a savvy, tough operator in the unsentimental world of film production and finance, and he was often hard on his associates. Nevertheless, the pleasure he experienced in making movies seems to have been infectious. Harry Baer recalled in 1992: "At the beginning, it was just fun—fun, fun, fun. . . . Then it became hard work, and that also attracted us. We worked very hard until the end."[82] Fassbinder said in 1974: "There is a mania in film-making. It's not like an ordinary eight-hour-a-day job. Film has to do with everything . . . your normal life disappears when you're filming."[83] Shortly before his death Fassbinder claimed that the first take he made with a movie camera was "more fantastic than the most fantastic orgasm I ever had."[84] And he spoke movingly of the sheer joy he and his crew had experienced in making *Veronika Voss,* pleasure that he said meant much more to him than the Golden Bear the film received at the Berlin Film Festival.[85]

Fassbinder's amazing productivity can thus be accounted for in part by what seems to have been an unusually strong personal delight in transforming his experiences and fantasies, and his observations of life around him, into cinematic images. Obviously important also were his visual imagination and visual memory—essential qualities in any filmmaker, of course, but apparently extraordinarily developed in Fassbinder. His interviews are full of recollections of films he had seen years earlier, and many of his coworkers marveled at how concretely he imagined the visual form and structure of his films before he began shooting.

Other personal qualities that contributed to Fassbinder's productivity were his decisiveness and his ability to inspire artistic commitment and discipline from actors and other coworkers. For all the problems of his private life, he was a highly disciplined director. As he said in 1977, he recognized that discipline was essential in the work of making films: "When I work I demand discipline and punctuality of my colleagues and co-workers, and from myself as well. . . . I submit to the terror of self-imposed deadlines."[86] Bavaria Studios producer Günther Rohrbach summed up the professional manner of the Fassbinder he knew: "However chaotic might have been the conditions among which he lived— in the studio he was a precise worker who projected calm and certainty." During shooting, Fassbinder usually sketched out each night the shots for the next day's filming on his copy of the script. Unlike most directors, he almost always filmed a shot in only one way, often in only one take.[87] Furthermore, he rarely rehearsed his actors, being convinced that the first performance of an action for the camera was usually the most convincing and dynamic.[88] Increasingly, as his acting troupe grew more professional, he gave minimal instructions to his players, usually talking only about the general effect he wanted and trusting their ability to interpret his desires.[89]

Probably the most important external factor in Fassbinder's productivity was the relatively stable entourage of actors, artists, and technicians with whom he worked from project to project—"the most impressive stock company in films outside of Ingmar Bergman's," Andrew Sarris observed in 1976.[90] At the personal level, the Fassbinder team seems to have served the director's psychological needs, as a sort of extended family, as he has pointed out,[91] just as he met the need in many of the early members of the group for an authoritarian and/or supportive parent figure.[92] Beyond that, the group provided him with a well known and fairly constant pool of talent, which could move quickly with him from project to project. Early in the antitheater days, Fassbinder seems to have genuinely hoped that the entourage would function as a utopian artistic collective. But that idea did not work out—apparently because of both the forcefulness of his creative personality and the unwillingness or inability of many in the troupe to assume necessary responsibilities. During the first few years of his filmmaking career, roles were created and parts were assigned with the director's understanding of the actors' own personalities and their relationship with him in mind, as he said.[93] This personalized approach to casting became less significant, however, as the group evolved into a body of mature professionals to whom Fassbinder granted freedom to exercise their creative abilities. While there was considerable continuity in the membership of the group, Fassbinder made many changes from project to project, and increasingly he brought in actors and artistic and technical staff with national and international reputations.[94]

The Fassbinder legend has been constructed to a considerable degree around the central image of the director as "monster," as master of a literal "theater of cruelty," tyrannizing over his technicians and actors, gleefully exploiting their psychological weaknesses and their dependence on him, and, in turn, emotionally dependent on them. Fassbinder seemed to be admitting a penchant for such behavior in *Beware of a Holy Whore,* 1970. Such a characterization, however, insofar as it is true, seems to apply much more to the early years of his career as a film director than to his later years. And it seems to derive in large part from the embittered and self-serving book published shortly after Fassbinder's death by Kurt Raab, whom Fassbinder had dismissed from his team in 1976, and from the scandalous stories supplied by the producer Peter Berling, an often untrustworthy biographical source.[95] Dirk Bogarde has written that the cast and crew of *Despair* were "shit terrified" of Fassbinder during their work in 1977. Still, Bogarde favorably compared Fassbinder, at age thirty-two, to the best European directors, claimed that he had enabled Bogard in *Despair* "to do my best work for the Cinema . . . the best I have ever done," and said that he would go anywhere to work with him again. Bogarde was also moved by Fassbinder's belief that he had learned from the older man how to inspire "authority without fear."[96] In other work about that time, Fassbinder seems to have inspired more authority than fear. A German critic who observed him during the shooting of three films in 1976 was impressed by the calm professionalism Fassbinder exhibited on the set and by his ability to elicit trust from his professional staff.[97] Two reporters who spent two days on the set of *Querelle* in 1982 were struck by the director's openness to suggestion and his ability to motivate the cast and crew to develop their own creativity, in a relaxed and trusting atmosphere.[98]

Three of Fassbinder's major artistic collaborators, interviewed in the late 1980s by Juliane Lorenz, have emphasized the balance he was able to maintain between demanding expectations and a warm collegiality. The cinematographer Xaver Schwarzenberger was surprised by the difference between Fassbinder's reputation as a tyrant and the disciplined but humane professional manner he observed once they began working together. He said that in the first three weeks of work on their first project, *Berlin Alexanderplatz,* Fassbinder seemed to be testing his new cameraman's limits, working extremely fast, as if in a kind of "showdown to see who would collapse first." Then, sensing Schwarzenberger's discouragement without the cameraman's having spoken of it, Fassbinder slowed down the pace. This event began what was "certainly the most fruitful, agreeable, and joyous work as cameraman that I ever had," Schwarzenberger said. He added that he knew of no other director who combined so effectively an extemporaneous working style and attention to detail, with a clear sense from the beginning of the rhythm he wanted to achieve. The art director Rolf Zehetbauer was also impressed by the precision of Fassbinder's imagination and his ability to communicate his general intentions concisely and quickly—often by reference to other films, which they sometimes looked at together. The costume designer Barbara Baum spoke of Fassbinder's subtle style of communicating with her, and his ability to challenge her and to inspire in her confidence in her own professionalism. "It was such a varied and great time with Rainer. Each film a new challenge . . . a fantastic time."[99]

One is struck by the contrast between such accounts of Fassbinder's professional and supportive directorial style during his later years and the troubling themes of the films he was making. If, as seems clear, these late films touched on issues of profound personal significance to the director, this fact did not seem to interfere with his artistic self-assurance. For example, no other Fassbinder project gives a more moving account of emotional exploitation and suffering, or was more intently engaged with the director's psyche, than *Berlin Alexanderplatz,* which Schwarzenberger found such pleasure in shooting with him over many months. The situation was similar with *Veronika Voss.* Fassbinder's next-to-last film is perhaps his most pointed dramatization of emotional exploitation in an intimate personal relationship, and it offers a damning condemnation of official corruption in the Federal Republic. But the film is also a strikingly beautiful and complex tribute to the cinematic medium, and Fassbinder's affection for the project seems to have permeated the ensemble who worked on it with him. The producer Thomas Schühly reported that the whole crew "were always in love with him and they would work for twenty-four hours. . . . When we started production, it was like an explosion for four or six weeks."[100]

If the atmosphere on a Fassbinder movie set during his later years was less traumatic than the legend has suggested, it was never without tension, however, as Schühly's comment suggests. There are many reports of an intense, almost erotic, creative ambiance during the shooting of his films, which may account for some of the unusual intensity that the viewer often senses in the finished product. The actors Ulli Lommel and Anna Karina spoke of the strong "magnetic field" generated by Fassbinder during shooting.[101] Macha Méril, who played the governess in *Chinese Roulette,* compared acting under Fassbinder's direction to making love: "often at such times you shouldn't say anything, you yourself understand . . . ."[102] Hanna Schygulla recalled in 1991: "He didn't have to say much and I would somehow, to a certain degree, totally give in to his fantasy—but also resisting it at some point. His big talent was provocation."[103] When he deemed it appropriate, even in his later work Fassbinder would employ with experienced actors the kind of intense psychological strategies that he had often used with less accomplished actors in the early years—as in the extreme discomfort he deliberately caused Margit Carstensen during the shooting of *Satan's Brew*[104] and the interpersonal tension among all members of the cast and crew that he created during the shooting of *Chinese Roulette* (as noted in chapter seven). Hans Günther Pflaum has pointed out that an actor who expected only limited involvement would not be comfortable as part of the Fassbinder team. But he said that he certainly did not find the director to be the "animal-trainer" on the set that his critics had often accused him of being.[105]

Fassbinder's Legacy and the Decline of the New German Cinema

The end result of Fassbinder's unusually fast-paced and intense work as a film director is a remarkable, if uneven, corpus of cinematic art. Not many of his films have attained the status of unquestioned masterpiece. Even those that have received the most enthusiastic and widespread critical acclaim—*The Marriage of Maria Braun, Despair, Berlin Alexanderplatz, In a Year of 13 Moons,* and *Veronika Voss,* for example—exhibit in places symptoms of Fassbinder's distaste for polish (which he shared with Italian Neo-realist and some French New Wave directors), and of his impatience to move on to the next, often distinctly different, project. He preferred to learn by doing, he said, correcting the mistakes of one film in the next. "Certainly the last [of my films] is the best . . . since I always learn something from it," he said in 1974.[106] Asked in 1982 if his films suffered in quality because he worked so quickly, as some critics had alleged, Fassbinder answered: "They have the depth and meaning they have. Some people take time to make shallow films. . . . I know I am quicker than the others. This is the kind of work for our times—who knows how much time we have? Life is precarious. Films have to reflect the changing and fast pace of our lives."[107]

In spite of their uneven quality (and of those self-deprecating comments by the director), it should be emphasized that a considerable number of Fassbinder's films rank among the most interesting examples of cinematic art produced anywhere in the postwar world. All of them bear marks of the director's extraordinary visual and aural imagination; his intensely personal involvement in his work; his sympathy for individuals, both victims and oppressors; and his commitment to employ the most popular modern art form to expose the emotional, economic, and political mechanisms by which people exploit and oppress each other in both their private and public lives. Although his career was cut short in midstream, Fassbinder's films, in all their variety, certainly fulfill a wish he once expressed: "I would like to build a house with my films. Some are the cellar, others the walls, still others the windows. But I hope that in the end it will be a house."[108]

Fassbinder's work after 1970 constitutes a unique effort among major filmmakers to bridge the gap between popular and oppositional cinema. After his apprenticeship, he generally eschewed the avant-garde cinematic strategies of such experimental West German film artists as Alexander Kluge, Werner Schroeter, and Edgar Reitz. Yet for all his interest in creating the "German Hollywood-film," he never made merely uncomplicatedly "popular" films such as the war melodrama *Das Boot,* 1981 (*The Boat*), and the children's fantasy *Die unendliche Geschichte,* 1984 (*The Neverending Story*) of his contemporary Wolfgang Peterson.

Moreover, of the four best-known directors of the New German Cinema, Fassbinder focused most intently, by far, on German material and themes. Wim Wenders regularly ventured into American themes and locales, while Werner Herzog explored romantic-existential themes in Mexico, South America, Africa, Australia and other non-German locales. Since the mid-1980s Volker Schlöndorff has been directing plays for American television, and in 1983 and 1985, respectively, he made adaptations of non-German novels, the French novelist Marcel Proust's *Swann in Love* and the American playwright Arthur Miller's *Death of a Salesman.* Admittedly, Fassbinder's final film was an adaptation of a French novel, with no reference to Germany; perhaps this was another way in which *Querelle* would have marked a transition in his career. In any case, virtually all of his films prior to that last one are distinctly German. Fassbinder's early death surely deprived the world of provocative cinematic explorations of the tumultuous—and in many respects deeply disturbing—changes that have occurred in Germany since its sudden unification in 1989 and 1990.

What may be most impressive about Fassbinder's films apart from aesthetic considerations is their lack of conformity to any version of what has lately been called Political Correctness. His insistence on filming his independent artistic vision led to difficulties with many shapers of public taste and opinion in the Federal Republic with whom he was for the most part in sympathy—the political left, gay and lesbian and feminist activists, and the West German Jewish community and its supporters—not to mention political conservatives and upholders of bourgeois privilege and propriety. That independence of artistic vision went hand in hand with the director's tendency to treat his characters as distinct individuals rather than as ciphers in contemporary political and cultural discourse. His films project empathetic understanding of misogynistic gangsters, cold-blooded killers, overbearing parents and wives and husbands, and even nascent and unreconstructed fascists. Correspondingly, they dramatize the self-centeredness and pettiness of even his most sympathetic characters, such as Emmi and Ali of *Fear Eats the Soul.*

Fassbinder's death in 1982 has often been interpreted as the most significant factor in the subsequent decline of a distinctly New German Cinema, even as European and American cinema has been enriched by the actors, cinematographers, and other creative film workers whose talents had developed substantially in working under his direction. In his obituary of the director who seemed to him "the dominant artistic personality" of contemporary West German film, the critic Wolfram Schütte observed that the "beating heart" of the New German Cinema had been stilled when Fassbinder died.[109] Another German critic, Peter Buchka, recalled in 1992 that "on the very day of his death it was obvious, even to his enemies, that he left a hole in the German film scene" and added: "No one, not even the most pessimistic, anticipated that this hole would become so large, so unfillable."[110] Thomas Elsaesser wrote in 1989 of the New German Cinema largely in the past tense, concluding that it had "dispersed itself to the four corners of the earth and fragmented whatever unity" it may have had in the 1970s. As Elsaesser notes, the "obvious absence" is Fassbinder, whose "loss not only for the New German Cinema is incalculable."[111]

Whatever conclusions one might draw about the current state of the New German Cinema or of the impact of Fassbinder's death upon it, there is no doubt that his films constitute a major achievement in the history of both German and international cinema. As commentators have often observed, filmmakers survive death as long as their films continue to be seen. Considering the growing and increasingly sophisticated interest in Fassbinder's work among film critics and cultural theorists, and the enthusiastic response of audiences at retrospectives around the world following the tenth anniversary of his death in 1992, it seems likely that these films will continue to reverberate in the imaginations of cineastes for a long time to come. This is as it should be. For the creative legacy of Rainer Werner Fassbinder bears unique testimony to the power of the cinema simultaneously to explore the most personal fantasies of its makers and to engage in provocative critique of the social sphere, in forms that both delight the eye and spur us to question our own lives, private and public.

Notes

1. Baer 184. *Querelle de Brest* (Querelle of Brest) was the fourth and final novel Genet wrote. Textual citations are to the 1974 English translation by Anselm Hollo.

2. In 1948, after Genet was convicted for his tenth burglary and threatened with automatic life imprisonment, the avant-garde writer and filmmaker Jean Cocteau and several other important French writers secured a pardon for him from the President of the French Republic. These supporters included Jean-Paul Sartre, who in 1952 published an influential "existentialist treatise" on Genet, *Saint Genet: Comédien et Martyr*. Edmund White's 1993 biography of Genet deconstructs some aspects of the Genet legend inspired by Sartre's book, pointing out, for example, that Genet preferred talking and writing about sex to engaging in it (Kaufmann 24–25).

3. Sikov 41.

4. Richard Dyer, *Now You See It* 48.

5. Genet 10, 14.

6. *Anarchy* 169.

7. Dyer, *Now You See It* 57.

8. *Anarchy* 168. Fassbinder admitted that his personal approach may have made it more difficult for the viewer to understand his adaptation of *Querelle*. But he said he hoped it would stimulate the viewer's own imagination (Steinborn Int 4). According to the filmmaker Monica Treut, the film "does not translate literature into the cinema," but rather exposes "the distance between the two."

9. The final shot of *Querelle,* which follows the one just described, seems ominous when we recall that Fassbinder died about two months after he finished shooting the film. The narrator reads aloud a note seen on the screen (purportedly in Genet's handwriting), in which the author mentions the date of his birth and then adds that the date of his death is "unknown" though it seems near.

10. In 1974 Fassbinder commented, "There are always brothers in my films" (which is nearly true, figuratively speaking, if not literally). He added that he "probably would have liked having one, what they call a brother, someone who would have offered a possibility of contact that I otherwise wouldn't have." (Wiegand Int 58).

11. The song is based on a line from "The Ballad of Reading Gaol" by Oscar Wilde, the Irish-born English author and dandy who had been sent to prison in 1895 after his homosexuality was made public. Monica Treut reads Lysiane as "a beautiful but passive outsider, excluded from the brother rituals of power and eros . . . a cross between the eternal mother who loves unconditionally and a saint who forgives all."

12. Dyer, *Now You See It* 91–93.

13. MacBean 18–19. Monika Treut, while admitting the film is "hard to love," gives a more appreciative reading of Fassbinder's portrayal of these male sexual power games, seeing the director as "ahead of his times . . . one of the first queer film-makers" who "did not care about portraying homosexuals in a politically correct way."

14. Baer 186–90. Fassbinder's companion Juliane Lorenz said she realized after ten days of the shooting of the film that it was better if she withdrew from the set, considering the "theme he was working on" (Int). Later she added: "Rainer didn't feel free enough having me around" (Let 3 June 1994).

15. *Anarchy* 71.

16. *Anarchy* 72.

17. Baer 194–95.

18. The film was shot in English, and the copy distributed in this country has an English sound track. The voices of the German actors and of Italian Franco Nero were presumably dubbed into English to avoid their accents. Jeanne Moreau's French-accented voice seems to be her own. The American Brad Davis speaks in an oddly unreal style, apparently in his own voice.

19. Carrassco 112.

20. According to Juliane Lorenz, Fassbinder was dissatisfied with an oratorio which he asked Peer Raben to write for the film, and to which he listened at the end of May 1982. Instead of an oratorio, he told her, Raben had written "a very sentimental homoerotic love-song arrangement." He asked Lorenz "to think about a special sound score, reminding me of the city noises of New York, the subways, and other noises." After Fassbinder's death (on 10 June), "I did exactly what he told me, after I was able to go on working." She used only three or four of the musical themes from Raben, and added the Handel organ music (recalling Fassbinder's use of it in his first short film, *Der Stadtstreicher* and in the slaughterhouse scene in *In a Year of 13 Moons*) in the scenes in which Querelle murders Vic and when he betrays Gil to the police. Lorenz asserts that Raben has not accepted the fact "that is was Rainer who decided not to use the whole music score he had prepared for *Querelle*" (Let 3 June 1994).

21. MacBean 13.

22. Lorenz, *Das ganz normale Chaos* 388. Some of the problems with *Querelle* may derive from the fact that, after dubbing, the film was cut from about two and a half hours to less than two (Juliane Lorenz, Let 3 June 1994).

23. According to Katz, the decision not to move ahead with *Kokain* earlier was made by the producer: "Wendlandt, cutting his losses, shelved *Cocaine*" (172). Juliane Lorenz, however, asserts that it was Fassbinder who delayed the project and that he intended to take it up again. She writes that Fassbinder chose to go ahead with *Lili Marleen* after finishing *Berlin Alexanderplatz* because the producer of *Lili Marleen*, Luggi Waldleitner, "had three versions of a script, and all the money was ready to start shooting soon." After Wendlandt asked him to shorten his script for *Kokain,* Fassbinder decided to start on *Lola* (for which Wendlandt was now the producer), primarily because the screenplay was complete and the studio and locations had already been arranged. He

also decided to make *Veronika Voss* (for which Wendlandt was also a major producer). Nevertheless Zehetbauer started working on his ideas for the set of *Kokain* and met with Fassbinder at least a few times to discuss them. Wendlandt kept the rights to *Kokain* and Fassbinder's screenplay. "So it was Rainer who decided which film he wanted to make, and Wendlandt agreed with him, because he really wanted him to be free in his decisions about the order in which he wanted to make his films." (Lorenz Let 3 June 1994). Fassbinder's handwritten screenplay and some of his specific plans for the film were included in the 1992 Berlin exhibition.

24. *Anarchy* 144–45.

25. Peter Märthesheimer and Pea Fröhlich, who had written a partial scenario for a film on Rosa Luxemburg entitled *Der Ruf der Lerche* (The Call of the Lark), were to have written the screenplay for Fassbinder's *Rosa L.* (RWFF Cat 248, 264). Margaretta von Trotta later bought the rights to the project, and her 1986 film, *Rosa Luxemburg,* was shot from her own script (Lorenz Let 22 June 1993). Von Trotta's film stars Barbara Sukowa, who had played major roles in Fassbinder's *Berlin Alexanderplatz* and *Lola.*

26. RWFF Cat 264.

27. Fassbinder dictated a screenplay for *Hurra, wir leben noch* to a tape recorder in 1980 (RWFF Cat 263).

28. Katz xv.

29. Along with the directors Alexander Kluge and Volker Schlöndorff, and Theo Hinz of the Filmverlag der Autoren, Fassbinder signed a telegram (dated December 23, 1981) to the well-known Polish filmmaker Andrzej Wajda inviting him to meet them in Munich or Warsaw to discuss the project. (The telegram to Wajda was among the Fassbinder material held in the Deutsches Kinemathek in Berlin in 1990, now in the RWF Foundation archives). This project was presumably brought to completion in the 1982–93 film, *Krieg und Frieden,* codirected by Schlöndorff, Kluge, Stefan Aust, and Axel Engstfeld (mentioned in Elsaesser, *New German Cinema* 412). Two additional major unrealized projects, which Fassbinder had in mind in 1974, would have treated contrasting aspects of modern psychology. One was a television series, to be called *Man Moses,* named after Sigmund Freud's final major work, *Der Man Moses und die monotheistische Religion* (*Moses and Monotheism,* 1938; Fassbinder discusses this project in Thomsen Int 100). The other was to have been a film based on B. F. Skinner's *Walden II;* in 1980 Fassbinder said that he was fascinated with Skinner's behaviorist model of a society in that book, though he did not approve of it, particularly because of its dependence upon a single leader (Limmer 77).

30. "Sein Name" 72.

31. *Anarchy* 28.

32. Elsaesser, "Cinema of Vicious Circles" 24–25.

33. Steinborn Int 7.

34. Fassbinder once said he wanted his films to "liberate the mind," as Douglas Sirk's films did (*Anarchy* 84).

35. Thomsen Int 93.

36. *Anarchy* 30; see also Limmer Int 78. For a "dialectical" analysis of the utopian dynamic between Fassbinder films and the spectator (focussing on readings by Elsaesser, Dyer, and Judith Mayne), see Ruppert, "Fassbinder, Spectatorship, and Utopian Desire."

37. Wüstensand Int 5. Jane Shattuc has noted how the viscerally "pleasurable" nature of Fassbinder's films induces in the viewer a "utopian moment" which "moves human beings to act" (*"Contra* Brecht" 51).

38. Shattuc, *"Contra* Brecht" 48–49.

39. See Rentschler, *West German Film* 83–84, and Sontag "Notes on 'Camp,'" 280.

40. In a 1971–72 interview, Fassbinder said that an unusually long-running shot or very slow camera movement produces a "kind of alienation." At such moments, audiences can "see what is happening between the characters involved. If I started cutting within a scene like that, then no one would see what it was all about" (Thomsen Int 83).

41. Nevers 54.

42. Wiegand Int 79–80.

43. Rayns 79.

44. In 1981, Fassbinder defined various functions of his mirror shots, including the following: to break the viewer's identification with characters, by revealing that an initial and presumably "real" image is in fact a mirror-image; to offer a commentary; and to create a distance between a character and his mirror-image (Limmer Int 87–88). Discussing the ubiquity of mirrors in the films of Jean Cocteau, Richard Dyer notes how they function both to imply homosexual desire and to "aestheticise" reality (*Now You See It* 67). Both of these observations are applicable also to Fassbinder's use of mirrors in a number of films.

45. The twenty-year-old Ballhaus was present at the filming in 1955 of his uncle's elegantly styled *Lola Montez* (Scorsese 99, 115 n. 2), one of Fassbinder's favorite films.

46. Rayns 80.

47. Fassbinder said that he and Ballhaus learned together how to use light more expressively than he had done in his earlier films, to establish atmosphere rather than merely to highlight action (Pflaum 82–83). Ballhaus's Hollywood work has included *The Last Temptation of Christ* (1988) and other films for Martin Scorsese and Francis Ford Coppola's *Bram Stoker's Dracula* (1992); he won an Oscar nomination for his work with Robert de Niro in *Goodfellas* (1990). See Scorsese 115, n. 2. Juliane Lorenz has speculated that Fassbinder stopped working with Ballhaus because "they had experienced all they could together. . . . It was just a time of separation—for Ballhaus as well." She recalled Fassbinder having once said to her: "I don't want him to force me to hurt him anymore. We have to part ways." (Int)

48. Steinborn Int 14. Harry Baer has summarized usefully the new visual effects Fassbinder was able to achieve with Schwarzenberger in *Berlin Alexanderplatz, Lili Marleen, Lola,* and *Veronika Voss* (170). Schwarzenberger has directed more than ten films since 1983 and continues to work as cinematographer as well.

49. Lorenz characterized Raab as one among "many weak people—mainly men" Fassbinder had around him in his earlier years. She said Fassbinder told her that he had

to separate from Raab when Raab hired someone to kill the director. (Int)

50. Barbara Baum has worked with more than a score of other German directors. In 1988 she won the prize for best costume design at the Venice film festival (for Andrew Birkin's *Brennendes Geheimnis*) and in 1994 won the Bavarian Film Prize for her total work.

51. For his work as film editor, Fassbinder almost always credited himself as "Franz Walsch," apparently alluding both to Franz Biberkopf of Döblin's novel *Berlin Alexanderplatz* and American director Raoul Walsh. Juliane Lorenz has written that in the later years of their work together Fassbinder often credited himself as coeditor of a film on the strength of only a few suggestions to her ("I have to laugh today about this little ego-mania of his"). She explained that she edited *Maria Braun* by herself during shooting and worked together with Fassbinder on the final scenes, in a manner similar to their reediting of *Despair* (see chapter 8, note 25). After that, as she became increasingly experienced, Fassbinder left the editing of all his films up to her, seeing them for the first time when her first cut was shown in a projection room. "From *Berlin Alexanderplatz* on, he shot only one or two takes (printing only one take, so there was no need to see rushes). Every day after shooting, I presented him the *final cut* of the scenes which were shot three days before." (Let 3 Jun 1994)

52. Pflaum and Fassbinder 129–32.

53. Pflaum and Fassbinder 131–36.

54. Lorenz had worked in a film laboratory for six months and had been assistant or coeditor on several film projects—including *Chinese Roulette* (1976) and *Bolwieser* (1976–77)—before Fassbinder asked her to take over the editing of *Despair* in 1977, when she was twenty-one. She said that while film cutters usually have to "pull the artistic potential out of the material," Fassbinder didn't need such creative editing work: "He created very precisely during shooting." She said she had no trouble understanding how he wanted his films to be edited. (Int) Lorenz has continued to work as a film editor since Fassbinder's death; she won the National Film Prize for cutting Werner Schroeter's 1991 film *Malina*.

55. Thomsen Int 85–86, 100–101. In 1980, Fassbinder said that only in the movie theatre can film portray "new experiences," leaving for television the "discussion-thesis films" (*Anarchy* 51). See also Bronner/Brocher Int 180.

56. The four films shot on videotape were: *The Coffeehouse, Bremen Coffee, Nora Helmer,* and the Brigitta Mira vehicle, *Wie ein Vogel auf dem Draht* (the last made in 1974).

57. Steinborn Int 11.

58. DIF 40.

59. An interesting instance of Fassbinder's penchant for acting out self-conscious versions of himself is the 1981 film, *Kamikaze '89,* directed by Wolf Gremm, a camp mixture of science-fiction and crime melodrama. Robert Katz, who rewrote the screenplay of the film for Gremm, discusses the project in some detail (xvi–xvii, 176–8, 195).

60. Eckhardt 151.

61. Pflaum and Fassbinder 145–46.

62. Limmer Int 72.

63. "The Doubled Individual" 60–61. See also Shattuc, "R. W. Fassbinder as a Popular *Auteur*" 52.

64. "The Doubled Individual" 64. The childlike directness with which emotions are presented in Fassbinder's films seems to be a significant aspect of their often-noted melodramatic quality—particularly when we recall Peter Brooks' point that the stylistic excess of melodrama "represents a victory over repression." In this mode, "the characters stand on stage and utter the unspeakable, give voice to their deepest feelings . . . assume primary psychic roles . . . and express basic psychic conditions" (4–5).

65. Fassbinder reportedly avoided doctors as much as possible, ate and drank heavily, with little regard to his health, and insisted that he could control the use of drugs which brought about his death at age thirty-seven (see *Anarchie* 171). One recalls also Fassbinder's imprudent flooding of the West German film market with his movies during the first eighteen months of his filmmaking career; his failure to anticipate how offensive his play about a "rich Jew" in Frankfurt would seem in post-Holocaust Germany; and his decision to create for his long-awaited adaptation of *Berlin Alexanderplatz* a horrific epilogue which was guaranteed to disturb the mass television audience at which it was aimed.

66. See Baer 36–37, 49.

67. Pflaum and Fassbinder 114.

68. Hayman 17; Katz 7–9.

69. *Anarchy* 72.

70. *Anarchy* 21.

71. Müller Int 184.

72. Limmer 75–76.

73. In her interview and correspondence with the author, Juliane Lorenz traced the history of her personal relationship with Fassbinder, as follows: She noticed early on that Fassbinder was attentive to her views ("He was the first man in my life who took me seriously") and was "amazed" that he quoted her to other people. After they cut *Despair,* they were "together more and more." She was "very focussed on him . . . interested in his feelings and in his life," and she was "very sorry about his loneliness" after Armin Meier died (May 1978). Following the shooting of *In a Year of 13 Moons* (July and August 1978), the director asked her to live with him, and she agreed. "So he started another kind of relationship. I didn't force him."

Considering how often the director discussed the "desolation one often feels in personal relationships, mainly in marriages," she was surprised that he often pressed her to marry him, starting with their first trip alone to Tangier at the beginning of June 1979. She did not encourage this, being skeptical of such ties herself because of her parents' bad marriage and her "romantic" notion that a genuine love relationship should not be "disturbed by official papers." He asked her again when they took a trip to Fort Lauderdale, Florida, at the end of that year, and this time she took his wish "more seriously than the impression I may sometimes have given." She located a Justice of the Peace, who told her that they would have to have a blood test, a possibility Fassbinder rejected: "I'm not going to have a blood test. Never, never, never!" The situation now seemed to her "amusing" and "more bearable." At her suggestion, they went through a marriage ceremony with the justice of the peace, who agreed to their "show" but made clear that they would have to repeat it in a country where a blood test was not required if they wanted to be married officially. After this they returned to their hotel and "had fun," though later they quarreled over his allegation that women desire marriage only for financial reasons. Lorenz said that the account of these events reported in Katz 158–62, and attributed to her, is incorrect in many respects.

She discouraged Fassbinder's later suggestions that they marry, in part because of her fear of being "overwhelmed" by publicity. But they continued to live together, and she didn't see any use for having a marriage certificate. Perhaps she was "afraid of being 'grown up'." In any case, she needed more time to get used to the idea of being "Mrs. Fassbinder" officially. In March 1982, understanding its importance to him, she suggested to Fassbinder that they marry on her brother's birthday, December 31, and they set this date. Fassbinder said that he wanted Rosel Zech and Thomas Schühly, the star and coproducer of *Veronika Voss,* who were then a couple, to marry at the same time; he wanted "to make a big event out of it." But he died in June. "Today I know what it meant for Rainer. He wanted to have order and structure. Maybe he thought that something could happen to him. Maybe."

She was not disturbed that the man she loved also loved men. "I understand very well the complementary parts of a person. We have both male and female possibilities in us." She was surprised by his "sensitiveness, his shyness, his carefulness" with her when they first slept together in Tangier. She knew of only three times he had sex with men in the time they were together, all one-night affairs. He was jealous of a brief affair she had with a man during this time. "There was a time when he lived as a gay man, and there was a time he lived as a bi-sexual person. I think he preferred to sleep with men. With a woman . . . it was more work for him, and he was also more afraid of it. I was happy when he slept with a man, because I knew it was easier for him. I was happy with the way we lived together. He was always very open about his attractions, which I think showed more respect for me than if he had tried to hide them. I was always certain of his love for me. He treated me like his wife. . . . I will feel for Rainer until the last day of my life. He was a part of me, no matter what relationship I have with another person. I am, and will remain, his life-companion." She was once pregnant by him, but had a miscarriage and never told him.

74. "Je ferai" 65.

75. Limmer Int 46–47.

76. Limmer 67–68.

77. *Anarchie* 173.

78. Al LaValley has argued that the treatment of gay themes is central to Fassbinder's work, and that it becomes particularly explicit and "autobiographical" in the films "starring or dedicated to his male lovers" (paper read at November 1992 RWF conference at Dartmouth College; see his "Gay Liberation"). In a January 1982 interview for the gay

American magazine *Christopher Street,* Fassbinder speaks at points as an advocate for gay rights, and even suggests that the protagonist of *Fox and his Friends* is a victim of a homophobic society. But he also seems to be distancing himself from the gay rights movement, which he characterizes as being interested primarily in "legislating new official attitudes" (Haddad-Garcia Int 53, 55).

79. Berling 20.

80. Müller Int 182.

81. Thomsen Int 94–95; see also Limmer Int 83. In 1977 Fassbinder said that he had definitely matured beyond the time when people might fear he would behave like a "psychopath," and hoteliers might expect that he and his team were likely to trash their rooms (Fischer Int 17).

82. Interview with author.

83. Thomsen Int 90.

84. *Anarchy* 71.

85. Steinborn and Naso 6.

86. Fischer Int 17.

87. Pflaum and Fassbinder 129–35; Jansen Int 113.

88. Baer 65. According to many accounts, Fassbinder was quite willing to rehearse inexperienced actors he felt needed more direct guidance—including his mother and his lovers El Hedi Salem and Armin Meier (see Pflaum and Fassbinder 96).

89. The virtually wordless direction of which Günther Lamprecht complained in *Berlin Alexanderplatz* had been anticipated in Fassbinder's mostly silent direction of Dirk Bogarde in *Despair* and was followed by his concise instructions to Jeanne Moreau when she asked for direction in *Querelle:* "Just be great!" (Baer 182)

90. Sarris 57.

91. Jansen Int 97.

92. According to Juliane Lorenz, the expectations of early members of the group for Fassbinder's attention were intense: "It was unbelievable how much love Rainer had for people who really were not so talented in the beginning, or were mistreating him. . . . Because Rainer was so sensitive and attentive to people who were close to him, you could get accustomed to this, and you felt really alone if he went to another person. It was unbelievable how long he sometimes stayed with someone. . . . Sometimes he was much too understanding." (Int)

93. Wiegand Int 66.

94. In 1978 Fassbinder said that he had not used personal friends in his early low-budget projects nearly as much as legend would have it. He said he would have much preferred even then to hire professionals and pay them well, noting the difficulty of telling friends that they are not suited for particular parts (Jansen Int 107–108).

95. Berling worked with Fassbinder primarily in his early years, although this is not made clear in Katz's book or his own (in which, like Kurt Raab earlier, he includes substantial accounts of his own life and career in a book purportedly about Fassbinder). Berling's exploitation of Fassbinder's reputation is indicated also in his attempts to sell

unauthorized copies of a death mask of the director at the Venice Film Festival in 1982 (Katz xvii; Spaich 109).

96. Bogarde to Fassbinder, 24 Sept. 1977, in Watson, "Bitter Tears." Bogarde had worked with such major European directors as Joseph Losey, Luchino Visconti, and Alain Resnais. In a letter to the author, Bogarde made an emphatic distinction between Fassbinder's relationship with the "un-disciplined . . . Inner Gang" ("they liked to be bullied and he liked to bully") and the mutual respect between Fassbinder and "the first professional players he had ever worked with"—himself, Andrea Ferréol, and Bernhard Wicki (29 May 1991).

97. Pflaum and Fassbinder 61–66.

98. Steinborn and Naso 3–4.

99. Lorenz, *Das ganz normale Chaos* 384–386 (Schwarzenberger), 374–381 (Zehetbauer), 289 (Baum).

100. Hayman 54. Hilmar Thate, the East German actor whom Fassbinder cast as the reporter in *Veronika Voss,* was surprised to discover how far Fassbinder's treatment of him during the production differed from the legend: "Everything was exceedingly easy-going and relaxed" and Fassbinder gave the actors plenty of rein to take responsibility for their performance within a general directorial framework (52–53).

101. Pflaum and Fassbinder 144–45; see also Henrichs 17.

102. Pflaum and Fassbinder 92.

103. Emerson 73.

104. Pflaum and Fassbinder 114.

105. Pflaum and Fassbinder 141.

106. Scherer Int 99.

107. Fassbinder added that, except for "special effects spectaculars," there is no need for films to "cost millions upon millions and take months to shoot. The details are more real if they are not planned a year in advance" (Haddad-Garcia Int 55). In 1982, in response to a question about his favorites among the films had made, Fassbinder mentioned six which he characterized as "beautiful"—*Despair, Lola, Veronika Voss, Gods of the Plague, Berlin Alexanderplatz,* and *Effi Briest*—and three which he called "important"—*Beware of a Holy Whore, In a Year of 13 Moons,* and *The Third Generation* (Steinborn Int 14).

108. *Anarchy* xv.

109. Jansen and Schütte 63–64.

110. Buchka 13.

111. According to Elsaesser, Fassbinder paradoxically may have contributed more to the demise of the New German Cinema during his life than in his death: "It was his work, the restless exploration of different conditions and possibilities of filmmaking which, if it did not inaugurate, then at any rate accelerated the changes that have led to the transformations of the New German Cinema into *the* German Cinema, and of the German Cinema into a host of rather heterogenous forms of film-making, in television and in the cinema, at home and abroad." (*New German Cinema* 310). See also Kilb and Pflaum, *Germany on Film* 144–45.

APPENDIX
LATER THEATER WORK

Note: Following is brief information on Fassbinder's theater work following the productions described in chapter two. Unless otherwise indicated, the scripts were written and the plays directed by Fassbinder (S: script; D: director); place and date indicate premiere performance. Production information is from Hans Helmut Prinzler's data in Jansen and Schütte 274–5.

Werewolf. S: Fassbinder and Harry Baer. Berlin, December 1969. Fassbinder and Baer wrote their parts of the play separately, in an experiment that Fassbinder found unsatisfactory. As with *Pre-Paradise Sorry Now,* parts of this play may be performed in any order. The play treats the legend of a sixteenth-century German peasant mass murderer who reputedly drank his victims' blood, examining the causes of his behavior in his isolation and neglect as a child.[1]

Das brennende Dorf (The Burning Village), based on *Fuenteovejuna* (ca. 1612, the title being the name of the village), by Lope de Vega (Spain 1562–1635). Adapted by Fassbinder (presumably from a German translation); D: Peer Raben. Bremen, November 1970. In the original, villagers rise up against an unjust king's deputy, but because of their solidarity and the justice of their complaints they are forgiven by the king, in a gesture which supports hierarchical order; the play has also frequently been interpreted as supporting the Marxist class struggle. Fassbinder departs drastically from both interpretations, presenting what Iden describes as a frenzied "collective orgasm" based on the "socially untenable position" that the rebellion is only a form of "release of [the peasants'] sexual energy."[2] Fassbinder's subtitle was, appropriately: "Revolt as an Obscene Gesture."

Pioniere [Military Engineers] *in Ingolstadt,* adapted by Fassbinder from the 1929 play by Marieluise Fleisser (Germany 1901–74). Bremen, January 1971. This was a considerably more faithful version of the play than the February 1968 *Zum Beispiel Ingolstadt* discussed in chapter two.[3]

Blood on a Cat's Neck (Blut am Hals der Katze). S: Fassbinder; D: Fassbinder and Peer Raben. Nuremburg, March 1971. This dark comedy is a series of vignettes in which Phoebe Zeitgeist, a visitor from outer space who has come to earth to learn about democracy, mimics the phrases she hears from an assortment of unhappy, sadomasochistic human stereotypes, which she then repeats back to them (in new contexts) as she bites their necks, vampire-fashion. Major themes are the misery of human existence, exploitation of relationships, and language as an instrument of oppression. Phoebe is based on an American comic-strip character.

Petra von Kant. S: Fassbinder; D: Peer Raben. Frankfurt, June 1971. The basis of the 1972 Fassbinder film *The Bitter Tears of Petra von Kant.* See chapter six.

Bremer Freiheit (Bremen Freedom). Bremen, December 1971. Fassbinder made a videotape version of this production in September 1972. See chapter six.

Liliom, from the 1909 play by Ferenc Molnár (Hungary, 1878–1952). Bochum, December 1972. This most popular of Molnár's plays was the basis of the American musical *Carousel,* 1945.

Bibi, adapted by Fassbinder from the 1928 musical play by Heinrich Mann (Germany, 1871–1950). Bochum, January 1973. Hayman writes that Fassbinder lost interest in this project but was unable to get out of his commitment to it, and that "little of Mann's text remained" in the production.[4] The production reportedly satirized Peter Zadek, the Bochum theater producer with whom Fassbinder was in conflict at this time.

Hedda Gabler, from the 1890 play by Henrik Ibsen (Norway, 1828–1906). Berlin, December 1973. The well-known realist tragedy of a spirited woman trapped within a marriage to a pedant and social conventions of her society which she dares not defy, except finally through suicide.

Die Unvernünftigen sterben aus (*They* [the irrational ones] *Are Dying Out,* 1973), by the Austrian playwright Peter Handke (born in 1942 in Germany). Frankfurt, May 1974. A parodic tragedy about a big-city capitalist entrepreneur, Hermann Quitt, who eventually commits suicide. The play "examines the use of subjectivity, veracity, and especially 'poetic thought' as tools of the irrational (life-saving) forces that Quitt tries to employ against the programmatic business world."[5] Fassbinder's version was one of the first five productions of the play, all performed early in 1974—in Zurich and in four German cities; these productions are reviewed in *Theater heute* 15, 7 (July 1974): 25–34.

Germinal, adapted by Yaak Karsunke from the 1885 novel by Émile Zola (France, 1840–1902). Frankfurt, Theater am Turm, September 1974. Zola's novel is a bleak, naturalistic account of an exploited miner who fails in his efforts to incite his comrades to strike against their inhuman working conditions; in spite of many setbacks, he dreams of a "germinal" (seed-time) which will lead to a utopian era. Peter Iden found Fassbinder's direction of Karsunke's adaptation of the novel "almost friendly, softening the social impact of the novel: Zola's gesture of accusation was turned into melodrama."[6]

Onkel Wanja (*Uncle Vanya*), the 1899 play by Anton Chekhov (Russia, 1860–1904). Frankfurt, Theater am Turm, December 1974. This mixture of comedy, tragedy, and elegy evokes the psychological exhaustion of the end-of-the-century Russian aristocracy, dramatizing the failure of both an idealist doctor and his cynically materialist rival (the title character) to respond effectively to the inspiration brought into their lives by the young wife of a professor. "Though lovingly attempted by the director and his actors [the production] deteriorated into mournful melodrama."[7]

Women in New York (*Women in New York*), adaptation of *The Women* (1936) by American magazine editor, playwright, and politician Clare Boothe Luce (1903–87) Hamburg, September 1976. In March 1977 Fassbinder filmed this production for television broadcast. See chapter six.

Der Müll, die Stadt, und der Tod (*Garbage, the City, and Death*). In 1975, Fassbinder was prevented from staging this controversial play (which he had written the late in 1974) at the Theater am Turm. Seven additional attempts were made to produce it in Frankfurt before 1985, when Günther Ruhle, newly appointed director of the city's prestigious Schauspielhaus, tried to stage it as a gesture indicative of the "normalization" of relations between West Germany and the state of Israel. (As feuilleton editor of the *Frankfurter Allgemeine Zeitung*, Ruhle had earlier vociferously opposed efforts to produce the play.) But a stormy protest, culminating in a takeover of the stage on opening night by members of the Frankfurt Jewish community, prevented that planned premiere.[8] What has been called a "world premiere of sorts" did take place on a Monday afternoon, 4 November 1985, before a few theater critics and other media representatives and some representatives of the Jewish community, with the public excluded.[9] The following year the play officially premiered in Copenhagen, Denmark, "without anyone getting excited about it."[10] The play is discussed in chapter seven.

Notes

1. Töteberg, "Theaterarbeit" 162.
2. Iden 18–19.
3. See Karsunke 3.
4. Hayman 50.
5. Firda 36.
6. Iden 23.
7. Iden 23.
8. Markovits 9; Lichtenstein 12, 21–24, 61ff.
9. Markovits 9, Lorenz Let 8 August 1994.
10. Juliana Lorenz in Braun 38.

FILMOGRAPHIES

Italicized English titles in parentheses are English-language release titles; roman-type titles in parentheses are translations of German titles not yet released in the United States. Initial dates indicate month(s) and year(s) during which the film was shot. Fassbinder was sole author of the screenplay and sole director, unless otherwise indicated. For ease of reading, *antiteater* is here spelled *antitheater*. Production credits and cast lists are incomplete.[1] Most cost figures are approximate. Following cast lists, premieres at film festivals are indicated, along with month and year of theatrical release (TR) and/or initial television broadcast (TV) in West Germany. West German television broadcasting corporations (which were all publicly funded during Fassbinder's life) are abbreviated as follows: ARD (Arbeitsgemeinschaft der öffentlich-rechtlichen Rundfunkanstalten Deutschlands—an association of regional broadcast corporations which transmits programs nationally), NDR (Norddeutscher Rundfunk, Hamburg), SDR (Süddeutscher Rundfunk, Stuttgart), SFB (Sender Freies Berlin), SR (Saarländischer Rundfunk, Saarbrücken), S3 (Sender Drei, Bremen), WDR (Westdeutscher Rundfunk, Cologne), ZDF (Zweites Deutsches Fernsehen, Mainz).

For more details, the reader is referred to one or more of the following, which are sources for the data given below: for list A—Hans Helmut Prinzler's filmography of Fassbinder's films in Jansen and Schütte (1992) 277–300; corrections by Juliane Lorenz (as indicated in notes); the chronological summary of Fassbinder's works in the 1992 Fassbinder exhibition catalogue (RWFF Cat) 257–64; and the filmography in Thomsen, *Rainer Werner Fassbinder,* 404–21; for List B—RWFF Cat 257–64 and Thomsen 404–21; for List C—Rüdiger Kischnitzki's filmography in Spaich, *Rainer Werner Fassbinder,* 384–413 and RWFF Cat 98–99.

Availability of 16 mm films for rental and video cassettes for sale and/or rental in the United States at the time of this writing is indicated at the end of each entry; films recently available for rental but currently out of distribution are indicated by [F]. (New Yorker Films, which has released several Fassbinder films on videocassette, intends to release additional ones in the future.)

The major distributor of Fassbinder films in the United States is New Yorker Films (16 West 61st Street, New York, NY 10023). Additional titles are available from Leisure Time Films (P. O. Box 1201, New York, NY 10009) and Films Inc. (5547 N. Ravenswood, Chicago, IL 60640). West Glen Films (1430 Broadway, New York, NY 10018-3396) rents at modest rates prints of several Fassbinder films provided by the German Embassy, for classroom showing. Three films (*Despair, The Marriage of Maria Braun,* and *In a Year of 13 Moons*) may be viewed by scholars at the Museum of Modern Art, New York, by prior arrangement. Forty hours of Fassbinder television films may be studied at The Museum of Television and Radio, 25 West 52nd Street, New York NY 10019, by prior arrangement. A good source for Fassbinder and other foreign films in videocassette format is Facets Multimedia, 1517 W. Fullerton Avenue, Chicago IL 60614.

The Goethe House New York/German Cultural Center (1014 Fifth Avenue, New York NY 10002) is a useful source of current information on the availability of German films in the United States.

A Films Directed by Fassbinder

This Night. July 1966, 8 mm color (lost).

Der Stadtstreicher (The City Tramp). Nov. 1966, 16 mm black and white, 10 min. Produced by Roser-Film. Cinematographer: Josef Jung. Cast: Christoph Roser (tramp), Susanne Schimkus (waitress), Michael and Thomas Fengler (two men), Irm Hermann (woman), RWF (young man in leather jacket).

Das kleine Chaos (The Little Chaos). Jan. 1967, 35 mm black and white, 9 min. Produced by Roser-Film. Cinematographer: Michael Fengler. Cast: RWF (Franz), Marite Greiselis (Marite), Christoph Roser (Theo), Lilo Pempeit, Greta Rehfeld, Susanne Schimkus.

Liebe ist kälter als der Tod (*Love Is Colder Than Death*). April 1969, 35 mm black and white, 88 min. Produced by antitheater-X-Film, production managers: Christian Hohoff, Wil Rabenbauer (Peer Raben); cost 95,000 DM. Cinematographer: Dietrich Lohmann; film editor: Franz Walsch; music by Peer Raben, Holger Münzer; art direction: Ulli Lommel, RWF. Cast: Ulli Lomel (Bruno), Hanna Schygulla (Joanna), RWF (Franz), Hans Hirschmüller (Peter), Katrin Schaake (woman in train), Peter Berling (shoemaker), Gisela Otto (first prostitute), Ingrid Caven (second prostitute), Ursula Strätz (third prostitute), Irm Hermann (sales clerk), Peter Moland (syndicate questionner), Rudolf Waldemar Brem (motorcycle policeman), Yaak Karsunde (police inspector). Berlin Film Festival, 26 June 1969; TR: 16 January 1970; TV: 18 January 1971. U.S./film (West Glen).

Katzelmacher. August 1969, 35 mm black and white, 88 min. Literary source: play by RWF. Produced by antitheater-X-Film; production manager: Wil Rabenbauer (Peer Raben); cost 80,000 DM. Cinematographer: Dietrich Lohmann; film editor: Franz Walsch; music by Peer Raben (after Franz Schubert); art director: RWF. Cast: RWF (Jorgos), Hanna Schygulla (Marie), Lilith Ungerer (Helga), Elga Sorbas (Rosy), Doris Mattes (Gunda), Irm Hermann (Elisabeth), Rudolf Waldemar Brem (Paul), Hans Hirshmüller (Erich), Harry Baer (Franz), Peter Moland (Peter), Hannes Gromball (Klaus). Mannheim Film Week, 8 October 1969; TR: 22 November 1969; TV: 17 September 1973 (ARD). U.S./film.

Götter der Pest (*Gods of the Plague*). October–November 1969, 35 mm black and white, 91 min. Produced by RWF, Michael Fengler for antitheater-X-Film; cost 180,000 DM. Cinematographer: Dietrich Lohmann; film editors: Franz Walsch, Thea Eymèsz; music by Peer Raben; art director: Kurt Raab. Cast: Harry Baer (Franz), Hanna Schygulla (Joanna), Margarethe von Trotta (Margarethe), Günther Kaufmann (Günther), Carla Aulaulu (Carla), Ingrid Caven (Magdalena Fuller), Jan George (police inspector), Marian Seidowski (Marian), Yaak Karsunke (police superintendent), Lilo Pempeit (mother), RWF (pornography seller). Vienna Film Festival, 4 April 1970; TR: 24 July 1970; TV: 8 August 1972 (ZDF). U.S./film, videocassette.

Warum läuft Herr R amok? (*Why Does Herr R Run Amok?*). December 1969, 16 mm blown up to 35 mm color, 88 min. Improvisation outline by Michael Fengler and RWF. Directors: Michael Fengler, RWF. Produced by antitheater for Maran-Film (commissioned by SDR); production manager: Wilhelm Rabenbauer; cost 135,000 DM. Cinematographer: Dietrich Lohmann; film editors: Franz Walsch, Michael Fengler; music by Peer Raben, song by Christian Anders; art director: Kurt Raab. Cast: Kurt Raab (Herr R.), Lilith Ungerer (his wife), Amadeus Fengler (their son), Franz Maron (boss), Harry Baer/Peter Moland/Lilo Pempeit (office colleagues), Hanna Schygulla (wife's school friend), Peer Raben (Herr R.'s school friend). Berlin Film Festival, 28 June 1970; TR: 5 February 1971; TV: 28 December 1971 (ARD). U.S./film.

Rio das Mortes. January 1970, 16 mm black and white., 84 min. Produced by Janus Film und Fernsehen and antitheater-X-Film; production manager Michael Fengler; cost 125,000 DM. Cinematographer: Dietrich Lohmann; film editor: Thea Eymèsz; music by Peer Raben; art director: Kurt Raab. Cast: Hanna Schygulla (Hanna), Michael König (Michel), Günther Kaufmann (Günther), Katrin Schaake (Hanna's friend Katrin), Joachim von Mengerhausen (Joachim, Katrin's friend), Lilo Pempeit (Günter's mother), Hanna Axmann-Rezzori (patroness), RWF (dances with Hanna in discotheque). TV: 15 February 1971.

Das Kaffeehaus (*The Coffeehouse*). February 1970, videotape, black and white, 105 min. Literary source: play by Carlo Goldini. Produced by WDR. Camera operators: Dietbert Schmidt, Manfred Förster; music by Peer Raben; art director: Wilfred Minks. Cast: Margit Carstensen (Vittoria), Ingrid Caven (Placida), Hanna Schugulla (Lisaura), Kurt Raab (Don Marzio), Harry Baer (Eugenio), Hans Hirschmüller (Trappolo), Günther Kaufmann (Leander), Peter Moland (Pandolfo), Wil Rabenbauer (Ridolfo). TV: 18 May 1970.

Whity. April 1970, 35 mm color, CinemaScope, 95 min. Produced by Atlantis Film and antitheater-X-Film; production manager: Peter Berling; cost 680,000 DM. Cinematographer: Michael Ballhaus; film editor: Franz Walsch, Thea Eymèsz; music by Peer Raben; art director: Kurt Raab. Cast: Günther Kaufmann (Whity), Hanna Schygulla (Hanna), Ulli Lommel (Frank), Harry Baer (Davy), Katrin Schaake (Katherine), Ron Randell (Mr. Nicholson), Thomas Blanco (fake Mexican doctor), Stefano Capriati (judge), Elaine Baker (Whity's mother), RWF (saloon guest). U.S./film.

Die Niklashauser Fart (The Niklashausen Journey). May 1970, 16 mm color, 86 min. Produced by Janus Film und Fernsehen for WDR; cost 550,000 DM. Screenplay by RWF, Michael Fengler; directors: RWF, Michael Fengler; cinematographer: Dietrich Lohmann; film editors: Thea Eymèsz, Franz Walsch; music by Peer Raben, Amon Düül II; art director: Kurt Raab. Cast: Michael König (Hans Böhm), Gochel Gordon (Antonio), RWF (black monk), Hanna Schygulla (Johanna), Walter Sedlmayr (pastor), Margit Carstensen (Magarethe), Franz Maron (her husband), Kurt Raab (bishop), Günther Rupp (his adviser), Karl Scheydt (Niklashausen citizen), Günther Kaufmann (leader of the farmers). TV: 26 October 1970.

Der Amerikanischer Soldat (The American Soldier). August 1970, 35 mm black and white, 80 min. Produced by antitheater; production manager Peer Raben; cost 280,000 DM. Cinematographer: Dietrich Lohmann; film editor: Thea Eymèsz; music by Peer Raben; song by RWF/Raben, sung by Günther Kaufmann; art directors: Kurt Raab, RWF. Cast: Karl Scheydt (Ricky), Elga Sorbas (Rosa), RWF (Franz), Jan George (Jan), Margarethe von Trotta (maid), Hark Bohm (Doc), Ingrid Caven (singer), Eva Ingeborg Scholz (Ricky's mother), Kurt Raab (Ricky's brother), Katrin Schaake (Magdalena Fuller), Ulli Lommel (gipsy), Irm Hermann (whore). Mannheim Film Week, 9 October 1970; TR: 27 November 1970; TV: 19 September 1972 (ZDF). U.S./film, videocassette.

Warnung vor einer heiligen Nutte (Beware of a Holy Whore). Sept. 1970, 35 mm widescreen, color, 102 min. Produced by antitheater-X-Film and Nova International, Rome; production manager: Peter Berling; cost 1,100,000 DM. Cinematographer: Michael Ballhaus; film editors: Franz Walsch, Thea Eymèsz; music by Peer Raben; songs by Gaetano Donizetti, Elvis Presley, Ray Charles, Leonhard Cohen, Spooky Tooth; art director: Kurt Raab. Cast: Lou Castel (Jeff, the director), Eddie Constantine (himself), Hanna Schygulla (Hanna, actress), Marquard Bohm (Ricky, actor), RWF (Sascha, prodution manager), Ulli Lommel (Korbinian, sound recordist), Katrin Schaake (scriptgirl), Benjamin Lev (Candy, Spanish sound recordist), Moniker Teuber (Billi, make-up woman), Margarethe von Trotta (Babs, production secretary), Kianni di Luigi (camera operator), Rudolf Waldemar Brem (lighting supervisor), Thomas Schieder (Jesus, lighting crew member), Kurt Raab (Fred), Ingrid Caven (extra), Harry Baer (her husband), Magdalena Montezuma (Irm), Werner Schroeter (Dieters, photographer). Venice Film Festival, 28 August 1971; TR (Germany): 2 June 1992; TV: 22 January 1972 (NDR III). U.S./film, videocassette.

Pioniere in Ingolstadt (Army Engineers in Ingolstadt). Nov. 1970, 35 mm color, 84 min. Literary source: play by Marieluise Fleisser. Produced by Janus Film und Fernsehen and antitheater for ZDF; production manager Kurt Raab; cost 550,000 DM. Cinematographer: Dietrich Lohmann; film editor: Thea Eymèsz; music by Peer Raben; art director: Kurt Raab. Cast: Hanna Schygulla (Berta), Harry Baer (Karl), Irm Hermann (Alma), Rudolf Waldemar Brem (Fabian), Walter Sedlmayr (Fritz), Klaus Löwitsch (sergeant), Günther Kaufmann (Max), Carla Aulaulu (Frieda), Elga Sorbas (Marie), Burghard Schlicht (Klaus), Gunther Krää (Gottfried). TV: 19 May 1971.

Händler der vier Jahreszeiten (*The Merchant of Four Seasons*). August 1971, 35 mm color, 89 min. Produced by Tango-Film; production manager: Ingrid (Caven) Fassbinder; cost 325,000 DM. Cinematographer: Dietrich Lohmann; film editor: Thea Eymèsz; music: songs by Rocco Granata and RWF; art director: Kurt Raab. Cast: Hans Hirschmüller (Hans Epp), Irm Hermann (Irmgard, his wife), Andrea Schober (their daughter), Hanna Scygulla (first sister of Hans), Heide Simon (second sister), Klaus Löwitsch (Harry), Karl Scheydt (Ansell), Ingrid Caven (Hans's great love), Lilo Pempeit (customer), El Hedi ben Salem (Arab), RWF (friend eating with Hans in restaurant). Paris Cinémathèque, 10 February 1972; TR: 10 March 1972; TV: 10 March 1972 (ZDF). U.S./film, videocassette.

Die bitteren Tränen der Petra von Kant (*The Bitter Tears of Petra von Kant*). January 1972, 35 mm color, 124 min. Literary source: play by RWF. Produced by Tango-Film; cost 325,000 DM. Cinematographer: Michael Ballhaus; film editor: Thea Eymèsz; music: songs by The Platters, The Walker Brothers, Giuseppe Verdi; art director: Kurt Raab. Cast: Margit Carstensen (Petra von Kant), Hanna Schygulla (Karin Thimm), Irm Hermann (Marlene), Eva Mattes (Gabriele von Kant), Katrin Schaake (Sidonie von Grasenabb), Gisela Fackeldey (Petra's mother, Valerie). Berlin Film Festival, 25 June 1972; TR: 5 October 1972; TV: 11 November 1973 (ARD). U.S./film, videocassette.

Wildwechsel (Wild Game Crossing). March 1972, 35 mm color, 102 min. Literary source: play by Franz Xaver Kroetz. Produced by Intertel for SFB; producer Gerhard Freund; cost 550,000 DM. Cinematographer: Dietrich Lohmann; film editor: Thea Eymèsz; music by Ludwig van Beethoven; song by Paul Anka; art director: Kurt Raab. Cast: Jörg von Liebenfels (Erwin), Ruth Drexel (Hilda, his wife), Eva Mattes (Hanni, their daughter), Harry Baer (Franz), Rodolf Waldemar Brem (Dieter), Hanna Schygulla (doctor), El Hedi ben Salem (friend). TR: 30 December 1972; TV: 9 January 1973 (SFB).

Acht Stunden sind kein Tag (Eight Hours Don't Make a Day). April–August 1972, 16 mm color; five episodes—101, 100, 92, 89, 89 min. Produced by WDR; cost 1,335,000 DM. Cinematographer: Dietrich Lohmann; video editor: Marie Anne Gerhardt; music by Jean Gepoint; art director: Kurt Raab. Cast: Gottfried John (Jochen), Hanna Schygulla (Marion), Luise Ullrich (Oma), Werner Finck (Gregor), Anita Bucher (Käthe), Wolfried Lier (Wolf), Christine Oesterlein (Klara), Renate Roland (Monika), Kurt Raab (Harald), Andrea Schober (Sylvia), Irm Hermann (Irmgard), Rudolf Waldemar Brem (Rolf), Hans Hirshmüller (Jürgen), Karl Scheydt (Peter). TV: 29 October 1972–18 March 1973.

Bremer Freiheit. (Bremen Freedom). September 1972, videotape, color, 87 min. Screenplay by RWF, Dietrich Lohmann. Literary source: play by RWF. Produced by Telefilm Saar for SR; cost 240,000 DM. Camera operators: Dietrich Lohmann, Hans Schugg, Peter Weyrich; video editors: Friedrich Niquet, Monika Solzbacher; music by Archive; art director: Kurt Raab. Cast: Margit Carstensen (Geesche), Ulli Lommel (Miltenberger), Wolfgang Schenck (Gottfried), Hanna Schugulla (Luise Maurer), RWF (Rumpf), Lilo Pempeit (mother), Walter Sedlmayr (pastor), Wolfgang Kieling (Timm), Rudolf Waldemar Brem (cousin Bohm), Kurt Raab (carpenter), Fritz Schediwy (Johann). TV: 12 December 1972 (S3). U.S./film (West Glen).

Welt am Draht (World on the Wire). January–March 1973, 16 mm color; two parts: 99 (cut to 91), 106 min. Screenplay by Fritz Müller-Scherz, RWF. Literary source: novel by Daniel F. Galouye. Produced by WDR; cost 950,000 DM. Cinematographer: Michael Ballhaus; film editor: Marie Anne Gerhardt; music by Gottfried Hüngsberg, Archive; art director: Kurt Raab. Cast: Klaus Löwitsch (Fred Stiller), Mascha Rabben (Eva), Adrian Hoven (Vollmer), Ivan Desny (Lause), Barbara Valentin (Gloria), Karl-Heinz Vosgerau (Siskins), Günther Lamprecht (Wolfgang), Margit Carstensen (Schmidt-Gentner), Kurt Raab (Holm), Karl Scheydt (Lehner). TV: 14 October 1973 (I), 16 October 1974 (II).

Nora Helmer. May 1973, videotape, color, 101 min. Screenplay/literary source: Bernhard Schulze's translation of Ibsen, *A Doll's House.* Produced by Telefilm Saar for SR; cost 550,000 DM. Camera operators: Willi Raber, Wilfried Mier, Peter Weyrich, Gisela Loew, Hans Schugg; video editors: Anne-Marie Bornheimer, Friedrich Niquet; music by Archive; art director: Friedhelm Boehm. Cast: Margit Carstensen (Nora), Joachim Hansen (Torvald), Barbara Valentin (Frau Linde), Ulli Lommel (Krogstadt), Klaus Löwitsch (Dr. Rank), Lilo Pempeit (Marie), Irm Hermann (Helene). TV: 3 February 1974 (SR).

Angst essen Seele auf (Ali: Fear Eats the Soul). September 1973, 35 mm wide-screen, color, 93 min. Produced by Tango-Film; cost 260,000 DM. Cinematographer: Jürgen Jürges; film editor: Thea Eymèsz; music by Archiv; art director: Kurt Raab. Cast: Brigitta Mira (Emmi), El Hedi ben Salem (Ali), Barbara Valentin (Barbara), Irm Hermann (Krista), RWF (Eugen, her husband), Karl Scheydt (Albert), Walter Sedlmayr (Angermayer, grocer), Doris Mattes (his wife), Liselotte Eder (Frau Münchmeyer). TR: 5 March 1974; TV: 25 July 1977 (ZDF). U.S./film, videocassette.

Martha. July–September 1973, 16 mm color, 111 min.; Produced by WDR; cost 500,000 DM. Cinematographer: Michael Ballhaus; film editor: Liesgret Schmitt-Klink; music by Archive; art director: Kurt Raab. Cast: Margit Carstensen (Martha Hyer/Salomon), Karlheinz Böhm (Helmut Salomon), Gisela Fackelday (mother), Andrian Hoven (father), Barbara Valentin (Marianne), Ingrid Caven (Ilse), El Hedi ben Salem (hotel guest). TV: 28 May 1974 (ARD). A 35 mm film version (blown up) premiered at the Venice Film Festival in September 1994, and was released 18 November in Germany in October. U.S./film.

Fontane Effi Briest (Effi Briest). September–October 1972, October–November 1973, 35 mm black and white 141 min. Literary source: novel by Theodor Fontane. Produced by Tango-Film; production manager: Christian Hohoff; cost 750,000 DM. Cinematographers: Dietrich Lohmann, Jürgen Jürges; film editor: Thea Eymèsz; music: motif from Camille Saint-Saens and others; art director: Kurt Raab; Cast: Hanna Schygulla (Effi), Wolfgang Schenck (Baron Geert von Innstetten), Karlheinz Böhm (Councillor Wüllersdorf), Ulli Lommel (Major Crampas), Ursula Strätz (Roswitha), Irm Hermann (Johanna), Lilo Pempeit (Luise von Briest, Effi's mother), Herbert Steinmetz (Herr von Briest, Effi's father), Hark Bohm (Gieshübler, pharmacist), Rudolf Lenz (Councillor Rummschüttel), Barbara Valentin (Maria Tripelli, singer), Andrea Schober (Annie), RWF (narrator). Berlin Film Festival, 17 June 1974; TR: 5 July 1974; TV: 31 October 1979 (ZDF). U.S./film, videocassette.

Faustrecht der Freiheit (*Fox and His Friends*).[2] April, July 1974, 35 mm color, 123 min. Produced by Tango-Film and City Film, Berlin; production manager Christian Hohoff; cost 450,000 DM. Cinematographer: Michael Ballhaus; film editor: Thea Eymèsz; music by Peer Raben, songs by Elvis Presley, Leonard Cohen; art director: Kurt Raab. Cast: RWF (Franz Biberkopf), Peter Chatel (Eugen), Karlheinz Böhm (Max), Karl Scheydt (Klaus), Adrian Hoven (Eugen's father), Ulla Jacobsen (Eugen's mother), Christiane Maybach (Franz's sister). TR: 30 May 1975. U.S./film, videocassette.

Wie ein Vogel auf dem Draht (Like a Bird on the Wire). July, 1974, videotape color, 44 min. Screenplay by RWF, Christian Hohoff; song texts by Anja Hauptmann. Produced by WDR; cost 150,000 DM. Camera operator: Erhard Spandel; art director: Kurt Raab; music by Ingfried Hoffman (arrangements), Kurt Edelhagen orchestra. Cast: Brigitte Mira, Evelyn Künneke. TV: 5 May 1975 (ARD).

Mutter Küsters Fahrt zum Himmel (*Mother Küsters Goes to Heaven*). February–March 1975, 35 mm color, 120 min. Screenplay by RWF, in collaboration with Kurt Raab; Produced by Tango-Film; production manager Christian Hohoff; cost 750,000 DM. Cinematographer: Michael Ballhaus; film editor: Thea Eymèsz; music by Peer Raben; art director: Kurt Raab. Cast: Brigitta Mira (Emma Küsters), Ingrid Caven (Corinna), Karlheinz Böhm (Tillmann), Margit Carstensen (Frau Tillmann), Irm Hermann (Helene), Gottfried John (Niemeyer), Armin Meier (Ernst). TR: 2 January 1976 (preview showing 7 July 1975, Berlin); TV: 14 June 1982 (ARD). U.S./film, videocassette.

Angst vor der Angst (*Fear of Fear*). April–May 1975, 16 mm color, 88 min. Screenplay by RWF, based on an idea by Asta Scheib. Produced by WDR; cost 375,000 DM. Cinematographers: Jürgen Jürges, Ulrich Prinz; film editor: Liesgret Schmitt-Klink, Beate Fischer-Weiskirch; music by Peer Raben; art director: Kurt Raab. Cast: Margit Carstensen (Margot), Ulrich Faulhaver (Kurt), Brigitta Mira (Mutter), Irm Hermann (Lore), Armin Meier (Karli), Adrian Hoven (Dr. Merck), Kurt Raab (Herr Bauer). TV: 8 July 1975.

Ich will doch nur, dass ihr mich liebt (*I Only Want You to Love Me*). October–November 1975, 16 mm color, 104 min. Literary source: Klaus Antes and Christiane Erhardt, *Lebenslänglich*. Produced by Bavaria Atelier for WDR; producer: Peter Märthesheimer; cost 800,000 DM. Cinematographer: Michael Ballhaus; film editor: Liesgret Schmitt-Klink; music by Peer Raben; art director: Kurt Raab. Cast: Vitus

Zeplichal (Peter), Elke Aberle (Erika), Alexander Allerson (father), Ernie Mangold (mother), Johanna Hofer (grandmother), Katharina Buchhammer (Ulla), Wolfgang Hess (construction supervisor), Armin Meier (foreman), Erika Runge (interviewer). TV: 23 March 1976. U.S./film, videocassette.

Satansbraten (*Satan's Brew*). October 1975, January–February 1976, 35 mm color, 112 min. Produced by Albatros Produktion for Trio-Film; producer: Michael Fengler; cost 600,000 DM. Cinematographers: Jürgen Jürges, Michael Ballhaus; film editors: Thea Eymèsz, Gabi Eichel; music by Peer Raben; art directors: Kurt Raab, Ulrike Bode. Cast: Kurt Raab (Walter Kranz), Margit Carstensen (Andrée), Helen Vita (Luise Kranz), Volker Spengler (Ernst), Ingrid Caven (Lilly), Marquard Bohm (Rolf, her husband), Ulli Lommel (Lauf), Y Sa Lo (Lana). TR: November 1976. U.S./film, videocassette.

Chinesisches Roulette (*Chinese Roulette*). April–June 1976, 35 mm color, 86 min. Produced by Albatros Produktion and Les Films du Losange; producer: Michael Fengler; cost 1.1 million DM. Cinematographer: Michael Ballhaus; film editors: Ila von Hasperg, Juliane Lorenz (ass.); music by Peer Raben; art director: Kurt Melber. Cast: Margit Carstensen (Ariane), Anna Karina (Irene), Alexander Allerson (Gerhard), Ulli Lommel (Kolbe), Andreas Schober (Angela), Macha Mèril (Traunitz), Brigitte Mira (Kast), Volker Spengler (Gabriel), Armin Meier (service station attendant), Roland Henschke (beggar). Paris Film Festival, 16 November 1976; TR: April 22, 1977; TV: 24 August 1982 (ZDF). U.S./film, videocassette, videodisk.

Bolwieser (*The Stationmaster's Wife*). October–December 1976; 16 mm color, 104 min. (Pt. I), 97 min. (Pt. II); theatrical version: 35 mm widescreen color (blown up from 16 mm format), 112 min. Literary source: novel by Oskar Maria Graf. Produced by Bavaria Atelier for ZDF; producer: Herbert Knopp; cost 1.8 million DM. Cinematographer: Michael Ballhaus; film editors: Ila von Hasperg, Juliane Lorenz; also Franz Walsch for theatrical version; music by Peer Raben; art directors: Kurt Raab, Nico Hehrhan. Cast: Kurt Raab (Xaver Bolwieser), Elisabeth Trissenaar (Hanni Bolwieser), Bernhard Helfrich (Merkl), Udo Kier (Schaffthaler), Volker Spengler (Mangst), Armin Meier (Scherber). New York Film Festival, 1983. TR: 10 June 1983; TV: 31 July 1977 (ZDF). U.S./film.

Frauen in New York (*Women in New York*). March 1977, 16 mm color, 111 min. Literary source: Clare Boothe Luce play *The Women* (translated by Nora Gray). Produced by NDR; cost 320,000 DM. Cinematographer: Michael Ballhaus; film editor: Wolfgang Kerhutt; art director: Rolf Glittenberg. Cast: Christa Berndl (Mary), Margit Carstensen (Sylvia), Anne-Marie Küsters (Peggy), Eva Mattes (Edith), Angela Schmit (Nancy). TV: 21 June 1977.

Despair—Eine Reise ins Licht (*Despair*). April–June 1977, 35 mm color, 119 min. Screenplay by Tom Stoppard from novel by Vladimir Nabokov. Produced by Bavaria Atelier for NF Geria II Film and SFP (Paris); producer: Peter Märthesheimer; cost 6 million DM. Cinematographer: Michael Ballhaus; film editors: Juliane Lorenz, Franz Walsch; music by Peer Raben; art director: Rolf Zehetbauer. Cast: Dirk Bogarde (Hermann), Andrea Ferréol (Lydia), Volker Spengler (Ardalion), Klaus Löwitsch

(Felix), Alexander Allerson (Mayer), Bernhard Wicki (Orlovius), Peter Kern (Müller), Gottfried John (Perebrodov), Hark Bohm (doctor), Y Sa Lo (Elsie), Liselotte Eder (secretary), Armin Meier (foreman; twin brothers in film). Cannes Film Festival, 19 May 1978; TR: 19 May 1978; TV: 30 August 1981 (ARD). U.S./videocassette.

Deutschland im Herbst (*Germany in August*). October 1977–February 1978 (RWF episode: October 1977); 35 mm color and black and white, 124 min (RWF episode: 26 min). Produced by Project Filmproduktion, Filmverlag der Autoren and Hallelujah Film/Kairos Film; production managers: Heinz Badewitz, Karl Melmer, Herbert Herz; cost 450,000 DM. RWF episode—cinematographer: Michael Ballhaus; film editor: Juliane Lorenz; cast: RWF, Liselotte Eder, Armin Meier. Berlin Film Festival (rough cut), 3 March 1978; TR: 17 March 1978. U.S./film, videocassette.

Die Ehe der Maria Braun (*The Marriage of Maria Braun*), January–March 1978, 35 mm wide-screen color, 120 min. Screenplay by Peter Märthesheimer, Pea Fröhlich, from idea by RWF. Produced by Albatros Produktion, Trio-Film, and WDR; producer: Michael Fengler; cost 1,975,000 DM. Cinematographer: Michael Ballhaus; film editors: Franz Walsch, Juliane Lorenz; music by Peer Raben; art director: Helga Ballhaus. Cast: Hanna Schygulla (Maria), Klaus Löwitsch (Hermann), Ivan Desny (Oswald), Gottfriend John (Willi), Gisela Uhlen (mother), Günther Lamprecht (Wetzel), George Byrd (Bill), Elixabeth Trissenaar (Betti). Private preview screening at Cannes Film Festival, 22 May 1978; Berlin Film Festival, 20 February 1979; TR: 23 March 1979; TV: 13 January 1985. U.S./film, videocassette.

In einem Jahr mit 13 Monden (*In a Year of 13 Moons*). July–August 1978, 35 mm wide-screen color, 124 min. Produced by Tango-Film and Project Filmproduktion, Filmverlag der Autoren; cost 700,000 DM. Cinematographer and film editor: RWF[3]; music by Peer Raben, songs by Suicide and from Roxy Music. Cast: Volker Spengler (Elvira Weishaupt), Ingrid Caven (Zora), Gottfried John (Anton Saitz), Elisabeth Trissenaar (Irene), Eva Mattes (Marie-Ann), Liselotte Pempeit (Sister Gudrun). TR: 17 November 1978; TV: 21 January 1985. U.S./film.

Die Dritte Generation (*The Third Generation*). December 1978–January 1979, 35 mm wide-screen color, 110 min. Produced by Tango-Film and Project Filmproduction, Filmverlag der Autoren; cost 800,000 DM. Cinematographer: RWF; film editor: Juliane Lorenz; music by Peer Raben; art directors: Raùl Gimenez, Volker Spengler. Cast: Volker Spengler (August Brem), Eddie Constantine (P. J. Lurz), Bulle Ogier (Hilde Krieger), Hanna Schygulla (Susanne Gast), Harry Baer (Rudolf Mann), Vitus Zeplichal (Berhnard von Stein), Udo Kier (Edgar Gast), Margit Carstensen (Petra Vielhaber), Günther Kaufmann (Franz Walsch), Lilo Pempeit (mother Gast). Cannes Film Fest., 13 May 1979; TR: 14 September 1979. U.S./film.

Berlin Alexanderplatz. June 1979–April 1980, 16 mm color, 15 hours in 14 parts (Pt. 1: 81 min; Pts. 2–13: 58–59 min; Pt. 14: 111 min). Screenplay by RWF, from novel by Alfred Döblin. Produced by Bavaria Atelier and RAI for WDR; producer: Peter Märthesheimer; cost 13 million DM. Cinematographer: Xaver Schwarzenberger; film editors: Juliane Lorenz, Franz Walsch; music by Peer Raben; art directors: Helmut Gassner, Werner Achmann, Jürgen Henze. Cast: Günther Lambrecht (Franz

Biberkopf), Hanna Schygulla (Eva), Barbara Sukowa (Mieze), Gottfried John (Reinhold), Franz Buchrieser (Meck), Claus Holm (pub keeper), Brigitte Mira (Mrs. Bast), Robert Fritz (Herbert), Karin Baal (Minna), Axel Bauer (Dreske), Hark Bohm (Lüders), Marquard Bohm (Otto), Margit Carstensen (Terah),[4] Ivan Desny (Pums), Jürgen Draeger (sausage seller), Annemarie Düringer (Cilly), Liselotte Eder (Mrs. Pums), Raul Gimenez (Konrad), Helmut Griem (Sarug), Irm Hermann (Trude), Traute Hoess (Emmy), Klaus Höhne (Nazi sympathizer in New World cafe), Helmut Petigk (old man in bar), Fritz Schediwy (Willy), Volker Spengler (Bruno), Herbert Steinmetz (news dealer in subway), Elisabeth Trissenaar (Lina), Barbara Valentin (Ida), Helen Vita (Fränze), Gerhard Zwerenz (Baumann). Venice Film Fest., 28 August–8 September 1980; TV: 12–29 December 1980. U.S./videocassette.

Lili Marleen. July–September 1980, 35 mm wide-screen color, 120 min. Screenplay by Manfred Purzer and RWF, from autobiography of Lale Anderson, *Der Himmel hat viele Farben*. Produced by Roxy-Film, Rialto-Film, CIP (Rome), and Bayerischer Rundfunk; producer: Luggi Waldleitner; cost 10.5 million DM. Cinematographer: Xaver Schwarzenberger; film editors: Juliane Lorenz, Franz Walsch; music by Peer Raben, song by Norbert Schultze; art director: Rolf Zehetbauer; costume designer: Barbara Baum. Cast: Hanna Schygulla (Willie), Giancarlo Giannini (Robert Mendelsohn), Mel Ferrer (David Mendelsohn), Karl-Heinz von Hassel (Hans Henkel), Christine Kaufmann (Miriam Glaubrecht), Hark Bohm (Taschner), Lilo Pempeit (Tamara Mendolsohn), RWF (Günther Weisenborn). TR: 15 January 1981; TV: 16 January 1985 (ARD). U.S./film.

Lola. April–May 1981, 35 mm wide-screen, color, 113 min. Screenplay by Peter Märthesheimer, Pea Fröhlich. Produced by Rialto-Film, Trio-Film, and WDR; producer: Horst Wendlandt; cost 3.5 million DM. Cinematographer: Xaver Schwarzenberger; film editor: Juliane Lorenz; music by Peer Raben, songs sung by Freddy Quinn, Rudi Schuricke; art directors: Raul Giminez, Udo Kier; costume designers: Barbara Baum, Egon Strasser. Cast: Barbara Sukowa (Lola), Armin Mueller-Stahl (von Bohm), Mario Adorf (Schuckert), Matthias Fuchs (Esslin). TR: 20 August 1981; TV: 20 January 1985 (ARD). U.S./film.

Theater in Trance, June 1981, 16 mm color, 91 min. Screenplay by RWF (with texts from Antonin Artaud, *The Theater and Its Double*), Produced by Laura-Film for ZDF; producer: Thomas Schühly; cost 220,000 DM. Cinematographer: Werner Lüring; film editors: Juliane Lorenz, Franz Walsch. Documentary with performances by 8 dance and theatrical performers and groups. Mannheim Film Week, 8 October 1981; TV: 11 November 1981.

Die Sehnsucht der Veronika Voss (*Veronika Voss*). November–December 1981, 35 mm wide-screen black and white, 104 min. Screenplay by Peter Märthesheimer, Pea Fröhlich, RWF. Produced by Laura-Film, Tango-Film, Rialto-Film, Trio-Film, and Maran-Film; producer: Thomas Schühly; cost 2.6 million DM. Cinematographer: Xaver Schwarzenberger; film editor: Juliane Lorenz; music by Peer Raben; art director: Rolf Zehetbauer; costume designer: Barbara Baum. Cast: Rosel Zech (Veronika Voss), Hilmar Thate (Robert Krohn), Cornelia Froboess (Henriette), Annemarie

Düringer (Dr. Katz), Doris Schade (Josefa), Armin Mueller-Stahl (Max Rehbein), Johanna Hofer and Rudolf Platte (old couple), Eric Schuman (Dr. Edel), Peter Berling (film producer), Günther Kaufmann (American soldier), Lilo Pempeit (jewelry store clerk), Volker Spengler (first film director), Peter Zadek (second director), Juliane Lorenz (producer's secretary), RWF (film viewer in theater). Berlin Film Festival (Golden Bear), 18 February 1982; TR: 19 February 1982; TV: 16 January 1985. U.S./[F], videocassette.

Querelle—ein Pakt mit dem Teufel (Querelle). March 1982, 35 mm CinemaScope color, Dolby-Stereo, 106 min. Screenplay by RWF, from Jean Genet novel, *Querelle de Brest*. Produced by Planet-Film, Albatros Produktion, and Gaumont (Paris) in cooperation with Sam Waynberg; producer: Dietor Schidor; cost 4.4 million DM. Cinematographer: Xaver Schwarzenberger; film editors: Juliane Lorenz, Franz Walsch; music by Peer Raben; art director: Rolf Zehetbauer; costume designer: Barbara Baum. Cast: Brad Davis (Querelle), Franco Nero (Lt. Seblon), Jeanne Moreau (Lysiane), Laurent Malet (Roger), Hanno Pöschl (Robert/Gil), Günther Kaufmann (Nono), Burkhard Driest (Mario), Dieter Schidor (Vic). Venice Film Fest., 31 August 1982; TR: 17 September 1982. U.S./videocassette.

B. Selected Fassbinder Performances and Production Responsibilities in Films Directed by Others

Tonys Freunde (Tony's Friends). 1967. Director: Paul Vasil. RWF plays Mallard.

Der Bräutigam, die Komödiantin und der Zuhälter (The Bridegroom, the Comedienne, and the Pimp). 1968. Director: Jean-Marie Straub, Danièle Huillet. RWF plays Freder, the pimp.

Al Capone im deutschen Wald (. . . in the German Forest). 1969. Director: F. P. Wirth. RWF plays Heini.

Fernes Jamaica (Distant Jamaica). 1969. Screenplay by RWF; director: Peter Moland. Produced by antitheater-X-Film.

Baal. 1969. Screenplay by Bertolt Brecht/Volker Schlöndorff. D. Schlöndorff. RWF plays Baal.

Sonja und Kirilow haben sich entschlossen, Schauspieler to werden und die Welt zu verändern (Sonja and Kirilow Have Decided to become Actors and to Change the World). 1969. Screenplay by Ursula Strätz, RWF; director: Strätz. Produced by antitheater-X-Film.

Der plötzliche Reichtum der armen Leute von Kombach (The Sudden Wealth of the Poor People of Kombach). 1970. Director: Volker Schöndorff. RWF plays a farmer.

Matthias Kneissl. 1970. Screenplay by Martin Speer, Reinhardt Hauff; director: Hauff. RWF plays Flecklbauer.

Zärtlichkeit der Wölfe (Tenderness of the Wolves). 1972. Screenplay by Kurt Raab; director: Ulli Lommel. Produced by Tango Film. RWF plays Wittkowski.

Schatten der Engel (*Shadow of Angels*). October–November 1975. 35 mm color, 101 min. Screenplay by Daniel Schmid, RWF. Literary source: RWF play, *Der Müll, die Stadt und der Tod* (*Garbage, the City, and Death*). Produced by Albatros Produktion, Tango-Film, and Artco; producer: Michael Fengler; cost 600,000. Director: Daniel Schmid; cinematographer: Renato Berta; film editor: Ila von Hasperg; music by Peer Raben, Gottfried Hüngsberg; art director: Raùl Gimenez. Cast: RWF (Raoul), Ingrid Caven (Lily), Klaus Löwitsch (the Jew), Annemarie Düringer (Mrs. Müller), Adrian Hoven (Müller), Ulli Lommel (little prince), Irm Hermann (Emma). Solothurn Festival, 1 January 1975; TR: 3 September 1976. U.S./film, videocassette.

Bourbon Street Blues. 1977. Group production, Munich Film and Television Academy. Director: Douglas Sirk. RWF plays a writer.

Der kleine Godard an das Kuratorium junger deutscher Film (The Little Godard at the Commision for Young German Film). 1977. Director: Hellmuth Costard. RWF plays himself.

Kamikaze 89. 1981. Screenplay by Robert Katz, Wolf Gremm. Director: Gremm. RWF plays the protagonist, police lieutenant Jansen. U.S./videocassette.

C. Selected Films and Television Programs about Fassbinder

Note: Items marked with an asterisk were included in 1992 Fassbinder Exhibition and Retrospective in Berlin. For those items, the program of the exhibition (Rainer Werner Fassbinder Foundation, *Rainer Werner Fassbinder Werkschau Programm* [Berlin: Argon, 1992] 98–99) is the source of the production and broadcast information (the program does not contain specific credits for direction, cinematography, etc.). Sources of other information are indicated in brackets and notes at the ends of entries.

*Ende einer Kommune (End of a Commune). 1969–70. 16 mm black and white, 50 min. Joachim von Mengerhausen. Documentary about the antitheater. TV: 2 February 1970.

*Fassbinder produziert (Fassbinder Produces). 1970–71. 16 mm black and white. Michael Ballhaus and Dietmar Buchmann. Fassbinder directing. TV: 27 January 1971 (WDR III).

*Rainer Werner Fassbinder. 1972. 16 mm black and white, 30 min. Christian Braad Thomsen. Interview with RWF during 1972 Venice Film Festival. Denmark Radio/TV.

*Je später der Abend. 1976. Television talk show with RWF and Reinhard Münchenhagen. TV: 20 March 1976 (WDR).

*Lebensläufe: Rainer Werner Fassbinder im Gespräch (Résumés: Talking with RWF). 1977. 16 mm color, 45 min. Interview with Peter W. Jansen. TV: 18 March 1978 (S3).

Filmarbeit mit Douglas Sirk (Film work with . . .). 1978. Director: Gustavo Gräf Marino. Television documentary about the shooting of *Bourbon Street Blues* (Spaich 406).

*Berlin Alexanderplatz. 1980. Hans-Dieter Hartl. Documentation of filming. Made for television.

Zum Tode von Rainer Werner Fassbinder (On the Death of . . .). 1982. 38 min. With Werner Schroeter and Wolfgang Gremm, moderated by Jürgen Kritz.

Gespräche über Rainer Werner Fassbinder (Conversations about RWF). 1982. Live television program with friends and coworkers of RWF, hosted by Hans Christoph Blumenberg (Spaich 413).[5]

Letze Arbeiten (Last Works). 1982. 16 mm color, 56 min. Wolfgang Gremm. Documentation of shooting of *Kamikaze 89* and *Querelle.*

Portrait: Rainer Werner Fassbinder. 1982. Director: Michael Straven. Produced by SFB. Juliane Lorenz describes this program as "really wonderful" (letter to the author 3 June 1994).

Der Bauer von Babylon: Rainer Werner Fassbinder dreht "Querelle" (*The Wizard of Babylon*). 1982. Director: Dieter Schidor. Television documentary of the director at work on *Querelle* and in an interview a few hours before his death (Spaich 413). 16 mm film distributed by New Yorker Films.

Ein Mann wie Eva/Haus der Begierde (A Man like Eva/House of Desire). 1983–84. 92 min. Director: Radu Gabrea (Spaich 413). Exploitation of the legend of RWF as driven artistic genius and "monster" in his personal relationships, starring frequent Fassbinder-actress Eva Mattes (in Fassbinder-beard) as the director. U.S./videocassette.

Der Mensch ist ein hässliches Tier (The Human Being Is a Nasty Beast). 1984–85. Director: Rosemarie Stenzel-Quast (Spaich 413). Juliane Lorenz describes this piece as "an exploitation of the Fassbinder legend as a bad person, in the form of a documentary, with interviews with very unimportant people—like Frank Rippolah [director of *Taxi zum Klo,* a commercially successful 1981 film depicting the homosexual subculture]" (letter to the author 3 June 1994).

Ich will nicht nur, dass ihr mich liebt. 1992. Director: Hans Günther Pflaum; Produced by Filmverlag der Autoren. Two-hour television retrospective (Richard C. and Maria E. Helt, *West German Cinema Since 1945: A Reference Handbook.* Metuchen, N.J.: Scarecrow, 1985; Lorenz letter to the author 7 April 1994).

Aspekte-Ausschnitte (Aspects-Excerpts). 1992. 40 min. Compilation by Juliane Lorenz showing various periods in the life of RWF.

Notes

1. Juliane Lorenz has pointed out some of the difficulties in defining the function of "producers" of Fassbinder's films. "A producer like Peter Märthesheimer, when he was *Redakteur* [editor] at the WDR, was responsible for the money within the internal structure of the WDR. When the antitheater produced a film, as in the case of *Whity* and *Beware of a Holy Whore,* the money came mainly from the Federal Ministry of the Interior and from the German Film Prizes. (Rainer later paid off the debts for such films, so he was in a way the producer.) Peter Berling was just the *Herstellungsleiter* [production

manager] for those two films; he didn't bring in any money, but rather only handled the money the antitheater was getting" (Let 3 June 1994).

2. For an explanation of the German title, see chapter 5, note 42.

3. For Juliane Lorenz's role in editing this film, see chapter 7, note 96.

4. Identification of the actors for the angels Terah and Sarug is here corrected from the Jansen and Schütte filmography, which lists Magdalena Montezuma and Werner Schroeter, respectively, for the roles. They were originally cast, and performed in one scene. But since Schroeter was not available for a later shooting date, Fassbinder replaced them with Margit Carstensen and Helmut Griem and reshot the original scene (Lorenz Let 3 June 1994).

5. Kurt Raab, Peer Raben, Harry Baer, and Irm Hermann appear in this program. Juliane Lorenz writes that Raab monopolizes the discussion, "talking bullshit the whole time" (Let 3 June 1994).

BIBLIOGRAPHY

Note: This selected bibliography includes all works cited in the text and notes. Abbreviations given in brackets before the Fassbinder interviews and several other frequently cited items are used for citations in the text and notes.

1. Fassbinder Plays

Anarchie in Bayern & andere Stücke. Frankfurt am Main: Verlag der Autoren, 1985. Also includes *Tropfen auf heisse Steine, Der Amerikanische Soldat, Werwolf,* an essay on Fassbinder's theater work by Michael Töteberg, and notes.

Antiteater (Katzelmacher, Preparadise sorry now, Die Bettleroper). Frankfurt am Main: Suhrkamp, 1970.

Antiteater: Funf Stücke nach Stücken. Frankfort am Main: Verlag der Autoren, 1986. Contains *Iphigenie auf Tauris, Ajax, Die Bettleroper, Das Kaffeehaus,* and *Das brennende Dorf,* an essay on Fassbinder's theater work by Michael Töteberg, and notes.

Antiteater 2 (Das Kaffeehaus, Bremer Freiheit, Blut am Hals der Katze). Frankfurt am Main: Suhrkamp, 1972.

Die bitteren Tränen der Petra von Kant, Der Müll, die Stadt und der Tod: Zwei Stücke. Frankfurt am Main: Verlag der Autoren, 1980.

The Bitter Tears of Petra von Kant/Blood on the Neck of a Cat. Tr. Anthony Vivis. Oxford: Amber Lane Press, 1984.

Bremer Freiheit, Blut am Hals der Katze: Zwei Stücke. Frankfurt am Main: Verlag der Autoren, 1983.

Katzelmacher, Preparadise sorry now. Frankfurt am Main: Verlag der Autoren, 1982.

Nur eine Scheibe Brot. Frankfurt am Main: Verlag der Autoren, 1992. Reprinted, with introduction by Michael Töteberg, *Theater Heute* (May 1994): 29–33.

Plays. Ed. and tr. by Denis Calandra. NY: PAJ [*Performing Arts Journal*] Publications, 1985. Contains *The Bitter Tears of Petra von Kant, Bremen Freedom, Katzelmacher, Blood on a Cat's Neck, Pre-Paradise Sorry Now,* and *Garbage, the City and Death,* and an introduction by Calandra, "The Antiteater of R. W. Fassbinder" (9–15). In English.

Sämtliche Stücke. Frankfurt am Main: Verlag der Autoren, 1991. Contains all the plays in the individual Verlag der Autoren volumes listed above, plus two radio plays, as well as notes by Michael Töteberg (but not his essays on Fassbinder's theater work published in *Anarchie in Bayern* and *Antiteater*).

Stücke 3. Frankfurt am Main: Suhrkamp, 1976. Contains *The Bitter Tears of Petra von Kant, Das brennende Dorf,* and *Der Müll, die Stadt und der Tod.*

2. Fassbinder Film Scripts

Die Ehe der Maria Braun. Ed. Lars Bardrum. Copenhagen: Gjellerup & Gad, 1987. Film script in German, commentary in Danish.

Die Erde is unbewohnbar wie der Mond. Frankfurt am Main: April! April!, 1986. Screenplay for a film (not produced) based on a novel by Gerhard Zwerenz.

Fassbinders Filme 2. Ed. Michael Töteberg. Frankfurt am Main: Verlag der Autoren, 1990. Continuity scripts for *Warum läuft Herr R. Amok, Rio das Mortes, Whity, Die Niklashauser Fart, Der amerikanische Soldat,* and *Warnung vor einer heiligen Nutte,* with background information and commentary.

Fassbinders Filme 3. Ed. Michael Töteberg. Frankfurt am Main: Verlag der Autoren, 1990. Continuity scripts for *Händler der vier Jahreszeiten, Angst essen Seele auf,* and *Fontane Effi Briest,* with background information and commentary.

Fassbinders Filme 4/5. 2 vols. Frankfurt am Main: Verlag der Autoren, 1991. Continuity script for the five episodes of *Acht Stunden sind kein Tag* broadcast on television and scripts for episodes 6–8, which were not produced. Volume 5 contains an essay by, and two interviews with, Fassbinder, two essays by the series editor for WDR, Peter Märthesheimer, and other material.

Der Film Berlin Alexanderplatz: Ein Arbeitsjournal. Rainer Werner Fassbinder and Harry Baer. Frankfurt am Main: Zweitausendeins, 1980. Continuity script of Fassbinder's 15-hour television mini-series, generously illustrated.

In a Year of Thirteen Moons. Tr. Joyce Rheuban. *October* 21 (Summer 1982): 5–50. Continuity script, in English translation.

Die Kinofilme 1. Ed. Michael Töteberg. Munich: Schirmer/Mosel, 1987. Continuity scripts of *Der Stadtstreicher, Das kleine Chaos, Liebe is kälter als der Tod, Katzelmacher,* and *Götter der Pest,* with more than 250 frame enlargements and an introduction by the editor.

Lili Marleen. Ed. Lars Bardram. Copenhaven: Gad, 1983. German script, with Danish commentary.

The Marriage of Maria Braun. Tr. and ed. Joyce Rheuban. New Brunswick, N. J., 1986. Continuity script in English translation, with commentary, notes, and interviews by several hands.

Querelle Filmbuch. Ed. Dietor Schidor and Michael McLernon. Munich: Schirmer/Mosel, 1982. English translation: *Querelle: The Film Book.* Tr. Arthur S. Wensinger and Richard H. Wood. Munich: Shirmer/Mosel/Grove, 1982. Continuity script, profusely illustrated (in color).

Schatten der Engel. Script by Daniel Schmid and RWF based on RWF's play *Der Müll, die Stadt und der Tod.* Frankfurt am Main: Zweitausendeins, 1976.

3. Fassbinder Interviews, Essays, and Other Writing

[*Anarchie*] *Die Anarchie der Phantasie: Gespräche und Interviews.* Ed. Michael Töteberg. Frankfurt am Main: Fischer Taschenbuch, 1986. Primarily, interviews with Fassbinder. See next item.

[*Anarchy*] *The Anarchy of the Imagination: Interviews, Essays, Notes.* Ed. Michael Töteberg and Leo A. Lensing. Tr. Krishna Winston. Baltimore: Johns Hopkins UP, 1992. Selection of materials from *Anarchie* and *Kopf,* with additional notes, in English.

[Brocher Int I] "Gruppen sind ja vieles: Gespräche mit Rainer Werner Fassbinder über die Geschichte des Antiteaters—Ein Fragment." 130-page typescript of Fassbinder's taped discussions in 1973 with Corinna Brocher for a planned book by RWF on the antitheater; forthcoming in *Fassbinder Interviews: Ungekürzt;* quoted by permission of Juliane Lorenz.

[Brocher Int II] "Da hab ich Regieführen gelernt." *Anarchie* 15–29. Selections from Brocher Int I.

[Bronner/Brocher Int]. Bronner, Barbara and Corinna Brocher, eds. *Die Filmmacher.* Munich: Bertelsman, 1973. Interviews with 17 directors, including Fassbinder (171–185, by Brocher).

"The Cities of Humanity and the Human Soul: Some Unorganized Thoughts on Alfred Döblin's *Berlin Alexanderplatz.*" *Anarchy* 160–7. First published in *Die Zeit,* 14 March 1980.

[Färber Int] "Revolution im Privaten: Gespräch mit Rainer Werner Fassbinder." Interviewed by Helmut Farber, Urs Jenny, and Wilhelm Roth. *Filmkritik* 13, 8 (1 Aug 1969): 471–6. One of the earliest Fassbinder interviews (in which Ursula Strätz, Ingrid Caven, and Peer Raben also comment briefly), focussing on the film *Love is Colder than Death,* the antitheater, and political implications of RWF's work.

Fassbinder-Interviews: Ungekürzt. Ed. Juliane Lorenz. Berlin: Henschel-Verlag, forthcoming. Will contain major interviews made abroad (translated into German), Brocher Int I and other interviews excerpted in *Anarchie,* and all interviews made with Christian Braad Thomsen.

[Fischer Int] "Fassbinder oder: Der Mut, die Schiffe hinter sich zu verbrennen—Gespräch mit einem, der auszog, die Bürger zu erschrecken." Interviewed by Kurt Joachim Fischer. *Kirche und Film* 30, 8 (Aug 1977): 15–18.

[Fründt Int] "Egal was ich mache, die Leute regen sich auf." Interviewed by Bodo Fründt and Michael Jürgs. *Anarchie* 167–85. Conducted in 1980, primarily concerns *Berlin Alexanderplatz* and *Lili Marleen.*

[Haddad-Garcia Int] "The Final Tears of Rainer Werner Fassbinder." Interviewed by George Haddad-Garcia. *Christopher Street* 6, 5 (1982): 48–55. One of the director's last interviews, for an American magazine directed at gay readers.

"Ich habe kein Sex gesehen." *Abendzeitung* (Munich), 7 August 1980. Brief comments about *Berlin Alexanderplatz* in a call-in program.

"Imitation of Life: Über die Filme von Douglas Sirk," *Fernsehen und Film,* February 1971, No. 2. Reprinted in *Filme befreien den Kopf* 11–24 and, in English translation ("On the Films of . . ."), in *Anarchy* 77–89; the latter version is cited in the text and notes. RWF's major statement on Sirk.

[Jansen Int] "Interview 2" by Peter W. Jansen. Jansen and Schütte 95–118. Transcript of a wide-ranging 1978 television interview (in German).

[Jansen Int/"Exile"] "Exile würde ich noch nicht sagen." Interviewed by Peter W. Jansen. *Cinema* [Zurich] 24, 2 (May 1978): 13–14.

[Jauch Int]. "Herr Fassbinder, lieben Sie die Menschen?" Interviewed by Eric Olaf Jauch and Ulrich Gehner. *Szene Hamburg,* 1 July 1977. DIF 27.

[*Kopf*] *Filme befreien den Kopf.* Ed. Michael Töteberg. Frankfurt am Main: Fischer Taschenbuch, 1984. RWF's writings on his work and other topics. See *Anarchy.*

[Limmer Int] "Alles Vernünftige interessiert mich nicht." Comprehensive, candid interview with Wolfgang Limmer (1980). Limmer 43–138.

[*Med* Int] "Zum Beispiel: Rainer Werner Fassbinder." Interview. *Medical Tribune,* 12 July 1974: 6.

[Müller Int] Three wide-ranging interviews with André Müller (1971, 1973, 1976). *Entblössungen.* Munich: Wilhelm Goldman, 1979. 178–98.

[Ponkie Int] "Die Ausbeutung von Gefühlen." Interviewed by "Ponkie." *Abendzeitung* [Munich] 29 April 1977.

[Röhl Int]. "Kommt die Polet-Welle?" Interviewed by Wolfgang Röhl. *Konkret* 13, 1973. Repr. *Fassbinders Filme 5,* 238–41.

[Scherer Int] "An einem Sonntagmorgen bei Rainer Werner Fassbinder." Interviewed by Theres Scherer and Bernhard Giger. *Innen ist warm und draussen kalt: Kino der 70er Jahre.* Gunligen: Keller Kino Bern: 1974. 97–9.

[Schütte Int] "Wenn ich nicht arbeite—ich weiss gar nicht, wie das so richtig ist." Interviewed by Wolfram Schütte (1976). *Anarchie* 67–81.

[Schygulla/RWF] "Hanna Schygulla. Kein Star, nur ein schwacher Mensch wie wir alle." Schygulla, *Bilder aus Filmen von Rainer Werner Fassbinder* 169–87. Reprinted *Kopf* 97–114 and in English translation by A. S. Wensinger and Richard Wood ("Hanna Schygulla—Not a Star, Just a Vulnerable Human Being Like the Rest of Us: Disorderly Thoughts about an Interesting Woman") in *Anarchy* 199–214; the latter is cited in the text and notes. Substantial commentary on Schygulla and on RWF's Action-Theater and antitheater work.

[Sparrow Int] Interviewed by Norbert Sparrow. *Cinéaste* 8, 2 (Fall 1977): 20–21.

[Steinborn Int] "Ich bin das Glück dieser Erde: Ach wär' das schön wenn's so wäre." Interviewed by Bion Steinborn and Rüdiger von Naso. *Filmfaust* 24, 9 (April-May 1982): 2–16.

"Sybille Schmitz: Geschichte für einen Spielfilm." *Text + Kritik* 103 (July 1989): 11–19. Initial brief scenario for *Veronika Voss.*

[Thomsen Int] "Five Interviews with Fassbinder." Selections from interviews with Chris-

tian Braad Thomsen (1971/1972, 1973, 1974, 1975, 1977). Tr. Soren Fischer with
   Tony Rayns. Rayns, *Fassbinder* 82–101. Substantial discussions about life and work.
[Wiegand Int] Interviewed by Wilfrid Wiegand. McC 37–82. English translation of a
   1974 interview dealing with life and films through *Effi Briest* (the first five pages
   were cut, for space reasons, in the fifth edition of Jansen and Schütte).
[Wüstensand Int] "Verzweiflung? Fast ein Monolog von Rainer Werner Fassbinder."
   Interviewed by Amalia Wüstensand. *Kirche und Film* 5 (May 1977): 4–7.

4. Secondary Materials

Alvarado, Manuel Alvarado. "Eight Hours Are Not a Day (and Afterword)." Rayns 70–
   78.
Anderson, Lale. *Der Himmel hat viele Farben: Leben mit einem Lied.* Munich: Deutscher
   Taschenbuch: 1974. Literary source for *Lili Marleen.*
Artaud, Antonin. *The Theater and Its Double.* Tr. Mary Caroline Richards. New York:
   Grove, 1958.
Babuscio, Jack. "Camp and the Gay Sensibility." Dyer, *Gays and Film* 49–50.
Baer, Harry. Personal Interview. 16 June 1992.
[Baer] *Schlafen kann ich, wenn ich tot bin: Das atemlose Leben des Rainer Werner
   Fassbinder.* Cologne: Kiepenheuer and Witsch, 1982. Paperback edition, 1990. Lively,
   insightful personal memoir, by a friend and frequent co-worker.
Bathrick, David. "Inscribing History, Prohibiting Desire: Fassbinder and Fascism." In
   forthcoming Fassbinder issue of *New German Critique.*
Bayer, Eva-Suzanne. "Naivität mit Widerhaken." *Stuttgarter Zeitung,* 24 December 1975.
   On *I Only Want You to Love Me.*
Berling, Peter. *Die 13 Jahre des Rainer Werner Fassbinder: Seine Filme, seine Freunde,
   seinde Feinde.* Bergisch Gladbach: Gustav Lübbe, 1992. Anecdotal account, emphasizing personal relations within the group and production arrangements (as well as
   the author's own work) by a German film producer, actor, and writer based in Rome,
   who worked with Fassbinder primarily during his early years. Much of this material
   is in Katz. On Berling's untrustworthiness as a biographer of Fassbinder, see Chap.
   11, n. 95.
Blumenberg, Hans C. "Der Rest sind Tränen." *Die Zeit* 13 June 1975.
Bogarde, Sir Dirk. Letters to the author. 2 May 1991, 1 July 1992.
———. *An Orderly Man.* New York: Knopf, 1983. Memoirs, including discussion of
   his work on *Despair.*
Braun, Karlheinz. Interview with Juliane Lorenz (15 December 1993). Forthcoming in
   Lorenz, *Rainer Werner Fassbinder: Leben und Werk.*
Brooks, Peter. *The Melodramatic Imagination: Balzac, Henry James, and the Mode of
   Excess.* New Haven: Yale UP, 1976.
Buchka, Peter. "Das Phänomen Fassbinder." *Süddeutsche Zeitung,* 10 June 1992, 13.

———. "Geschichte einer Erziehung." *Süddeutsche Zeitung,* 17 Nov. 1994, 18. On the theatrical release of *Martha.*

Burgoyne, Robert. "Narrative and Sexual Excess." *October* 21 (Summer 1982): 56–7. On *In a Year of 13 Moons.*

Byars, Jackie. *All that Hollywood Allows: Re-reading Gender in 1950s Melodrama.* Chapel Hill: University of North Carolina Press, 1991.

Calandra, Denis. "The Antiteater of R. W. Fassbinder." Fassbinder, *Plays* 9–15.

Carrasco, Candide. "Fassbinder's *Querelle:* An Iconography of Desire." *Sex and Love in the Motion Pictures.* Ed. Douglas Radcliff-Umstead. Kent Ohio: Kent State University Romance Languages Dept., 1984. 111–16.

Caven, Ingrid. "Entretien avec Ingrid Caven." Interviewed by Camille Nevers. *Cahiers du Cinéma* 469 (June 1993): 59–61.

Chatman, Seymour. *Story and Discourse: Narrative Structure in Fiction and Film.* Ithaca: Cornell UP, 1978.

———. *Coming to Terms: The Rhetoric of Narrative in Fiction and Film.* Ithaca: Cornell UP, 1990.

Coe, Richard. *The Vision of Jean Genet.* New York: Grove Press, 1968.

Collins, Richard and Vincent Porter. "Westdeutscher Rundfunk and the Arbeiterfilm (1967–1977)." *Quarterly Review of Film Studies* 5, 2 (Spring 1980): 233–251.

Cook, David A. *A History of Narrative Film.* Second edition. New York: Norton, 1990.

Corrigan, Timothy. *New German Film: The Displaced Image.* Austin: Texas UP, 1983. Includes discussion of *Petra von Kant.*

———. "The Temporality of Place, Postmodernism, and the Fassbinder Texts." In forthcoming special Fassbinder issue of *New German Critique.*

Demetz, Peter. *After the Fires: Recent Writing in the Germanies, Austria, and Switzerland.* New York: Harcourt Brace Jovanovich, 1986.

———. *Postwar German Literature: A Critical Introduction.* New York: Schocken, 1970. More detailed discussion of the immediate post-war period than his 1986 study.

[DIF] Deutsches Institut für Filmkunde. *R. W. F. Die Information,* Heft 1. Frankfurt am Main: DIF, 1982. Articles on RWF from German newspapers and magazines, 1969–82.

Doane, Mary Ann. *The Desire to Desire: The Woman's Film of the 1940s.* Bloomington: Indiana UP, 1987.

Döblin, Alfred. *Berlin Alexanderplatz: Die Geschichte vom Franz Biberkopf.* Olten: Walter-Verlag, 1961.

———. *Berlin Alexanderplatz: The Story of Franz Biberkopf.* Tr. Eugene Jolas. New York: Frederick Ungar, n. d.

Dollenmayer, David. *The Berlin Novels of Alfred Döblin.* Berkeley: University of California Press, 1988.

Dornberg, John. "West Germany's Embattled Democracy: The Antiterrorist Menace from the Right." *Saturday Review* 5 (10 June 1978): 18–21.

Duren, Brien. "Fassbinder's Trilogy of Vamps." *Sex and Love in the Motion Pictures.* Ed. Douglas Radcliff-Umstead. Kent Ohio: Kent State University Romance Languages Dept., 1984. 105–10.

Dyer, Richard, ed. *Gays and Film*. London: British Film Institute, 1977.

————. *Now You See It: Studies in Lesbian and Gay Film*. New York: Routledge, 1990.

————. "Reading Fassbinder's Sexual Politics." Rayns, *Fassbinder* 54–64.

Ebert, Roger. "Fassbinder: The Final Days," *Gentlemen's Quarterly,* December 1983, 54, 57, 247–8.

Eckhardt, Bernd. *Rainer Werner Fassbinder, in 17 Jahren 42 Filme*. Munich: Wilhelm Heyne, 1982. Uncritical biographical study, but with useful quotations from film reviews, and information on Fassbinder's early theater work (including photographs and programs).

Eder, Liselotte. "Der Tote Sohn." Interviewed by André Müller. *Die Zeit* 18 (24 April 1992): 55–56.

[Eder Int] Personal interview. 21 and 24 September 1990, unpublished. German translation, augmented by discussions with Juliane Lorenz, in Lorenz, *Das ganz normale Chaos* 252–68.

Ehrhard, Christiane and Klaus Antes, ed. *Lebenslänglich-Protokolle aus der Haft*. Munich: R. Piper, 1972. Literary source for *I Only Want You to Love Me*.

Eichinger, Bernd. "Some Thoughts on West German Cinema in the Eighties." Interview (March 29, 1985) with Richard E. Welt. Helt and Helt, *West German Cinema Since 1945.* 16–22.

Eisner, Lotte. *The Haunted Screen*. Berkeley: Univ. of California Press, 1969. Study of Weimar era German cinema.

Elsaesser, Thomas. "A Cinema of Vicious Circles." Rayns 24–36.

————. "Filming Fascism: Is History Just an Old Movie?" *Sight and Sound* 2, 5 NS (Sept. 1992): 18–21.

————. "Forgetting Fassbinder?" In forthcoming Fassbinder issue of *New German Critique*.

————. *"Lili Marleen:* Fascism and the Film Industry." *October* 21 (Summer 1982): 121.

————. "Murder, Merger, Suicide: The Politics of *Despair.*" Rayns 37–53.

————. *New German Cinema: A History*. New Brunswick, New Jersey: Rutgers UP, 1989.

————. "The Postwar German Cinema." Rayns 1–16.

————. "Rivette and the end of cinema." *Sight and Sound* 1, 12 NS (April 1992): 20–23.

Emerson, Jim. "Regarding Hanna." *Film Comment* 27, 4 (July 1991): 72–4. Based on an interview with Hanna Schygulla in Hollywood during the filming of Kenneth Branagh's *Dead Again*.

Faletti, Heidi. "The Doomed Moralist in *The Blue Angel* and *Lola.*" *National Traditions in Motion Pictures* (Proceedings of the Third Annual Conference on Film). Kent, Ohio: Kent State University Department of Romance Languages, 1985. 80–84.

Fest, Joachim. "Reicher Jude von links." *Frankfurter Allgemeine Zeitung,* 19 March 1976.

Film und Fernsehen 20, 4 (1992). This issue of the Berlin film and television journal contains a 26-page section on Fassbinder (on the occasion of the tenth anniversary of his death).

Filmverlag der Autoren (Munich). Press kit for *Chinesisches Roulette* (March 18, 1977).

Firda, Richard A. *Peter Handke*. New York: Twayne, 1993.

Fischer, Robert and Joe Hembus. *Der neue deutsche Film, 1960–1980*. Munich: Goldman, 1981.

Fischetti, Renate. *Das neue Kino—Acht Porträts von deutschen Regisseurinnen*. Frankfurt am Main: Tende, 1992.

Fleisser, Marieluise. "All meiner Söhne: Über Martin Speer, Rainer Werner Fassbinder und Franz Xaver Kroetz." *Gesammelte Werk*. Vol. 2. Frankfurt am Main, 1982. 508–513.

Fontane, Theodor. *Effi Briest*. Ed. Walter Keitel and Helmuth Nürnberger. Frankfurt am Main: Ullstein, 1989.

Foss, Paul. *Fassbinder in Review*. Sydney: Australian Film Institute, 1983.

Franklin, James. *New German Cinema: From Oberhausen to Hamburg*. Boston: Twayne, 1983. General survey and separate chapters on eight major filmmakers, including Fassbinder (through 1979).

Galouye, Daniel F. *Welt am Draht: Ein utopisch-technischer Roman*. Munich: Wilhelm Goldman, 1964. Literary source for the 1973 RWF film.

Gemünden, Gerd. "Re-Fusing Brecht: The Cultural Politics of Rainer Werner Fassbinder's German Hollywood." In forthcoming special Fassbinder issue of *New German Critique*.

———. "Remembering Fassbinder in a Year with 13 Moons." Introduction to forthcoming special Fassbinder issue of *New German Critique*.

Genet, Jean. *Querelle*. Tr. Anselm Hollo. New York: Grove Weidenfeld, 1974.

Gilliatt, Penelope. "The Current Cinema." *The New Yorker* (June 14, 1976): 94–5. On *The Bitter Tears of Petra von Kant*.

Gledhill, Christine, ed. *Home is Where the Heart Is: Studies in Melodrama and the Women's Film*. London: British Film Institute, 1987.

Grayson, Jane. *Nabokov Translated: A Comparison of Nabokov's Russian and English Prose*. Oxford: Oxford UP, 1977.

Grimm, Reinhold. "The Jew, the Playwright, and Trash: West Germany's Fassbinder Controversy." *Monatshefte* 83, 1 (1991): 17–28.

Haag, Achim. *"Deine Sehnsucht kann keiner Stillen"*: *Rainer Werner Fassbinders Berlin Alexanderplatz—Selbstbildreflexion und Ich-Auflösung*. Munich: Trickster, 1992. Study of the autobiographical aspects of Fassbinder's magnum opus.

Hake, Sabine. "New German Cinema." *Monatshefte* 82, 3 (Fall 1990), 267–25. Pedagogical approaches.

Haskell, Molly. *From Reverence to Rape: The Treatment of Women in the Movies,* 2nd ed. Chicago: University of Chicago Press, 1987.

Hayman, Ronald. *Fassbinder: Film Maker*. London: Weidenfeld and Nicolson, 1984. Biographical study with limited interpretation of the films, largely and often uncritically interpreted as commentary on the life, drawing heavily from Raab; useful discussion of the theater work.

Helt, Richard C. and Maria E. Helt. *West German Cinema Since 1945: A Reference Handbook*. Metuchen, N.J.: Scarecrow, 1985.

————. *West German Cinema, 1985–1990: A Reference Handbook*. Metuchen, N.J.: Scarecrow, 1992. Continuation of previous item.

Hembus, Joe. *Der deutscher Film kann gar nicht besser sein; Ein Pamphlet von gestern, eine Abrechnung von heute*. Munich: Rogner and Bernhard, 1981.

Henrichs, Benjamin. "Müder Wunderknabe—Rainer Werner Fassbinder: Von der Theaterkommune zur Kunstfabrik." *Zeitmagazin* 8 June 1973. DIF 16–17.

Hoffmeister, Donna L. "Drugs as Metaphor: Fassbinder's *Veronika Voss* as Dance of Death." Unpublished essay read at 1991 Conference of the South Atlantic Modern Language Association.

————. *The Theater of Confinement: Language and Survival in the Milieu Plays of Marieluise Fleisser and Franz Xaver Kroetz*. Columbia, S. C.: Camden House, 1983.

Holden, Stephen. "A Grim Fassbinder on the Marriage Bond." *New York Times*, 24 Sept. 1994.

Iden, Peter. "The Impact-Maker." McC 13–23. On RWF's theater work through 1975.

Insdorf, Annette. *Indelible Shadows: Film and the Holocaust*. Second edition. Foreword by Elie Wiesel. New York: Cambridge UP, [1983] 1989.

Jacobsen, Wolfgang, Anton Kaes, and Hans-Helmut Prinzler. *Geschichte des Deutschen Films*. J. B. Metzler, 1993.

Jansen, Peter W., and Wolfram Schütte, eds. *Rainer Werner Fassbinder*. Reihe Film 2 (five editions). Munich: Carl Hanser Verlag, 1974–85. Expanded fifth edition, Frankfurt: Fischer Taschenbuch 1992. Single most important Fassbinder research tool, including commentary on the films, production stills, detailed filmography, bibliography of Fassbinder's writings and of criticism of his work by German, French, and English-language writers. (In German; for English translation, see McC below.)

Jenkins, Steve. "*Veronika Voss*." *Monthly Film Bulletin*, January 1983. Reprinted *Film Review Annual*, 1983: 1297–8.

Jenny, Urs. "Der Händler der vier Jahreszeiten," *Filmkritik* 16, 5 (May 1972): 270–71.

Jeremias, Brigitte. "Franz Biberkopfs Geschichte neu erzählt." *Frankfurter Allgemeine Zeitung* 6 Oct. 1975.

Johnston, Sheila. "The Author as a Public Institution." *Screen Education* 32/33 (1979/80), 67–78. The myth of the *auteur/Autor* in the New German Cinema.

————. "A Star is Born: Fassbinder and the New German Cinema." *New German Critique* 24–5 (Fall-Winter 1981–2): 57–72.

Kaes, Anton. *From Hitler to Heimat: The Return of History as Film*. Cambridge: Harvard UP, 1989. Includes commentary on *The Marriage of Maria Braun*.

————. "History, Fiction, Memory: Fassbinder's *The Marriage of Maria Braun*." *Persistence of Vision* 2 (Fall 1985): 52–60. Also Eric Rentschler, ed. *German Film and Literature* 276–288.

Kaplan, E. Ann. "Fassbinder as Political Voyeur: `Lola' and `Veronika Voss'." *Social Policy* 14, 1 (summer 1983): 60–62.

————. *Motherhood and Representation: The Mother in Popular Culture and Melodrama*. New York: Routledge, 1992.

————. *Psychoanalysis and Cinema*. AFI Film Readers. New York: Routledge, 1990.

————. *Women and Film: Both Sides of the Camera*. New York: Metheun, 1983.

Karsunke, Yaak. "History of Anti-Teater: The Beginnings." McC 2–9.

[Katz] Katz, Robert and Peter Berling. *Love is Colder than Death: The Life and Times of Rainer Werner Fassbinder*. New York: Random House, 1987. London: Paladin, 1989. (The cover of the 1989 paperback edition gives the sub-title as *Life and Work*.) Lively but sensationalistic, largely undocumented, and often erroneous biographical study, with slight attention to the artistic work. Katz (author of the screenplay for *Kamikaze '89*, the 1989 Wolf Gremm film starring RWF) appears to be the primary author, except for an appendix and several other sections written by Berling, whose file on RWF is acknowledged as the major source of the book (xi). See Berling, above.

Katzenstein, Peter J. *West Germany's Internal Security Policy: State and Terrorism in the 1970s and 1980s*. Ithaca: Cornell UP, 1991.

Kaufman, David. "The Fugitive." *The Nation* 3/10 Jan. 1994: 22–5. Review of White, *Genet*.

Kaufmann, Stanley. "Latter-day Lola." *The New Republic*, 2 August 1982: 24–5.

Kawin, Bruce. *Mindscreen: Bergman, Godard, and First-Person Film*. Princeton: Princeton UP, 1978.

Kilb, Andreas. "Die Hölle? Die Unsterblichkeit." *Die Zeit*, 25 (12 June 1992): 67–8.

————. "Hoaxes and hopes." *Sight and Sound* 2, 1 NS (May 1992): 5.

Kirby, Lynne. "Fassbinder's Debt to Poussin." *Camera Obscura* 13–14 (1985–86): 5–27. On *The Bitter Tears of Petra von Kant*.

Knight, Julia. *Women and the New German Cinema*. New York: Verso, 1992.

Koch, Gertrud. "Torments of the Flesh, Coldness of the Spirit: Jewish Figures in the Films of Rainer Werner Fassbinder." *New German Critique* 38 (Spring/Summer 1986): 28–38.

Kort, Wolfgang. *Alfred Döblin*. New York: Twayne, 1974

Kracauer, Siegfried. *From Caligari to Hitler: A Psychological History of the German Film*. Princeton: Princeton UP, 1947.

Kroetz. Franz Xaver. *Wildwechsel*. Munich: Georg-Lentz-Verlag, 1973.

Kuhn, Anna K. "Rainer Werner Fassbinder: The Alienated Vision." Phillips, 76–123. Brief discussion of the films through *Berlin Alexanderplatz*.

————. *Women's Pictures: Feminism and Cinema*. New York: Routledge and Kegan Paul, 1982.

Lardeau, Jean. *Rainer Werner Fassbinder*. Paris: Editions de l'Étoile, *Cahiers du cinéma*, 1990. Discussion of the life and work, emphasizing sociological and esthetic topics, with a chapter on *Berlin Alexanderplatz;* in French.

LaValley, Al. "The Gay Liberation of Rainer Werner Fassbinder: Male Subjectivity, Male Bodies, Male Lovers." In forthcoming special Fassbinder issue of *New German Critique*.

Lawrence, Amy. "Erotic Cruelty: Dirk Bogarde in *Providence, The Damned,* and *Despair.*" Essay read at Dartmouth College Fassbinder Conference, Hanover, New Hampshire, 1992.

Lenssen, Claudia. *Women's Cinema in Germany.* Munich: Goethe Institute, 1980.

Lichtenstein, Heiner, ed. *Der Fassbinder-Kontroverse, oder, Das Ende der Schönheit.* Afterword by Julius H. Schoeps. Königstein/Ts.: Athenäum, 1986. Sixty-five German newspaper articles on RWF's controversial play *Der Müll, die Stadt und der Tod,* including his responses to charges of anti-Semitism.

Lieb, Rebecca. "Fassbinder's Films are Back, Maybe." *New York Times* 29 August 1993, H 12.

Limmer, Wolfgang. *Rainer Werner Fassbinder, Filmemacher.* Hamburg: *Spiegel* Verlag, 1981. Spiegel-Buch 8. Reinbeck bei Hamburg: Rowohlt Taschenbuch, 1981. Includes 44-page biographical-critical essay and 95-page interview.

Literature/Film Quarterly. Special issues on New German Cinema. 7, 3 (1979) and 13, 4 (1985).

Lorenz, Juliane. Interview with Erika Richter. *Film und Fernsehen.* February 1982: 59–61.

———. "Je ferai tous mes films avec toi." Interviewed by Eugène Andréanszky. *Cahiers du cinéma,* 469 (June 1993): 65–7. Discussion of RWF and the work of the Rainer Werner Fassbinder Foundation.

———. [Let] Letters to the author. 1 September 1991; 22, 23 June 1993; 7 April, 24 May, 30 May, 3 June, 6 June, 21 June, 24 June, 29 July, 8 August 1994.

———. [Int] Personal Interview. 10 June 1992. German translation in Lorenz ed., *Das ganz normale Chaos,* 418–28.

———. Personal Interview with Donna L. Hoffmeister (unpublished). 8 August 1993.

———, ed. *Das ganz normale Chaos: Gespräche über Rainer Werner Fassbinder.* Berlin: Henschel Verlag, 1995. Important interviews with forty-two former Fassbinder actors and other coworkers, most conducted by Lorenz.

MacBean, James Roy. "Between Kitsch & Fascism: Notes on Fassbinder, Pasolini, (Homo)sexual Politics, the Exotic, the Erotic & Other Consuming Passions." *Cinéaste* 13, 4 (1984): 12–19.

Markovits, Andreis, Seyla Benhabib, and Moishe Postone. "Rainer Werner Fassbinder's *Garbage, The City and Death:* Renewed Antagonisms in the Complex Relationship between Jews and Germans in the Federal Republic of Germany." *New German Critique* 38 (Spring/Summer 1986): 3–27.

Märthesheimer, Peter. "Der geordnete Gang ist, erzählerisch gegeben, weniger ergiebig als der aufrechte." Fassbinder, *Fassbinders Filme 5.* 254–6. On *Acht Stunden sind kein Tag.*

———. "A Letter to the Editor." Fassbinder, *The Marriage of Maria Braun* (tr. and ed. Joyce Rheuban). 188–9.

———. "Die Okkupation eines bürgerlichen Genres." Fassbinder, *Fassbinders Filme 5.* 242–250. On *Acht Stunden sind kein Tag.*

Mast, Gerald. *A Short History of the Movies,* 5th ed., rev. by Bruce F. Kawin. New York: Macmillan, 1992.

McCormick, Richard. *Politics of the Self: Feminism and the Postmodern in West German Literature and Film.* Princeton: Princeton UP, 1991.

McCormick, Ruth. "Fassbinder's Reality: An Imitation of Life." McC 85–109.

[McC] McCormick, Ruth, tr. *Fassbinder.* New York: Tanam Press, 1981. English translation of Jansen and Schütte, with additional essays by McCormick and Wolfram Schütte. Important research tool for non-German readers, although the synopses and commentary in the "Annotated Filmography" by Wilhelm Roth (with supplementary contributions by Wilfriend Wiegand and Ruth McCormick) do not cover the four Fassbinder films made after *Lili Marleen* (1980).

Micheu, Anne. "*Mutter Krause ct Mutter Küsters.*" *Les Cahiers de la Cinématheque,* 32 (Spring 1981): 165–7.

Moeller, H.-B. "Fassbinder's Use of Brechtian Aesthetics." *Jump Cut* 35 (April 1990): 102–7. Focusses particularly on *Maria Braun.*

Moltke, Johannes von. "Camping in the Art Closet: The Politics of Camp and Nation in German Film." In forthcoming special Fassbinder issue of *New German Critique.*

Müller, André. See Liselotte Eder, "Der tote Sohn."

Murray, Bruce. *Film and the German Left in the Weimar Republic, from "Caligari" to "Kuhle Wampe."* Austin. University of Texas Press, 1990.

Nabokov, Vladimir. *Despair.* New York: Viking Penguin, 1981. Reprint of 1965 G. P. Putnam edition, New York.

Nevers, Camille. "R. W. F., la rumeur du monde." *Cahiers du cinéma* 469 (June 1993). 52–8.

New Germana Critique 24–25 (Winter/Fall 1981–2). Special issue on New German Cinema. Ed. David Bathrick and Miriam Hansen.

———. 38 (Spring/Summer 1986). Special Issue on the German-Jewish Controversy. Ed. David Bathrick, Helen Fehervary, Miriam Hansen, Andreas Huyssen, Anson Rabinback, and Jack Zipes. Several essays pertinent to RWF's play, *Garbage, the City, and Death.*

———. Special Fassbinder Issue, forthcoming. Essays (mostly from a November 1992 conference at Dartmouth College).

Niroumand, Miriam. "German as a Foreign Language: Fassbinder on Video." *Cinéaste* 20, 1 (1993): 52–3.

October [Massachusetts Institutute of Technology] 21 (Summer 1982). Special Fassbinder issue, including continuity script of *In a Year of 13 Moons* and critical essays.

Persistence of Vision 2 (Fall 1985). Special Issue on New German Cinema.

Petley, Julian. *Capital and Culture: German Cinema 1933–1945.* London: British Film Institute, 1979.

Pflaum, Hans Günther. *Germany on Film.* Contemporary Film and Television Studies and Readers Series. Ed. Robert Picht. Tr. Richard C. Helt and Roland Richter. Detroit: Wayne State UP, 1990. Brief survey of West German Film since the early 1960s.

————. "Der Händler der vier Jahreszeiten" *Suddeutsche Zeitung* 12 November 1972.

————. *Rainer Werner Fassbinder: Bilder und Dokumente.* Munich: Edition Spangenberg, 1992. Brief overview of the career, illustrated.

————. "Reise ins Land des Wahnsinns." *Süddeutsche Zeitung* 5 May 1978. On *Despair.*

————. "Wie fleischfressende Pflanzen." *Süddeutsche Zeitung* 15 June 1975. On *Fox and His Friends.*

Pflaum, Hans Günther and Rainer Werner Fassbinder. *Das bisschen Realität, das ich brauche: Wie Film entstehen.* Munich: Carl Hanser, 1976. Pflaum's account of the shooting and some post-production work on *I Only Want You to Love Me, Satan's Brew,* and *Chinese Roulette,* based on first-hand observation and discussions with RWF and others, illustrated.

Pflaum, Hans Günther and Hans Helmut Prinzler. *Cinema in the Federal Republic of Germany.* Bonn: InterNationes, 1983. First edition: *Film in der Bundesrepublik Deutschland* (Munich: Carl Hanser Verlag and InterNationes 1979). Brief survey, with additional information on West German film archives, periodicals, etc., and data on twenty-five filmmakers (in English).

Phillips, Klaus, ed. *New German Filmmakers: From Oberhausen through the 1970's.* New York: Ungar, 1984. General essay by the editor, and articles on twenty filmmakers by various hands.

Pluta, Ekkehard. "Die Sachen sind so, wie sie sind." *Fernsehen + Film* Dec. 1970. Reprinted in DIF 11–15. Discussion of five of the earliest antitheater films.

Praunheim, Rosa von. "Schwul, pervers, kontrovers." *Berliner Zeitung,* 10 June 1992: 2.

Prinzler, Hans Helmut and Eric Rentschler. *Augenzeugen: 100 Texts neuer deutscher Filmemacher.* Frankfurt am Main: Verlag der Autoren, 1988.

Quarterly Review of Film Studies 5, 2 (Spring 1980). Special issue on New German Cinema. Ed. Eric Rentschler.

Raab, Kurt. "My Life with Rainer." *Village Voice.* 3 May 1983, 43–45.

[Raab] Raab, Kurt and Karsten Peters. *Die Sehnsucht des Rainer Werner Fassbinder.* Munich: Bertelsmann, 1982. Unreliable account of the life and career of the director (and the life of the author) which admits to reporting "not the truth about Rainer Werner Fassbinder, but Kurt Raab's very subjective truth about RWF" (9); includes discussions by several other members of Fassbinder group.

Rayns, Tony, ed. *Fassbinder,* rev. edition. London: British Film Institute, 1980. In its original edition (1976), the first English-language book on the director, with still-useful essays by Thomas Elsaesser, Peter Iden, Richard Dyer, and others, and Christian Braad Thomsen's five interviews with Fassbinder.

Reimer, Robert C. "*Veronika Voss:* Fassbinder's Ambivalent Homage to Ufa/Hollywood Film Magic," *Sex and Love in Motion Pictures,* Proceedings of the Second Annual Film Conference, ed. Douglas Radcliff-Umstead (Kent, Ohio: Romance Languages Dept., Kent State University: 1984): 101–4.

Rentschler, Eric, ed. *German Film and Literature: Adaptations and Transformations.* New York: Methuen, 1986. Twenty essays by various hands.

―――. "Terms of dismemberment: the body in/and/of Fassbinder's *Berlin Alexanderplatz* (1980)." Rentschler, *German Film and Literature* 305–21.

―――. *West German Film in the Course of Time: Reflections on the Twenty Years since Oberhausen.* Bedford Hills, N. Y: Redgrave 1984. Extends the discussion beyond Phillips and Franklin, emphasizing historical and cultural contexts, with an epilogue on Fassbinder.

―――, ed. *West German Filmmakers on Film: Visions and Voices.* New York: Holmes and Meier, 1988. Documents and personal statements by a wide variety of people associated with the Young and New German Cinema, with introductions and commentary.

Rheuhan, Joyce. "*The Marriage of Maria Braun:* History, Melodrama, Ideology," "Notes on the Shooting Script," and "Reviews." Fassbinder. *The Marriage of Maria Braun.* 3–20, 163–80, 211–2.

Rohrback, Günther. "Ich will doch nur, dass Ihr mich liebt." *Filmecho/Filmwoche,* 19 June 1982. DIF 40.

[Roth/AF] Roth, Wilhelm. "Annotated Filmography." McC 111–218.

[Roth/KF] "Kommentierte Filmographie." Jansen and Schütte 119–269.

Roud, Richard. "Biter Bit." *Sight and Sound* 51, 4 (1982), 288–9. Reminiscences of RWF by the director of the New York Film Festival.

Ruppert, Peter. "Fassbinder's *Despair:* Hermann Hermann through the Looking Glass." *Post script* 3, 2 (winter 1984): 48–64.

[RWFF Cat] Rainer Werner Fassbinder Foundation. *Rainer Werner Fassbinder: Dichter, Schauspieler, Filmemacher—Werkschau 28.5–19.7.1992* Berlin: Argon, 1992. Catalogue of seven-weeks Fassbinder exhibition at the Alexanderplatz in Berlin, June-July 1992, with articles by various hands and a detailed chronology; illustrated (over 50 pages in color).

[RWFF/Prog] *Rainer Werner Fassbinder Werkschau Programm.* Berlin: Argon, 1992. A companion to the preceding item, listing schedule of screenings and other programs; includes information on films and television programs about RWF and notes on 50 of his favorite films by other directors.

Sanders-Brahms, Helma. "Eine Erinnerung." *Film und Fernsehen* 20, 4 (1992): 70–1.

Sandford, John. *The New German Cinema.* New York: Da Capo, 1980. The chapter on Fassbinder (63–103) deals in detail only with films through *Despair* (1977).

Santner, Eric L. *Stranded Objects: Mourning, Memory, and Film in Postwar Germany.* Ithaca: Cornell UP, 1990.

Sarris, Andrew. "Can Fassbinder Break the Box-Office Barrier?" *The Village Voice,* Nov. 22, 1976: 57.

Schäfer, Horst. *Film im Film: Selbstportäts der Traumfabrik.* Frankfurt am Main: Fischer Taschenbuch, 1985. Survey of European and American films-about-film, films, including *Holy Whore, Veronika Voss,* and *A Man Like Eva.*

Scheib-Rothbart, Ingrid. "German Film Distribution and Exhibition in the United States: A Chronology." *Persistence of Vision* 2 (Fall 1985): 76–83. Information primarily on film programs in New York City 1961–83, by the head of the Goethe House film department.

Schidor, Dieter. "The Wizard of Babylon." Interviewed by Gregory Solman. *Cinéaste* 12, 4 (1983): 17–19. Recollections of RWF by the producer of *Querelle* and maker of a documentary film, *The Wizard of Babylon*.

Schütte, Wolfram. "Ich—was ist das? Oder: Ästhetic als Widerstand." *Frankfurter Rundschau* 5 May 1978.

———. "Respekt für sein `Cheyenne autumn'." *Frankfurter Rundschau,* 1 July, 1974. On *Effi Briest*.

———. "Sein Name: eine Ära, Rückblicke auf den späten Fassbinder (1974–82)." Jansen and Schütte, 63–74.

Schygulla, Hanna. *Bilder aus Filmen von Rainer Werner Fassbinder*. Munich: Schirmer/ Mosel, 1981. Autobiographical narrative by the star of many RWF films, focussing on her work with the director. Includes RWF essay on Schygulla (Schygulla/RWF).

Scorsese, Martin. *Scorsese on Scorsese*. Ed. David Thompson and Ian Christie. Intro. Michael Powell. Boston: Faber and Faber, 1990.

Shattuc, Jane. "*Contra* Brecht: R. W. Fassbinder and Pop Culture in the Sixties." *Cinema Journal* 33, 1 (Fall 1993): 35–54.

———. "R. W. Fassbinder's Confessional Melodrama: Towards Historicizing Melodrama within the Art Cinema." *Wide Angle* 22, 1 (June 1990): 44–59.

———. "R. W. Fassbinder as a Popular *Auteur:* The Making of an Authorial Legend." *Journal of Film and Video* 45, 1 (Spring 1993): 40–57.

———. *Television, Tabloids, and Tears: R. W. Fassbinder and Popular Culture*. Madison: University of Wisconsin Press, forthcoming.

Sikov, Ed. "*Querelle*." *Cinéaste* 13, 1 (1983): 40–2.

Silverman, Kaja. "Fassbinder and Lacan: A Reconsideration of Gaze, Look and Image." *Camera Obscura* 19 (Jan. 1989): 55–84.

———. *Male Subjectivity at the Margins*. New York: Routledge, 1992.

Smith, James L. *Melodrama*. The Critical Idiom Series. London: Metheun, 1973.

Sontag, Susan. "Notes on `Camp'." *Against Interpretation and Other Essays*. New York: Octagon, 1978. 275–292.

Spaich, Herbert. *Rainer Werner Fassbinder: Leben und Werk*. Weinheim: Beltz, 1992. A 104-page summary of Fassbinder's life and career, followed by discussion of the films (organized by themes); a number of photographs and other illustrations not previously published.

Stam, Robert. *Reflexivity in Film and Literature: From "Don Quixote" to Jean-Luc Godard*. New York: Columbia University Press, 1992.

Stoppard, Tom. Letters to Dirk Bogarde. 1 Nov., 17 Dec., 1976; 9 March, 11 April 1977; 10 Dec., 1978. Bogarde Papers. Mugar Memorial Library, Boston University.

———. Letter to the author. 1 March 1993.

Stuart, Dabney. *Nabokov: The Dimensions of Parody*. Baton Rouge: Louisiana University Press, 1978.

Text + Kritik, 103, July 1989. Special Fassbinder issue of a Munich-based periodical usually treating German authors.

Thate, Hilmar. "Das macht nichts, das lassen wir." Interviewed by Margit Voss. *Film und*

Fernsehen 20, 4 (1992): 92–3. Reminiscence of RWF, by an East German actor who played in *Veronika Voss*.

Thieringer, Thomas. "Memories of Fassbinder's Television Work." Rayns 65–9.

Thomsen, Christian Braad. "The Doubled Individual." Tr. Joseph Burns. *Wide Angle* 12, 1 (June 1990): 60–5. Originally published as "Der doppelte Mensch," *Text + Kritik* 103 (July 1989) 3–9.

———. *Rainer Werner Fassbinder: Leben and Werk eines masslosen Genies*. Tr. from Danish by Ursula Schmalbruch. Hamburg: Rogner and Bernhard, 1993. Comprehensive study by Danish filmmaker who frequently interviewed RWF.

Töteberg, Michael. "Einführung." Fassbinder. *Die Kinofilme 1*, 9–22.

——— —. "Fassbinders Theaterarbeit." Fassbinder. *Anarchie in Bayern & andere Stücke*, 151–67.

———. "Nachwort." Fassbinder. *Antiteater*, 231–42,

——— —. "Nachwort." Fassbinder. *Fassbinders Filme 2* 241–54.

———"Das Theater der Grausamkeit als Lehrstück. Zwischen Brecht und Artaud: Die experimentellen Theatertexte Fassbinders." *Text + Kritik* 103 (July 1989): 20–34.

———. "Wie man einen Film verstümmelt: R. W. Fassbinder's 'Warnung vor einer heiligen Nutte' (1970) und was Peer Raben daraus gemacht hat. Eine Kriminalgeschichte." *taz* [Berlin], 21 June 1990.

Treut, Monika. "Man to Man." *Sight and Sound* 4, 5 NS (May 1994): 69. Primarily on *Querelle*.

Turner, Henry Ashby, Jr. *The Two Germanies since 1945*. New Haven: Yale UP, 1987.

Watson, Wallace. "The Bitter Tears of RWF." *Sight and Sound* 2, 3 NS (July 1992): 24 9. Summary of Fassbinder's career, accompanied by a previously unpublished note from RWF to Dirk Bogard (20 June 1977) and two letters in response from Bogarde to RWF (24 June and 24 September 1977). The note from RWF as published here is corrected in chapter 4, note 14.

———. "'Sexuality Wanders Dark Paths': Fassbinder's Romanticization of *Berlin Alexanderplatz*." *Literature/Film Quarterly* 18,4 (1990): 245–50.

White, Edmund. *Genet: A Biography*. New York: Knopf, 1993.

Wide Angle, 12, 1 (Jan. 1990): "The Other Fassbinder: The Popular/The Historical/The International." Ed. Jane Shattuc. Special issue of an American film quarterly, with essays on Fassbinder reflecting recent gender, genre, and psychoanalytical theories.

Wiegand, Wilfriend. "Hans ohne Glück." *Frankfurter Allgemeine Zeitung*, 31 May 1972. On *The Merchant of Four Seasons*.

[Zwerenz] Zwerenz, Gerhard. *Der langsame Tod des Rainer Werner Fassbinders: Ein Bericht*. Munich: Schneekluth, 1982. Sympathetic personal reminiscences and commentary by a former East German writer who acted in two RWF films and collaborated with the director on several projects.

———. *Die Ehre der Maria Braun*. Munich: Goldmann, 1979. Novelistic version of the film *The Marriage of Maria Braun;* originally serialized in *Stern* magazine starting February 1979.

INDEX

Note: Unless otherwise indicated, italicized titles refer to Fassbinder films; *motif* and *theme* refer to treatment in Fassbinder plays or films.